Encyclopædia
of World Architecture

Henri Stierlin

Encyclopædia of
World Architecture

2

M

Layout: Henri Stierlin
Jacket: Marcel Wyss SWB
Production: Suzanne Meister

Printing:
Imprimeries Réunies, Lausanne
Binding:
Mayer & Soutter, Renens
Photolithos (colour and jacket):
Schwitter Reproduction, Basle
Photolithos (black and white):
Aberegg-Steiner & Co AG, Berne, and
Atesa Argraf S.A., Geneva

Second edition 1979

© Macmillan Press Ltd., London
First published in English 1977
Translation © 1977 by Office du Livre
ISBN 0 333 23209 7

Printed in Switzerland

Inde　　　Indien　　　India

Si l'architecture indienne naît vers 2500 avant notre ère, tant à Mohenjo-daro qu'à Harappa, sur le cours de l'Indus, la civilisation hindouiste ne débute qu'un millénaire plus tard avec l'invasion aryenne. Elle trouve son expression écrite dans les Védas, consignés vers le IXᵉ siècle av. J.-C. Des premiers édifices de bois, rien ne nous est parvenu. Les débuts de l'architecture de brique et de pierre sont l'œuvre du bouddhisme, qui constitue une réforme de l'hindouisme primitif. Au IIIᵉ siècle av. J.-C., les sanctuaires de Sanchi commémorent l'œuvre du Gautama Bouddha (563–483), et remontent au règne de l'empereur Ashoka. C'est à Sanchi qu'apparaît la forme du stupa, tertre funéraire hémisphérique, qui sera appelé à une extraordinaire ferveur dans tout le monde bouddhique. Le parasol-arbre du monde qui le surmonte donnera naissance aux diverses formes de pagodes de tout l'Extrême-Orient. Les bas-reliefs décorant les torana, ou portails de pierre, nous renseignent sur les édifices de bois de cette époque, qui trouveront leur transcription dans les sanctuaires nommés chaitya, creusés par les moines bouddhiques dans les falaises de Lomas Rishi, Karli ou Ajanta, entre le IIIᵉ siècle av. J.-C. et le VIᵉ siècle de notre ère.

Dès le Vᵉ siècle, une véritable renaissance de l'hindouisme se produit au sud de l'Inde, qui va donner le jour à la grande architecture médiévale. Tant les édifices taillés dans le roc de Mahabalipuram (vers 650) que les temples rupestres d'Ellora (VIIIᵉ s. pour la Kailasa) perpétuent les techniques bouddhiques. Mais auparavant, vers 450, l'Inde méridionale avait vu la construction en pierre de taille des temples dravidiens

Die frühesten indischen Bauten stammen aus der Zeit um 2500 v.Chr. (Mohenjo-Daro und Harappa), die Hindu-Kultur begann jedoch erst etwa tausend Jahre später mit der Arier-Invasion. Sie fand ihren Niederschlag in den Veden, die um das 9.Jahrhundert v.Chr. aufgezeichnet wurden. Von den ersten hölzernen Bauten ist nichts erhalten. Die Ziegel- und Steinarchitektur wurde durch den Buddhismus, eine Reform des ursprünglichen Hinduismus, eingeführt. Im 3.Jahrhundert wurden unter König Ashoka in Sanci Heiligtümer zum Gedenken an das Wirken des Gautama Buddha erbaut. Hier tritt zum ersten Mal die architektonische Form des Stupa, eines halbkugelförmigen Grabhügels, auf, der dann in der buddhistischen Welt weiteste Verbreitung fand. Aus dem ihm aufgesetzten Weltenbaum entwickelten sich die verschiedenen Pagodenformen des Fernen Ostens. Die Reliefs auf den Torana, den Steintoren, geben uns Aufschluß über die Holzbauten jener Zeit, deren Formen auch auf die von buddhistischen Mönchen zwischen dem 3.vorchristlichen und dem 6.nachchristlichen Jahrhundert aus dem Fels gehauenen Heiligtümer übertragen wurden (Lomas-Rishi, Karli, Ajanta).

Im 5.Jahrhundert setzte in Südindien eine eigentliche hinduistische Renaissance ein, in deren Folge die großartige mittelalterliche Architektur entstand. Sowohl in den Felsentempeln von Mahabalipuram (um 650) als auch in den Höhlentempeln von Ellora (Großer Kailasa-Tempel, 8.Jahrhundert) wurden die buddhistischen Techniken weiter angewandt. Doch bereits um 450 wurden in Südindien die drawidischen Tempel von Lad Khan und Durga aus

Although the earliest Indian architecture dates from 2500 B.C. (Mohenjo-daro and Harappa), Hindu civilisation proper did not begin until a thousand years later with the Aryan invasion. It found literary expression in the Vedas, which were committed to writing around the ninth century B.C. Of the earliest wooden buildings nothing has survived. The beginnings of brick and stone architecture were the work of Buddhism, which was in effect a reformation of primitive Hinduism. In the third century B.C., under Emperor Ashoka, shrines were built at Sanchi to commemorate the work of Gautama Buddha (563–483 B.C.). It was at Sanchi that the stupa made its appearance as an architectural form. Originally a hemispherical burial mound, the stupa was to enjoy a most exuberant future in Buddhist architecture. The umbrella-shaped 'world-tree' surmounting it was the origin of the various types of pagoda developed throughout the Far East. The bas-reliefs adorning the *torana*s or stone gateways tell us something about the wooden buildings of the period, which were also copied in the shrines known as *chaityas* that Buddhist monks hollowed out of the cliffs at Lomas Rishi, Karli and Ajanta between the third century B.C. and the sixth century A.D.

Starting in the fifth century there was a veritable renaissance of Hinduism in southern India, which ushered in the great period of medieval architecture. Buddhist techniques survived in the buildings carved out of the rock at Mahabalipuram (*c.*650) as well as in the cave temples of Ellora (the Kailasa temple is eighth-century). But before this, around 450, freestone had been

261

de Ladh Khan ou de Durga, dont vont découler les vastes réalisations de Buvaneshvar, Tanjore, Khajuraho, Konarak ou Somnathpur. Dans une enceinte sacrée formant «temenos», le sanctuaire se compose généralement d'une haute tour, symbolisant la cité des dieux édifiée en plusieurs étages sur le sommet du mont Mérou, et d'une salle de réunion. La technique de construction recourt à la voûte en encorbellement. Le plan s'établit à partir d'un tracé magique, dit mandala, fondé sur des formes géométriques simples. L'apogée de cette architecture médiévale se situe entre le X\(^e\) et le XIII\(^e\) siècle. Par la suite s'élèveront encore, au sud de la péninsule, les immenses cités sacrées, surmontées de leurs hauts gopuram (ou portes) à étages, comme à Madurai ou Kanchipuram.

Stein errichtet, ihnen folgten die gewaltigen Tempelbauten von Bhuvaneshvar, Tanjore, Khajuraho, Konarak und Somnathpur. Ein Heiligtum besteht in der Regel – innerhalb eines geheiligten Bezirks – aus einem hohen Turm, Symbol der in mehreren Ebenen auf dem Meru-Berg errichteten Stadt der Götter, und einer Versammlungshalle. Die Bauten sind nach dem System des Kraggewölbes konstruiert. Der Grundriß beruht auf der magischen Figur der Mandala, die aus einfachen geometrischen Formen gebildet ist. Diese mittelalterliche Architektur erreichte ihren Höhepunkt zwischen dem 10. und 13. Jahrhundert. Auch später noch entstanden im Süden der Halbinsel große heilige Städte mit hochaufragenden mehrstöckigen Stadttoren (Gopura) wie in Madurai und Kanchipuram.

used to build the Dravidian temples of Ladh Khan and Durga, from which stemmed the colossal achievements of Bhuvanesvar, Tanjore, Khajuraho, Konarak and Somnathpur. Set in a sacred precinct, the shrine usually consisted of a tall tower, which symbolised the city of the gods built on several levels at the summit of Mount Meru, and an assembly hall. The technique of construction relied on the corbelled vault. The plan was based on a magical diagram known as a mandala, which used simple geometrical forms. The heyday of this medieval architecture was between the tenth and the thirteenth century, but even later enormous sacred cities continued to be built in the south, cities crowned with tall *gopuras* or gatehouses several storeys high, such as those at Madurai and Kanchipuram.

1 Le grand stupa bouddhique de Sanchi (Inde centrale), construit entre 273 et 150 av. J.-C. Le torana au premier plan date de 25 av. J.-C.
2 Le grand temple de Kandariya Mahadeo, à Khajuraho (Inde centrale), sanctuaire hindou datant de 1050 de notre ère.
3 L'ensemble rupestre de Mahabalipuram, sur la côte orientale de l'Inde, datant du VII\(^e\) siècle de notre ère. Tous les édifices sont taillés dans le granit.

1 Sanci (Zentralindien), der große Stupa (zwischen 273 und 150 v. Chr.); im Vordergrund der Torana (25 v. Chr.)
2 Khajuraho (Zentralindien), der hinduistische Kandariya-Mahadeo-Tempel (um 1050)
3 Mahabalipuram, Tempelanlage an der südindischen Ostküste; alle Bauten sind in situ aus dem Granit gehauen (7. Jh.)

1 The Great Stupa, Sanchi (central India), a Buddhist shrine built between 273 and 150 B.C. The *torana* in the foreground dates from 25 B.C.
2 Temple of Khandariya Mahadeo, Khajuraho (central India), a Hindu shrine dating from A.D *c.* 1050.
3 The cave complex of Mahabalipuram (east coast of south India), dating from the seventh century A.D. All the buildings were carved *in situ* from the granite.

1

2

3

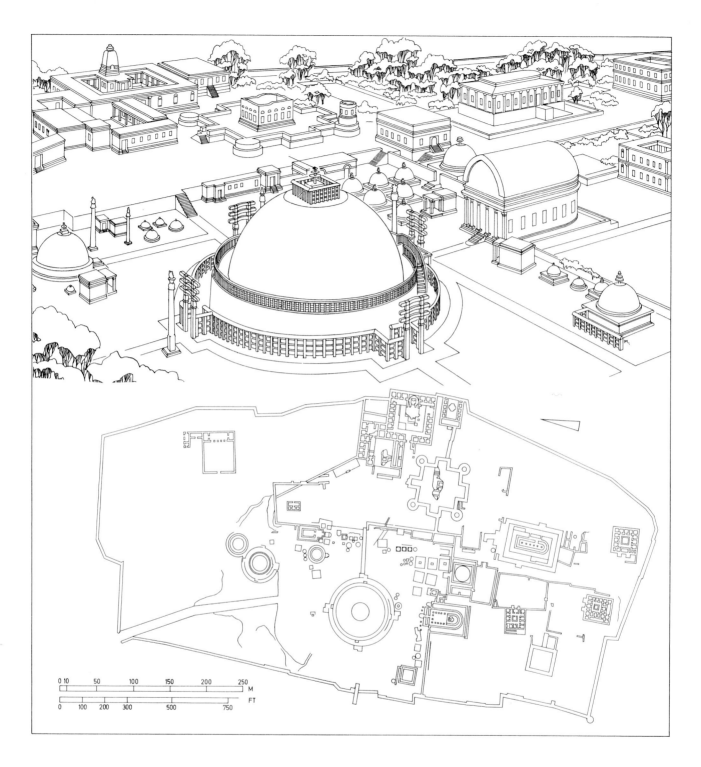

Monastère de Sanchi (Inde centrale), sanctuaire bouddhique fondé par le roi Ashoka (273–232 av.J.-C.) et construit entre le IIIᵉ siècle avant notre ère et le IIᵉ s. de notre ère. Vue reconstituée et plan d'ensemble 1:5000. Au premier plan de la vue, le grand stupa, agrandi en 150 av.J.-C. et dont les torana furent édifiés en 25 av.J.-C.

Kloster Sanci (Zentralindien), zwischen dem 3.Jh. v.Chr. und dem 2.Jh. n.Chr. erbaut. Das buddhistische Heiligtum wurde von König Ashoka (273–232 v. Chr.) gestiftet. Im Vordergrund der große, 150 v.Chr. erweiterte Stupa mit den 25 v.Chr. erbauten Torana (Steintoren). Rekonstruktion der Anlage; Lageplan 1:5000.

Sanchi monastery (central India), a Buddhist shrine founded by King Ashoka (273–232 B.C.) and built between the third century B.C. and the second century A.D. Reconstructed view and overall plan 1:5000. In the foreground of the view is the Great Stupa, enlarged in 150 B.C. and with *toranas* (carved gateways) erected in 25 B.C.

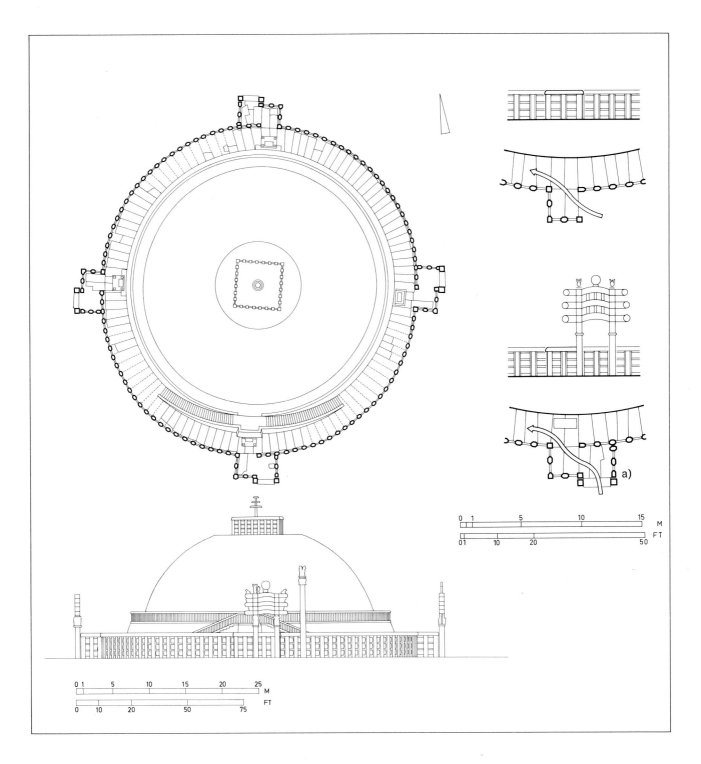

Grand stupa de Sanchi. Plan et élévation 1:500 et détail des balustrades ou thabha 1:300 avant et après la pose des torana ou portails sculptés datant de 25 av. J.-C. L'enclos de pierre entoure la base du stupa, permettant le rite de la circumambulation. Une double rampe mène au déambulatoire supérieur. Au sommet, l'arbre cosmique symbolisé en pierre.

Sanci, Großer Stupa. Das Steingitter umschließt die Basis des Stupa und bildet einen Umgang für den Ritus des Umschreitens. Eine doppelläufige Treppe führt zu einem oberen Umgang. Den Bau krönt das Symbol des «kosmischen Baums». Grundriß und Aufriß 1:500; Detail des Steingitters vor und nach der Errichtung der Torana im Jahr 25 v. Chr. 1:300.

Great Stupa, Sanchi. Plan and elevation 1:500; detail of the *thabhas* (balustrades) (1:300) before and (a) after the addition of the gateways in 25 B.C. The stone enclosure round the base of the *stupa* was for ritual circumambulation. A double ramp gives access to the upper ambulatory. The *stupa* is crowned by a symbolic world tree in stone.

265

Grand stupa de Sanchi. Détail des balustrades 1:60 et d'un portique 1:40; à droite, détail du sommet de la colonne d'Ashoka. Une balustrade de pierre, haute de 3,13 m, entoure le stupa, et une balustrade plus petite (représentée ici) borde le déambulatoire supérieur. Les somptueux portiques sont couverts de reliefs représentant la vie du Bouddha.

Sanci, Großer Stupa. Die um den Stupa laufende Balustrade ist 3,13 m hoch, diejenige des oberen Umgangs niedriger. Die reich skulptierten Steintore tragen Szenen aus dem Leben Buddhas. Details der oberen Balustrade 1:60; Detail eines Steintores 1:40; rechts: Spitze der Ashoka-Säule.

Great Stupa, Sanchi. Detail of the balustrades 1:60 and of a *torana* 1:40. Right, detail of the top of Ashoka's column. A stone balustrade, 3.13 m. high, runs round the base of the *stupa* and a smaller balustrade (shown here) surrounds the upper ambulatory. The elaborate gateways are covered with reliefs depicting the life of the Buddha.

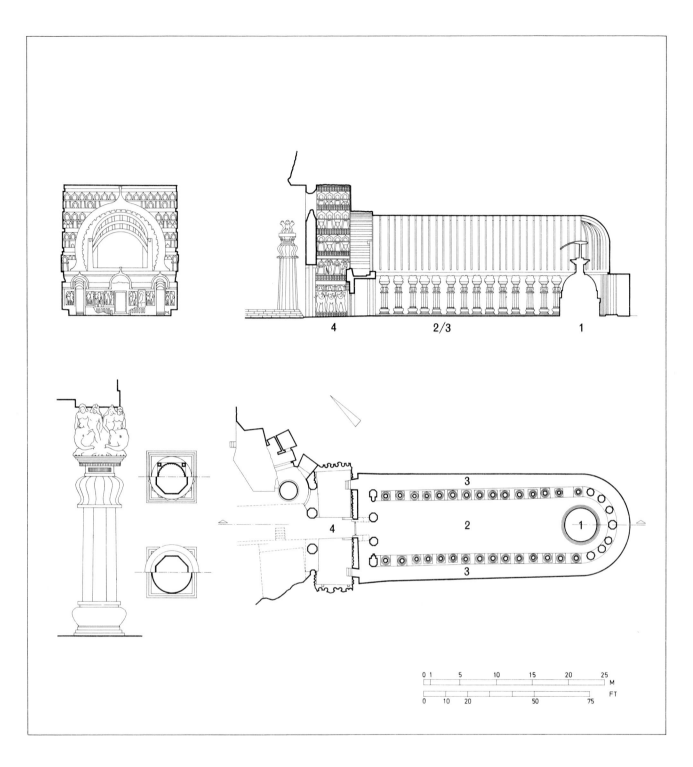

4   2/3   1

3

2   1

4

3

0 1   5   10   15   20   25
                              M
0   10   20   50   75   FT

Chaitya bouddhique de Karli (côte ouest de l'Inde), œuvre rupestre datant du Ier siècle av. J.-C. Elévation de la façade, coupe longitudinale et plan 1:500, détails d'une colonne 1:80. C'est la plus grande «basilique» monolithique excavée de l'Inde. Le fond, semi-circulaire, permettait le rite ambulatoire autour du stupa. 1) Stupa, 2) Nef centrale, 3) Nefs latérales, 4) Vestibule.

Karli (Westküste Indiens), Buddhistische Chaitya-Halle, 1. Jh. v. Chr. Das Höhlenheiligtum ist die größte der in Indien aus dem Fels gehauenen Hallen. Der halbkreisförmige Abschluß erlaubt das rituelle Umschreiten des Stupa. 1) Stupa, 2) Mittelschiff, 3) Seitenschiffe, 4) Vorhalle. Fassadenaufriß, Längsschnitt, Grundriß 1:500; Details einer Säule 1:80.

Buddhist chaitya, Karli (west coast), a rock shrine dating from the first century B.C. Façade elevation, longitudinal section, and plan 1:500; details of a column 1:80. This is India's largest 'basilica' carved out of the solid rock. The semicircular termination allowed ritual circumambulation of the *stupa*. 1) stupa, 2) nave, 3) side aisles, 4) vestibule.

Dharmaraja Ratha hindou de Mahabali-puram (côte orientale de l'Inde du Sud), édifice taillé dans le roc vers 650 de notre ère. Vue verticale, plan, coupe, élévation et axonométrie 1:200. Les «ratha» ou chars célestes sont traités à la manière de maquettes monolithiques, sans espace interne. De plan carré, selon le motif du mandala, cet édifice influera sur le style dravidien.

Mahabalipuram (südindische Ostküste), Hinduistischer Dharmaraja Ratha, um 650 n. Chr. Die aus dem Fels gehauenen Rathas oder himmlischen Fahrzeuge sind Monolithe ohne Innenraum. Der Grundriß ist quadratisch und entspricht dem Mandala-Motiv; diese Bauform beeinflußte den Drawida-Stil. Aufsicht, Grundriß, Schnitt, Aufriß, Axonometrie 1:200.

Hindu Dharmaraja Ratha, Mahabalipuram (east coast of south India), carved out of the rock *c.*A.D. 650. Vertical view, plan, section, elevation, and axonometric projection 1:200. The *rathas* or heavenly chariots are treated as monolithic maquettes: they are solid. Square in plan (following the *mandala* motif), this building had an influence on the Dravidian style.

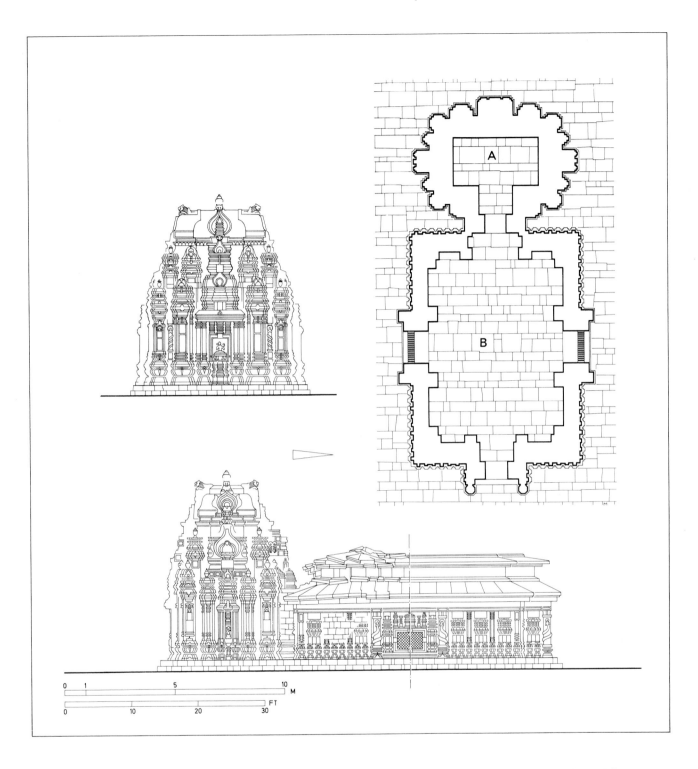

Temple de Varahi, à Caurasi (côte orientale de l'Inde), édifié au XIIe s. Elévation du «chevet», plan et élévation latérale 1:150. A) Garbha griha, ou cella du temple hindou, B) Mukhashala, ou salle de réunion. Les espaces de cet édifice de pierre sont entièrement bâtis à l'aide de voûtes en encorbellement. Les parois sont décorées de reliefs tantriques.

Caurasi (indische Ostküste), Varahi-Tempel, 12. Jh. Alle Räume dieses Steinbaus sind von Kraggewölben überdeckt. Tantrische Reliefs schmücken die Wände. Aufriß der Cella-Front, Grundriß des Tempels und Aufriß einer Seite 1:150: A) Garba Griha (Cella), B) Mukhashala (Versammlungsraum).

Temple of Varahi, Caurasi (east coast), built in the twelfth century. Elevation of the 'apse', plan, and side elevation 1:150. A) garbha griha or cella of the Hindu temple, B) mukhashala or assembly hall. The interiors of this stone building are contrived entirely with corbelled vaults. The walls are decorated with Tantric reliefs.

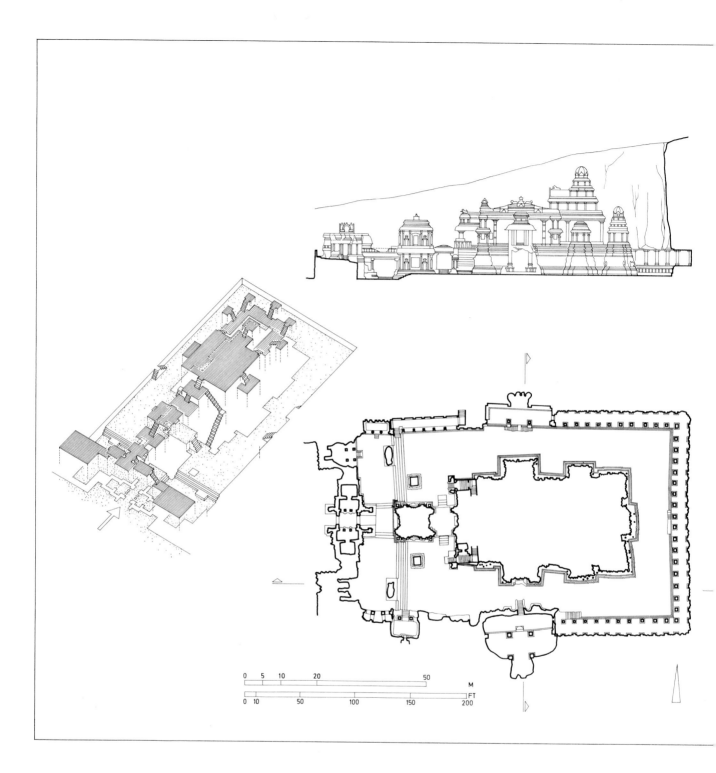

Grand Temple du Kailasa, à Ellora (Inde centrale), édifice entièrement excavé dans la falaise au VIIIᵉ s. de notre ère. Axonométrie montrant l'aménagement sur deux étages, élévation latérale, plan au niveau inférieur, coupe transversale, plan au niveau supérieur 1:1000, et colonne monolithique de la cour 1:100. Ce temple a été fondé par Krishna Iᵉʳ, dans le style méridional dravidien.

Ellora (Zentralindien), Großer Kailasa-Tempel, 8.Jh. n.Chr. Der aus den Felsen gehauene Tempel im südlichen Dra-wida-Stil wurde von Krishna I. gestiftet. Axonometrie, Aufriß einer Seite, Grund-riß des Untergeschoßes 1:1000; Neben-seite: Querschnitt, Grundriß des Ober-geschosses 1:1000; Monolithsäule im Hof 1:100.

The Kailasa temple, Ellora (central India), was carved entirely out of solid rock in the eighth century A.D. Axonometric projection showing the two-storeyed arrangement, side elevation, plan of the lower level, cross section, and plan of the upper level 1:1000; monolithic column in the courtyard 1:100. Founded by Krishna I, the temple exemplifies the southern Dravidian style.

Pour réaliser cet énorme édifice rupestre consacré à Shiva, avec sa tour principale haute de 30 m, et qui constitue le plus grand sanctuaire monolithique de l'Inde, il a fallu creuser et évacuer 150000 m³, soit quelque 400000 tonnes de matériaux.

Um dieses gewaltige, Shiva geweihte Felsheiligtum, die größte monolithische Anlage in Indien mit einem 30 m hohen Turm, zu schaffen, mußten 150000 m³ Fels ausgehauen und transportiert werden, das heißt ungefähr 400000 Tonnen.

In order to construct this enormous rock-cut temple dedicated to Shiva, which is the largest monolithic sanctuary in India and whose principal tower is 30 m. high, 150,000 m³ of rock, i.e. some 400,000 tons of material, had to be dug out and removed.

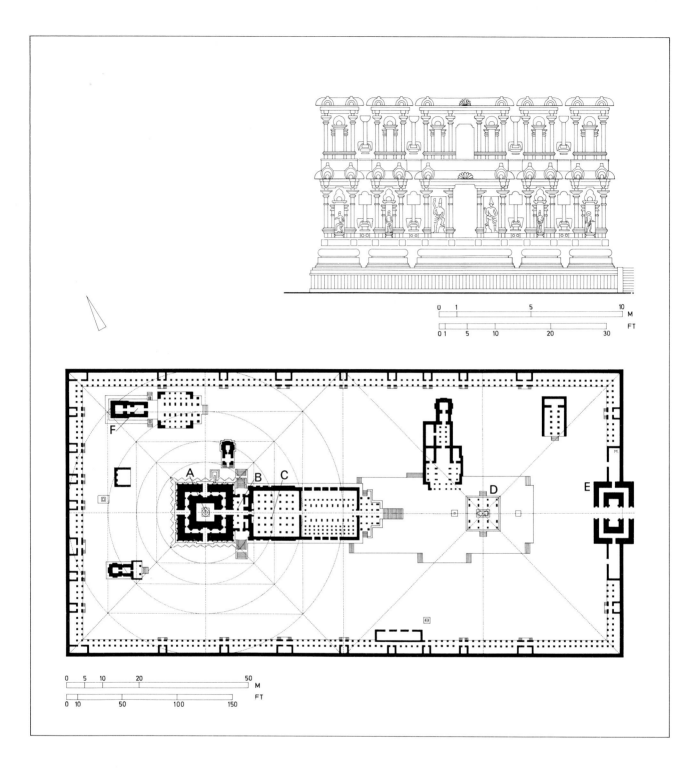

Temple de Brihadeshvara, à Tanjore (Inde méridionale), construit en six ans seulement vers 1010 par la dynastie des Chola. Elévation de la cella (sans la tour) 1:200 et plan général 1:1000. A) Sanctuaire, B) Artha mandapa, ou vestibule de réunion, C) Maha mandapa ou second vestibule, D) Nandi mandapa, ou vestibule contenant la statue du taureau, monture de Shiva, E) Gopuram, F) Sanctuaire de Subrahmanya.

Tanjore (Südindien), Brihadeshvara-Tempel, um 1010. Der Tempel wurde von den Cholas in nur sechs Jahren erbaut. Aufriß der Cella (ohne Turm) 1:200; Grundriß 1:1000: A) Cella, B) Artha mandapa (Versammlungshalle), C) Maha mandapa (zweite Vorhalle), D) Nandi mandapa (Vorhalle mit dem Standbild des Nandi-Stiers, des Reittiers Shivas), E) Gopura, F) Subrahmanya-Heiligtum.

Temple of Brihadeshvara, Tanjore (south India), c.1010; built by the Chola dynasty in the space of only six years. Elevation of the cella (without the tower) 1:200; overall plan 1:1000. A) shrine, B) artha mandapa or meeting vestibule, C) maha mandapa or second vestibule, D) nandi mandapa or vestibule containing the statue of the bull, the sacred mount of Shiva, E) gopuram, F) shrine of Subrahmanya.

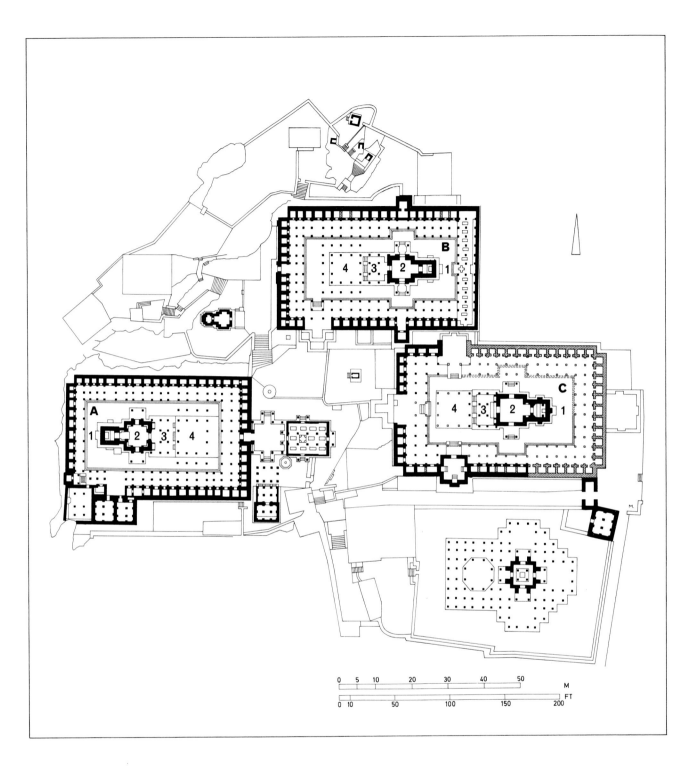

Temples jaïna de Mont Abu (Inde occidentale). A) Temple de Vimala, datant de 1021, B) Temple de Tejapala, de 1230, C) Temple d'Adinatha. Plan d'ensemble 1:1000. 1) Garbha griha ou sanctuaire, 2) Gudha mandapa ou vestibule, 3) Nav choki ou portique intermédiaire, 4) Ranga mandapa ou pavillon de danse. Les pavillons de danse sont couverts de coupoles plates en encorbellement.

Mount Abu (Westindien), Jainistische Tempel. A) Vimala-Tempel, 1021, B) Tejapala-Tempel, 1230, C) Adinatha-Tempel. Die Tanzpavillons dieser Tempel sind mit flachen Kragkuppeln überwölbt. Lageplan 1:1000: 1) Garba-Griha (Cella), 2) Gudha mandapa (Vorhalle), 3) Nav choki (Zwischenportikus), 4) Ranga mandapa (Tanzpavillon).

Jain temples, Mount Abu (western India). A) temple of Vimala, built 1021, B) temple of Tejapala, built 1230, C) temple of Adinatha. Overall plan 1:1000. 1) garbha griha or shrine, 2) gudha mandapa or vestibule, 3) nav choki or middle gateway, 4) ranga mandapa or dancing pavilion. The dancing pavilions are roofed with shallow corbelled domes.

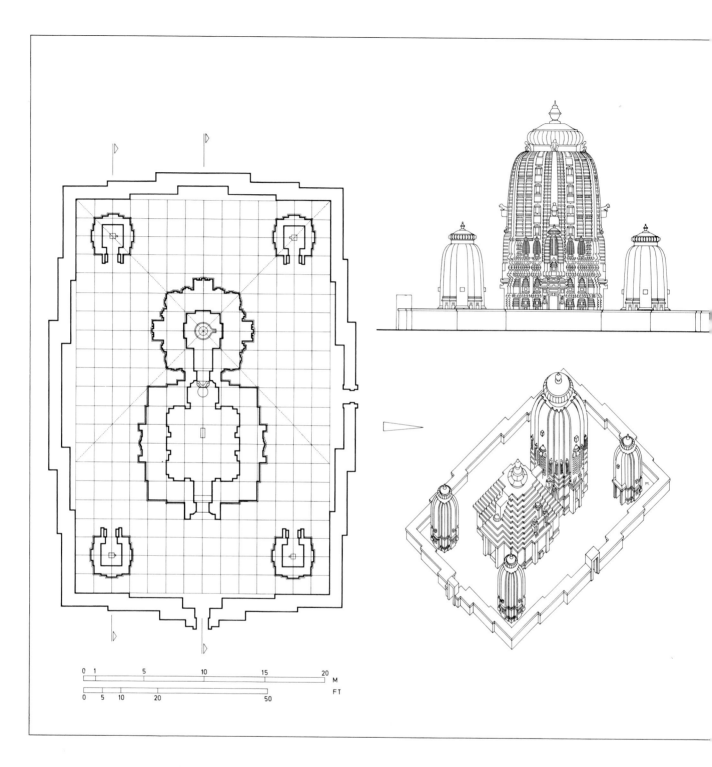

Temple de Brahmeshvara, à Bubaneswar (Inde orientale), datant de 1075. Plan général, élévation de la face antérieure, élévation latérale et coupe longitudinale 1:300, axonométrie. Résidence des souverains du Kalinga, Bubaneswar compte plus de cent temples érigés entre le VIIIᵉ et le XIIIᵉ s. Le temple principal de Brahmeshvara est entouré de quatre sanctuaires secondaires.

Bhuvaneshvar (Ostindien), Brahmesh-vara-Tempel, 1075. In der einstigen Residenz der Könige von Kalinga stehen mehr als hundert zwischen dem 8. und dem 13. Jh. erbaute Tempel. Der Brahmeshvara-Haupttempel ist von vier kleinen Tempeln umgeben. Grundriß, Aufriß der Vorderfassade 1:300; Axonometrie; Nebenseite: Aufriß einer Seite, Längsschnitt 1:300.

Temple of Brahmeshvara, Buvaneshvar (eastern India), built 1075. Overall plan, elevation of the front, side elevation, and longitudinal section 1:300; axonometric projection. Buvaneshvar was the residence of the kings of Kalinga and has more than a hundred temples built between the eighth and thirteenth centuries. The main temple of Brahmeshvara is surrounded by four secondary shrines.

A droite, plan du **Temple de Raja Rani, à Bubaneswar,** datant de 1200 environ. Plan très découpé et complexe du sanctuaire par rapport à l'aspect massif du vestibule ou salle de réunion, 1:300.

Bhuvaneshvar, Raja-Rani-Tempel, um 1200. Die Mauern der Cella sind im Vergleich zu denen der Versammlungshalle vielfältig und kleinteilig gegliedert. Grundriß 1:300.

Right, plan of the **Temple of Raja Rani, Buvaneshvar,** built *c*. 1200. Plan 1:300. The shrine is built on a jagged and complex plan compared with the massive quality of the vestibule or assembly hall.

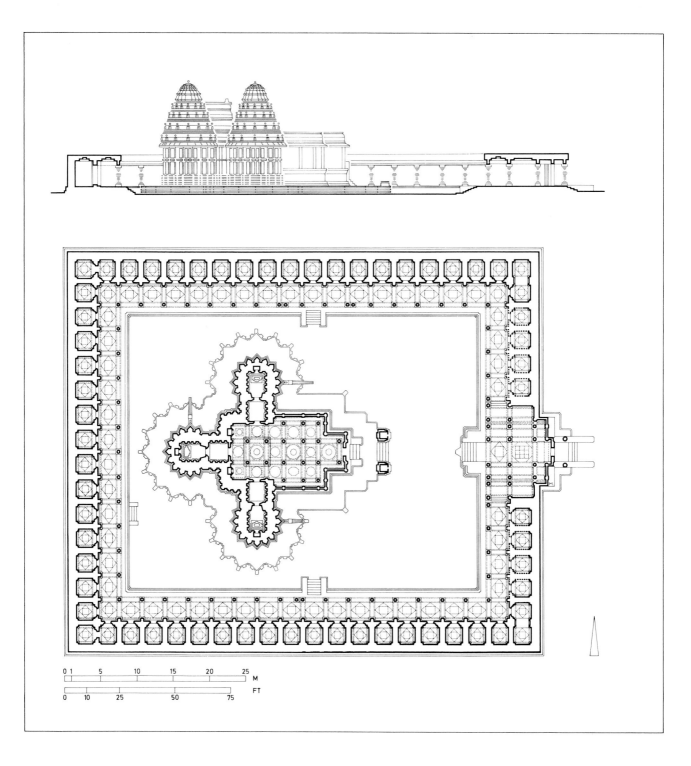

0 1   5   10   15   20   25   M

0   10   25   50   75   FT

Temple de Keshava, à Somnathpur (Inde méridionale), datant de 1268. Elévation du temple avec coupe des galeries pourtournantes, plan général 1:500. La cour, entourée de galeries qui protègent des cellules, contient un temple où le vestibule conduit à trois sanctuaires, selon une disposition cruciforme, consacrés à trois aspects de Vishnou.

Somnathpur (Südindien), Keshava-Tempel, 1268. Der Hof ist von den Mönchszellen mit davorliegendem Säulengang umschlossen. In der Mitte des Hofes der Tempel, an dessen Vorhalle kreuzförmig drei Sanktuarien anschließen, die drei Inkarnationen Vishnus geweiht sind. Aufriß des Tempels mit Schnitt durch die umlaufende Galerie, Grundriß 1:500.

Temple of Keshava, Somnathpur (south India), built 1268. Elevation of the temple with section through the galleries and overall plan 1:500. The courtyard, surrounded by galleries that protect the cells, contains a temple in which a vestibule leads to three shrines, arranged in a cruciform pattern and consecrated to the three aspects of Vishnu.

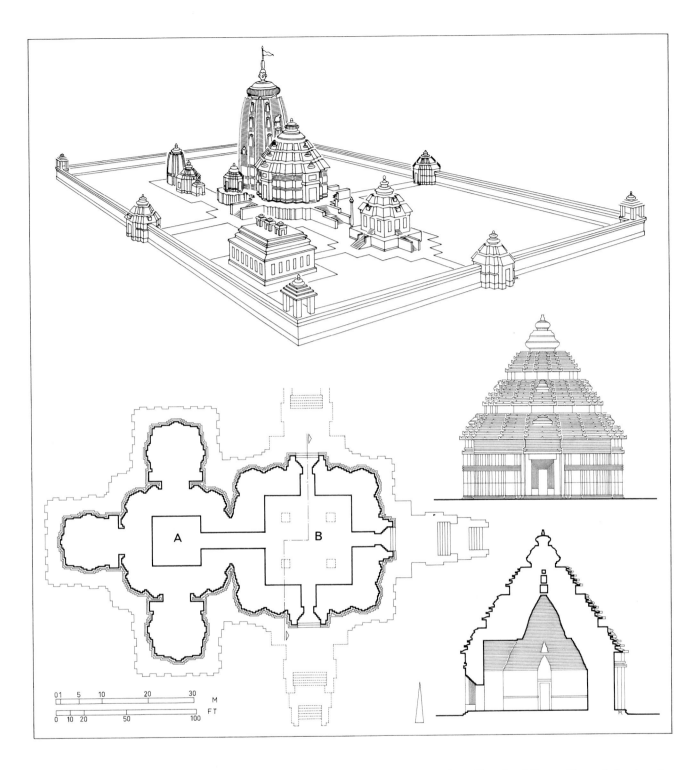

Temple de Surya, à Konarak (Inde orientale), reconstitution de l'ensemble datant de 1250. Plan, élévation et coupe transversale de la salle de réunion 1:800. Ce pavillon de la danse (jagamohan) précédait le plus haut des shikhara, ou tour du temple, de toute l'Inde. Il s'effondra au cours de la construction et ne fut jamais achevé.

Konarak (Ostindien), Surya-Tempel, 1250. Dieser Jagamohan stand vor dem höchsten Tempelturm, der je in Indien geplant wurde. Er stürzte während der Bauarbeiten ein und wurde nie vollendet. Rekonstruktion der Gesamtanlage; Grundriß 1:800; Aufriß und Querschnitt der Versammlungshalle 1:800.

Temple of Surya, Konarak (eastern India), reconstruction of the complex, which dates from 1250. Plan, elevation, and cross section of the assembly hall 1:800. This dancing pavilion *(jagamohan)* stood in front of the highest *shikhara* or temple tower in all India. It collapsed during construction and was never completed.

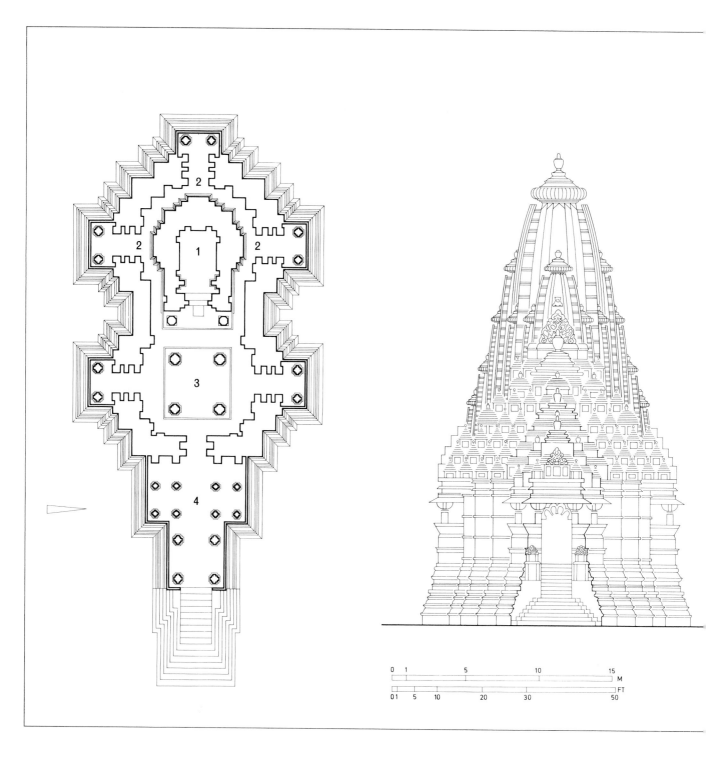

Temple de Kandariya Mahadeo, à Khajuraho (Inde centrale), datant du XIᵉ s. Plan et élévation de la façade d'entrée 1:250. 1) Garbha griha ou sanctuaire, 2) Couloir de circumambulation, 3) Mandapa ou salle de réunion, 4) Artha mandapa ou véranda couverte. La construction est entièrement réalisée en assises en encorbellement, qui n'autorisent pas les grands espaces internes.

Khajuraho (Zentralindien), Kandariya-Mahadeo-Tempel, 11. Jh. Der Bau wurde gänzlich mit überkragenden Steinlagen ausgeführt, so daß keine großen Innenräume möglich waren. Grundriß 1:250: 1) Garba-Griha (Cella), 2) Umgang, 3) Mandapa (Versammlungssaal), 4) Artha mandapa (überdachte Veranda); Aufriß der Eingangsfassade 1:250.

Temple of Khandariya Mahadeo, Khajuraho (central India), mid-eleventh century. Plan and elevation of the entrance façade 1:250. 1) garbha griha or shrine, 2) ambulatory, 3) mandapa or assembly hall, 4) artha mandapa or covered veranda. The whole building is constructed of corbelled courses, which do not allow of large interiors.

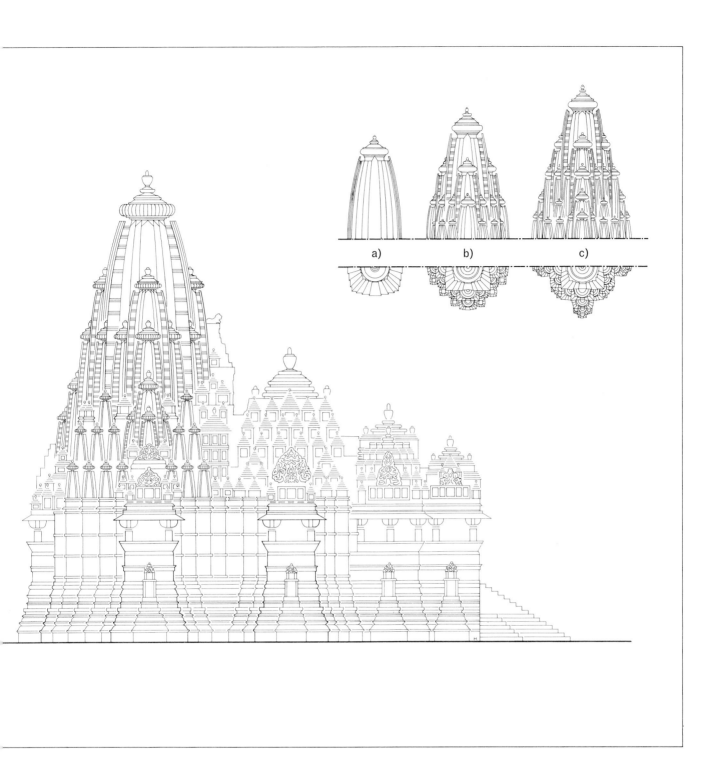

a)　　　　　b)　　　　　c)

Elévation latérale du **Temple de Kandariya Mahadeo, à Khajuraho,** 1:250. Depuis l'entrée, l'édifice présente une série de jaillissements soulignés par des assises horizontales. A droite, passage du shikhara simple aux shikhara complexes à Khajuraho: a) Temple d'Adinatha, jaïna, 950 apr. J.-C. b) Temple de Paraswanatha, jaïna, 970 apr. J.-C. c) Temple de Kandariya Mahadeo, hindou, 1050 apr. J.-C.

Khajuraho, Kandariya-Mahadeo-Tempel. Vom Eingang her erweitert sich der Bau in einer Folge von Abstufungen, die durch vorkragende Steinlagen betont werden. Aufriß einer Seite 1:250. Rechts oben: Die Entwicklung vom einfachen zum vielteiligen Shikara in Khajuraho: a) Adinatha-Tempel, 950 n. Chr., jainistisch, b) Paraswanatha-Tempel, 970 n. Chr., jainistisch, c) Kandariya-Mahadeo-Tempel, 1050 n. Chr., hinduistisch.

Side elevation of the **Temple of Khandariya Mahadeo, Khajuraho,** 1:250. From the entrance the building widens in a series of sharp projections underlined by horizontal courses. Right, the progression from simple to complex *shikharas* at Khajuraho: a) temple of Adinatha (Jain), A.D. 950, b) temple of Paraswanatha (Jain), 970, c) temple of Khandariya Mahadeo (Hindu), mid-eleventh century.

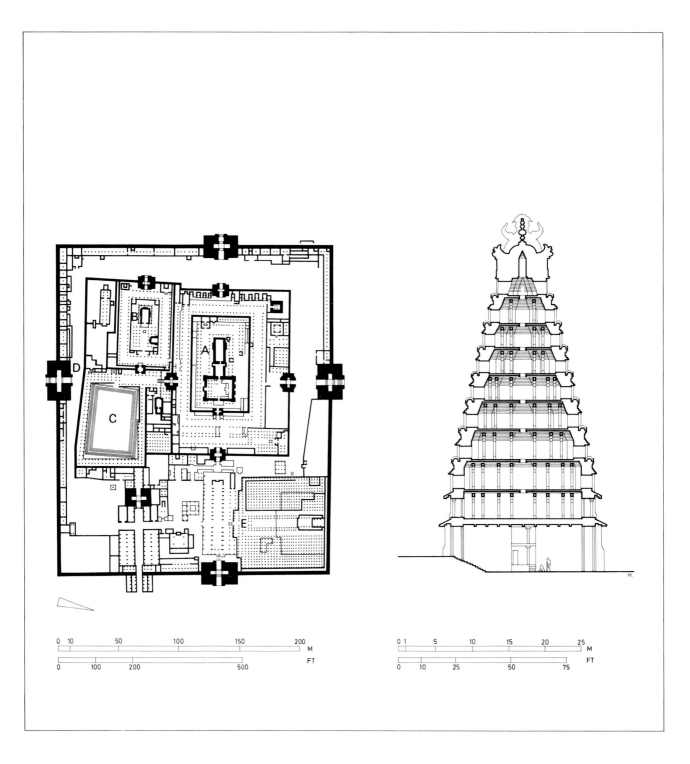

Ville-Temple de Madurai (Inde du Sud), centre religieux mentionné dès le VIIIe s., agrandissements du XIIe au XVIe s. Plan d'ensemble 1:3000. A) Sanctuaire de Sundareshvara, B) Sanctuaire de Meenakshi, C) Etang sacré, D) Gopuram sud, E) Salle aux mille piliers. A droite: coupe du gopuram sud 1:500. Les gopuram, ou portes de la ville, sont couverts de sculptures multicolores.

Tempelstadt Madurai (Südindien), erste Erwähnung des religiösen Zentrums im 8. Jh., im 12.–16. Jh. erweitert. Die Stadttore (Gopura) sind mit bemalten Skulpturen geschmückt. Gesamtplan 1:3000: A) Sundareshvara-Tempel, B) Meenakshi-Tempel, C) Heiliger Teich, D) südliches Gopura, E) Saal der tausend Säulen; Schnitt durch das südliche Gopura 1:500.

Temple city of Madurai (south India), a religious centre mentioned from the eighth century and enlarged in the twelfth to sixteenth centuries. Overall plan 1:3000. A) shrine of Sundareshvara, B) shrine of Meenakshi, C) sacred pond, D) south gopuram, E) Hall of the Thousand Pillars. Right, section of the south *gopuram* 1:500. The *gopurams* or gate-towers of the city are covered with multi-coloured sculpture.

Sud-Est asiatique   Südostasien   South-east Asia

L'aire d'influence de la civilisation indienne – bouddhique et hindouiste – est considérable dans le Sud-Est asiatique. Dès Ashoka (IIIe s. av. J.-C.) Ceylan se convertit au bouddhisme. La Birmanie, l'Indochine et les îles de Java et Bali seront atteintes au IIe siècle de notre ère. L'essor de l'art javanais a lieu sous les Çailendra (VIIe s.), tout spécialement à Borobudur, vaste stupa de pierre édifié vers 800 sur un plan carré de 110 × 110 m à cinq plates-formes culminant à 45 m de haut. Puis l'hindouisme s'instaure à Java, ainsi qu'en témoignent les sanctuaires de Pram Banam. Les plans redentés issus du mandala et les hautes tours à étages symbolisant la cité divine sur le mont Mérou annoncent l'art indochinois.

C'est dans le Cambodge khmer que se développe la plus importante floraison de temples suscitée par les religions indiennes. Dès le VIIe siècle, à Sambor Prei Kuk, s'élabore un style original qui trouvera son expression parfaite dans la zone angkorienne, d'abord aux Kulen, puis à Roluos au IXe siècle avec l'apparition du système hydraulique des barays qui va commander tout l'urbanisme et la riziculture: cités en quadrilatères, entourées de douves et que des digues axiales rattachent aux campagnes irriguées. Au centre, le grand sanctuaire de pierre ou de brique, temple-montagne avec ses tours ou prasat et leur décor sculpté de dieux et de déesses hindouistes.

Par Phnom Bakheng, Pré Rup, Banteay Srei, Takéo, on suit l'évolution qui conduit à l'apothéose classique: Angkor Vat. Une douve large de 200 m enferme un quadrilatère de 1,5 × 1,3 km. La chaussée qui franchit la douve atteint des propylées larges de 235 m et se pour-

Der Einfluß der indischen Kultur – sowohl der buddhistischen wie der hinduistischen – in Südostasien ist beachtlich. Im 3. Jahrhundert vor Christus, zur Zeit Ashokas, wurde Ceylon buddhistisch; im 2. Jahrhundert griff der Buddhismus auch auf Burma, Indochina und die Inseln Java und Bali über. Unter den Shailendras (7. Jahrhundert) setzte der Aufschwung der javanischen Kunst ein, deren großartigste Leistung der um 800 erbaute Stupa von Borobudur ist, ein 45 m hoher fünfstufiger Bau auf quadratischem Grundriß (110 × 110 m). Zeugen für das folgende Eindringen des Hinduismus in Java sind die Heiligtümer von Prambanan. Auf der Mandala beruhende Grundrisse und hohe Stufentürme, Symbol der Götterstadt auf dem Berg Meru, künden die indochinesische Kunst an.

Die Khmer-Kunst von Kambodscha schuf die schönste Gruppe von indischen Religionen beeinflußter Tempel. Beginnend mit Sambor Prei Kuk im 7. Jahrhundert entwickelte sich ein eigenständiger Stil, der im Gebiet von Angkor, zunächst in Kulen, dann in Roluos (9. Jahrhundert), mit der Ausbildung des auf den Baray beruhenden hydraulischen Systems seinen vollkommensten Ausdruck fand. Dieses Bewässerungssystem wurde für den Städtebau und die Reiskultur entscheidend: rechteckig angelegte, von Wassergräben umgebene Städte, durch axiale Deiche mit dem bewässerten Land verbunden; im Zentrum der Stadt das große Heiligtum – in Ziegeln oder Stein erbaut –, ein Tempelberg mit Turmheiligtümern (Prasat) und reichem Skulpturenschmuck, hinduistischen Göttern und Göttinnen.

Phnom Bakheng, Pre Rup, Banteay

Indian civilisation, both Buddhist and Hindu, spread its influence over much of south-east Asia. Ceylon was converted to Buddhism in Ashoka's time (third century B.C.); Burma, Indochina, and the islands of Java and Bali followed in the second century A.D. Javanese art sprang up under the Sailendra dynasty (seventh century), particularly at Borobudur, a vast stone *stupa* built around 800 on a 110 m. by 110 m. ground plan and rising in five platforms to a height of 45 m. Subsequently Hinduism took root in Java, as witness the shrines of Prambanan. The mandala-based ground plans and the tall towers symbolising the divine city on Mount Meru heralded the art of Indochina.

It was the Khmer civilisation of Cambodia that produced the finest crop of temples inspired by the religions of India. Beginning in the seventh century (Sambor Prei Kuk) the Khmers evolved an original style that reached its culmination in the Angkor region, first at Kulen and later, in the ninth century, at Roluos, where they developed the hydraulic system of *barays* that was to govern both their town-planning and the way they grew their rice. Quadrilateral, moated cities were linked with the irrigated countryside around them by means of radial dykes. At the centre was a great shrine of stone or brick, a temple-mountain with towers or *prasats* carved with all the gods and goddesses of Hinduism.

Phnom Bakheng, Pre Rup, Banteay Srei and Takeo are stages in an evolution leading to the classic apotheosis of Angkor Vat. Here a 200 m. wide moat surrounds a quadrilateral measuring 1.5 km. by 1.3 km. The causeway over the moat leads to propylaea that

suit sur 350 m jusqu'au formidable édifice. Surmonté de ses cinq tours en tiares culminant à 65 m, il est enserré par des galeries en fausses voûtes, ouvertes sur l'extérieur, qui mesurent 187 × 215 m. Œuvre de Suryavarman II (1113–1150) ce sanctuaire, contemporain du gothique français, est une véritable cathédrale de la jungle.

Un raid des Chams fait s'effondrer la culture classique. Une renaissance d'inspiration baroque, animée par le souverain bouddhique Jayavarman VII donnera au Cambodge un nouvel et ultime chef-d'œuvre: le Bayon, avec ses tours-visages symbolisant l'omniprésence du Bouddha, au centre de la ville murée d'Angkor Thom. Puis les incursions des Thaïs conduiront à l'abandon de la cité d'Angkor qui connut, à son apogée, une population de 800000 habitants.

Srei und Ta Keo sind Stationen auf dem Weg zum klassischen Höhepunkt Angkor Vat: ein 200 m breiter Wassergraben umschließt ein Rechteck von 1,5 × 1,3 km; eine Straße führt über den Deich zu den 235 m breiten Propyläen und zum 350 m entfernten gewaltigen Heiligtum, auf dem fünf Türme 65 m über dem Erdboden aufragen; nach außen geöffnete Galerien mit Kraggewölben schließen eine Tempelfläche von 187 × 215 m ein. Dieses zur Zeit der französischen Gotik unter Suryavarman II. (1113–1150) errichtete Werk ist eine wahre Kathedrale im Dschungel.

Ein Einfall der Cham führte das Ende der klassischen Kultur herbei. Die von dem buddhistischen Herrscher Jayavarman VII. eingeleitete «barocke» Renaissance schenkte Kambodscha ein neues und letztes Meisterwerk, den Bayon im Zentrum der ummauerten Stadt Angkor Thom. Seine Gesichtertürme symbolisieren die Allgegenwart Buddhas. Im Gefolge der Thai-Einfälle wurde Angkor, das in seiner Blütezeit 800000 Einwohner zählte, aufgegeben.

are 235 m. wide and continues for a further 350 m. to the massive building. Crowned by five tiara towers reaching a height of 65 m., it is enclosed by false-vaulted galleries open towards the outside and measuring 187 m. by 215 m. The cathedral of the jungle, built by Suryavarman II (1113–50), is contemporary with early Gothic architecture.

A raid by the Chams led to the collapse of the classical Khmer culture. A 'baroque' renaissance inspired by the Buddhist king Jayavarman VII gave Cambodia one last masterpiece—the Bayon temple in the middle of the walled city of Angkor Thom, its four-faced towers symbolising the omnipresence of the Buddha. Subsequently Thai invasions led to the abandonment of the Angkor complex, which in its heyday had housed a population of 800,000.

1 Le grand temple d'Angkor Vat (Cambodge), avec ses cinq tours, édifié par Sûryavarman II entre 1113 et 1150.
2 Les prasat de Préah Kô, à Roluos, près d'Angkor, édifiés en brique par Indravarman en 879.
3 Les tours à visages du Bayon, temple bouddhique construit au centre de la cité murée d'Angkor Thom par Jayavarman VII en 1200 environ.

1 Angkor Vat (Kambodscha), der unter Suryavarman II. erbaute Tempelberg mit den fünf Turmheiligtümern (1113–1150)
2 Roluos (Kambodscha), der unter Indravarman erbaute Prasat Preah Ko, ein Ziegelbau (879)
3 Angkor Thom, Bayon, einer der Gesichtertürme des unter Jayavarman VII. erbauten Tempels (um 1200)

1 The great temple of Angkor Vat (Cambodia) with its five towers, built by Suryavarman II between 1113 and 1150.
2 The prasats of Preah Ko, Roluos, near Angkor, built of brick by Indravarman in 879.
3 The face towers of the Bayon, a Buddhist temple built by Jayavarman VII in the centre of the walled city of Angkor Thom.

1

2

3

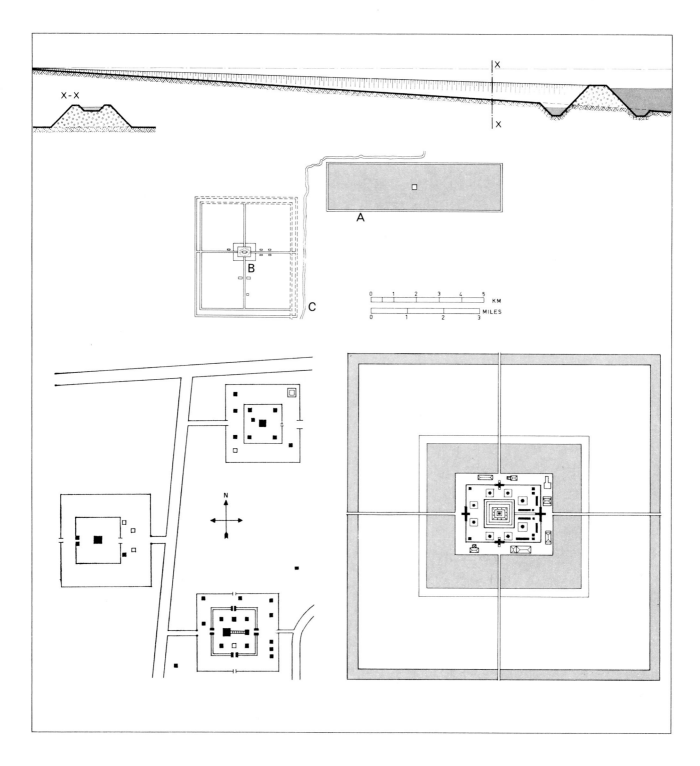

Angkor (Cambodge): système de mise en charge des barays, ou lacs artificiels, pour l'irrigation. Au centre: la **cité de Yasodharapura**: A) Baray oriental, B) Phnom Bakheng au centre de la cité, C) Rivière Siem Réap. En bas à gauche: plan de **Sambor Prei Kuk** au VIIe siècle. A droite, plan d'ensemble de la **cité de Bakong, à Roluos,** avec sa double ceinture de douves, sa pyramide centrale et ses voies axiales, 1:8000.

Oben: **Angkor,** Bewässerungssystem mit Kanälen und künstlichen Seen (Baray). Mitte: **Yashodharapura.** Lageplan: A) Östlicher Baray, B) Phnom Bakheng im Zentrum der Stadt, C) Stung Siem Reap. Unten links: **Sambor Prei Kuk** im 7.Jh. Lageplan. Unten rechts: **Roluos, Bakong.** In der Mitte der Stadt mit doppeltem Wassergraben und axial angelegten Straßen die Tempelpyramide. Plan 1:8000.

Angkor (Cambodia): System of filling the *barays* or artificial lakes for irrigation purposes. Centre, **City of Yasodharapura:** A) east baray, B) Phnom Bakheng at the centre of the city, C) Siem Reap river. Below left, plan of **Sambor Prei Kuk** in the seventh century. Right, overall plan of the **City of Bakong, Roluos,** with its double moat, central pyramid and axial streets 1:8000.

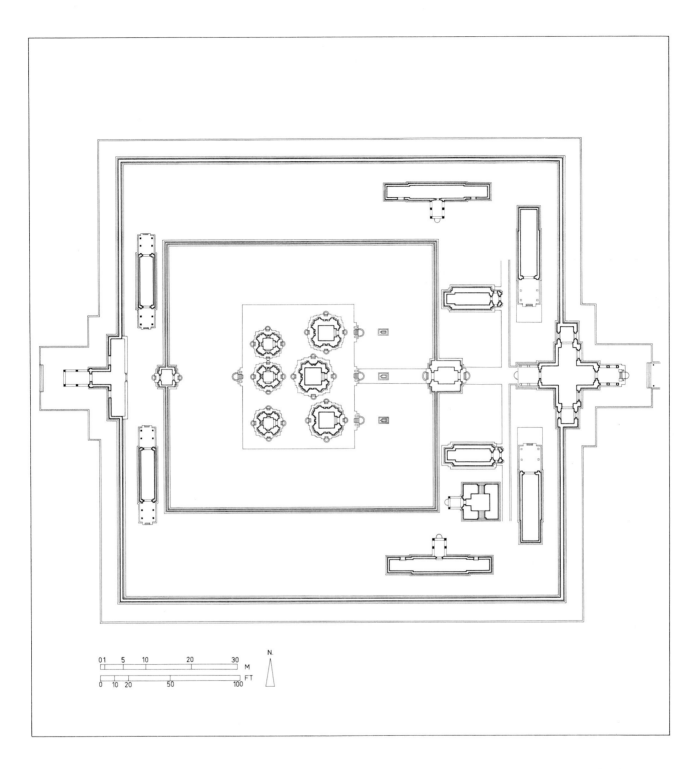

01 5   10   20   30 M

0 10 20   50   100 FT

N.

Ensemble de Préah Kô, à Roluos, près d'Angkor (Cambodge), datant de 879 et construit par Indravarman comme temple funéraire de Jayavarman II, consacré au culte de Shiva, 1:800. Au milieu d'une double enceinte, six prasat, ou sanctuaires, construits en brique, se dressent sur une terrasse unique. A droite, sur l'axe de pénétration, le gopuram, ou porte, donnant accès à l'ensemble cultuel.

Roluos (Kambodscha), Preah Ko, 879. Der Shiva geweihte Tempel wurde von Indravarman als Grabtempel Jayavarmans II. errichtet. Innerhalb der doppelten Einfriedung erheben sich auf einer Plattform sechs Tempeltürme (Prasat) aus Ziegeln. Das Gopura in der Achse (rechts) dient als Eingang. Grundriß 1:800.

Preah Ko, Roluos (near Angkor, Cambodia), begun 879 by Indravarman as a funerary temple for Jayavarman II and consecrated to the worship of Shiva. Plan 1:800. Surrounded by a double enclosure, six brick-built *prasats* or shrines stand on a single terrace. Right, on the axis of penetration, the *gopuram* or gate-tower that gives access to the ritual complex.

285

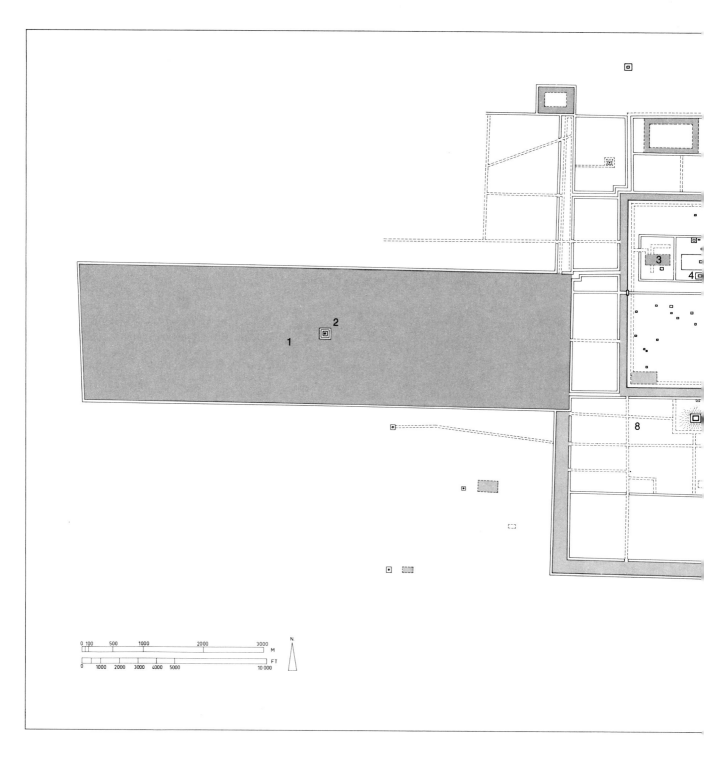

0 100 500 1000   2000   3000
                                        M
0   1000 2000 3000 4000 5000   10 000
                                        FT
N

Plan général des sites d'Angkor (Cambodge), au XIIᵉ s. 1:60000. Les lignes doubles sont des digues, les pointillés des canaux. 1) Grand Baray occidental, 2) Mébon occidental, 3) Phiméanakas, 4) Baphuon, 5) Bayon, 6) Porte d'Angkor Thom, 7) Baksei Chamkrong, 8) Phnom Bakheng, 9) Angkor Vat, 10) Préah Khan, 11) Takéo, 12) Ta Prohm, 13) Néak Péan, 14) Banteay Kdei, 15) Srah Srang, 16) Rivière Siem Réap, 17) Ta Som, 18) Mébon oriental,

Angkor im 12. Jh. Die Ebene von Angkor wurde dank eines überlegten Systems intensiv bewässert. Die Hauptstadt des Khmer-Reichs war nach einem rechtwinkligen Schema angelegt, die beiden Baray (künstliche Seen) spielten eine entscheidende Rolle. Lageplan 1:60000: Durchgezogene Linien bezeichnen Deiche, gestrichelte Kanäle bzw. den Fluß; 1) Westlicher Baray, 2) Westlicher Mebon, 3) Phimeanakas, 4) Baphuon, 5) Bayon, 6) Angkor Thom,

Overall plan of the **Angkor sites** (Cambodia) in the twelfth century 1:60,000. The double lines represent embankments, the dotted lines canals. 1) great west baray, 2) west mebon, 3) Phimeanakas, 4) Baphuon, 5) Bayon, 6) gate of Angkor Thom, 7) Baksei Chamkrong, 8) Phnom Bakheng, 9) Angkor Vat, 10) Preah Khan, 11) Takeo, 12) Ta Prohm, 13) Neak Pean, 14) Banteay Kdei, 15) Srah Srang, 16) Siem Reap river, 17) Ta Som, 18) east mebon,

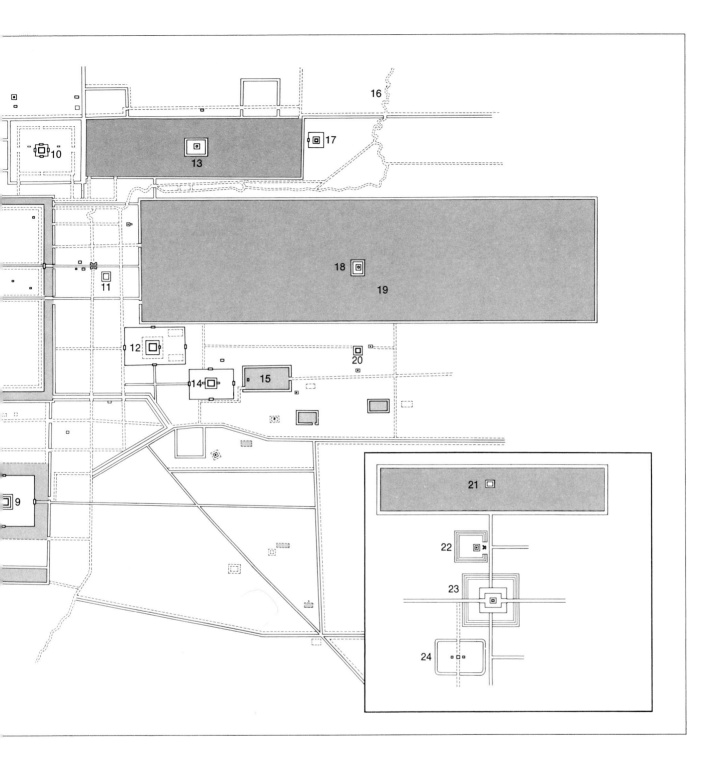

19) Grand Baray oriental, 20) Pré Rup; en médaillon, l'**ensemble de Roluos:** 21) Baray de Lolei, 22) Préah Kô, 23) Bakong, 24) Prasat Prei Monti. Toute la plaine angkorienne est aménagée pour l'irrigation intensive et la culture du riz. Un urbanisme orthogonal, où dominent les grands barays, ou réservoirs artificiels en charge, caractérise la capitale du royaume khmer.

Stadttor, 7) Baksei Chamkrong, 8) Phnom Bakheng, 9) Angkor Vat, 10) Preah Khan, 11) Ta Keo, 12) Ta Prohm, 13) Neak Pean, 14) Banteay Kdei, 15) Srah Srang, 16) Stung Siem Reap, 17) Ta Som, 18) Östlicher Mebon, 19) Östlicher Baray, 20) Pre Rup. Unten links (im Viereck): **Roluos.** Plan: 21) Baray von Lolei, 22) Preah Ko, 23) Bakong, 24) Prasat Prei Monti.

19) great east baray, 20) Pre Rup; inset, the **Roluos complex:** 21) Lolei baray, 22) Preah Ko, 23) Bakong, 24) Prasat Prei Monti. The whole Angkor plain was engineered for intensive irrigation and rice culture. A rectangular system of town planning dominated by the great *barays* or artificial heads of water characterised the capital of the Khmer kingdom.

287

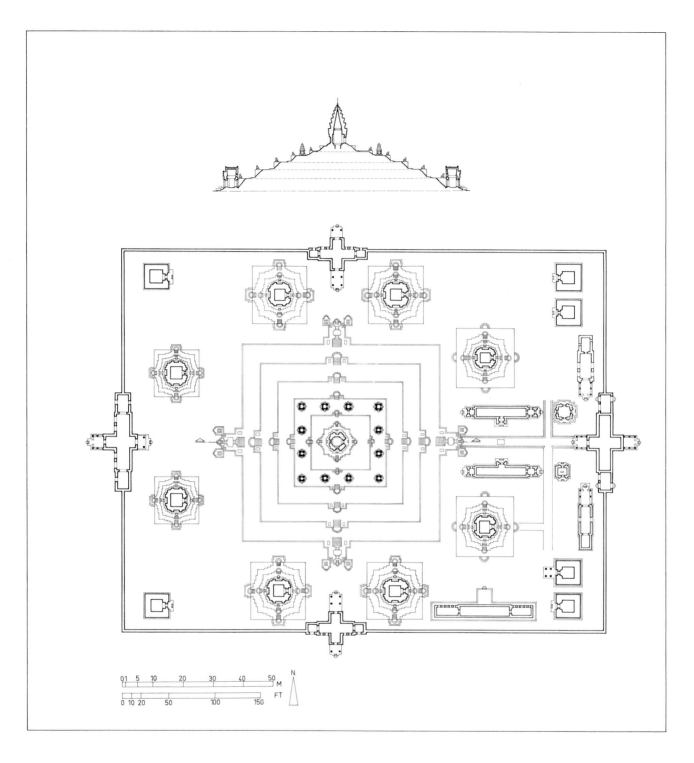

0 1 5 10 20 30 40 50 M
0 10 20 50 100 150 FT
N

Temple-montagne de Bakong, à Roluos, construit en 881 par Indravarman. Coupe et plan 1:1200. La ville proprement dite se nommait Hariharalaya. L'édifice est formé de cinq terrasses en grès, commandées par quatre escaliers axiaux. La cella originelle a été remplacée par un sanctuaire de XIIᵉ s. Autour de la pyramide, une série de prasats, ou sanctuaires secondaires en brique.

Roluos, Bakong, 881 von Indravarman errichtet. Die Stadt hieß ursprünglich Hariharalaya. Der Bakong ist als Tempelberg aus fünf Sandsteinterrassen mit vier axialen Treppen aufgebaut. Das Sanktuarium des 9. Jh. wurde im 12. Jh. durch einen Neubau ersetzt. Um den Terrassenbau sind acht Prasat aus Ziegelmauerwerk gruppiert. Schnitt und Grundriß 1:1200.

Temple mountain of Bakong, Roluos, built 881 by Indravarman. Section and plan 1:1200. The city proper was called Hariharalaya. The building consists of five sandstone terraces with four axial stairways. The original cella was replaced with another shrine in the twelfth century. Surrounding the pyramid are a series of *prasats* or secondary shrines in brick.

288

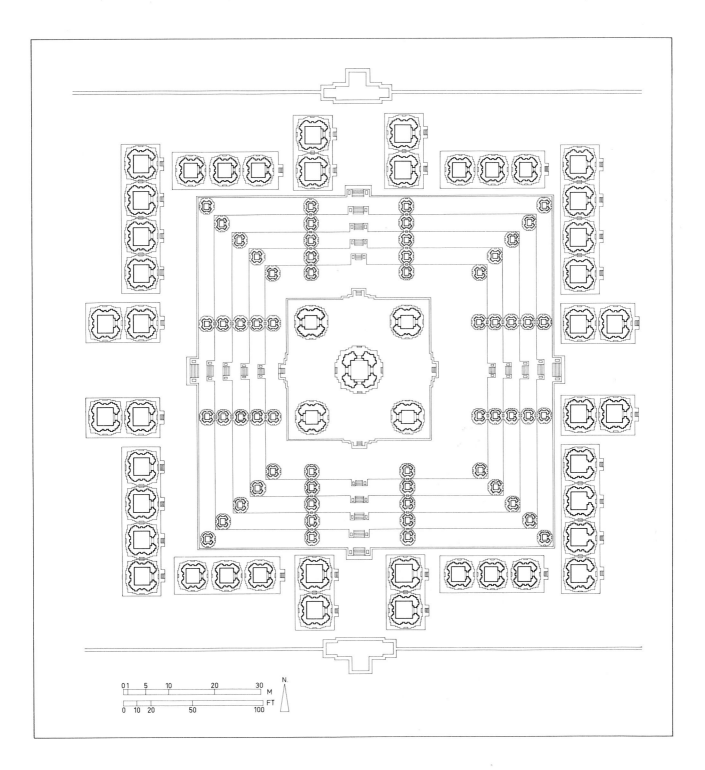

0 1   5   10   20   30   M
0 10 20   50   100 FT

N.

Temple-montagne de Phmon Bakheng, à Angkor, centre de la cité de Yasodharapura, fondée par Yasovarman en 893. Plan 1:800. Couronnant une colline dominant de 60 m la plaine, ce temple est entouré d'une première enceinte de 180 × 120 m. La pyramide se compose de cinq terrasses qu'entourent quarante-quatre prasats. Soixante templions en grès marquent les angles et bordent les escaliers axiaux.

Angkor, Phnom Bakheng, Mittelpunkt der 893 von Yashovarman gegründeten Stadt Yashodharapura. Das Heiligtum steht auf einem 60 m hohen, die Ebene beherrschenden Hügel, seine innere Umwallung schließt eine Fläche von 180 × 120 m ein. Auf der fünfstufigen, von 44 Prasat umgebenen Pyramide stehen fünf Turmheiligtümer, 60 Sandsteintempelchen an den Ecken und beidseits der Treppen jeder Stufe. Grundriß 1:800.

Temple mountain of Phnom Bakheng, Angkor, centre of the city of Yasodharapura founded by Yasovarman in 893. Plan 1:800. Crowning a hill 60 m. above the plain, this temple is surrounded by a first enclosure measuring 180 m. by 120 m. The pyramid consists of five terraces surrounded by forty-four *prasats*. Sixty small sandstone towers mark the corners and edge the axial stairways.

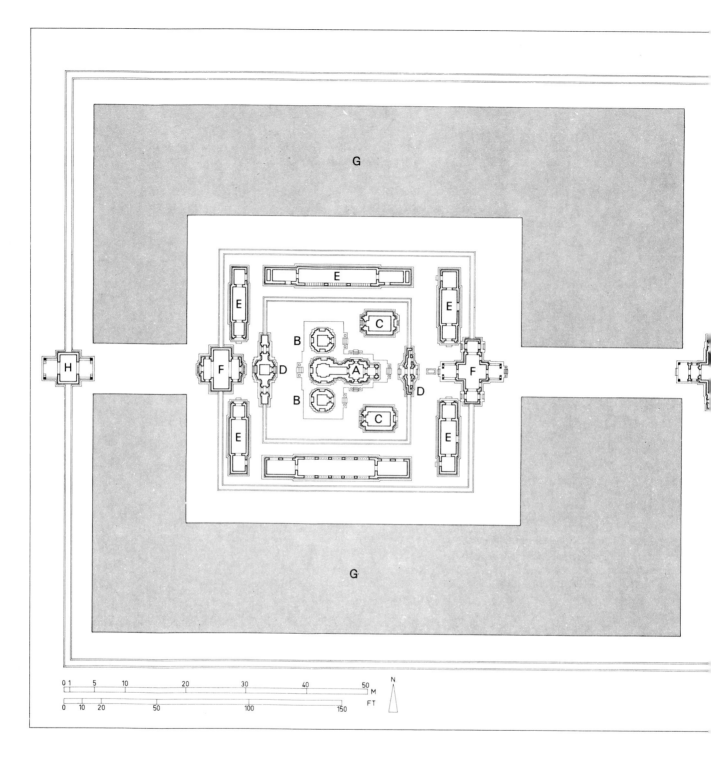

Temple de Banteay Srei, à Ishvarapura (Cambodge), construit en 967. Plan 1:600. Ce sanctuaire, dédié à Shiva, est situé à 20 km au nord-est d'Angkor. A) Sanctuaire principal à mandapa, B) Sanctuaires secondaires, C) Bibliothèques, D) Gopurams de la première enceinte, E) Bâtiments longs annonçant la galerie pourtournante, F) Gopurams de la deuxième enceinte, G) Douves, H) Gopurams de la troisième enceinte, I) Allée d'entrée, J) Galeries à portiques

Banteay Srei (Kambodscha), 967. Das Shiva-Heiligtum wurde in der untergegangenen Stadt Ishvarapura, 20 km nordöstlich von Angkor angelegt. Grundriß 1:600: A) Zentrales Sanktuarium mit Mandapa, B) Nebentempel, C) Bibliotheken, D) Gopura der ersten Einfriedung, E) Langsäle, Vorläufer der umlaufenden Galerien, F) Gopura der zweiten Einfriedung, G) Wassergräben, H) Gopura der dritten Einfriedung, I) Zugangsweg, J) einander gegenüber-

Temple of Banteay Srei, Ishvarapura (Cambodia), built in 967. Plan 1:600. This Shiva shrine is situated 20 km. north-east of Angkor. A) main mandapa shrine, B) secondary shrines, C) libraries, D) gopurams of the first enclosure, E) long buildings, forerunners of the peripheral gallery, F) gopurams of the second enclosure, G) moats, H) gopurams of the third enclosure, I) entrance avenue, J) facing porticoed

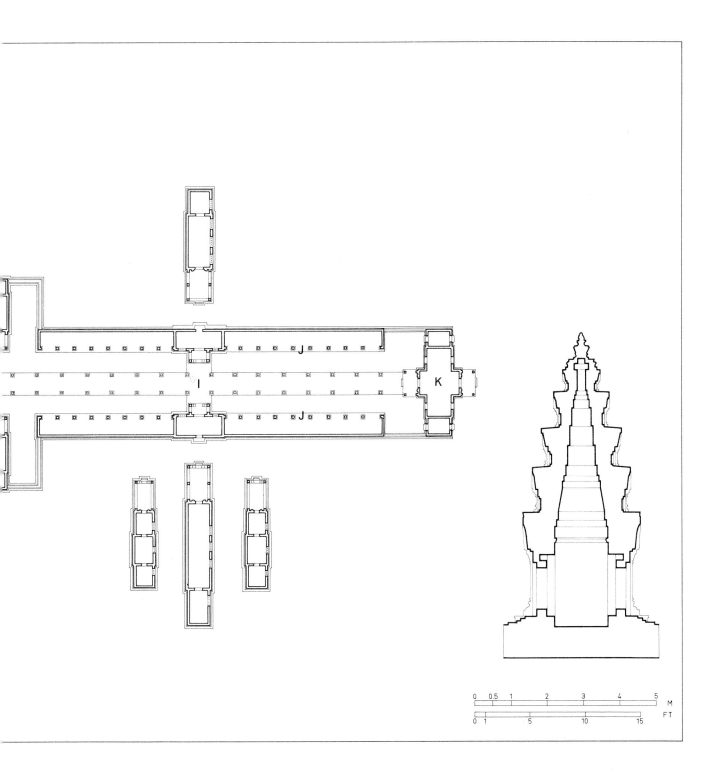

se faisant face, K) Gopuram d'entrée. A droite, coupe d'un **prasat de Banteay Srei,** avec ses cinq étages superposés, figurant la cité des dieux sur le mont Mérou, 1:100. La construction est réalisée en assises en encorbellement, ou fausse voûte, les Khmers n'ayant jamais connu la voûte à claveaux rayonnants.

liegende Pfeilergalerien, K) Haupteingang. **Banteay Srei, Prasat.** Der fünfgeschossige Turmtempel ist Symbol des Berges Meru, Sitz der Götter. Der Bau ist nach dem System des Kraggewölbes konstruiert; die Khmer kannten das Keilgewölbe nicht. Schnitt 1:100.

galleries, K) entrance gopuram. Right, section of a **prasat, Banteay Srei,** showing the five storeys representing the city of the gods on Mount Meru 1:100. The Khmers never knew the voussoir method of vaulting with wedge-shaped stones and the whole building is done with corbelled courses forming what are called 'false vaults'.

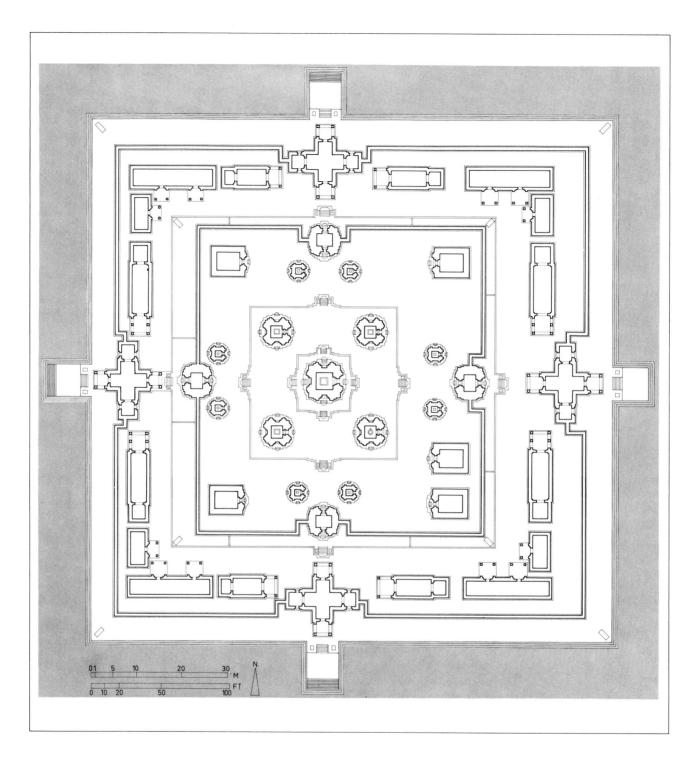

Mébon oriental, à Angkor, temple situé sur un îlot au centre du grand Baray oriental et construit par Rajendravarman II en 952. Plan 1:800. Ici, la couronne de salles longues doublant la muraille extérieure prépare plus nettement encore qu'à Banteay Srei la naissance de la galerie pourtournante. Les gopurams sont situés en retrait et les débarcadères sont saillants.

Angkor, Östlicher Mebon, 952 von Rajendravarman II. angelegt. Der Tempelbezirk ist auf einer Insel in der Mitte des Östlichen Baray erbaut. Die innerhalb der Umfassungsmauer umlaufenden Säle sind noch deutlicher als beim Banteay Srei eine Vorform der umlaufenden Galerien. Vor den etwas zurückgesetzten Gopura liegen Landungsstege. Grundriß 1:800.

East Mebon, Angkor, a temple built in 952 by Rajendravarman II on an island in the middle of the great east *baray*. Plan 1:800. Here the 'crown' of long buildings lining the outer wall heralds even more clearly than at Banteay Srei the later peripheral gallery. The *gopurams* are set back, while some of the landing-stages project forwards.

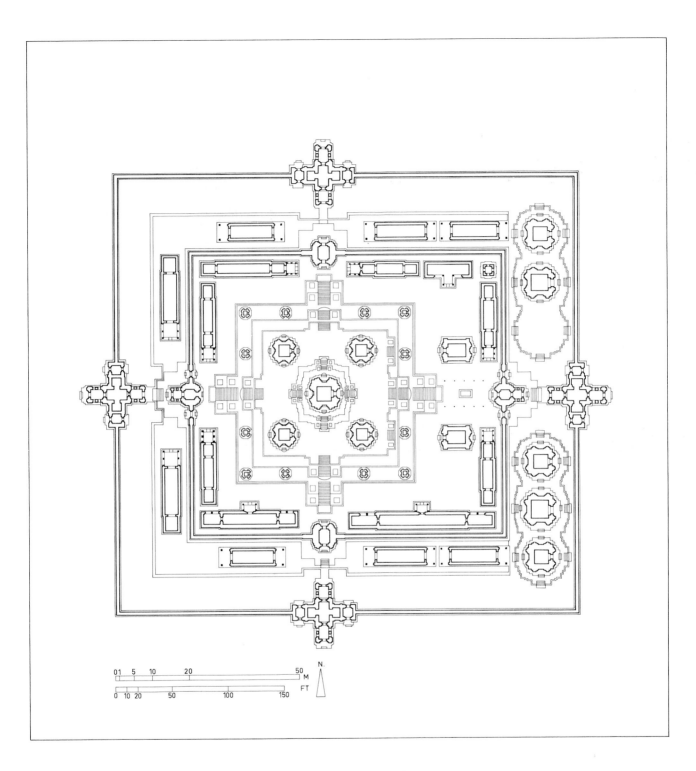

01 5 10 20 50 M

0 10 20 50 100 150 FT

N.

Temple-montagne de Pré Rup, à Angkor, édifié en 961 par Rajendravarman II (comme le Mébon oriental). Plan 1:1000. La pyramide à trois étages est en latérite. Sur la terrasse supérieure s'élèvent cinq prasats, selon une formule désormais classique (Phnom Bakheng et Mébon oriental). Entre le gopuram d'entrée et la seconde enceinte, de grands prasats en brique plus tardifs.

Angkor, Pre Rup, Tempelberg, 961 von Rajendravarman II., dem Erbauer des Östlichen Mebon, errichtet. Auf der dreistufigen, hohen Lateritpyramide stehen auf einer oberen Plattform fünf Turmheiligtümer in der klassischen kreuzweisen Anordnung (wie Phnom Bakheng und Östlicher Mebon). Die großen Türme aus Ziegelmauerwerk zwischen dem östlichen Gopura und der zweiten Mauer sind jünger. Grundriß 1:1000.

Temple mountain of Pre Rup, Angkor, built in 961 by Rajendravarman II, builder of the East Mebon. Plan 1:1000. The three-storeyed pyramid is built of laterite. Following the now standard formula (cf. Phnom Bakheng and the East Mebon) the upper terrace contains five *prasats*. Other large brick-built *prasats* were added later between the entrance *gopuram* and the second enclosure.

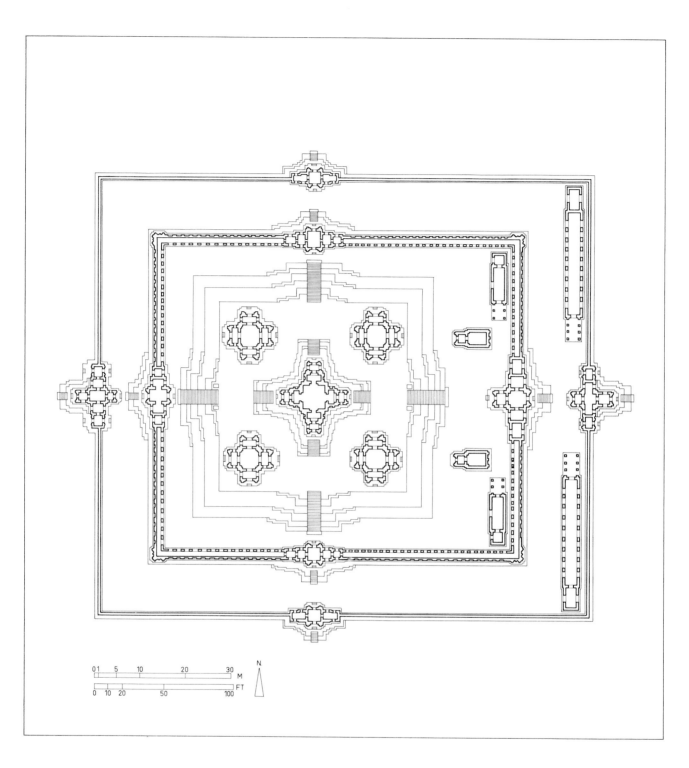

0 1 5   10   20   30   M
0 10 20   50   100   FT

N

Temple de Takéo, à Angkor, édifié entre 980 et 1013. Plan 1:800. Avec Takéo, on retrouve le type du grand temple-montagne à cinq gradins. Construit probablement dès la fin du règne de Jayavarman V et achevé par Suryavarman Ier, cet énorme édifice, qui culmine à 22 m au niveau de la dernière terrasse, présente l'un des premiers exemples de galerie pourtournante. Cinq prasats couronnent son sommet.

Angkor, Ta Keo, Tempelberg, 980–1013. Der gewaltige Tempelbau wurde wahrscheinlich gegen Ende der Regierungszeit Jayavarmans V. begonnen und unter Suryavarman I. vollendet. Auf der obersten Plattform der – jetzt wieder fünfstufigen – Pyramide, in 22 m Höhe, stehen fünf Turmheiligtümer. Um die zweite Stufe läuft eine Galerie, eines der ersten Beispiele dieser Bauform. Grundriß 1:800.

Temple of Takeo, Angkor, built between 980 and 1013. Plan 1:800. Takeo is another example of the large five-storeyed temple mountain. Begun probably at the end of the reign of Jayavarman V and completed by Suryavarman I, this enormous building—the last terrace is 22 m. high—contains one of the first examples of a peripheral gallery. Five *prasats* crown the summit.

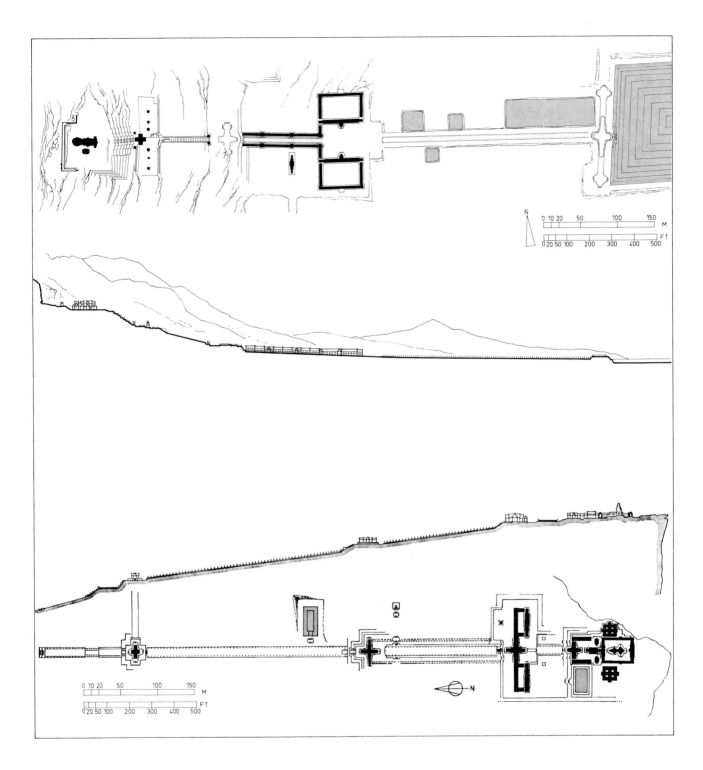

Plan et profil du grand temple de Vat Phu (Cambodge), construit par Jayavarman VI entre 1080 et 1107, 1:5000. En bas: **profil et plan du temple de Préah Vihear,** couronnant la chaîne des Dangrek (Cambodge), construit par Suryavarman I er et Suryavarman II (1050 à 1150) 1:5000. Deux types de temples édifiés sur un plan axé et non centré. Programme architectural énorme et audacieux.

Oben: **Heiligtum Vat Phu** (Kambodscha), der älteste Tempel, 1080–1107 unter Jayavarman VI. ausgebaut. Lageplan und Profil 1:5000. Unten: **Preah Vihear (Kambodscha),** 1050–1150 von Suryavarman I. und Suryavarman II. errichtet. Der Tempel ist über einem Steilhang des Dangrek-Gebirges angelegt. Profil und Lageplan 1:5000. Beide Tempel, gewaltige und kühne Anlagen, sind axial ausgerichtet.

Great temple of Vat Phu (Cambodia), built 1080–1107 by Jayavarman VI. Plan and profile 1:5000. Below, **Temple of Preah Vihear,** crowning the Dangrek chain (Cambodia), built 1050–1150 by Suryavarman I and Suryavarman II. Profile and plan 1:5000. Two types of temple built on a non-centralised axial plan: in terms of its architectural programme, an enormous and ambitious undertaking.

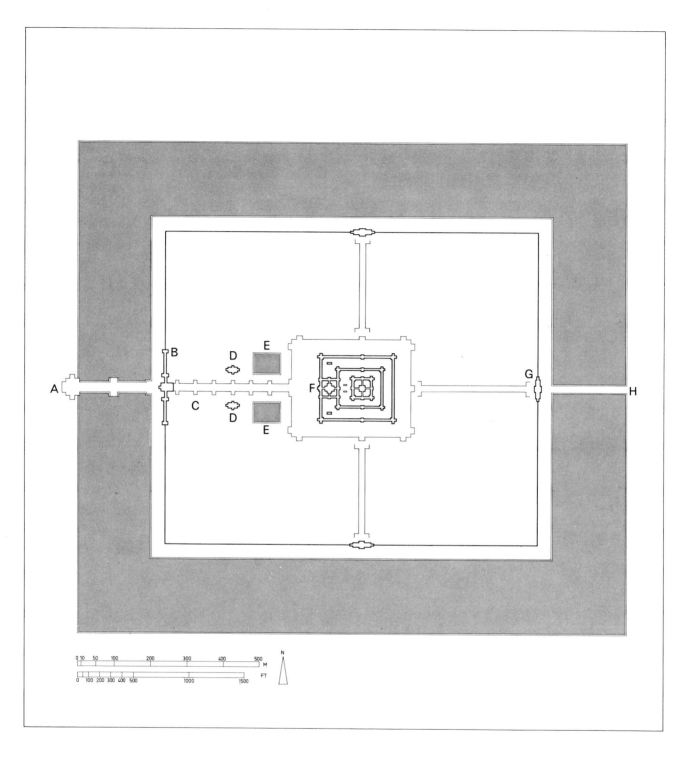

0 10 50   100   200   300   400   500   M

0 100 200 300 400 500   1000   1500   FT

N

Grand temple d'Angkor Vat, situation générale de l'édifice avec son enceinte extérieure et ses larges douves 1:10000. Construit par Suryavarman II (1113 à 1150). A) Digue sur la douve de 200 m de large, B) Propylées, C) Allée axiale de 350 m de long, D) Bibliothèques, E) Bassins, F) Grand Temple, G) Gopuram oriental, H) Digue de terre. A l'intérieur de l'enceinte, la ville occupait une surface de 1 km².

Angkor Vat, 1113–1150 von Suryavarman II. erbaut. Die Stadt (innerhalb der Mauern) bedeckte eine Fläche von 1 km². Lageplan mit Außenmauer und Wassergraben 1:10000: A) Dammstraße über den 200 m breiten Wassergraben, B) Haupteingang mit seitlichen Galerien, C) 350 m lange axiale Straße, D) Bibliotheken, E) Wasserbecken, F) Tempelberg, G) östliches Gopura, H) Deich.

Great temple of Angkor Vat, built by Suryavarman II (1113–1150). Site plan of the building with its outer enclosure and broad moats 1:10,000. A) causeway over the 200 m. wide moat, B) propylaea, C) axial avenue (350 m. long), D) libraries, E) pools, F) great temple, G) east gopuram, H) earth embankment. Within its enclosure the city occupies an area of 1 km².

Angkor Vat, détails de la construction des **galeries voûtées** en encorbellement 1:200. A) Galerie du préau cruciforme, sur son terrasson, avec sa «nef» centrale contre-butée par deux bas-côtés. B) Galerie du premier étage, présentant un profil asymétrique. C) Galerie du deuxième étage avec un seul contre-butement, mais dont la hauteur interne est moindre.

Angkor Vat, Galerien mit Kraggewölben. Schnitte 1:200: A) Galerie des kreuzförmigen Hofes, auf hohem Unterbau; an das mittlere Schiff sind beidseits niederere angelehnt, B) asymmetrische Galerie der ersten Pyramidenstufe, C) Galerie der zweiten Stufe; sie ist niedriger und nur von einem Seitenschiff begleitet.

Angkor Vat. Structural details of the corbel-vaulted galleries 1:200. A) gallery of the cruciform courtyard built on a little terrace with its 'nave' buttressed by two side aisles, B) first-storey gallery with its asymmetrical profile, C) second-storey gallery with a single buttress (but not so high inside).

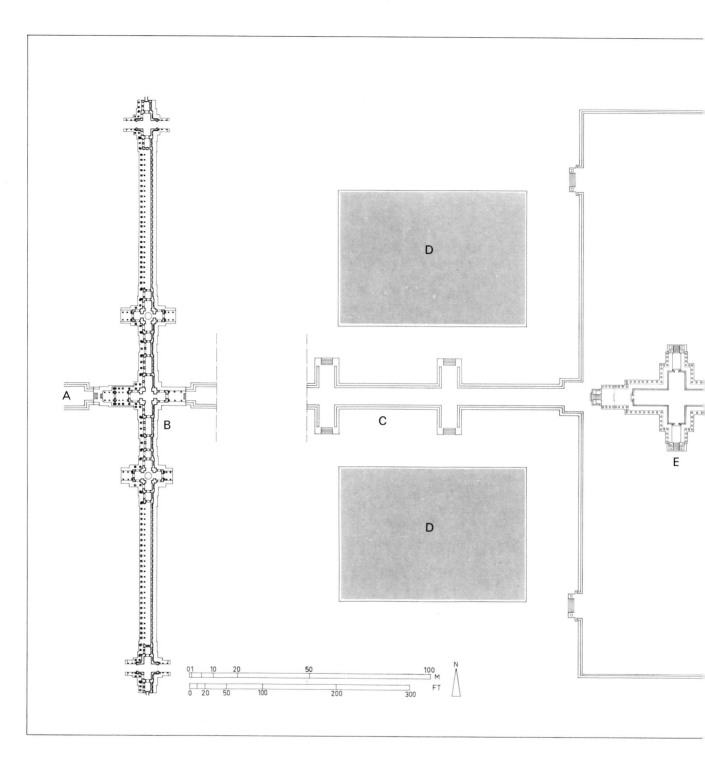

Angkor Vat (1113–1150), plan des propylées et du temple 1:1500. A) Digue franchissant la douve, B) Propylées en portique de 235 m de large, coupées par un triple gopuram, avec tours aux extrémités, C) Allée axiale (ici incomplète) de 350 m de long, surélevée et dallée, qu'entrecoupent douze perrons, D) Bassins, E) Plate-forme cruciforme à deux niveaux, disposée sur la première terrasse, F) Galerie des bas-reliefs, ou 3e enceinte, ouverte vers l'extérieur,

Angkor Vat, 1113–1150. Grundrisse des Haupteingangs und des Tempels 1:1500: A) Dammstraße, B) 235 m breiter Haupteingang mit Säulenhallen, in der Mitte Gopura mit drei Durchgängen, an den Enden Türme, C) 350 m lange axiale erhöhte Zugangsstraße (hier geschnitten), mit Steinplatten gepflastert, beidseits 12 Aufgänge, D) Wasserbekken, E) kreuzförmige zweistufige Plattform auf der untersten Tempelstufe, F) Reliefgalerie des dritten Mauergür-

Angkor Vat (1113–50). Plan of propylaea and temple 1:1500. A) causeway crossing the moat, B) portico of propylaea 235 m. wide, broken by a triple *gopuram* with towers at the extremities, C) axial avenue (incomplete here); this is 350 m. long, raised and paved, and cut by twelve stairways, D) pools, E) two-level cruciform platform on the first terrace, F) gallery of the bas-reliefs or third enclosure, open to the outside, G) cruciform courtyard, H) small libraries,

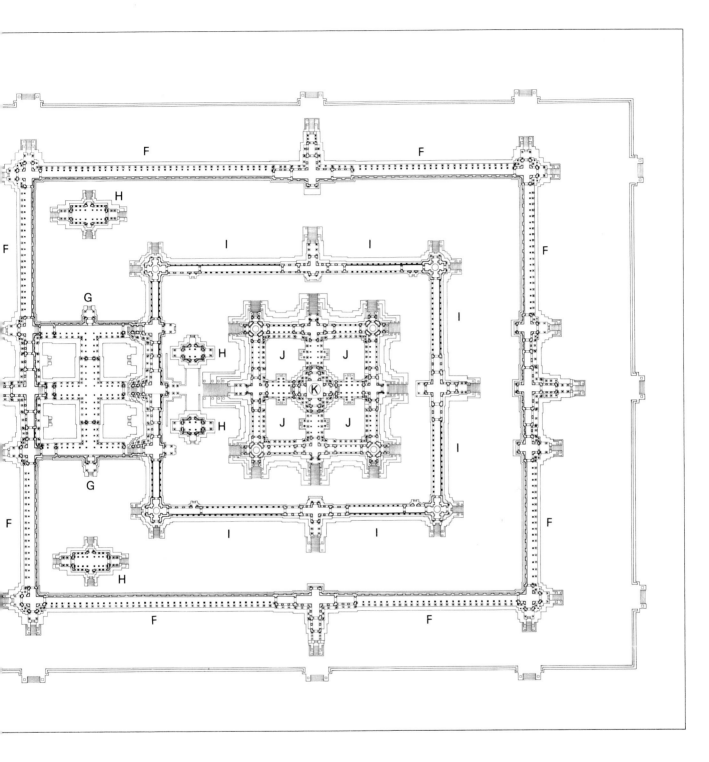

G) Préau cruciforme, H) Petites bibliothèques, I) Galeries de la 2ᵉ enceinte, ouvertes vers l'intérieur, J) Massif de la 3ᵉ enceinte, dont les galeries sont ouvertes tant vers l'extérieur que vers l'intérieur, K) Sanctuaire principal, érigé sous forme de tour jaillissant à 65 m au-dessus de la plaine et entourée de quatre tours secondaires.

tels, nach außen geöffnet, G) kreuzförmiger Hof, H) kleine Bibliotheken, I) Galerien des zweiten Gürtels, J) erster Gürtel mit beidseits offenen Galerien, K) Haupttheiligtum; der Tempelturm ragt 65 m über die Ebene; an den Plattformecken vier kleinere Tempeltürme.

I) galleries of the second enclosure, open to the inside, J) body of the third enclosure with galleries open both to the outside and to the inside, K) main shrine in the form of a tower rising 65 m. above the plain and surrounded by four secondary towers.

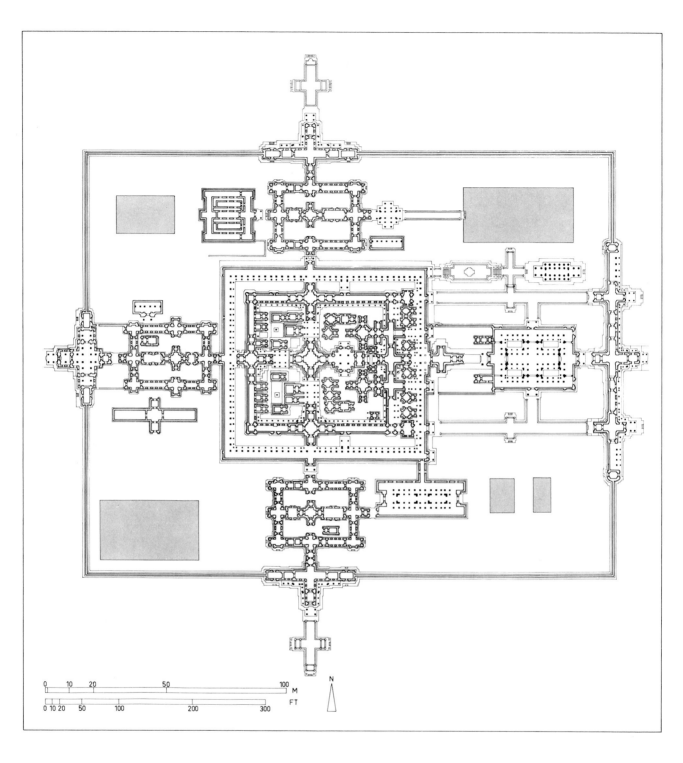

0 10 20 50 100 M

0 10 20 50 100 200 300 FT

N

Temple de Préah Khan, à Angkor, construit par Jayavarman VII entre 1184 et 1191. Plan 1:1500. Ce vaste temple plat sis au milieu d'une enceinte de 1000 × 750 m, entourée d'une douve de 40 m de large, représente un complexe d'édifices s'enchevêtrant sur 220 × 170 m. Il marque l'apparition du style «baroque» de la dernière période angkorienne, de culte bouddhique.

Preah Khan von Angkor, Tempel 1184 bis 1191 von Jayavarman VII. errichtet. Der riesige, auf einer Ebene angelegte Tempel mißt 220 × 170 m; er liegt in einem von einer Mauer und einem 40 m breiten Wassergraben umgebenen Stadtbezirk von 1000 × 750 m. Dieser buddhistische Tempel ist ein Beispiel des «barocken» Stils in der letzten Epoche von Angkor. Grundriß 1:1500.

Temple of Preah Khan, Angkor, built 1184–91 by Jayavarman VII. Plan 1:1500. This enormous low temple, situated in the middle of an enclosure measuring 1000 m. by 750 m. and surrounded by a 40 m. wide moat, comprises a complex of buildings occupying an area of 220 m. by 170 m. It marks the appearance of the 'baroque' style of the final, Buddhist period of Angkor culture.

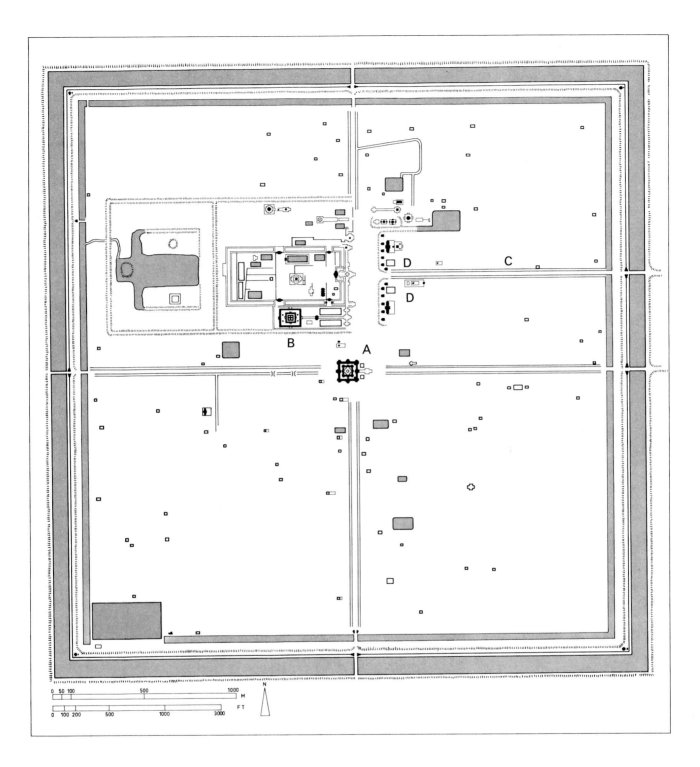

Plan de la cité d'Angkor Thom, construite par Jayavarman VII vers 1200, 1:20000. La double douve, créant un système hydraulique complexe, est franchie par les quatre digues axiales, auxquelles s'ajoute celle de la Porte des Victoires (C). Au centre, le temple du Bayon (A); au nord-ouest, le Baphuon, édifié par Udayadityavarman II vers 1060 (B); en face des terrasses royales, les Kléang (D).

Angkor Thom, um 1200 von Jayavarman VII. erbaut. Die Stadt ist von zwei Wassergräben umgeben, die zu einem raffinierten Be- und Entwässerungssystem gehören. Über die Gräben führen fünf Dammstraßen, vier in den Achsen und eine vor dem Siegestor. Stadtplan 1:20000: A) Bayon, B) Baphuon, um 1060 von Udayadityavarman II. erbaut, C) Siegestor, D) die beiden Kleang gegenüber den Königlichen Terrassen.

City of Angkor Thom, built c.1200 by Jayavarman VII. Plan 1:20,000. The double moat, key to a complex hydraulic system, is crossed by four axial causeways plus that of the Gate of Victories (C). Centre, the Bayon temple (A); to the north-west, the Baphuon, built c.1060 by Udayadityavarman II (B); opposite the royal terraces, the kleangs (D).

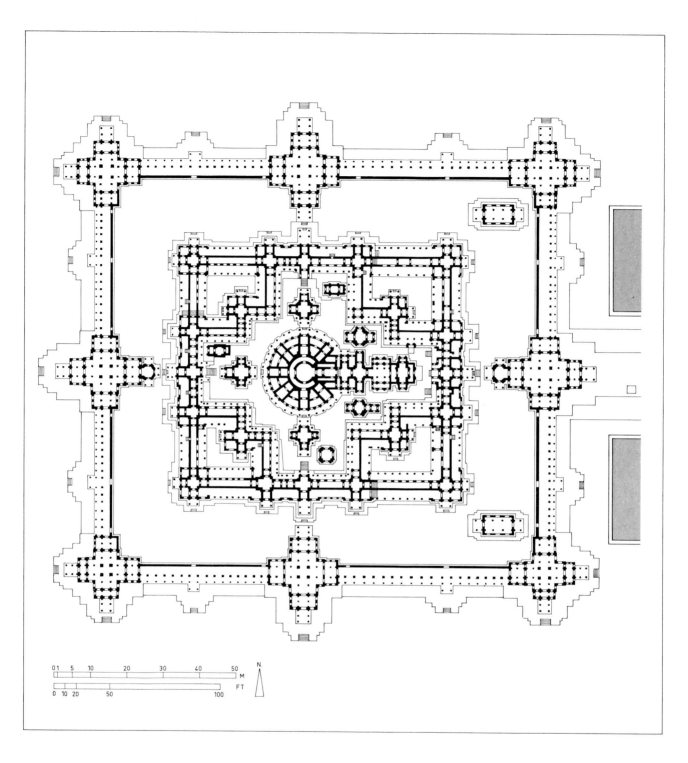

01 5   10   20   30   40   50
                                           M
                                        FT
0 10 20   50   100

N

Temple du Bayon, édifié par Jayavarman VII au centre d'Angkor Thom au
début du XIIIᵉ s. Plan 1:1000. Ce sanctuaire bouddhique, transformé par son
auteur en temple-montagne par l'adjonction de hauts massifs en forme de
tours à visages, figurant les traits du roi
en Boddhisattva, est l'édifice le plus
complexe d'Angkor: 54 tours-satellites
totalisent 216 visages.

Angkor Thom, Bayon, Anfang 13. Jh.
von Jayavarman VII. erbaut. Das buddhistische Heiligtum hat durch die sich
zur Mitte hin in der Höhe steigernden
Türme die Gestalt eines Tempelbergs
erhalten. Jedes Heiligtum trägt einen
Turm mit vier Gesichtern, dem des
Herrschers als Bodhisattva. Der Bayon
mit dem zentralen Turm und 54 Neben-
türmen mit 216 Gesichtern ist das kom-
plexeste Bauwerk von Angkor.

Bayon temple, Angkor Thom, built by
Jayavarman VII in the centre of the
city at the beginning of the thirteenth
century. Plan 1:1000. Transformed by
its architect into a temple mountain by
the addition of tall, solid towers carved
with faces (the king as bodhisattva), this
Buddhist shrine is the most complex
building on the Ankgor site. The 54
satellite towers bear a total of 216 faces.

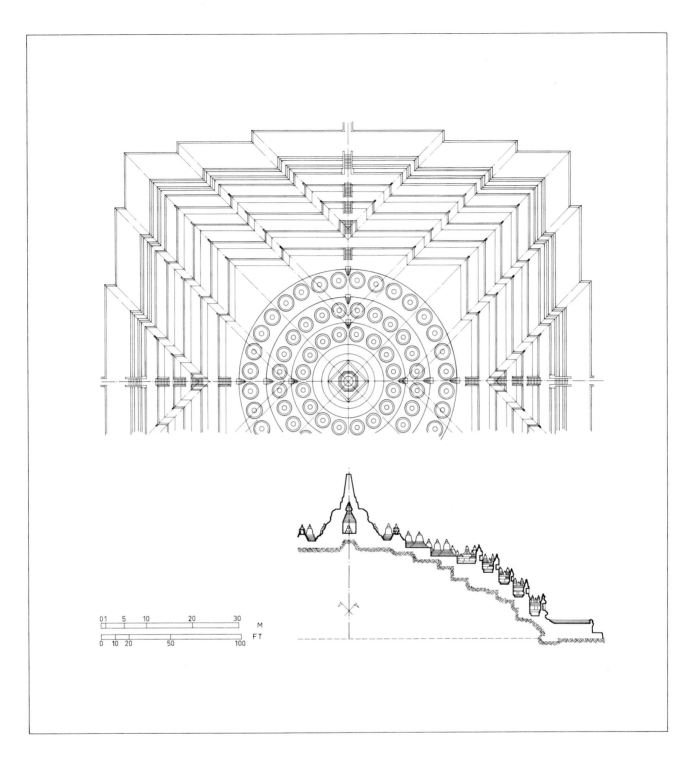

Grand temple-stupa de Borobudur (Java) construit entre 800 et 850. Plan et coupe 1:800. Structure centrée surmontée de 72 petits sanctuaires secondaires entourant le stupa central qui commémore le Bouddha. Cette énorme construction, avec ses escaliers axiaux, a probablement servi de modèle aux premiers temples-montagnes khmers.

Borobudur (Java), 800–850. Ein Zentralbau mit 72 Stupas rings um den großen mittleren Stupa zum Gedenken Buddhas. Vielleicht war der gewaltige Bau mit axialen Treppen das Vorbild für die ersten Tempelberge der Khmer. Grundriß und Schnitt 1:800.

Great stupa temple of Borobudur (Java), built between 800 and 850. Plan and section 1:800. A centrally planned structure surmounted by 72 small secondary shrines surrounding the central *stupa*, which commemorates the Buddha. This enormous building with its axial stairways was probably the model for the first Khmer temple mountains.

Temple d'Ananda, à Pagan (Birmanie), lieu de culte bouddhique édifié en 1090 par le roi Kyaunzittha. Demi-coupe et demi-élévation de l'une des façades et plan 1:500. Fondé sur une double symétrie, cet édifice reproduit la silhouette du stupa. Chacune des faces du carré comporte un porche en avancée. A l'intérieur, un double corridor concentrique. Au centre, quatre statues du Bouddha (H. 10 m).

Pagan (Burma), Ananda-Tempel, 1090 von König Kyanzittha errichtet. Das kreuzförmige (2 Symmetrieachsen) buddhistische Heiligtum hat im Aufriß die Silhouette eines Stupa. Jeder Seite ist ein Portal vorgelegt. Im zentralen Raum, um den zwei konzentrische Gänge führen, befinden sich vier 10 m hohe Buddhastatuen. Schnitt einer Hälfte, Aufriß einer halben Fassade, Grundriß (angeschnitten) 1:500.

Temple of Ananda, Pagan (Burma), a Buddhist shrine built in 1090 by King Kyanzittha. Half section and half elevation of one of the façades and plan 1:500. Using double symmetry, this building reproduces the silhouette of the *stupa*. Each side of the square carries a projecting porch. Inside is a double concentric corridor, and in the centre there are four statues of the Buddha 10 m. in height.

Chine

China

China

Dès les Han (206 av. J.-C. à 220 apr. J.-C.), la Chine connaît un extraordinaire essor architectural. Les tronçons de murs édifiés sous les Royaumes Combattants, qui protègent le pays au nord contre les incursions des Barbares nomades, sont réunis entre eux pour former la Grande Muraille, longue de 3000 km.

L'urbanisme revêt une importance considérable: fondées sur un plan rigoureusement rectangulaire, régi par une stricte axialité qui correspond à une vision cosmologique et hiérarchique, les capitales auront des proportions considérables. Au VIIe siècle, Changan compte plus d'un million d'habitants. Au cœur de l'ensemble s'édifie la Cité Impériale, véritable ville dans la ville, avec ses propres murailles, enserrant le palais et les édifices gouvernementaux. Sous les Sui et les Tang (VIe au Xe s.), Changan couvre un rectangle muré de 9,7 par 8,6 km, avec une enceinte de 35 km et des avenues de 100 à 150 m de large bordant des damiers de 25000 m². Cette architecture est destinée à exalter le pouvoir central.

A partir du Ier siècle, le bouddhisme pénètre dans l'empire, véhiculant certaines formes issues de l'Inde. Des pagodes en brique ou en pierre voient le jour dès le Ve siècle. Des grottes, à l'instar de celles d'Ajanta en Inde, sont creusées à Gunhuang, Yungang et Longmen, entre 350 et le VIIe siècle. Mais l'essentiel des édifices publics et impériaux est traditionnellement en bois, même dans le Pékin des Ming (XVe au XVIIe s.). Les bâtiments, construits sur de vastes esplanades ou terrasses, sont à piliers et à fermes, selon une technique très élaborée des charpentes, dont hériteront les Japonais à l'époque de Nara

Mit der Han-Dynastie (206 v. bis 220 n. Chr.) setzte in China ein außerordentlicher Aufschwung der Architektur ein. Die zur Zeit der Kämpfenden Reiche errichteten Mauerabschnitte, die den Norden des Landes vor Barbareneinfällen schützen sollten, wurden zur 3000 km langen Großen Mauer verbunden.

Die Bedeutung des Städtebaus nahm stark zu: Die Hauptstädte mit exakt rechtwinkligem Grundriß und streng axialem System – entsprechend den kosmologischen und hierarchischen Vorstellungen – nahmen imponierende Ausmaße an. Changan zählte im 7. Jahrhundert über eine Million Einwohner. Im Zentrum der Stadtanlage liegt die kaiserliche Stadt, eine Stadt in der Stadt mit eigener Mauer, die den Palast und die Regierungsgebäude umschließt. Unter den Sui und den Tang (6. bis 10. Jahrhundert) bildete Changan ein ummauertes Rechteck von 9,7 × 8,6 km und war von einer ungefähr 35 km langen Mauer umschlossen. 100 bis 150 m breite Straßen teilten die Stadt in Quartiere von 25000 m². Ziel und Sinn dieser Architektur war die Verherrlichung der Zentralgewalt.

Vom 1. Jahrhundert an drang der Buddhismus in China ein und brachte gewisse indische Formen mit. Im 5. Jahrhundert wurden die ersten Pagoden aus Stein oder Ziegeln erbaut; Höhlentempel nach dem Beispiel von Ajanta in Indien entstanden zwischen 350 und dem 7. Jahrhundert in Gunhuang, Yungang und Longmen. Die wichtigsten öffentlichen und kaiserlichen Bauten waren weiterhin der Tradition entsprechend Holzbauten, selbst im Peking der Ming (15. bis 17. Jahrhundert). Die auf großen Esplanaden oder Terrassen errichteten Gebäude sind Stützenkon-

The Han dynasty (206 B.C. to A.D. 220) saw the beginning of an extraordinary flowering of architecture in China. The sections of wall built under the Warring Kingdoms to protect the north against invasion by barbarian nomads were joined up to form the Great Wall, 3,000 km. long.

Town-planning took on considerable importance. Based on a rectangular plan and using a strictly axial system that corresponded to a particular cosmological and hierarchical vision, China's capitals grew to impressive proportions; seventh-century Ch'ang-an had a million inhabitants. The heart of the complex was the Imperial City; a veritable town within a town, this had its own walls enclosing the palace and the government buildings. Under the Sui and T'ang dynasties (sixth to tenth century) Ch'ang-an was a fortified rectangle of 9.7 km. by 8.6 km. with a wall measuring 35 km. around and avenues between 100 and 150 m. wide forming 25,000m² blocks. The purpose of Chinese architecture was to exalt the central power.

Buddhism began to penetrate the empire in the first century, bringing with it certain architectural forms of Indian origin. Brick or stone pagodas were built from the fifth century onwards. Cave temples on the model of those at Ajanta in India were dug at Gun-huang, Yün-kang and Lung-men between 350 and the seventh century. But the great majority of public and imperial buildings were traditionally built of wood, even in Ming Peking (fifteenth to seventeenth century). Erected on vast esplanades or terraces, such buildings employed posts and trusses in a highly elaborate framing technique, which the Japanese inherited in the Nara period

(VIIIᵉ s.): toitures incurvées, supportées par des jeux savants de corbeaux ou consoles en porte à faux. Les temples impériaux – Temple du Ciel à Pékin – sont les autels de sacrifice où l'empereur venait officier et prier les puissances naturelles. Ils relèvent de l'architecture traditionnelle en bois.

Les habitations, elles aussi, connaissent très tôt un développement remarquable, régi par une scrupuleuse hiérarchie sociale. Les jardins constituent un art du paysagisme d'une riche imagination qui ne cherche pas à imiter la nature, mais à créer un décor visant à des effets de surprise ou à favoriser la méditation.

struktionen mit hölzernen Dachstühlen in einer sehr ausgefeilten Zimmermannstechnik, die dann von den Japanern in der Nara-Zeit (8.Jahrhundert) übernommen wurde. Kaiserliche Tempel wie der Tempel des Himmels in Peking – Opferstätten, an denen der Kaiser Opfer darbrachte und zu den Naturmächten betete – sind Holzbauten im traditionellen System.

Der Wohnbau entwickelte sich früh in bemerkenswerter Weise, und zwar entsprechend der strengen sozialen und hierarchischen Ordnung. Die Gärten sind in einer phantasievollen Art der Landschaftsgärtnerei angelegt, ohne die Absicht, die Natur zu imitieren, sondern mit dem Ziel, Überraschungseffekte zu schaffen und die Meditation zu begünstigen.

(eighth century); their concave roofs were supported by skilful use of corbels and cantilevers. The imperial temples—such as the Temple of Heaven in Peking—were sacrificial altars at which the Emperor officiated to invoke the powers of nature, and were based on traditional timber architecture.

Housing also made great strides at a very early date; ideas of social hierarchy were important here. China also evolved a richly imaginative art of landscape gardening that sought not to imitate nature but to create a decor embodying surprise effects or offering aids to meditation.

1 Vue axiale du Taihe dian, dans la Cité Interdite de Pékin, édifice de bois construit sur un socle de marbre.
2 Sur de hauts socles de maçonnerie peinte en rouge, que couronnent des créneaux, les édifices de bois de la Cité Interdite de Pékin.
3 Le Qinian dian, ou salle de la prière pour les bonnes récoltes, du Temple du Ciel, à Pékin, construit en 1420 sur plan circulaire.

1 Peking, Verbotene Stadt, axiale Ansicht des Taihe dian: Holzbau auf marmornem Sockelbau
2 Peking, Verbotene Stadt, die hölzernen Bauten stehen auf hohen gemauerten Basen, die rot gestrichen sind und Zinnen tragen
3 Peking, Tempel des Himmels, Qinian dian (Halle der Gebete für gute Ernten), ein Rundbau (1420)

1 Axial view of the T'ai-ho Tien in the Forbidden City, Peking, a wooden building on a marble base.
2 The wooden buildings of Peking's Forbidden City stand on high masonry bases painted red and topped with crenellations.
3 The Chi Nien Tien or Hall of Prayer for Good Harvests, part of the Temple of Heaven, Peking, built on a circular plan in 1420.

1

2

3

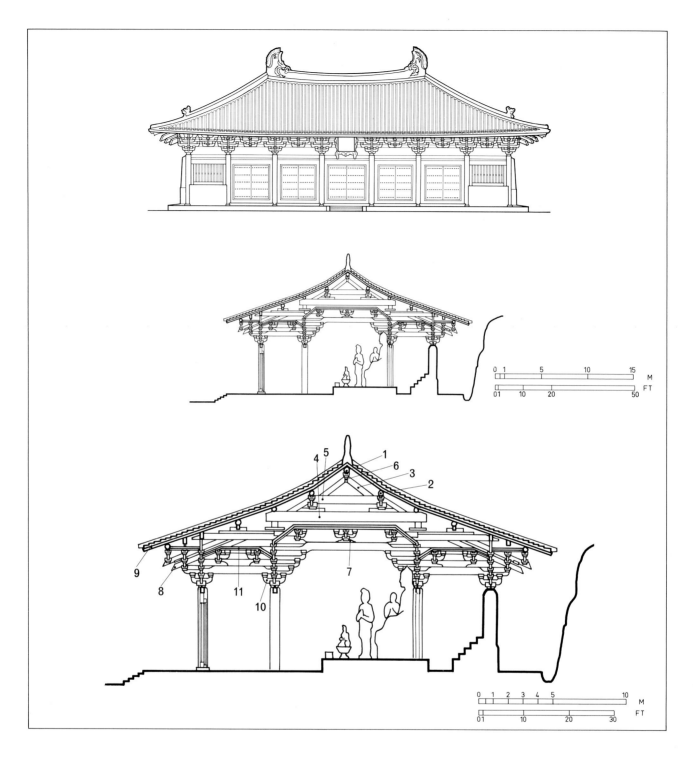

Temple du Foguang si, à Wutai shan (Shanxi), salle principale construite en bois entre 850 et 860. Elévation et coupe transversale 1:400. La plus ancienne construction en bois de Chine, remontant à l'époque Tang. En bas, coupe détaillée 1:250. 1) Panne faîtière, 2) Panne, 3) Contre-fiche, 4) Entrait, 5) Entrait retroussé, 6) Poinçon, 7) Console, 8) Bras de levier, 9) Chevrons, 10) Bras de console, 11) Plafond.

Foguang si am Wutai Shan (Shanxi), Haupthalle, zwischen 850 und 860. Der älteste erhaltene Holzbau in China, aus der Tang-Zeit. Aufriß und Querschnitt 1:400; unten: Querschnitt 1:250: 1) Firstpfette, 2) Pfette, 3) Strebe, 4) Querbalken, 5) oberer Querbalken, 6) kurze Säule, 7) Konsole, 8) sparrenartiger Hebelarm, 9) Sparren, 10) Konsolenarm, 11) Decke.

Fo Kuang temple (near Mount Wu T'ai, Shansi), main hall built of wood between 850 and 860. Elevation and cross section 1:400. This is the oldest wooden building in China, going back to the T'ang dynasty. Below, detailed section 1:250. 1) ridge purlin, 2) purlin, 3) brace, 4) tie-beam, 5) cocked tie-beam, 6) king post, 7) bracket, 8) lever arm, 9) rafters, 10) bracket arm, 11) ceiling.

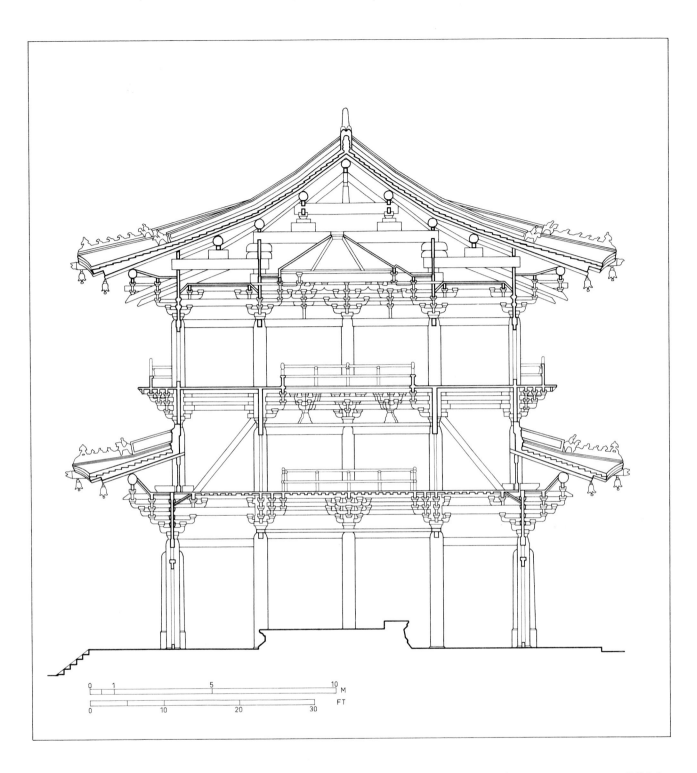

0 1 5 10 M
FT
0 10 20 30

Temple de Guanyin ge (Dule si), Jixian (Hebei), édifice de bois datant de 984. Coupe transversale 1:150. Ce temple à trois étages, de la dynastie des Liao, est encore construit dans l'esprit des Tang. Les consoles sont déjà apparentées aux créations des Song. La courbure incurvée des toitures est très caractéristique de l'architecture classique chinoise.

Jixian (Hebei), Guanayin-ge-Tempel, 984. Der Tempel, ein dreigeschossiger Holzbau der Liao-Dynastie, entspricht in der Konstruktion noch der Tang-Zeit. Die Konsolen ähneln bereits denen der Song-Bauten. Die Schwingung der Dächer ist eine Eigenheit der klassischen chinesischen Architektur. Querschnitt 1:150.

Kuan Yin hall, Tu Lo temple, Ch'i-hsien (Hopei), a wooden building dating from 984. Cross section 1:150. Erected under the Liao dynasty, this three-storeyed building is still T'ang in spirit. The brackets, however, already look forward to the Sung period. The concave line of the roof is very typical of classical Chinese architecture.

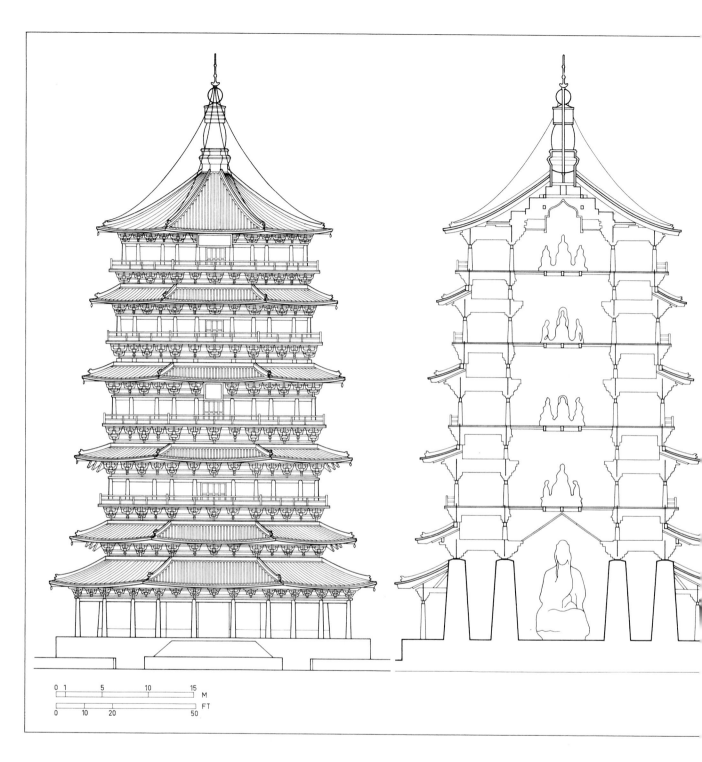

0 1   5   10   15
                         M
0   10   20   50
                         FT

Pagode Shijia du Fogong si, Ying xian (Shanxi), édifice datant de 1056. Elévation et coupe 1:400. Bâtiment octogonal à quatre étages, entièrement construit en bois, hormis le soubassement et le rez-de-chaussée. Le système de charpente, avec jeu complexe de corbeaux, caractérise l'architecture chinoise. La forme de la pagode dérive du stupa et des tours symbolisant le mont Mérou en Inde.

Yingxian (Shanxi), Shijia-Pagode des Fogong si, 1056. Der fünfgeschossige Bau mit oktogonalem Grundriß ist mit Ausnahme des Unterbaus und des Erdgeschosses aus Holz errichtet. Das komplizierte Holzwerk ist ein Charakteristikum der chinesischen Holzarchitektur. Die Form der Pagode ist aus dem Stupa und den indischen, den Berg Meru symbolisierenden Türmen abgeleitet. Aufriß und Schnitt 1:400.

Shi Chia pagoda, Fo Kung temple, Yinghsien (Shansi), built 1056. Elevation and section 1:400. An octagonal five-storeyed structure built entirely of wood except for the base and the ground floor. The beam frame system with its skilful use of brackets is a feature of Chinese architecture. The pagoda form derives from that of the *stupa* and of towers symbolising Mount Meru in India.

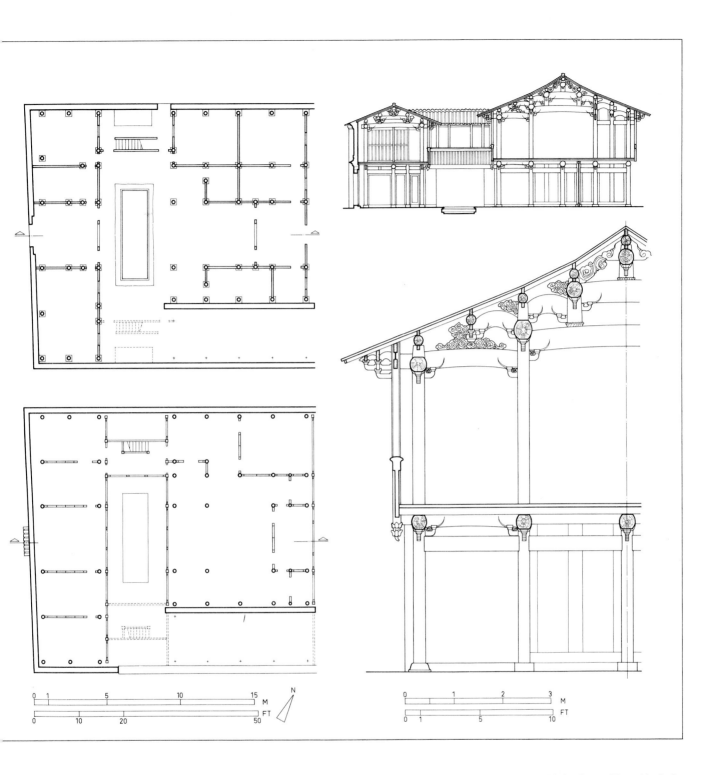

Maison Ming du village de Xijinan, au Huizhou (Anhui). Plan du rez-de-chaussée et du premier étage, coupe transversale 1:250. Détail de la coupe avec système de la charpente 1:75. Demeure chinoise close, entre ses murs de brique grise, qui symbolise la sécurité. Les jardins ouvrent sur l'univers naturel.

Xijinan am Huizhou (Anhui), Haus der Ming-Zeit. Die Außenmauern des Wohnhauses sind aus grauen Ziegeln. Die Geschlossenheit des vornehmen Wohnsitzes symbolisiert zugleich Sicherheit, seine Gärten sind dagegen der Natur geöffnet. Grundriß des Erd- und des Obergeschosses, Querschnitt 1:250; Detail des Querschnitts mit Struktur des Holzwerks 1:75.

Ming house, Hsi-chinan village (Anhui). Plan of the ground and first floors and cross section 1:250. Detail of the section showing the beam frame system 1:75. The Chinese dwelling-house was enclosed within walls of grey brick, symbolising security. The gardens open on to the world of nature.

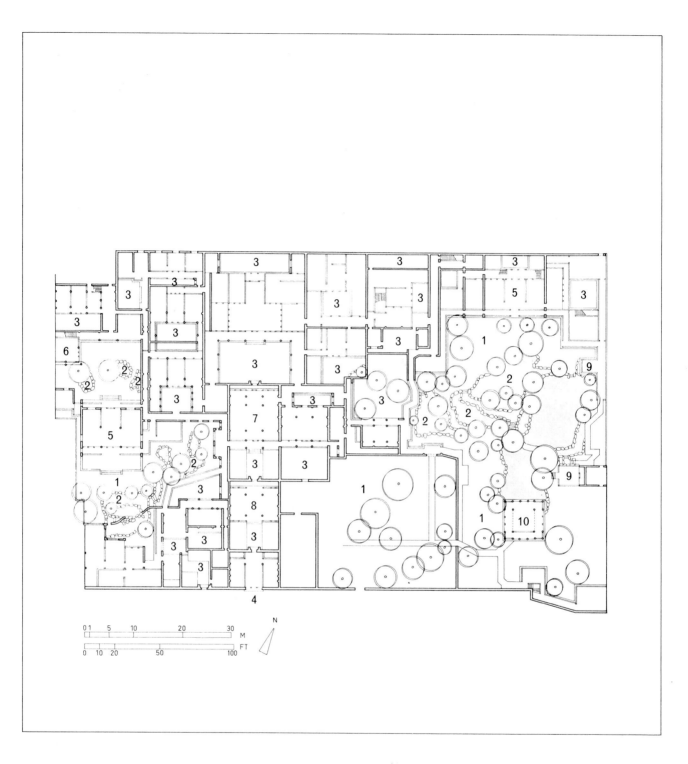

Jardin Ou, à Suzhou (Jiangsu), datant de l'époque Ming, en Chine du Sud, 1:75. Vaste demeure de lettré. 1) Jardin, 2) Rocaille, 3) Cour, 4) Entrée, 5) Salle de réception, 6) Bibliothèque, 7) Grande salle, 8) Salle des chaises à porteurs, 9) Kiosque, 10) Pavillon ouvert. Avec son «lac», ses «montagnes», ses «rivières» et ses ponts, le jardin est un microcosme, dans lequel s'inscrit l'habitation.

Suzhou (Jiangsu), Ou-Garten, Ming-Zeit. Der ausgedehnte Wohnsitz eines Gelehrten. Das Haus ist in den Mikrokosmos des Gartens mit «See», «Bergen», «Flüssen» und Brücken eingebettet. Plan 1:75: 1) Gärten, 2) Felsgruppen, 3) Höfe, 4) Haupteingang, 5) Empfangshallen, 6) Bibliothek, 7) große Empfangshalle, 8) Sänftenraum, 9) Gartenpavillon, 10) allseitig offener Pavillon. Plan 1:75.

Ow gardens, Soochow (Kiangsu, south China), the vast home of a Ming dynasty scholar. Plan 1:75. 1) gardens, 2) rock garden, 3) courtyard, 4) entrance, 5) reception room, 6) library, 7) great hall, 8) Hall of the Palankeens, 9) summerhouse, 10) open pavilion. With its 'lake', its 'mountains', its 'rivers', and its bridges the garden forms a microcosm of the universe around the dwelling-house.

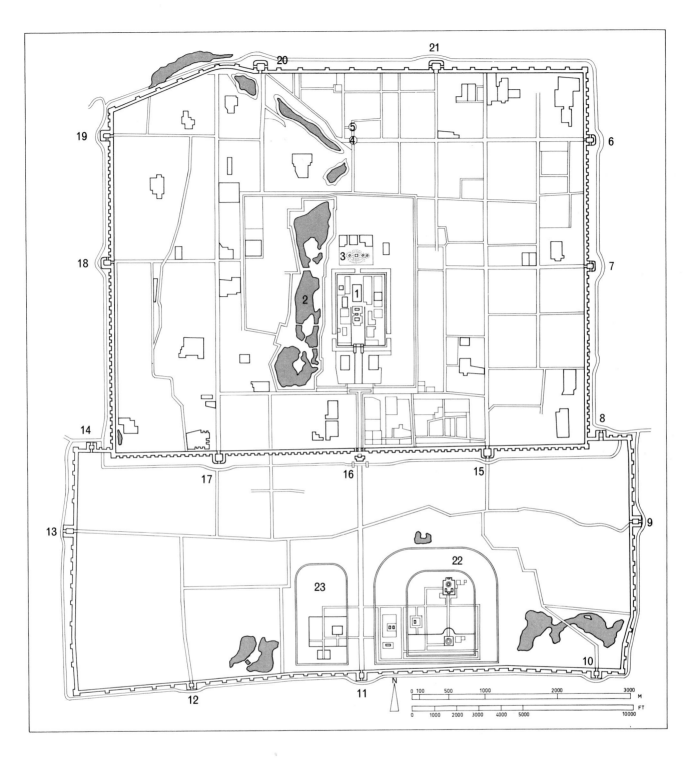

Plan de la cité de Pékin sous les Ming et les Qing (1366–1911), 1:50000. Au nord, la ville impériale, au sud, la ville extérieure. Les murs sont longs de 23,55 km et construits en brique. 1) Palais impérial, 2) Lacs, 3) Colline de charbon, 4) Tour du Tambour, 5) Tour de la Cloche, 6) à 21) Portes, 22) Temple du Ciel, 23) Temple de l'Agriculture.

Peking zur Zeit der Ming- und der Qing-Dynastie, 1366–1911. Im Norden liegt die Kaiserstadt, im Süden die Chinesenstadt; die Ziegelmauern sind im ganzen 23,55 km lang. Stadtplan 1:50000: 1) Kaiserpalast, 2) Westseen am Kaiserpalast, 3) Kohlenhügel, 4) Trommelturm, 5) Glockenturm, 6)–21) Tore, 22) Tempel des Himmels, 23) Tempel des Ackerbaus.

City of Peking under the Ming and Ch'ing dynasties (1366–1911). Plan 1:50,000. The northern part is the Inner City, containing the Imperial City; the southern part is the Outer City. The brick-built walls total 23.55 km. in length. 1) Imperial palace, 2) lakes, 3) Coal Hill, 4) Drum tower, 5) Bell tower, 6–21) gates, 22) temple of Heaven, 23) temple of Agriculture.

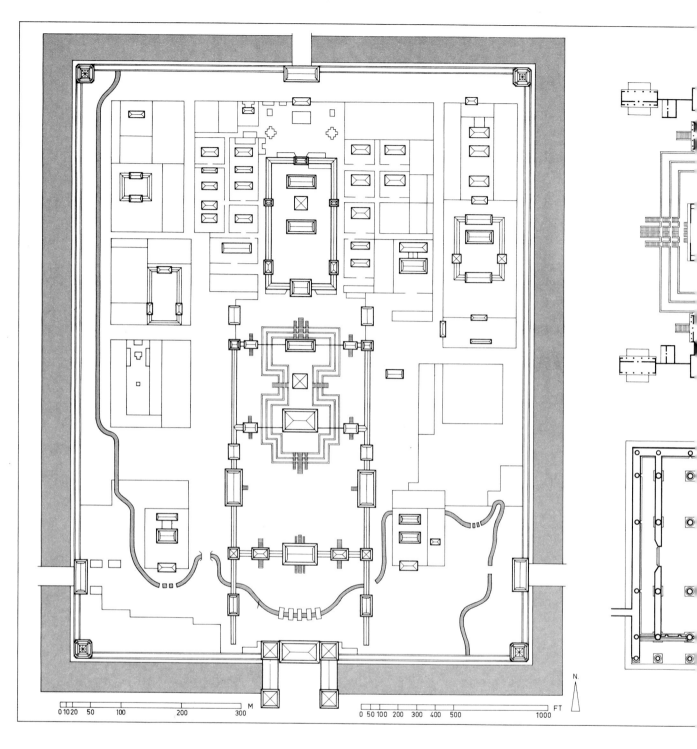

Cité Interdite de Pékin, ou quartier du Palais impérial, ceinte de douves larges de 50 m. Plan 1:6000. Une ordonnance strictement symétrique avec, au centre, la partie officielle du Palais impérial (page de droite) 1:3000. 1) Baohe dian, ou pavillon de l'Harmonie protectrice, 2) Zhonge dian, ou pavillon de l'Harmonie du milieu, 3) Taihe dian, ou pavillon de l'Harmonie suprême (trois édifices datant de 1627), 4) Taihe men, ou porte de l'Harmonie suprême,

Peking, die «Verbotene Stadt», Das von 50 m breiten Wassergräben umgebene Palastviertel ist nach einem nahezu symmetrischen Plan angelegt; in der Mittelachse der Kaiserpalast. Grundriß 1:6000. Rechts oben: **Kaiserpalast,** offizieller Teil. Grundriß 1:3000: 1) Baohe dian, Pavillon der schützenden Harmonie, 2) Zhonge dian, Pavillon der Harmonie der Mitte, 3) Taihe dian, Pavillon der höchsten Harmonie (alle drei Bauten 1627), 4) Taihe men, Tor der höch-

Forbidden City, Peking. Plan 1:6000. Ringed with a 50 m. wide moat, the palace quarter follows a strictly symmetrical arrangement centring on the official part of the imperial palace (facing page, 1:3000). 1) Pao-ho Tien or Hall of Protecting Harmony, 2) Sung-ho Tien or Hall of Middle Harmony, 3) T'ai-ho Tien or Hall of Supreme Harmony (all three buildings date from 1627), 4) T'ai-ho Men or Gate of

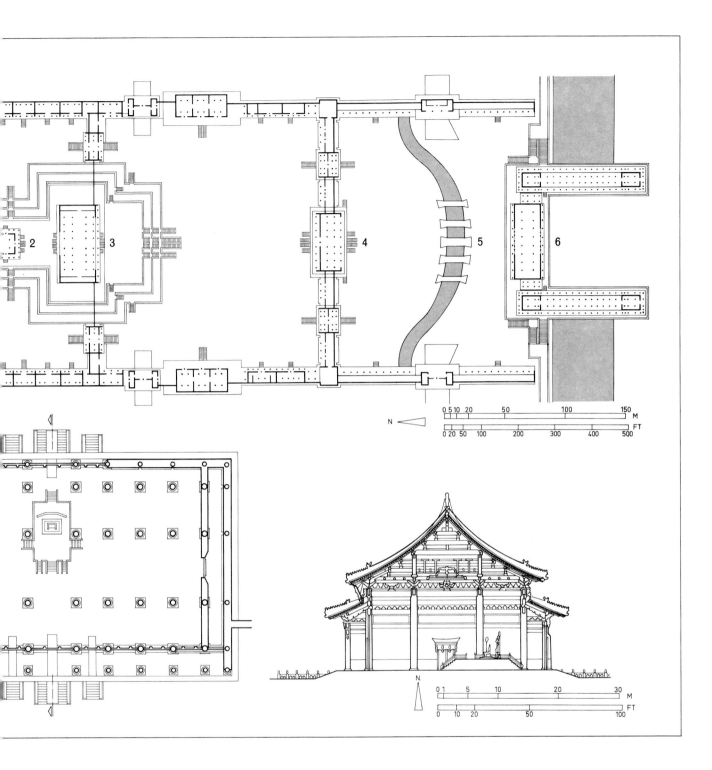

5) Pont de la rivière des Eaux d'Or,
6) Wu men, ou porte méridionale, construite en 1420 et relevée en 1647, longue
de 126 m. En bas, plan et coupe transversale du **Taihe dian,** construit en 1627,
reconstruit en 1697 et réparé en 1765,
1:600. L'édifice mesure 64 × 37 m. Il
est typique de l'architecture de bois à
corbeaux de la Chine.

sten Harmonie, 5) Brücke über den
Goldwasserfluß, 6) Wu men, südliches
Tor (1420 erbaut, 1647 aufgestockt;
126 m lang). Unten: **Taihe dian,** 1627
erbaut, 1697 Neubau, 1765 Reparatu-
ren. Für den chinesischen Holzbau typische Halle; Grundfläche 64 × 37 m.
Grundriß und Schnitt 1:600.

Supreme Harmony, 5) bridge over the
Golden Waters river, 6) Wu Men or
South Gate, built 1420 and restored
1647, 126 m. long. Below, the **T'ai-ho
Tien,** built 1627, rebuilt 1697, and restored in 1765. Plan and cross section
1:600. The building, a typical example
of Chinese wooden architecture, measures 64 m. by 37 m.

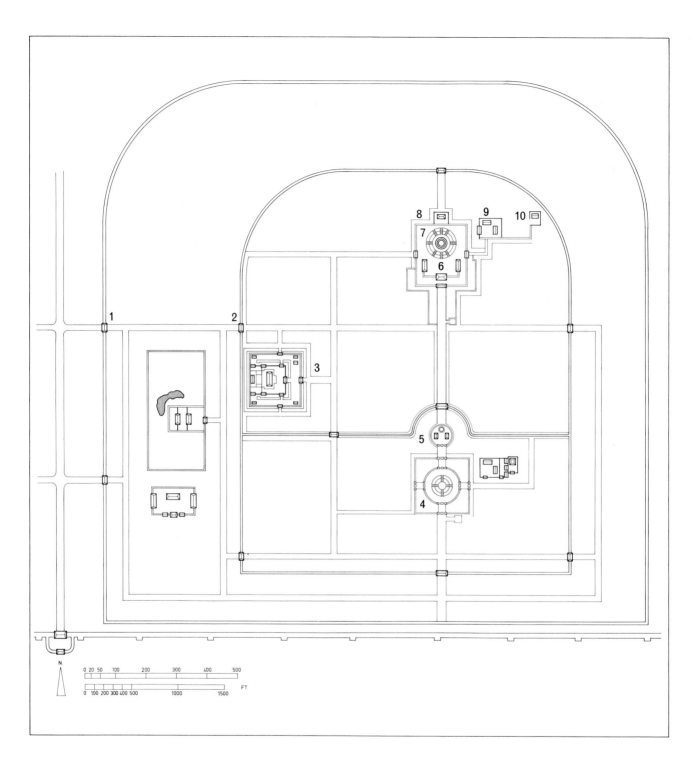

Temple du Ciel à Pékin, édifié en 1420, restauré en 1530 et en 1751. L'ensemble est entouré d'une double muraille (1700 × 1600 m). Plan 1:12000. 1) Porte principale, 2) Porte intérieure, 3) Zhai gong ou palais de la purification, 4) Autel du Ciel, 5) Abri des tablettes du Ciel, 6) Porte Qinian, 7) Qinian dian, salle de prière pour les bonnes récoltes, 8) Huangqian dian, 9–10) Cuisines et abattoirs.

Peking, Tempel des Himmels, 1420 erbaut, 1530 und 1751 restauriert. Der Tempel (Grundfläche 1700 × 1600 m) ist von zwei Mauern umschlossen. Grundriß 1:12000: 1) Äußeres Haupttor, 2) Inneres Haupttor, 3) Zhai gong (Palast der Reinigung), 4) Altar des Himmels, 5) Rundbau für die Tafeln des Himmels, 6) Qinian-Tor, 7) Qinian dian (Halle der Gebete für gute Ernten), 8) Huangqian dian, 9) und 10) Küchen, Schlachthäuser.

Temple of Heaven, Peking, built 1420, restored in 1530 and again in 1751. The complex is surrounded by a double wall (1700 m. by 1600 m). Plan 1:12,000. 1) main gate, 2) inner gate, 3) Chai Kung or Palace of Purification, 4) altar of Heaven, 5) shelter over the tablets of Heaven, 6) Chi Nien gate, 7) Chi Nien Tien or Hall of Prayer for Good Harvests, 8) Huang Chian Tien, 9–10) kitchens and abattoirs.

316

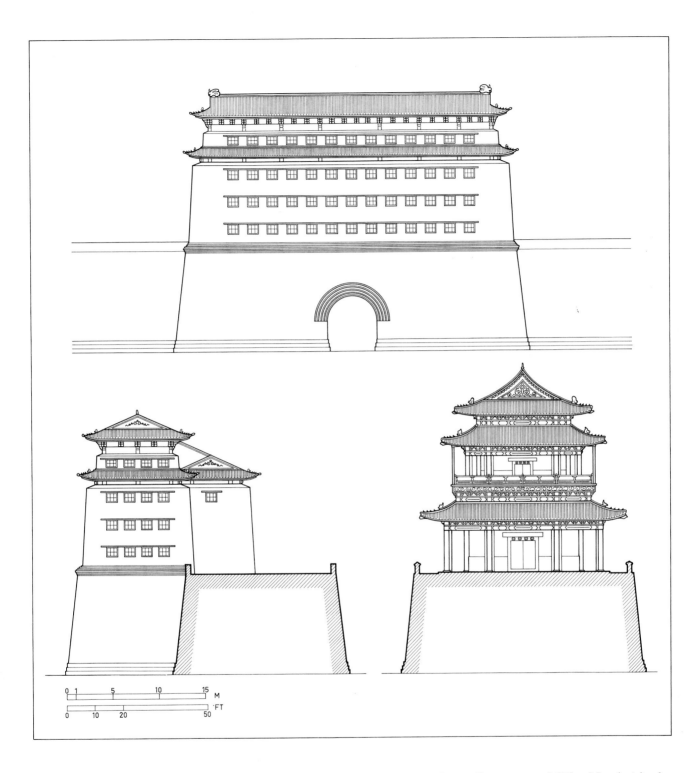

0 1   5   10   15   M
0   10   20   50   FT

Enceinte de Pékin, Tour extérieure de la porte de Qian men, ou Zhengyang men, au sud de la ville impériale. Elévation (avant restauration) et vue latérale 1:400. A droite en bas, **Tour intérieure de la porte de Pingzi, ou Fucheng men,** vue latérale 1:400. Ces portes fortifiées de l'époque Ming sont construites en brique.

Peking, Stadtmauer, Außenturm des Qian-men-Tors (früher Zhengyang men), Ming-Zeit. Haupttor, im Süden der Kaiserstadt. In der Mingzeit wurden die Außentürme der befestigten Tore aus Ziegelmauerwerk gebaut. Aufriß (vor der Restaurierung), Seitenansicht 1:400. Unten rechts: **Innenturm des Fuchengmen-Tors (früher Pingzi).** Seitenansicht 1:400.

Outer tower of Chien Men (gate), also known as Cheng Yang Men, part of the wall of Peking to the south of the Imperial city. Elevation (before restoration) and side view 1:400. Below right, **Inner tower of Ping Tse Men** (or Fu Cheng Men). Side view 1:400. These Ming dynasty fortified gates are built of brick.

Sépultures impériales des Ming, au nord-ouest de Pékin (Shisan ling). Plan général 1:50000. 1) Grande Porte Rouge qui ouvre la voie sacrée longue de 5,5 km, 2) Pavillon de la Stèle, 3) Chemin des Ames, bordé de statues de pierre, 4) Changling, ou tombeau de l'empereur Yong le, 5) Dingling, ou tombeau de l'empereur Wan li. Treize empereurs Ming reposent dans ce site funéraire.

Grabanlagen der Ming-Kaiser nordwestlich von Peking (Shisan ling). Hier wurden dreizehn Ming-Kaiser beigesetzt. Plan der Gesamtanlage 1:50000: 1) das große rote Tor am Anfang der 5,5 km langen Heiligen Straße, 2) Pavillon der Stele, 3) Seelenweg, von steinernen Statuen gesäumt, 4) Changling (Grab des Kaisers Yong le), 5) Dingling (Grab des Kaisers Wan li).

Imperial tombs of the Ming dynasty, north-west of Peking (Shisan-ling). Overall plan 1:50,000. 1) Great Red Gate, the start of the 5.5 km. long sacred avenue, 2) Pavilion of the Stele, 3) Way of Souls, bordered with stone statues, 4) Chang-ling or tomb of Emperor Kung Lo, 5) Ting-ling or tomb of Emperor Wan Li. Thirteen Ming emperors are buried on this site.

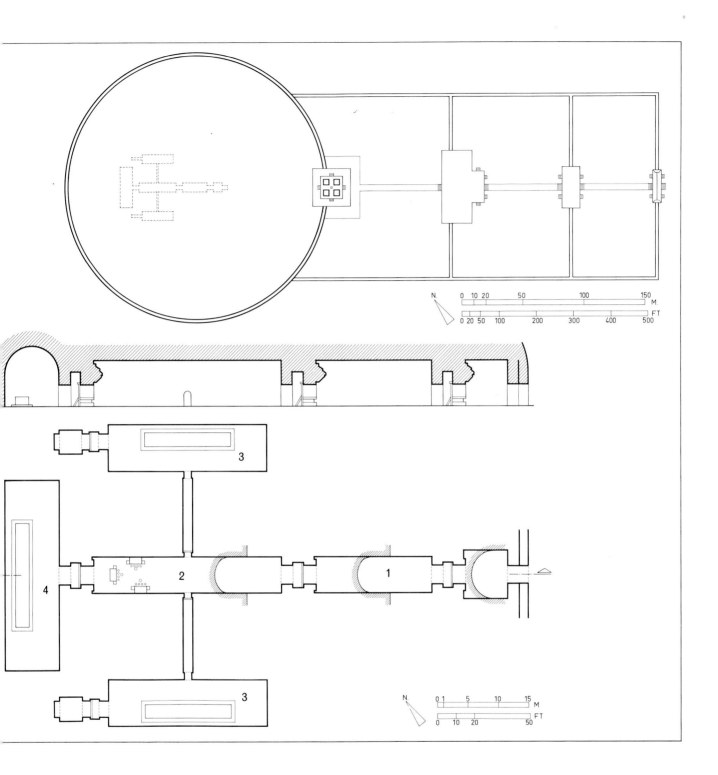

Dingling, tombeau de l'empereur Wan li, datant de 1584. Plan du tumulus et des trois cours 1:3000, coupe et plan du mausolée 1:600. 1) Antichambre, 2) Chambre sacrificielle, 3) Chambres annexes, 4) Chambre sépulcrale. Cette sépulture a été fouillée entre 1956 et 1958. Ce palais souterrain grandiose répond au style de la Cité interdite de Pékin.

Dingling (Grab des Kaisers Wan li), 1584. Das Grab wurde 1956–1958 ausgegraben. Der großartige unterirdische Palast ist im Stil der «Verbotenen Stadt» angelegt. Grundriß des Grabhügels und der drei Höfe 1:3000; Schnitt und Grundriß des Mausoleums 1:600: 1) Vorraum, 2) Opferraum, 3) Nebenräume, 4) Grabkammer.

Ting-ling, tomb of Emperor Wan Li, built 1584 (excavated 1956–8). Plan of the tumulus and the three courtyards 1:3000. Section and plan of the mausoleum 1:600. 1) antechamber, 2) sacrificial chamber, 3) annexe chambers, 4) burial chamber. This imposing underground palace echoes the style of Peking's Forbidden City.

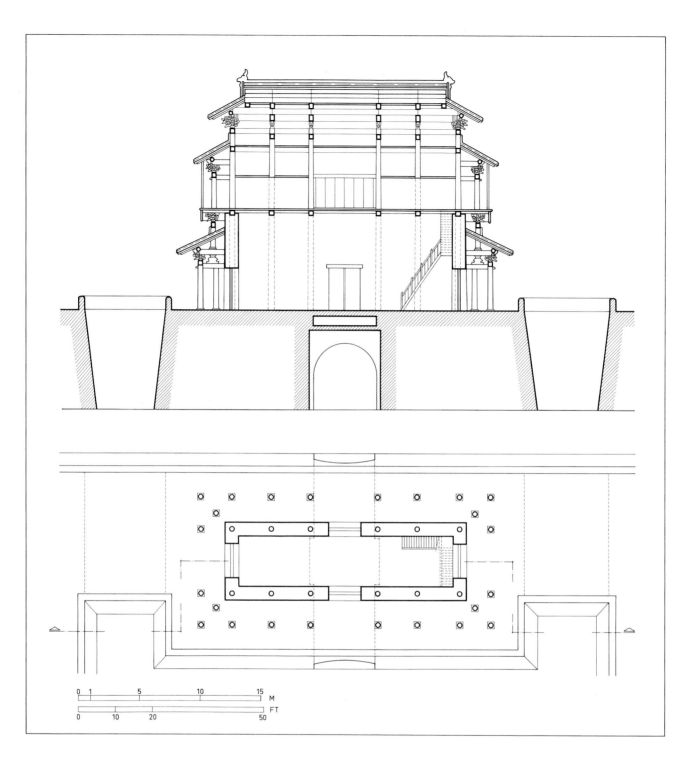

0 1   5   10   15
                                        M
0   10   20   50
                              FT

**Enceinte de Pékin, porte intérieure Yon-
ding men,** au sud de la ville extérieure,
époque Ming. Coupe longitudinale et
plan 1:300. Avec sa structure de bois et
son rez-de-chaussée entouré d'une sorte
de portique, cette porte diffère pro-
fondément de celles en maçonnerie de
brique qui sont disposées à l'extérieur
de la muraille.

**Peking, Stadtmauer, inneres Yonding-
men-Tor,** Ming-Zeit. Das Tor in der
Südmauer der Chinesenstadt mit hölzernen Aufbauten und einem von einer
Art Portikus umgebenen Untergeschoß
unterscheidet sich deutlich von den in
Ziegelmauerwerk gebauten Außentoren
der Mauer. Längsschnitt und Grundriß
1:300.

Inner gate of Yung Ting Men, Ming
period; part of the wall of Peking to the
south of the Outer City. Longitudinal
section and plan 1:300. Built of wood
and with a sort of portico running
round the ground floor, this gate differs
profoundly from the brick-built gates
around the outside of the wall.

Japon   Japan   Japan

L'histoire et l'architecture commencent tard au Japon: les premiers monuments sont des tertres funéraires ou «kofun». Ces tombeaux impériaux remontent au IIIᵉ siècle. Il s'agit de montagnes artificielles composées d'une butte circulaire précédée d'une plate-forme, et dont le plan revêt la forme d'un «trou de serrure». Le plus grand (Nintoku), qui atteint 500 m de long, totalise trois millions de tonnes de matériaux; une douve en eau de 3 km de pourtour en défend l'accès. Sous le tertre, une chambre funéraire en blocs mégalithiques contenait le sarcophage. Un édit impérial interdit l'édification des kofun en 646.

La plus ancienne tradition architecturale du Japon survit dans les sanctuaires shintoïstes d'Isé, qui perpétuent les formes de la maison de bois préhistorique. La couverture de chaume à deux pans est supportée par un poteau libre placé devant chaque mur-pignon en charpente. Les sanctuaires, construits dans des enclos sacrés, sont dédiés aux forces de la nature.

Le bouddhisme qui pénètre dès le Vᵉ siècle par la Chine et la Corée s'accompagne de l'apparition de temples de style continental. Des charpentiers coréens introduisent à Nara (Heijo-Kyō capitale dès 710) l'architecture de bois des Tang, tant au Hōryū-ji (670) qu'au Tōshōdai-ji (754): même corbeaux en porte à faux et mêmes toitures incurvées qu'en Chine. L'art des résidences reflète également à ses débuts l'influence continentale. Il subsiste de cette architecture aristocratique le pavillon du Hōo-dō du Byōdo-in, datant de 1053, caractérisé par son jeu de pilotis qui surélève l'édifice et ses galeries. En se transformant, le style des pavillons s'épanouira aux XVIIᵉ et XVIIIᵉ siècles

Geschichte und Architektur beginnen in Japan spät. Die ältesten Baudenkmäler, kaiserliche Grabhügel (Kofun), stammen aus dem 3. Jahrhundert. Es sind schlüssellochförmige Anlagen aus einem künstlichen runden Hügel mit vorgelagerter Plattform. Der größte dieser Grabhügel (Nintoku) ist 500 m lang, besteht aus 3 Millionen Tonnen Material und wird von einem 3 km langen Wassergraben geschützt. Die aus mächtigen Steinblöcken erbaute Grabkammer im Innern des Hügels enthielt den Sarkophag. Im Jahr 646 wurde die Anlage von Kofun durch kaiserlichen Erlaß verboten.

Die älteste japanische Bauweise hat sich im Shinto-Heiligtum von Ise erhalten, das die Formen prähistorischer Holzbauten tradiert. Ein frei vor jede der hölzernen Giebelwände gestellter Pfosten trägt das strohgedeckte Satteldach. Die innerhalb eines geschlossenen heiligen Bezirks errichteten Sanktuarien sind den Naturmächten geweiht.

Vom 5. Jahrhundert an drang der Buddhismus über China und Korea in Japan ein, mit ihm traten die ersten Tempel im kontinentalen Stil auf. Koreanische Zimmerleute führten die Holzbauweise der Tang in Nara (Heijo-Kyo, Hauptstadt seit 710) ein, und zwar sowohl beim Horyu-ji-Tempel (670) wie beim Toshodai-ji (754), wo wir die chinesische Konstruktion mit Konsolen finden und wie in China geschwungene Dächer. Auch der Palastbau spiegelt in seinen Anfängen kontinentalen Einfluß; von dieser aristokratischen Architektur ist der Hoo-do des Byo-do-in (1053) erhalten geblieben, ein auf Pfosten errichteter Pavillon mit Galerien. Der Pavillon-Typus breitete sich im 17. und 18. Jahrhundert in abgewandelter Form

Architecture, like history, began late in Japan. The first monuments—imperial burial mounds known as *kofuns*—date from the third century A.D. A *kofun* is a circular hillock with a platform in front of it, the whole thing being keyhole-shaped in plan. The largest (that of Nintoku) is 500 m. long, comprises three million tons of material, and is protected by a water-filled moat measuring 3 km. around. Beneath the mound is a burial chamber of megalithic masonry containing the sarcophagus. An imperial edict of A.D. 646 prohibited the erection of *kofun* tombs.

Japan's most ancient architectural tradition is embodied in the Shinto shrines at Ise, which perpetuate the forms of the prehistoric wooden dwelling. The thatched roof in two sections is supported by a free-standing post in front of each frame wall. Situated in sacred precincts, the shrines are dedicated to the forces of nature.

Buddhism started to enter Japan during the fifth century via China and Korea and was accompanied by the first temples built in the continental style. Korean carpenters brought the wooden architecture of the T'ang dynasty to Nara, which became the capital in 710. Examples of their work are the Horyu-ji (670) and the Toshodai-ji (754), both of which feature the Chinese system of cantilevered brackets and concave roofs. The first residences also reflect continental influence, a survivor of this aristocratic architecture being the Hoodo pavilion of the Byodo-in, built in 1053 and characterised by a system of piles raising the building and its galleries above the ground. The pavilion style evolved further and in the seventeenth and eighteenth centuries blos-

avec des réussites admirables, tel le « palais » de Katsura, près de Kyoto (Héian-Kyō, capitale de 794 à 1869).

Construits en grande partie en dur, avec des superstructures en bois, les châteaux forts du Japon médiéval se développent au XVe siècle et connaissent une vogue intense entre 1550 et 1615, date à laquelle la plupart sont rasés et leur édification interdite. Par opposition à ces rares constructions de pierre, l'habitation est restée traditionnelle jusqu'à une date récente et se caractérise par une structure en bois, une toiture en tuiles et des parois en papier, ainsi qu'un plan modulaire fondé sur les proportions du tatami (natte de paille de riz).

weiter aus; es entstanden so herrliche Anlagen wie die kaiserliche Villa Katsura bei Kyoto (Heian-Kyo, Hauptstadt von 794 bis 1869).

Die weitgehend aus dauerhaften Materialien mit hölzernen Aufbauten errichteten mittelalterlichen Burgen Japans entwickelten sich im 15. Jahrhundert, ihre Blütezeit lag zwischen 1550 und 1615, in welchem Jahr die meisten geschleift und der Neubau verboten wurde. Im Gegensatz zu diesen wenigen Steinbauten blieb die Bauweise der Wohnhäuser bis vor kurzem traditionell. Ihre Charakteristika sind: Holzkonstruktion, Ziegeldach, Papierwände, Modulsystem des Grundrisses mit dem Tatami (Reisstrohmatte) als Einheit.

somed in such magnificent achievements as the Katsura Imperial Villa near Kyoto (Heian-Kyo, the capital from 794 to 1869).

Built largely of stone with a wooden superstructure, the castles of medieval Japan emerged during the fifteenth century to enjoy a great vogue between 1550 and 1615, the date when most of them were razed to the ground and a ban placed on building new ones. The castles apart, domestic architecture remained traditional until quite recently. It was characterised by a wooden structure, a tile roof and paper walls and used a modular ground plan based on the proportions of the *tatami* (a mat of rice straw).

1 Un grenier du sanctuaire shintoïste d'Isé, avec son poteau extérieur typique, et dont la tradition remonte à 690 de notre ère.
2 Le donjon central du château du Héron Blanc à Himeji, construit en 1580.
3 Au bord d'une pièce d'eau, le Hōodō du Byōdō-in d'Uji, près de Kyoto, pavillon de plaisance (1053), transformé en sanctuaire bouddhique.

1 Ise, Shinto-Schrein, Schatzhaus mit den charakteristischen äußeren Pfosten; die Bautradition dieses Tempels reicht zurück bis 690
2 Himeji, Burg des Weißen Reihers, Hauptturm (1580)
3 Uji (Präfektur Kyoto), Byo-do-in, Hoo-do, ein später in einen Tempel umgewandelter Lustpavillon am Ufer eines Sees (1053)

1 A granary at the Shinto shrine of Ise with its characteristic outside post, a tradition of construction that goes back to A.D 690.
2 Main keep of Egret Castle, Himeji, built in 1580.
3 The Hoo-do, a lakeside pleasure pavilion dating from 1053 and forming part of the Byodo-ji, Uji. It subsequently became a Buddhist shrine.

1

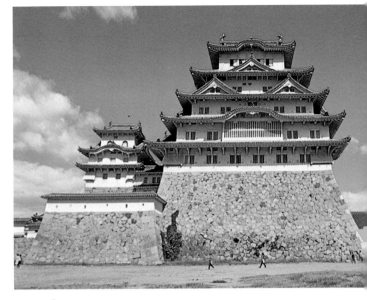

2

3

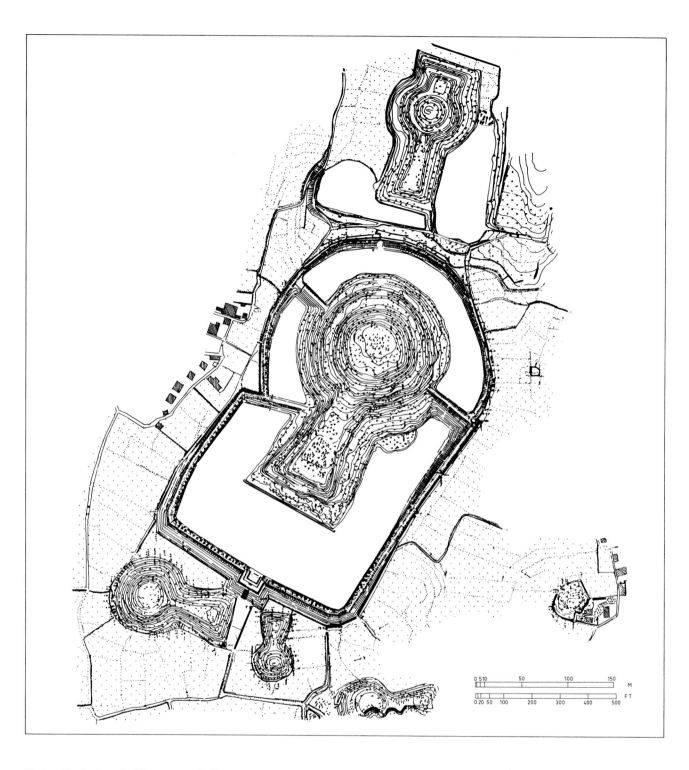

Tertre funéraire de l'empereur Sujin (préfecture de Nara), édifié au Vᵉ s. apr. J.-C. par le fondateur du gouvernement impérial du Yamato. Plan 1:4000. Le tertre, long de 240 m, est entouré d'une large douve en forme de «trou de serrure». Alentour, plusieurs tertres funéraires secondaires.

Grabhügel des Kaisers Sujin (Präfektur Nara), 5.Jh. n.Chr. Der von dem Begründer der Yamato-Herrschaft angelegte 240 m lange Tumulus wird von einem breiten Wassergraben umschlossen; die Gesamtform ist schlüssellochartig. Ringsum liegen mehrere kleine Tumuli. Grundriß 1:4000.

Kofun or burial mound of Emperor Sujin (Nara district), built in the fifth century A.D. by the founder of the imperial government of Yamato. Plan 1:4000. The mound, 240 m. long, is surrounded by a broad moat forming the shape of a keyhole. There are various secondary burial mounds nearby.

| 0 10 | 50 | 100 | 200 | 300 | M |
| 0 50 100 | 200 | 300 400 500 | | 1000 | FT |

Grand tertre funéraire de l'empereur Nintoku (préfecture de Nara), Vᵉ s. de notre ère. Plan 1:6000. Entouré de sa triple douve, le tertre à lui seul est long de 500 m et représente le plus vaste monument du Japon. Aujourd'hui encore le sol du tertre est sacré. La terre prélevée pour créer les douves a servi à réaliser l'île artificielle en forme de «trou de serrure» qui contenait la sépulture.

Grabhügel des Kaisers Nintoku (Präfektur Nara), 5. Jh. n. Chr. Den 500 m langen Tumulus, die größte Bauanlage in Japan, umschließen drei Wassergräben. Noch heute gilt der Bezirk des Tumulus als heilig. Mit dem Aushub der Wassergräben schüttete man die schlüssellochförmige Insel für das Grab auf. Grundriß 1:6000.

Great burial mound of Emperor Nintoku (Nara district), fifth century A.D. Plan 1:6000. The 500 m. long *kofun*—to this day a sacred site—is the largest monument in Japan. The earth dug out of the tomb on the keyhole-shaped artificial island was used to form the triple moat around it.

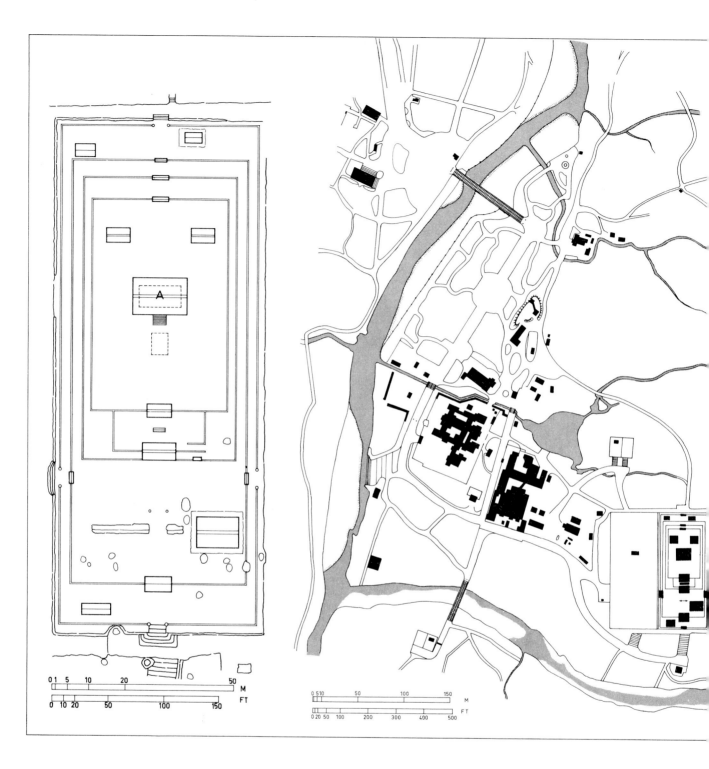

Sanctuaire shintoïste d'Isé (préfecture de Mié), reconstruit tous les 20 ans depuis l'année 690. Plan de l'enceinte sacrée 1:1000, A) Shōden. Situation au bord de la rivière Isuzu, présentant, en bas à droite, les deux aires sacrées sur lesquelles sont construits alternativement les sanctuaires de bois, 1:4000. Isé représente la survivance de la première architecture de bois du Japon.

Ise (Präfektur Mie), Shinto-Schrein, seit 690 alle 20 Jahre neu gebaut. Die beiden Tempelbezirke, auf denen die hölzernen Tempel abwechselnd gebaut werden, liegen am Ufer des heiligen Flusses Isuzu. In Ise hat sich die altjapanische Holzbauweise erhalten. Links: Plan des Tempelbezirks 1:1000: A) Shoden; rechts: Lageplan 1:4000.

Shinto shrine, Ise (Mie district), founded in 690 and rebuilt every 20 years since then. Plan of the sacred precinct 1:1000. A) shoden. Plan of the site on the bank of the River Isuzu, showing at bottom right the two sacred enclosures in which the wooden shrines are erected alternately, 1:4000. The Ise shrines represent a survival of Japan's earliest wooden architecture.

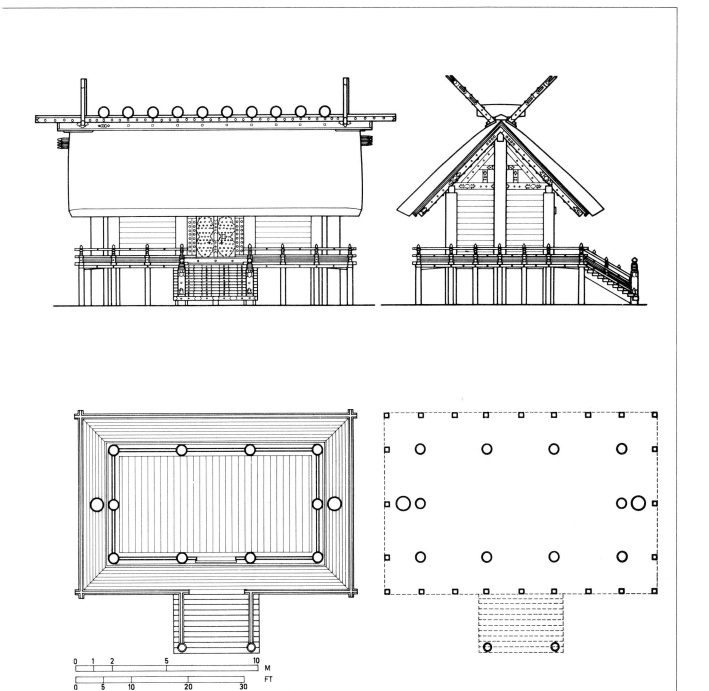

| 0 | 1 | 2 | | 5 | | 10 | M |
| 0 | | 5 | 10 | | 20 | 30 | FT |

Sanctuaire d'Isé, le Naigu. Elévation en façade et latérale, plan au niveau de la terrasse, plan au sol 1:200. Avec ses poteaux externes, situés devant les façades latérales, qui supportent la panne faîtière, son toit en chaume et son travail de charpente original, qui n'a pas subi l'influence chinoise, ce sanctuaire d'Isé remonte probablement aux techniques architecturales du Japon préhistorique.

Ise, Shinto-Schrein, der Innere Schrein (Naigu). Das von äußeren, vor den Seiten stehenden Stützpfosten getragene Dach, die Strohdeckung und das Holzwerk, das nicht von China beeinflußt ist, lassen vermuten, daß der Ise-Schrein in der bautechnischen Tradition des vorgeschichtlichen Japan steht. Fassadenaufriß, Aufriß einer Seite, Grundriß in Terrassenhöhe, Grundriß in Bodenhöhe 1:200.

Naigu shrine, Ise. Front and side elevations, plan at the terrace level, and ground plan 1:200. With its posts standing away from the side walls outside the building to support the ridge purlin, its thatched roof, and its original beam work uninfluenced by Chinese models, this shrine probably preserves the architectural techniques of prehistoric Japan.

Sanctuaire shintoïste d'Itsukushima (préfecture d'Hiroshima), mentionné au XIIe s. Plan d'ensemble 1:2500. Construit sur pilotis et s'avançant dans la mer, ce sanctuaire est l'un des plus pittoresques du Japon. A) Honden, B) Haiden, C) Plate-forme de danses sacrées, D) Estrade pour représentations de Nō, E) Torii.

Itsukushima (Präfektur Hiroshima), Shinto-Schrein, im 12. Jh. zum erstenmal erwähnt. Der auf Stützpfählen errichtete, ins Meer vorgeschobene Tempel ist einer der malerischsten in ganz Japan. Lageplan 1:2500: A) Honden, B) Haiden, C) Plattform für Sakraltänze, D) No-Bühne, E) Torii.

Shinto shrine, Itsuku-shima (Hiroshima district), mentioned in the twelfth century. Overall plan 1:2500. Built on piles to project out over the sea, this is one of the most picturesque shrines in Japan. A) honden, B) haiden, C) platform for sacred dances, D) stage for No performances, E) torii or gates.

328

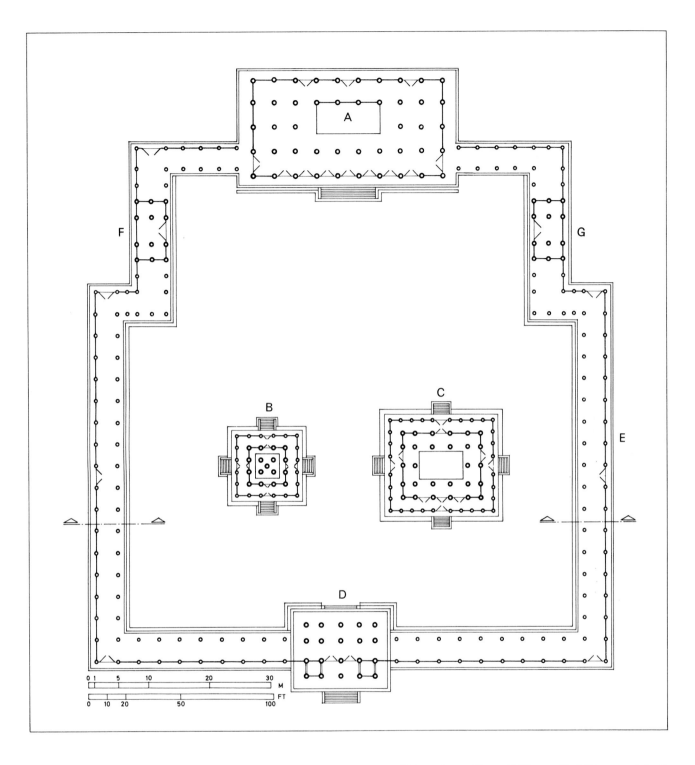

Temple bouddhiste de Hōryū-ji, à Nara.
Reconstruits sur les ruines d'un édifice de 607, les bâtiments actuels ont vu le jour entre 670 et 714. Plan 1:600. Ils sont l'œuvre de charpentiers bouddhistes de Paekche en Corée. A) Salle d'assemblée ou Kōdō, B) Pagode, C) Pavillon central ou Kondō, D) Portail intérieur ou chūmon, E) Passage couvert, F) Pavillon des soutras, G) Pavillon de la cloche.

Nara, Buddhistischer Horyu-ji-Tempel, 670–714 am Ort eines Tempels aus dem Jahr 607 erbaut. Ein Werk buddhistischer Zimmerleute aus Paekche (Korea). Grundriß 1:600: A) Versammlungsraum (Kodo), B) Pagode, C) Haupthalle (Kondo), D) Inneres Tor (Chumon), E) offener Umgang, F) Sutrenhalle, G) Glockenpavillon. Grundriß 1:600.

Horyu-ji, Nara, a Buddhist temple built on the ruins of a building of 607; the present fabric dates from between 670 and 714 and is the work of Buddhist carpenters from the Korean kingdom of Paekche. Plan 1:600. A) kodo or assembly hall, B) pagoda, C) kondo or central pavilion, D) chumon or inner gateway, E) covered passage, F) pavilion of the Sutras, G) Bell pavilion.

329

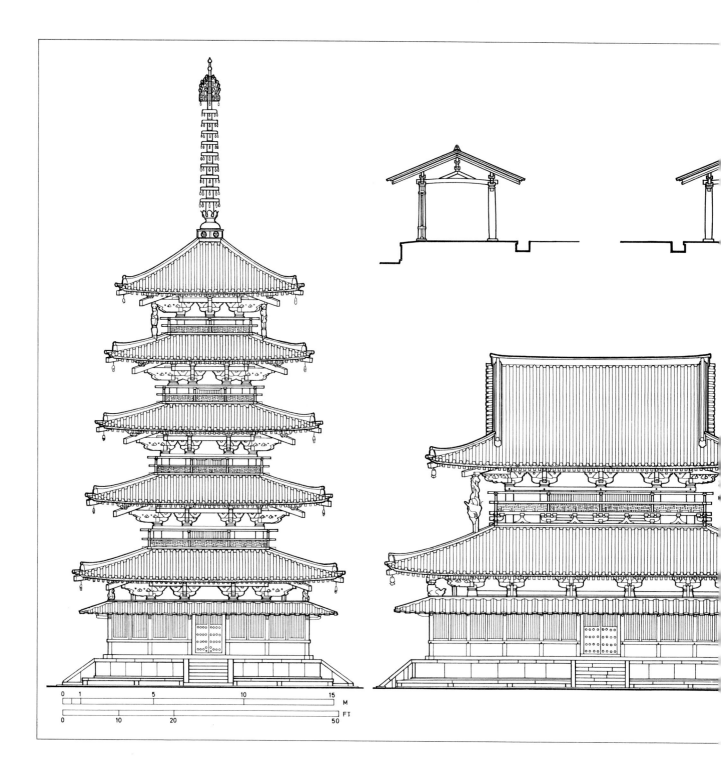

0 1 5 10 15 M
0 10 20 50 FT

Pagode de Hōryū-ji, élévation, **Kondō, ou pavillon central de Hōryū-ji,** élévation, **galeries couvertes de Hōryū-ji,** coupes 1:200. Architecture bouddhique où l'on retrouve les caractères des édifices chinois de l'époque Tang, tant pour les formes que pour les techniques de construction. Le recours, pour le travail de charpente, à des corbeaux ou consoles supportant l'avancée des toitures, est caractéristique.

Nara, Horyu-ji-Tempel, Pagode, Kondo (Haupthalle), offener Umgang. An dieser buddhistischen Architektur treten in den Formen und der Bautechnik charakteristische Eigenheiten chinesischer Bauten der Tang-Zeit auf. Bezeichnend ist die Verwendung von Konsolen als Stützen der Dachüberstände. Aufriß der Pagode und der Halle, Schnitt des Umgangs 1:200.

Horyu-ji: pagoda, elevation, **kondo or central pavilion,** elevation, and **covered galleries,** sections 1:200. This Buddhist architecture echoes many features of the Chinese architecture of the T'ang period as regards both form and structural technique. The use in the beam frame of brackets or consoles to support the projecting eaves of the roof is characteristic.

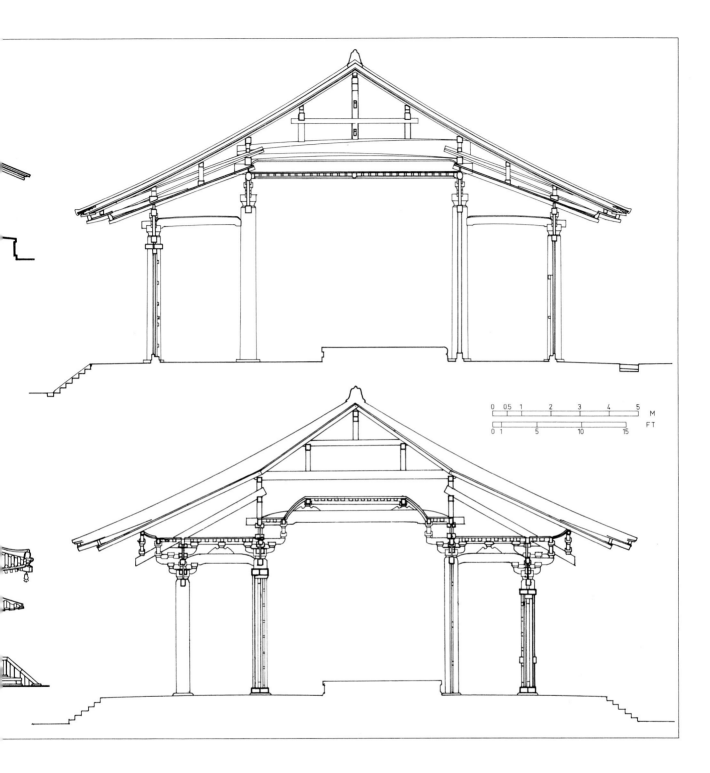

Kōdō ou salle d'assemblée du Temple de Hōryū-ji à Nara. Coupe transversale montrant le système de charpente 1:125. En bas, **Kondō ou pavillon central du Temple de Tōshōdai-ji, à Nara,** datant de 759. Coupe transversale 1:125. La formule plus complexe de la charpente s'apparente à la technique utilisée en Chine sous les Tang (voir par exemple le Foguang si).

Oben: Nara, Horyu-ji, Kodo (Versammlungsraum). Querschnitt zur Veranschaulichung der Holzkonstruktion 1:125. Unten: **Nara, Toshodai-ji, Kondo (Haupthalle),** 759. Das komplexere System des Holzwerks entspricht den chinesischen Techniken der Tang-Zeit, beispielsweise Foguang si. Querschnitt 1:125.

Horyu-ji: kodo or assembly hall, cross section showing the beam frame system 1:125. Below, **Kondo or central pavilion of the Toshodai-ji (temple), Nara,** which dates from 759. Cross section 1:125. This more complex type of beam frame resembles the technique used in T'ang dynasty China (cf. Fo Kuang temple).

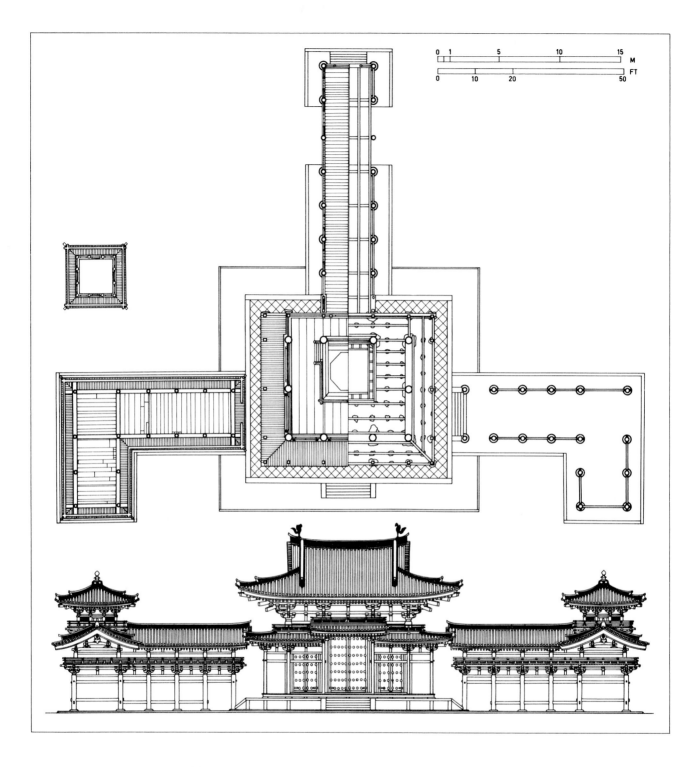

Hōo-dō du Byōdō-in, à Uji (préfecture de Kyoto), pavillon de plaisance édifié en 1053 à l'image des constructions aristocratiques de la Chine. Plan et élévation 1:300. Cet édifice, transformé par la suite en temple bouddhique, représente la vision de la Terre pure du Paradis. Son plan représente le Phénix volant.

Uji (Präfektur Kyoto), Byo-do-in, Hoo-do (Phönixhalle), 1053. Der nach dem Vorbild chinesischer Adelsbauten errichtete und später in einen Tempel umgewandelte Lustpavillon stellt den Palast im Reinen Lande Buddhas dar, der Grundriß bildet einen fliegenden Phönix nach. Grundriß und Aufriß 1:300.

Hoo-do pavilion of the Byodo-in, Uji (Kyoto district), a pleasure pavilion erected in 1053 on the model of Chinese aristocratic buildings. Plan and elevation 1:300. This building, subsequently converted into a Buddhist temple, represents a vision of the Pure Earth of paradise. Its plan forms the figure of a flying phoenix.

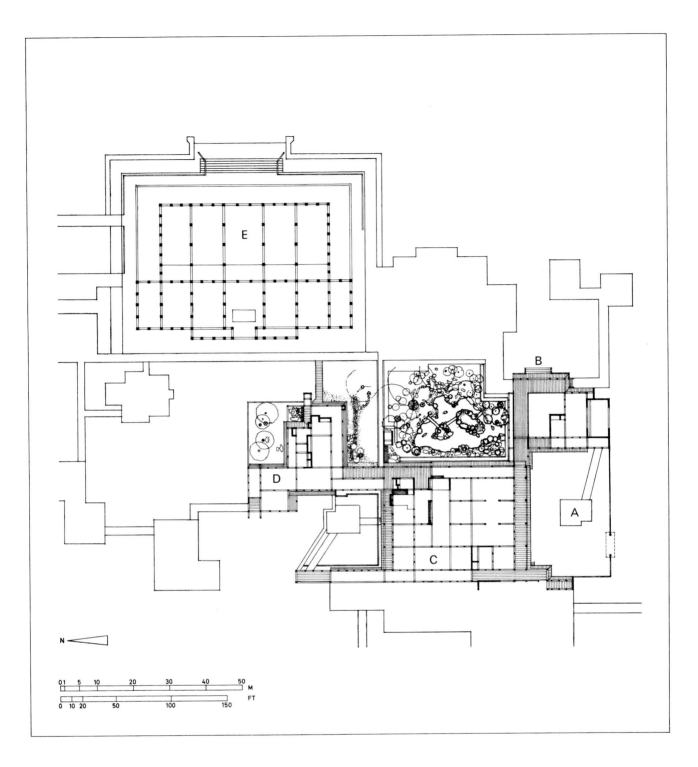

Temple de Nishi-Honganji, à Kyoto, édifié en 1657. Plan 1:1000. A) Estrade pour les représentations de Nō, B) Entrée, C) Salons de réception ou taimensho, D) Salons privés du Supérieur ou kuroshoin, E) Temple. Les diverses parties du temple se combinent avec un art des jardins très subtil.

Kyoto, Nishi-Hongan-ji-Tempel, 1657. Die verschiedenen Teile des Tempelkomplexes sind durch kunstvoll angelegte Gärten miteinander verbunden. Grundriß 1:1000: A) No-Bühne, B) Eingang, C) Audienzhalle (Taimensho), D) Privaträume des Hauptpriesters (Kuro-shoin), E) Tempel.

Nishi-Hongan-ji (temple), Kyoto, built 1657. Plan 1:1000. A) stage for No performances, B) entrance, C) taimensho or reception rooms, D) kuroshoin or private quarters of the Superior, E) temple. The different parts of the temple are linked by gardens of highly sophisticated layout.

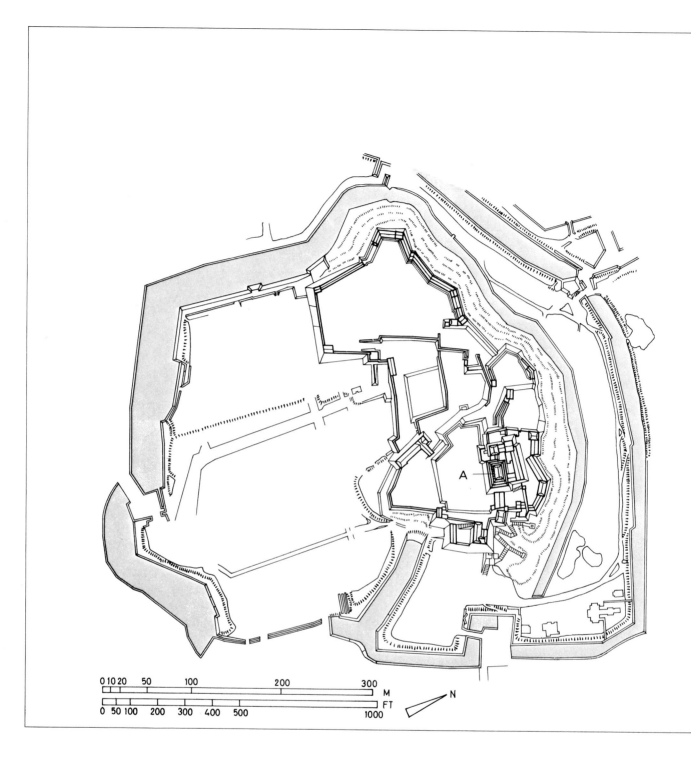

0 10 20 50   100   200   300
                                              M
0 50 100 200 300 400 500   FT
                                          1000

N

Château du Héron Blanc, Himeji (préfecture du Hyōgo), construit en 1580. Plan d'ensemble 1:4000. Dans un plan complexe, conçu comme un labyrinthe pour dérouter l'ennemi, environné de douves profondes, se dresse (A) le donjon principal de la forteresse centrale. Cette architecture militaire florissante au XVIe s. disparaît presque entièrement en 1615, sur ordre du pouvoir central.

Himeji (Präfektur Hyogo), Burg des Weißen Reihers, 1580. In der labyrinthartig verschachtelten, von Wassergräben umgebenen Befestigungsanlage, die Feinden die Orientierung erschweren sollte, erhebt sich der Hauptturm (A) der Hauptbefestigung. Die Festungsarchitektur erlebte ihre Blüte im 16. Jh. und wurde 1615 auf Befehl der Zentralgewalt praktisch eingestellt. Grundriß 1:4000.

Egret castle, Himeji (Hyogo district) built in 1580. Overall plan 1:4000. The main keep of the central fortress (A) is erected on a complex plan—designed as a maze to confuse the enemy—and surrounded by deep moats: an example of the military architecture that flourished in the sixteenth century, only to disappear almost completely in 1615 by order of the central government.

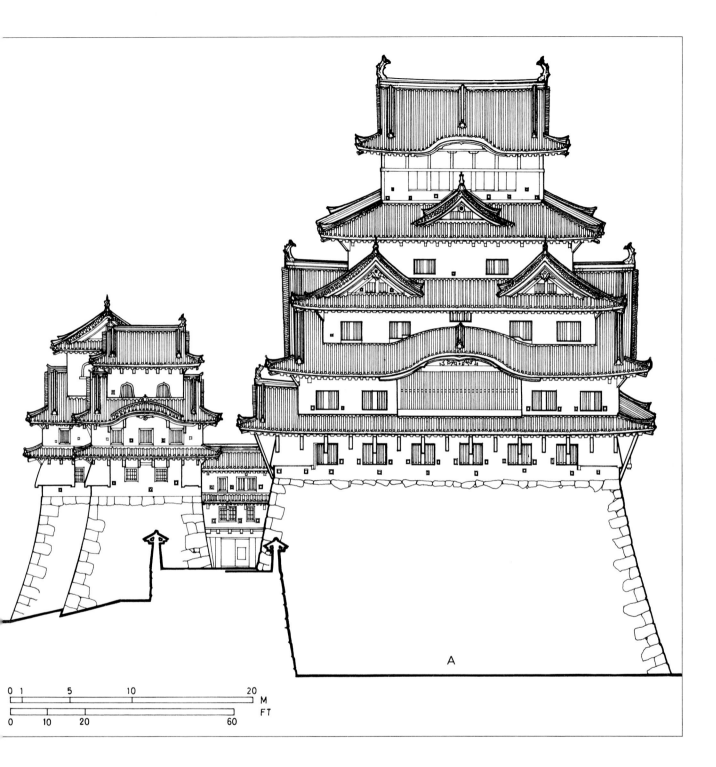

0	1	5	10	20	M
0	10	20		60	FT

A

Donjon principal du château de Himeji. Elévation 1:300. Sur une puissante infrastructure de pierre, aux murailles incurvées et dotées d'un fruit important se dressent des superstructures de bois dans le style traditionnel de l'architecture nipponne. Le donjon culmine à 50 m au-dessus de la plaine environnante.

Himeji, Burg, Hauptturm. Auf einem massiven Unterbau mit kurvig gebösch-ten Steinmauern erhebt sich der höl-zerne Turm im traditionellen japani-schen Stil mit einer Firsthöhe von 50 m über dem umliegenden Gelände. Aufriß 1:300.

Egret castle, Himeji: the main keep. Ele-vation 1:300. The powerful stone base has concave walls with a pronounced slope; the superstructure is built of wood in the traditional Japanese style. The keep rises to a height of 50 m. above the surrounding plain.

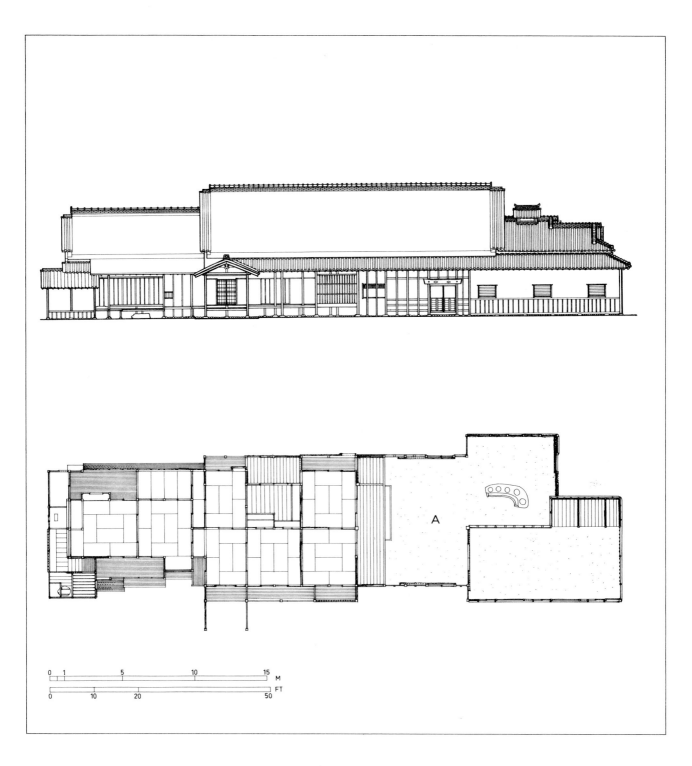

0 1   5   10   15 M
0   10   20   50 FT

Maison Yoshimura (préfecture d'Osaka), ferme construite au XVIIe s., où sont réunis sous le même toit des espaces de travail au sol (A) avec cuisine, et des pièces d'habitation, dont les proportions sont régies par le module du tatami, ou natte de paille de riz. Elévation de la façade et plan 1:250. On notera l'étroite parenté de cette architecture avec celle des villas impériales.

Haus Yoshimura (Präfektur Osaka), 17. Jh. Bei diesem Gehöft sind unter einem Dach die Wirtschaftsräume (A) mit der Küche und den Wohnräumen vereinigt. Das Grundmaß für die Aufteilung der Räume ist die Reisstrohmatte (Tatami). Diese Architektur ist derjenigen der kaiserlichen Villen eng verwandt. Fassadenaufriß und Grundriß 1:250.

Yoshimura house (Osaka district), a seventeenth-century farm-house uniting under one roof both utility rooms on the ground floor (A), including the kitchen and living quarters. The proportions of the latter are governed by the module of the *tatami*, a mat of rice straw. Front elevation and plan 1:250. Note how similar this is to the architecture of the imperial villas.

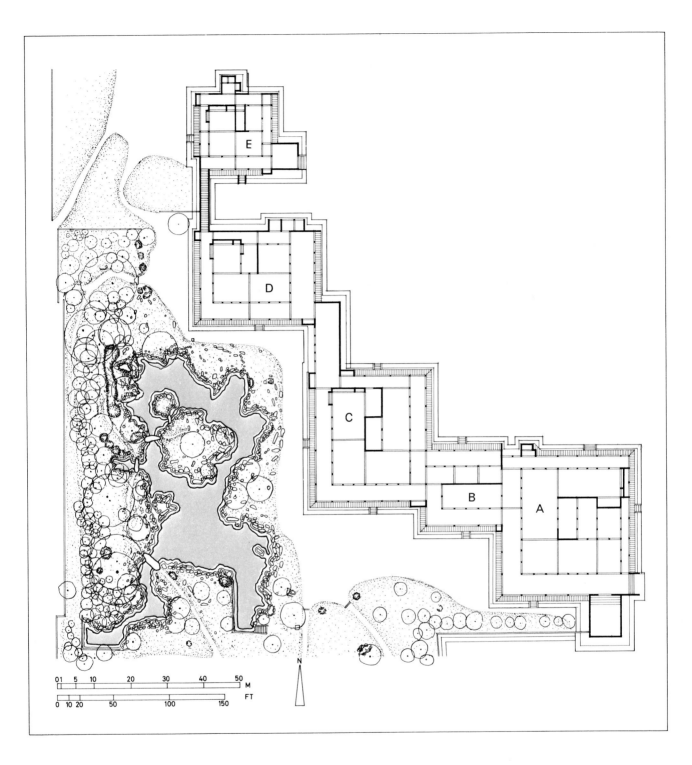

Scale bars:
0 1 5 10 20 30 40 50 M
0 10 20 50 100 150 FT

N

Château de Nijo, Ninomaru densha, à Kyoto, construit dès 1602 par Tokugawa Ieyasu. Plan du palais d'habitation 1:1000. A) Bâtiment d'attente, B) Salle des assemblées, C) Salons de réception, D) Salons privés, E) Séjour du shōgun. La disposition échelonnée des bâtiments et la liberté du plan, pourtant rigoureux, sont caractéristiques de cette architecture modulaire.

Kyoto, Schloß Nijo, Ni-no-maru densha, ab 1602 für Tokugawa Ieyasu erbaut. Die gestaffelte Anordnung der Gebäude und die freie, aber doch klare Gliederung der Anlage sind Kennzeichen dieser Modulbauweise. Grundriß des Wohnpalastes 1:1000: A) Halle für aufwartende Samurai, B) Versammlungssaal, C) Audienzräume, D) Privatgemächer, E) Wohnräume des Shogun.

Nijo castle, Kyoto, begun 1602 by Tokugawa Ieyasu. Plan of the *ninomaru densha* or dwelling-palace 1:1000. A) antechamber building, B) assembly hall, C) reception rooms, D) private quarters, E) Shogun's quarters. The staggered arrangement of the buildings and the apparent freedom of the plan (in fact it is strictly disciplined) are characteristic of this modular architecture.

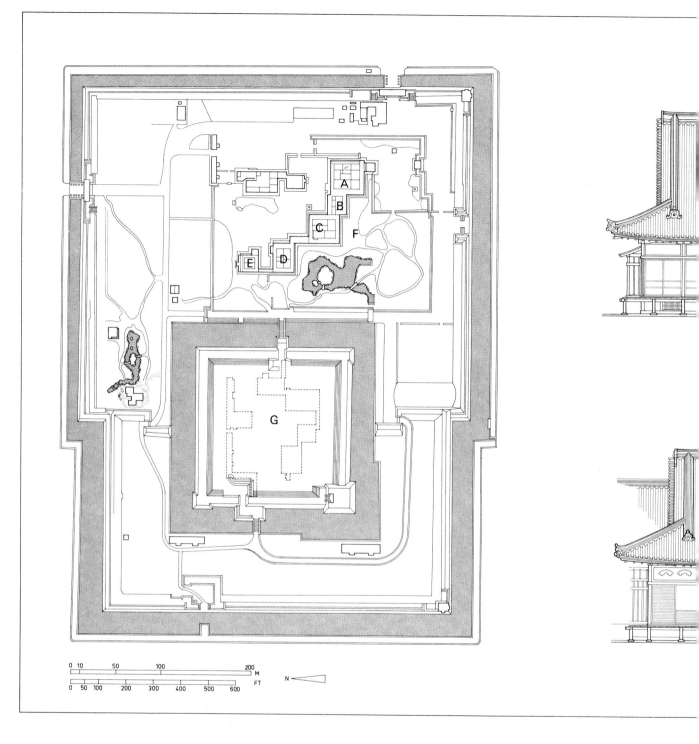

0 10   50   100   200
                                                     M
                                              FT
0 50 100   200   300   400   500   600

N

Château de Nijo, à Kyoto. Plan d'ensemble montrant la double douve à tracé rectiligne 1:4000. Pour les lettres A) à E), voir légende de la page précédente. F) Ninomaru, ou ensemble des bâtiments du palais d'habitation, G) Hon-maru ou château proprement dit, que surmontait un donjon, qui a été la proie des flammes et ne fut jamais reconstruit.

Kyoto, Schloß Nijo. Plan der Gesamtanlage mit den beiden rechtwinklig geführten Wassergräben 1:4000: A) bis E) vgl. vorstehende Legende, F) Ni-nomaru (Wohnpalast), G) Hon-maru, das Hauptschloß, über dem sich ein Turm erhob, der abbrannte und nicht wieder aufgebaut wurde.

Nijo castle, Kyoto. Overall plan showing the straight lines of the double moat 1:4000. A) to E) see caption on previous page, F) ninomaru or dwelling-palace complex, G) hon-maru or castle proper, originally surmounted by a keep, which burned down and was never rebuilt.

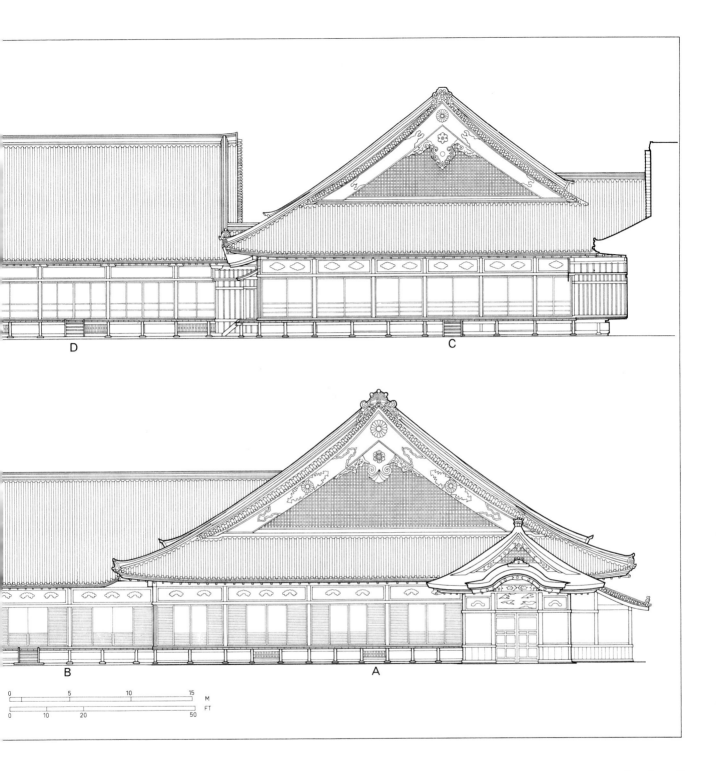

0	5	10	15	M
0	10	20		50 FT

Château de Nijo, à Kyoto. Elévation des façades des bâtiments A à D vus du sud 1:300. Outre la courbure des toitures, on remarquera la construction sur «pilotis» et l'articulation très légère de ces édifices pourtant vastes, dont la façade totalise 120 m de longueur.

Kyoto, Schloß Nijo. Außer der Schwingung der Dächer ist auch das Stützensystem bemerkenswert und die anmutige Leichtigkeit dieses recht ausgedehnten Komplexes, dessen Fassade insgesamt 120 m lang ist. Südfassaden-Aufrisse der Gebäude A bis D 1:300.

Nijo castle, Kyoto. Front elevation of buildings A) to D) seen from the south 1:300. As well as the curvature of the roofs, note the pile construction and the extremely light articulation of these buildings, despite their size (the façade totals 120 m. in length).

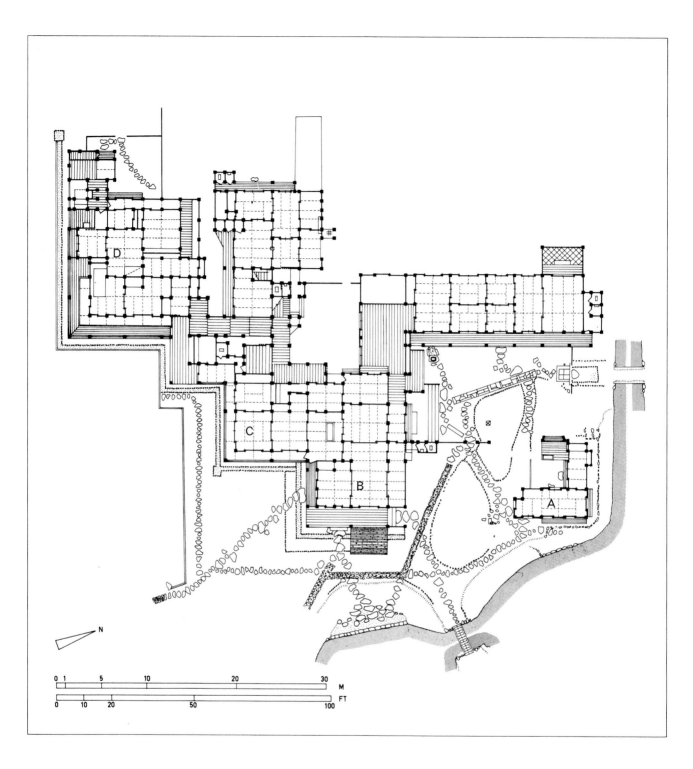

0 1   5   10   20   30   M

0   10 20   50   100 FT

Villa impériale de Katsura, près de Kyoto, construite entre 1620 et 1650. Plan d'esemble 1:400. A) Pavillon de thé (gepparo), B) Bâtiment le plus ancien (ko-shoin), C) Bâtiment du milieu (chû-shoin), D) Bâtiment le plus récent (shin-shoin). Disposition en diagonale analogue à celle du château de Nijo. Un plan très libre, mais régi par le module strict du tatami (natte en paille de riz).

Katsura bei Kyoto, Kaiserliche Villa, 1620–1650. Die Gebäude sind wie beim Schloß Nijo in der Diagonalen gestaffelt. Der Plan ist sehr frei, jedoch durch den Tatami- (Reisstrohmatten-) Modul bestimmt. Grundriß 1:400: A) Teepavillon (Geppa-ro), B) ältestes Gebäude (Ko-shoin), C) mittleres Gebäude (Chu-shoin), D) jüngstes Gebäude (Shin-shoin).

Katsura imperial villa (near Kyoto), built between 1620 and 1650. Overall plan 1:400. A) gepparo or tea pavilion, B) ko-shoin, the oldest building, C) chushoin, the middle building, D) shinshoin, the most recent building. The diagonal layout resembles that of Nijo castle. The plan is very free but again governed by the strict module of the *tatami* or rice-straw mat.

Islam classique

Islam

Classical Islam

Héritiers de l'acquis technologique et des formes byzantino-sassanides ainsi que des édifices romains et paléochrétiens, mais proposant des programmes neufs, en fonction de besoins religieux nouveaux nés du Coran et de modes de vie particuliers, les Arabes des premiers siècles de l'hégire vont créer des espaces totalement originaux. Omeyyades et Abbassides forgent un langage où subsistent tout d'abord les modes décoratifs et les organes byzantins: mosaïques, colonnes, chapiteaux, arcs, voûtes et coupoles (Grande Mosquée de Damas ou Dôme du Rocher à Jérusalem).

Mais si le Dôme du Rocher (692) dérive des plans centrés propres aux martyriums circulaires chrétiens, la mosquée classique, en revanche, apporte des espaces barlongs – plus larges que profonds – qui s'opposent à ceux en longueur des basiliques et des églises. L'orientation des édifices religieux est un impératif rigoureusement observé, fût-ce au prix de bouleversements dans la trame urbaine. La kibla ou mur du fond de la salle de prière, dans lequel s'inscrit le mihrab, est toujours perpendiculaire à la direction de La Mecque, où se trouve le vénéré Rocher Noir ou Kaaba.

Les hypostyles ouvertes sur cour de Samarra, Kairouan ou Cordoue créent, grâce à une forêt de supports, un environnement dont les limites sont insaisissables. L'usage de la brique, légué tant par Rome que par les Sassanides de Mésopotamie, va permettre rapidement d'immenses réalisations (Abou Dolaf: 859, Ibn Touloun: 876) et un urbanisme à l'échelle des plus vastes cités de l'Antiquité (Bagdad: 762).

Le refus de la façade, impliquant l'intégration des volumes dans le tout orga-

Die Araber übernahmen zwar byzantinisch-sassanidische Techniken und Formen, ließen sich auch durch römische und frühchristliche Bauten inspirieren, doch sie stellten, entsprechend den sich aus dem Koran ergebenden religiösen Erfordernissen und ihrer Lebensweise, neue Programme auf und schufen in den ersten Jahrhunderten der Hedschra völlig eigenständige Räume. Omaijaden und Abbasiden entwickelten eine Architektur, die sich zunächst byzantinischer Struktur- und Schmuckelemente bediente: Mosaiken, Säulen, Kapitelle, Bogen, Gewölbe und Kuppeln (Große Moschee in Damaskus, Felsendom in Jerusalem).

Der Felsendom (692) ist von den christlichen Zentralbauten der Martyrien abgeleitet, die Räume der klassischen Moschee sind jedoch - ganz im Gegensatz zur Längsrichtung der Basiliken und christlichen Kirchen - querrechteckig, also breiter als tief. Die Orientierung der religiösen Bauwerke wird streng eingehalten, auch wenn das städtebauliche Schema dadurch gestört wird. Die Qibla, die abschließende Mauer des Betsaals, in der sich der Mihrab befindet, steht stets im rechten Winkel zur Richtung nach Mekka, wo die Kaaba den meerverehrungswürdigen Schwarzen Stein steht.

Die auf einen Hof geöffneten Säulensäle von Samarra, Kairuan oder Córdoba bilden dank ihrer «Säulenwälder» Räume, deren Grenzen sich der Faßbarkeit entziehen.

Die sowohl von den Römern wie auch den mesopotamischen Sassaniden übernommene Ziegeltechnik ermöglichte schon früh den Bau gewaltiger Moscheen (Abu Dulaf, 859; Ibn Tulun, 876) und einen Städtebau im Maßstab

The Arabs of the early centuries of the Hegira (the Mohammedan era), heirs to the technological attainments and architectural forms of the Byzantines and Sassanids as well as to the buildings of the Roman and Early Christian periods, created totally original architectural forms by adding programmes of their own based on new religious requirements (the Koran) and distinctive modes of life. Umayyads and Abbasids forged a language that above all preserved the architectural features and decorative manner of Byzantium: mosaics, columns, capitals, arches, vaults and domes (the Great Mosque, Damascus; Dome of the Rock, Jerusalem).

The Dome of the Rock (692), however, owes its centralised plan to the Christian martyry. The classical mosque, in contrast to the basilica and the church, presented a lateral oblong—i.e. it was wider than it was deep. The orientation of Moslem religious buildings constitutes a rigorous imperative, complied with even at the cost of disturbing the layout of the town concerned. The qiblah or back wall of the mosque, which contains the mihrab, is always at right angles to the direction of Mecca, where the revered Black Stone or Caaba (ka'bah) is situated.

The hypostyles opening on to courtyards at Samarra, Kairwan and Cordoba create, with their forests of supports, environments whose limits are elusive. The use of brick, which was inherited from Rome as well as from the Sassanids of Mesopotamia, soon made it possible to erect vast mosques (Abu Dulaf, 859; Ibn Tulun, 876) and practise town-planning on the scale of the largest cities of antiquity (Baghdad, 762).

nique de l'urbanisme, donne naissance à de prodigieux ensembles généreusement articulés, rythmés d'avenues, de places, de portiques (quartiers-palais de Djawsak Khakani et de Balkuwara à Samarra, IXᵉ s.). Les résidences du désert, dérivant à la fois de réalisations comme Spalato (palais de Dioclétien) et de Ctésiphon, avec leur organisation orthogonale quadripartite, leurs allées, leurs salles voûtées, leurs enceintes, leurs bains et leurs jardins, marquent la recherche de luxe, d'apparat et de faste dont s'entourent les califes (Mshatta, Ukhaïdir, Khirbat al-Mafdjar).

Avec l'éclatement du monde islamique au Xᵉ siècle, les styles vont se diversifier dans chaque aire culturelle, contrairement à l'unité «internationaliste» de l'époque classique.

der größten antiken Anlagen (Bagdad, 762).

Der Verzicht auf die Ausbildung von Fassaden erlaubt die Eingliederung der Bauten in den Organismus der Stadt; dadurch können herrliche, durch breite Straßen, Plätze und Portiken großzügig gegliederte Anlagen entstehen (die Palastviertel von Djawsak Khakani und von Balkuwara in Samarra, 9. Jahrhundert). Die nach vierteiligem, rechtwinkligem Plan angelegten Wüstenresidenzen gehen sowohl auf den Diokletianspalast in Spalato wie auch auf Ktesiphon zurück. Ihre Alleen, überwölbten Säle, Umfassungsmauern, Badeanlagen und Gärten sind Zeichen des Strebens nach Luxus und der Pracht- und Prunkliebe der Kalifen (Mschatta, Ukhaidir, Khirbet el-Mefdschir).

Mit der Zersplitterung des Islam im 10. Jahrhundert entwickelten sich in jedem Gebiet eigene Stilvarianten, die nahezu «internationale» Geschlossenheit der klassischen Zeit ging verloren.

Rejection of the façade, implying as it did the integration of volumes in an organic urban whole, gave rise to prodigious complexes that were generously articulated and rationalised by means of avenues, squares and porticoes (the palace quarters of Djawsak Khakani and Balkuwara at Samarra, ninth century). Desert residences, derived from such buildings as Diocletian's Palace at Spalato as well as from Ctesiphon, typified, with their quadripartite rectangular organisation, broad walks, vaulted halls, precincts, baths and gardens, the luxury and pomp with which the Caliphs sought to surround themselves (Mshatta, Ukhaidir, Khirbat al-Mafdjar).

With the fragmentation of the Moslem world in the tenth century, architectural styles became diversified in each cultural area that was overrun, ending the 'internationalist' unity of the classic period.

1 La salle hypostyle de la grande mosquée de Cordoue (Espagne), construite entre 785 et 987, qui totalise 600 colonnes supportant un système d'arcades doubles superposées.
2 La salle hypostyle à piliers de briques de la mosquée d'Ibn Touloun, construite en 876 au Caire.
3 Voûtes à stalactites de la Cour des Lions à l'Alhambra de Grenade, construite en 1377 par la dynastie des Nasrides d'Espagne.

1 Córdoba, Hypostil der Großen Moschee; die 600 Säulen tragen ein übereinandergesetztes zweifaches Bogensystem
2 Kairo, Große Moschee des Ibn Tulun, das Innere des Hypostils; die Pfeiler sind in Ziegelmauerwerk erbaut (876)
3 Granada, Alhambra, Stalaktitengewölbe im Löwenhof (1377 unter der Nasriden-Dynastie erbaut)

1 The hypostyle interior of the great mosque, Cordoba (Spain; 785–987), where a total of 600 columns supports a system of double superposed arcades.
2 The brick-pillared hypostyle interior of Ibn Tulun mosque, Cairo, built in 876.
3 Stalactite vaults in the Lion court of the Alhambra, Granada, built by the Spanish-Moslem Nasrid dynasty in 1377.

1

2

3

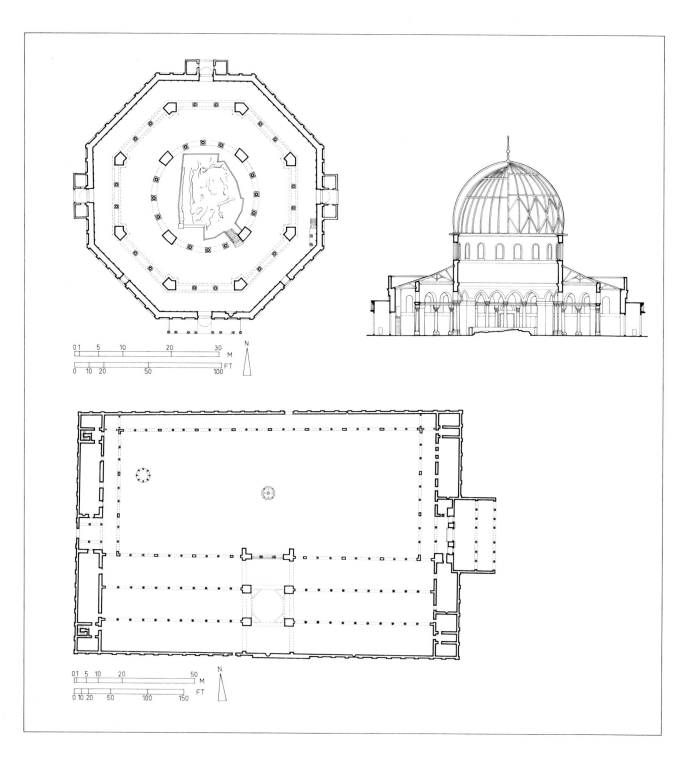

Dôme du Rocher, à Jérusalem, construit de 685 à 692. Plan et coupe 1:750. Edifice en forme de martyrium octogonal à plan centré et double déambulatoire, avec coupole à deux coques en bois. Ce vénérable monument islamique a été construit par des bâtisseurs byzantins. En bas, **Grande Mosquée des Omeyyades, à Damas** (Syrie), édifiée entre 706 et 715. Plan 1:1500. Cour à portiques.

Oben: **Jerusalem, Felsendom,** 685–692. Oktogonales Martyrium mit zentraler Kuppel und doppeltem Umgang. Die Kuppel ist eine zweischalige Holzkonstruktion. Das hochverehrte Heiligtum wurde von byzantinischen Baumeistern errichtet. Grundriß und Schnitt 1:750. Unten: **Damaskus, Große Omaijaden-Moschee,** 706–715. Moscheehof mit Säulengängen. Grundriß 1:1500.

Dome of the Rock, Jerusalem, built 685–92. Plan and section 1:750. This splendid Moslem monument was built by Byzantine craftsmen. It takes the form of a centrally-planned octagonal martyrium with a double ambulatory and a dome consisting of two wooden shells. Below, the **Great Mosque of the Ummayads,** Damascus (Syria), built 706–15. Plan 1:1500. Note the porticoed courtyard.

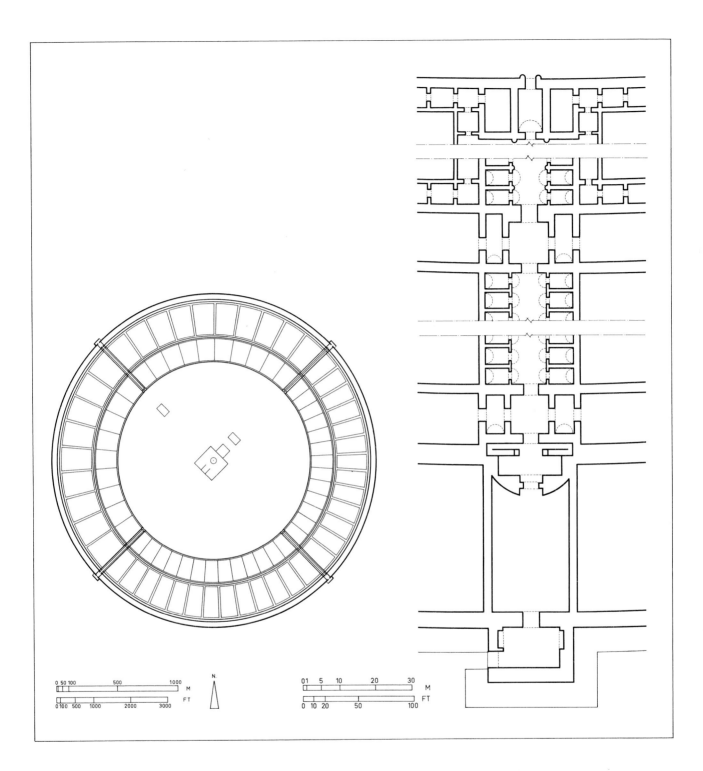

| 0 50 100 | 500 | 1000 | M |
| 0 100 500 | 1000 | 2000 3000 | FT |

N.

| 01 5 | 10 | 20 | 30 | M |
| 0 10 20 | 50 | | 100 | FT |

Ville Ronde de Bagdad (Irak), fondée par al-Mansur en 762. Plan 1:30000 et détail des portes et des murailles concentriques 1:1000. De bas en haut: l'une des quatre portes, avec chicane et pont, suivie d'un glacis conduisant à la seconde porte fortifiée; 54 arcades d'une rue marchande axiale, suivie d'une nouvelle porte, puis une trentaine d'arcades jusqu'à la dernière porte. Au centre, la mosquée et le palais.

Bagdad (Irak), die Rundstadt, 762 von el-Mansur gegründet. Im Zentrum Moschee und Palast. Stadtplan 1:30000; rechts: Detail eines der vier Zugänge mit den konzentrischen Stadtmauern 1:1000: von unten nach oben: äußerstes Tor mit Schikane und Brücke, dann Glacis, das zum zweiten befestigten Tor führt; 54 Arkaden einer Verkaufsstraße, drittes Tor, etwa 30 weitere Arkaden, innerstes Tor.

Round city of Baghdad (Iraq), founded by al-Mansur in 762. Plan 1:30,000 and detail of the gates and concentric walls 1:1000. From the bottom: one of the four gates, with zigzag and bridge, followed by a glacis leading up to the second fortified gate; 54 arches of an axial commercial street, followed by a new gate and a further thirty or so arches up to the last gate. Centre, the mosque and palace.

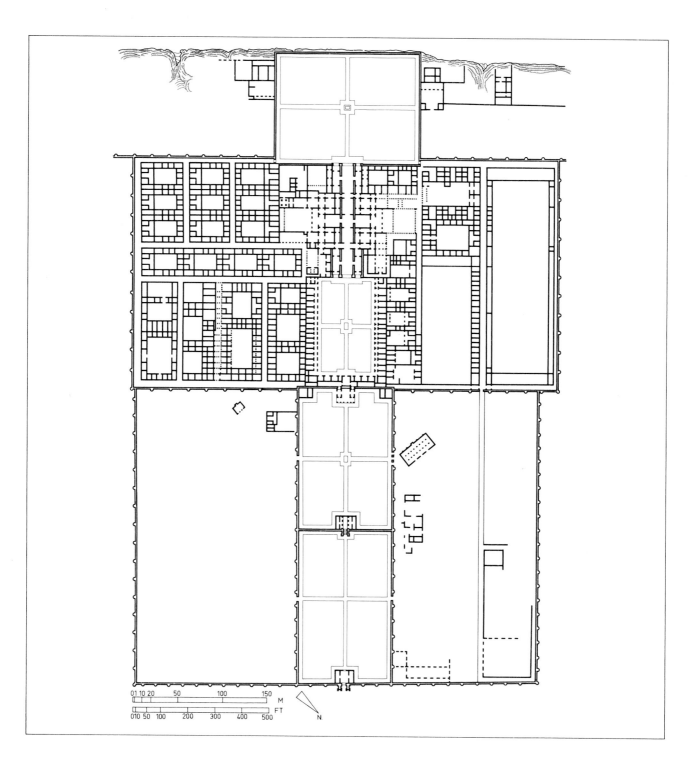

Palais califien de Balkuwara, à Samarra (Irak), construit par al-Mutawakkil pour son fils al-Mutazz, entre 850 et 860, sur la rive droite du Tigre. Plan 1:4000. Construction axée de 670 m de longueur, ceinte de murs flanqués de tours, ce quartier du palais constitue une ville dans la ville, avec ses places, ses iwâns, ses allées d'apparat et sa mosquée. Un exemple d'urbanisme islamique.

Samarra (Irak), Kalifenpalast Balkuwara, 850–860 von el-Mutawakkil für seinen Sohn el-Mu'tazz auf dem rechten Tigrisufer erbaut. Das von einer turmbewehrten Mauer umgebene Palastviertel mit 670 m langer Mittelachse bildet mit Plätzen, Iwanen, prächtigen Alleen und der Moschee eine Stadt in der Stadt; ein Beispiel für islamischen Städtebau. Grundriß 1:4000.

Balkuwara palace, Samarra (Iraq), built on the right bank of the Tigris by al-Mutawakkil for his son al-Mutazz, 850–60. Plan 1:4000. An axial arrangement 670 m. in length and surrounded by walls flanked with towers, this palace of the Caliphs constitutes a city within a city with its own squares, *iwans*, stately avenues and mosque. It is a good example of Moslem town-planning.

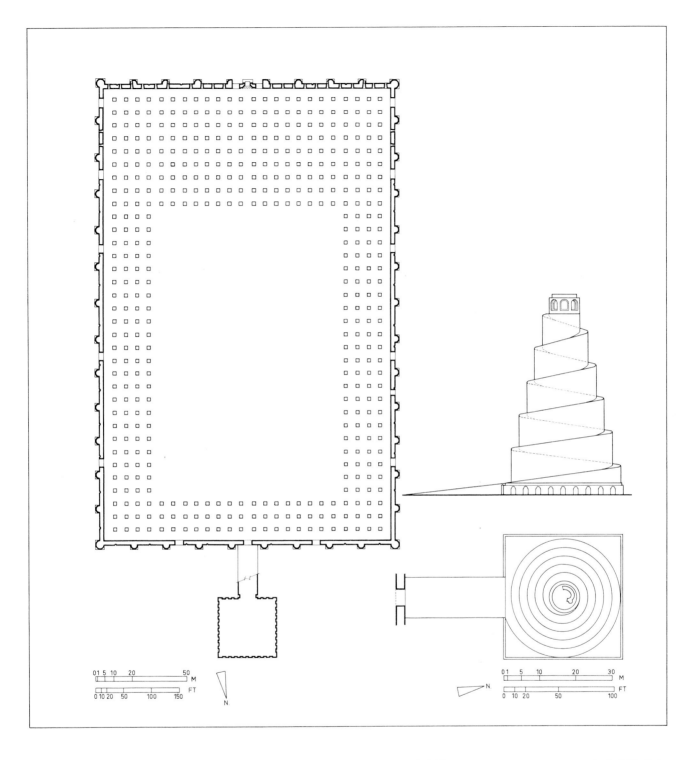

Grande Mosquée de Samarra (Irak), édifiée de 848 à 852, sous le califat de al-Mutawakkil. Plan 1:2000, élévation et plan du minaret hélicoïdal, dit Malawiyya 1:1000. C'est la plus vaste mosquée au monde. Construite entièrement en brique, dans une enceinte flanquée de tours, elle présente un minaret haut de 55 m avec rampe hélicoïdale qui rappelle des ziggourats mésopotamiennes.

Samarra (Irak), Große Moschee, 848 bis 852 unter dem Kalifen el-Mutawakkil erbaut. Die größte Moschee der Welt, vollständig aus Ziegelmauerwerk und von einer mit Türmen bewehrten Mauer umgeben. Das 55 m hohe Minarett mit spiralförmiger Rampe erinnert an mesopotamische Zikkurats. Grundriß 1:2000; Aufriß und Grundriß des Minaretts (Malawiyya) 1:1000.

Great mosque, Samarra, built 848–52 in the caliphate of al-Mutawakkil. Plan 1:2000; elevation and plan of the spiral al-Malwiyah minaret 1:1000. This is the largest mosque in the world. Built entirely of brick within a wall flanked with towers, it has a 55 m. high minaret with a spiral ramp that recalls the ziggurats of Mesopotamia.

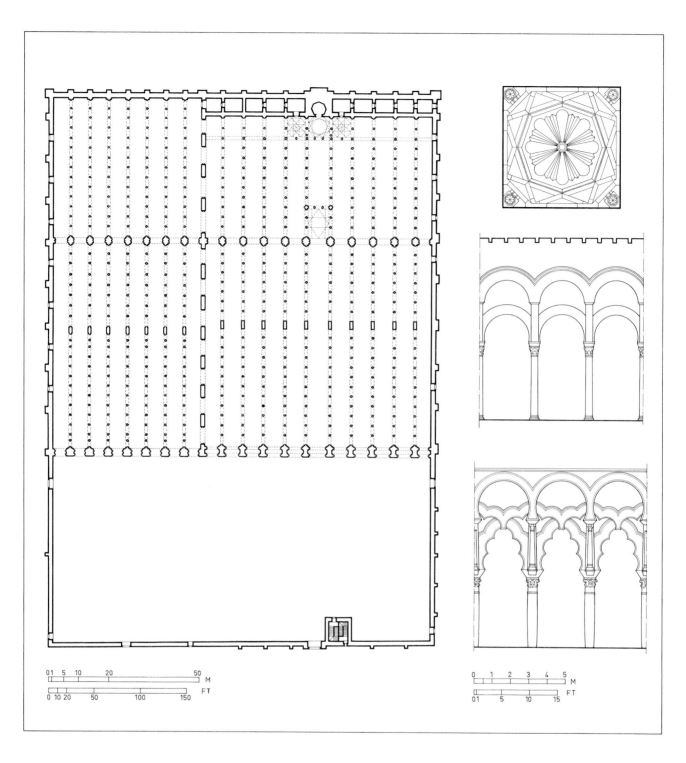

Grande Mosquée de Cordoue (Espagne), fondée en 785, agrandie en 833, 961 et 987. Plan 1:1200, détail de la coupole du mihrab (961), des arcades super-posées et des arcades entrelacées situées devant le mihrab 1:200. La salle hypo-style totalise 600 colonnes, souvent d'origine antique, réemployées. Les mosaïques ornant le mihrab sont l'œuvre d'artistes byzantins.

Córdoba (Spanien), Große Moschee, 785 begonnen, 833, 961, 987 vergrößert. Bei den 600 Säulen des Hypostils handelt es sich weitgehend um wiederverwen-dete antike Stücke (Spolien). Die Mo-saiken im Mihrab wurden von byzanti-nischen Künstlern geschaffen. Grund-riß 1:1200; Details der Kuppel über dem Mihrab (961), der zweigeschossi-gen Arkaden und der durchbrochenen Arkaden vor dem Mihrab 1:200.

Great mosque, Cordoba (Spain), found-ed in 785 and enlarged in 833, 961 and 987. Plan 1:1200. Detail of the *mihrab* dome (961), the superposed arcades, and the interlocking arches in front of the *mihrab* 1:200. The hypostyle interior contains a total of 600 columns, many of them re-used classical remains. The mosaics decorating the *mihrab* are the work of Byzantine artists.

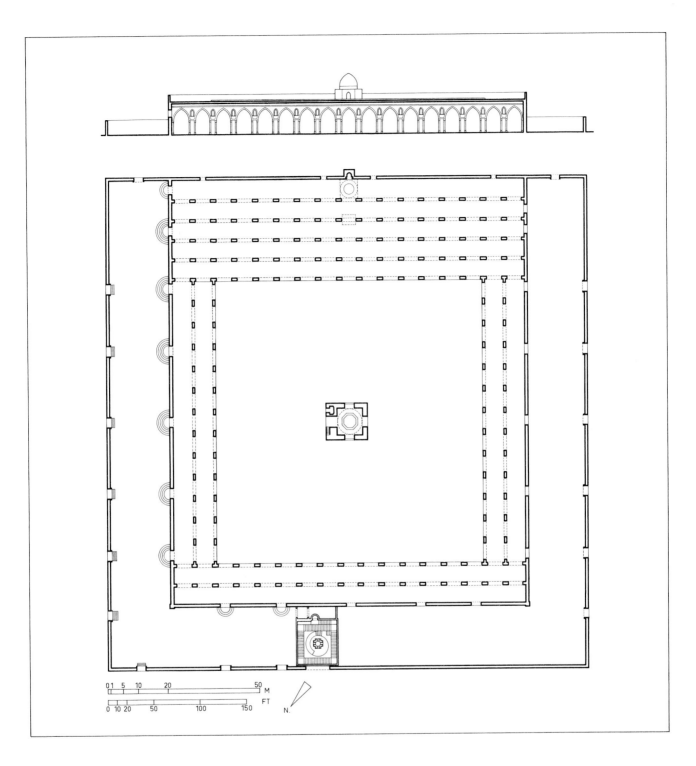

| M | 0 1 | 5 | 10 | 20 | | 50 |
| FT | 0 10 20 | | 50 | | 100 | 150 |

N.

Grande Mosquée d'Ibn Touloun, Le Caire (Egypte), édifiée de 876 à 879 par le général Ahmed Ibn-Touloun, fondateur de la dynastie des Toulounides d'Egypte. Coupe transversale dans la salle de prière et plan 1:1200. Edifice hypostyle à arcades en tiers-point couvertes en charpente, cette mosquée de brique s'inspire des réalisations de Samarra. Cour carrée de 92 m de côté.

Kairo, Große Moschee des Ibn Tulun, 876–879 von General Ahmed Ibn Tulun, dem Begründer der Tuluniden-Dynastie in Ägypten, erbaut. Die in Ziegelmauerwerk errichtete Moschee ist nach dem Vorbild von Samarra angelegt. Der quadratische Hof hat eine Seitenlänge von 92 m. Querschnitt durch den Betsaal und Grundriß 1:1200.

Great mosque of Ibn Tulun, Cairo (Egypt), built 876–9 by Ahmed Ibn Tulun, founder of the Tulunid dynasty that ruled Egypt. Cross section of the prayer-hall and plan 1:1200. A hypostyle with pointed arches and a beam roof, this brick-built mosque was inspired by the buildings of Samarra. The courtyard measures 92 m. by 92 m.

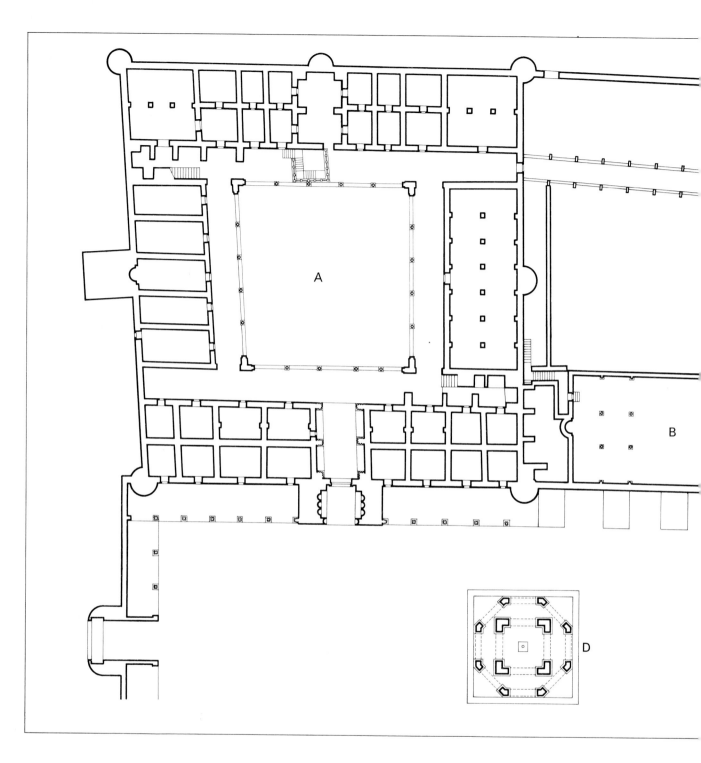

Palais omeyyade de Khirbat al-Mafdjar, près de Jéricho, probablement construit par le calife Hisham (724–743). Plan 1:600. Sur un château de plan carré, à cour centrale (A), se greffent une mosquée (B), un bain monumental (C) et un grand bassin (D). Fortifié à la manière des châteaux classiques, avec tours d'angles, le palais comporte au nord une grande salle de réception.

Khirbet el-Mefdschir (nahe Jericho), Omaijadenschloß, vermutlich von Kalif Hischam (724–743) erbaut. Der Palast ist in herkömmlicher Weise durch Ecktürme befestigt. Grundriß 1:600: Quadratisch angelegtes Schloß, A) innerer Arkadenhof, B) anschließend Moschee, C) weitläufige Badeanlage, D) großes Wasserbecken. Nördlich ein großer Audienzsaal.

Ummayad palace of Khirbat al-Mafjar, near Jericho, probably built by Caliph Hisham (724–43). Plan 1:600. A square castle with a central courtyard (A) is adjoined by a mosque (B), a monumental bath (C), and a large pool (D). To the north is a large reception room. The palace is fortified with angle towers in the manner of ancient castles.

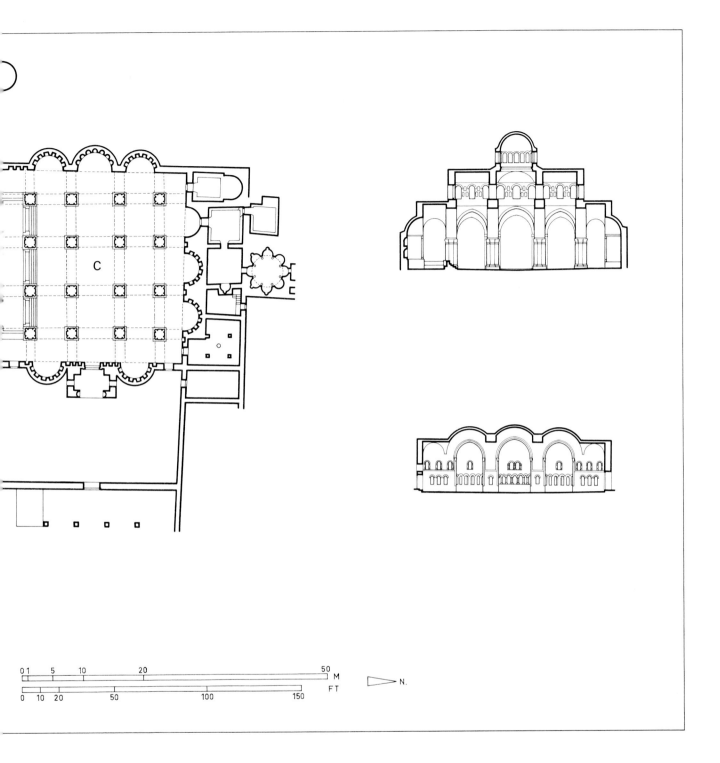

La vaste salle hypostyle voûtée des bains de **Khirbat al-Mafdjar,** dont on voit une coupe transversale et une coupe longitudinale latérale 1:600, précède l'étuve proprement dite, à plan tréflé, sise au nord. Par son échelle, cet établissement de bains s'apparente aux thermes de l'Antiquité. Le voûtement en coupoles représenté ici est une reconstitution hypothétique.

Khirbet el-Mefdschir, Badeanlage. An den großen überwölbten Säulensaal schließt im Norden das Caldarium an, dessen Grundriß einer achtblättrigen Rosette gleicht. In der Größe entspricht diese Badeanlage durchaus den Thermen der Antike. Querschnitt, seitlich gelegter Längsschnitt 1:600 (die Kuppelüberwölbung ist eine hypothetische Rekonstruktion).

Palace of Khirbat al-Mafjar: the enormous vaulted hypostyle of the baths. Cross section and lateral longitudinal section 1:600. This precedes the sweating-room proper, which is built on a trefoil plan to the north. In scale this bathing establishment rivals the thermae of antiquity. The domed vaulting represented here is a hypothetical reconstruction.

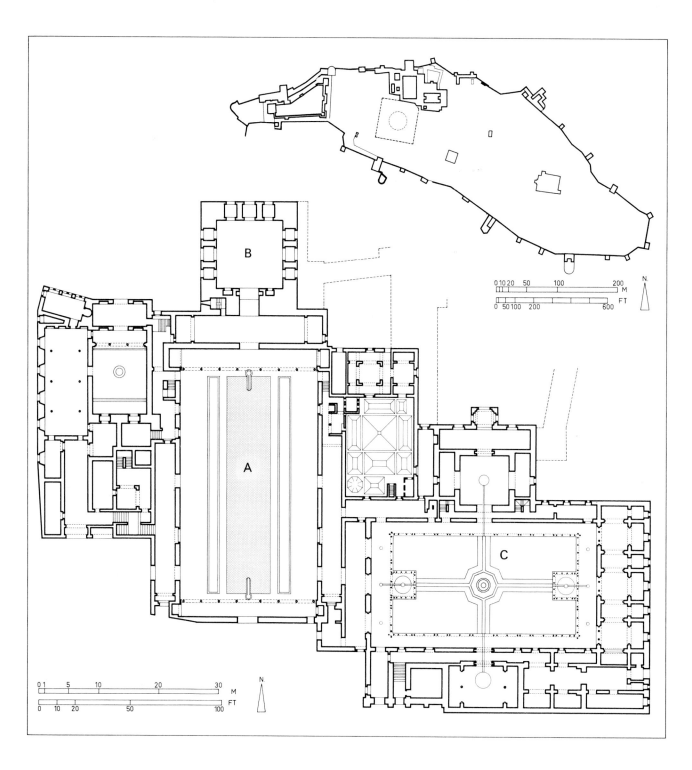

Alhambra de Grenade (Espagne), construite entre 1305 et 1377 par la dernière dynastie islamique d'Espagne, les Nasrides. Situation générale 1:6000, avec l'enceinte de la forteresse, et plan du palais 1:600. A) Cour des Myrthes, B) Salle des Ambassadeurs (1335–1340), C) Cour des Lions (1377). La «Forteresse Rouge» perpétue, à la fin du monde islamique occidental, les palais arabes classiques.

Granada, Alhambra, 1305–1377 unter den Nasriden, der letzten islamischen Dynastie in Spanien, erbaut. Die «Rote Festung» ist ein Beispiel klassischer arabischer Palastbaukunst am Ende der islamischen Herrschaft in Westeuropa. Lageplan (mit Festungsmauer) 1:6000; Grundriß des Palastes 1:600: A) Myrthenhof, B) Gesandtensaal (1335–1340), C) Löwenhof (1377).

Alhambra, Granada (Spain), built between 1305 and 1377 by the Nasrids, the last Moslem dynasty to rule in Spain. Site plan 1:6000 showing the wall of the fortress and plan of the palace 1:600. A) Myrtle court, B) hall of the Ambassadors (1335–40), C) Lion court (1377). The 'Red Fortress' is an echo, right at the end of the period of Moslem presence in the West, of the classical Arabian palace.

Perse

Persien

Persia

L'architecture des mosquées de la Perse se caractérise par l'utilisation de l'iwân (vaste niche voûtée, héritée des palais sassanides). L'iwân est présent au milieu de chacune des quatre façades sur cour de l'édifice de prière dès le XIe siècle. Ce grand porche à encadrement plat donne accès au sanctuaire principal et aux salles secondaires. Il accentue les quatre directions de la cour cruciforme, au centre de laquelle une pièce d'eau est destinée aux ablutions rituelles. Dès la période seldjoukide, au XIIe siècle, la Mosquée du Vendredi à Ispahan réalise l'exemple parfait de cette formule.

Le revêtement des structures de brique à l'aide de mosaïques (époque timouride), puis de carreaux de faïence polychrome (époque safavide) finit par couvrir toutes les surfaces visibles de la mosquée: après le sanctuaire et le mihrab, les iwâns et les arcades sur cour, c'est enfin la coupole en forme de dôme outrepassé (en bulbe) qui est habillée de ce décor rutilant et haut en couleur, où s'épanouissent les motifs floraux, les pampres et les ramures figurant l'impérissable végétation du paradis promis aux croyants.

L'époque safavide, avec Shah Abbas qui fait d'Ispahan sa capitale (1598), marque l'apogée de l'architecture propre à l'Iran shi'ite, dont l'aire culturelle s'étend de la Mésopotamie au Turkestan et des frontières de l'Empire ottoman à celles de l'Inde. Cet art culmine avec l'oratoire privé du souverain, ou Mosquée de Lotfallah, et surtout avec la grande Mosquée du Shah (1612), vaste édifice flanqué de deux madrasas et dont le sanctuaire est surmonté d'une coupole haute de 53 m. Sa parure de faïence a nécessité un million et demi de carreaux polychromes.

Die persischen Moscheen sind durch den Iwan gekennzeichnet, eine große überwölbte Nische, die aus der sassanidischen Palastarchitektur übernommen wurde. Vom 11. Jahrhundert an erhielt jede der vier Hoffassaden einen Iwan; die großen flach gerahmten Tore führen in das Hauptheiligtum und die Nebenräume. Dieses Schema betont die Kreuzform des Hofes, in dessen Zentrum sich ein Wasserbecken für rituelle Waschungen befindet. Seit der seldschukischen Epoche im 12. Jahrhundert ist die Freitagsmoschee in Isfahan das vollkommenste Beispiel einer solchen Anlage.

Unter den Timuriden verkleidete man die Ziegelmauern mit Mosaiken, unter den Safawiden mit bunten Fayencen. Schließlich wurden alle sichtbaren Flächen der Moschee – nach dem Betsaal und dem Mihrab, den Iwanen und Hofarkaden zuletzt auch die Zwiebelkuppeln – mit farbenprächtigen pflanzlichen Motiven, Weinranken und Laubwerk bedeckt, Symbolen der unvergänglichen Vegetation in dem den Gläubigen verheißenen Paradies.

Ihren Höhepunkt erreichte die Architektur des schiitischen Persien, dessen kultureller Einfluß von Mesopotamien bis Turkestan und von den Grenzen des Osmanischen Reiches bis nach Indien reichte, in der Safawidenzeit unter Schah Abbas, der 1598 Isfahan zu seiner Hauptstadt machte. Die großartigsten Bauten sind die Privatmoschee des Herrschers (Lutfullah-Moschee) und die Große kaiserliche Moschee (1612), eine gewaltige, von zwei Medresen flankierte Moschee mit 53 m hoher Kuppel. Für den Fayencenschmuck waren eineinhalb Millionen farbiger Plättchen notwendig.

The architecture of the Persian mosque is characterised by the use of the *iwan*, an enormous vaulted niche taken over from the Sassanid palace. It is placed in the centre of the four courtyard façades of the building from the eleventh century onwards. This large porch with a flat frame gives access to the main sanctuary and to the secondary rooms. It emphasises the four directions of the cruciform courtyard, at the centre of which is a pool for ritual ablutions. As early as the twelfth-century Seljuk period, the Friday Mosque at Isfahan embodied this formula to perfection.

The practice of facing brick structures with mosaic (Timurid period) and then with polychrome tiles (Safavid period) eventually led to the covering of all the mosque's visible surfaces: after the sanctuary and the *mihrab*, the *iwans* and the courtyard arcades and finally the onion-shaped dome were clad in this gleaming, highly coloured decor with its abundance of floral motifs, vine leaves and foliage symbolising the imperishable vegetation of the paradise of which believers were assured.

The Safavid period, and particularly the reign of Shah Abbas, who made Isfahan his capital in 1598, marked the architectural high point of this Shiite culture, whose sphere of influence extended from Mesopotamia to Turkestan and from the frontiers of the Ottoman Empire eastwards to India. The culmination was represented by the sovereign's private oratory, the Lutfullah Mosque, and above all by the great Mosque of the Shah (1612), an immense building flanked by two madrasahs or Koran schools and with a 53 m. high dome surmounting the sanctuary. Its decorative cladding called for one

A la fin de la dynastie safavide, une baroquisation des formes se fait jour dans le complexe de Shah Sultan Husain (1706), ensemble groupant un bazar long de 220 m, une madrasa avec sa mosquée et un grand caravansérail. L'architecture des palais et pavillons révèle une grâce décorative qui s'épanouit au milieu de jardins, de bassins et de jets d'eau. Car la capitale, oasis au cœur des hauts plateaux arides, est une véritable cité verte, avec ses places (Meidan-é Shah: 500 × 150 m) et ses allées d'apparat (Tchahar Bagh: 1,6 km) ainsi que ses ponts (Pont aux 33 Arches: 300 m de long).

Am Ende der Safawidenzeit, in der Medrese des Schah Sultan Husein (1706), tritt eine Barockisierung der Formen ein. Der Komplex umfaßt einen 220 m langen Basar, die Medrese mit der Moschee und eine große Karawanserei. Die Architektur der Paläste und Pavillons, die zwischen Wasserbecken und Springbrunnen in Gärten liegen, ist von dekorativer Anmut. Die Hauptstadt, eine Oase inmitten der unfruchtbaren Hochebene, ist mit ihren herrlichen Plätzen (Maidan-i-Schah: 500 × 150 m), prächtigen Alleen (Tschahar Bagh: 1,6 km) und Brücken (Brücke der 33 Bogen: 300 m) eine Stadt des Grüns.

and a half million polychrome tiles.
At the end of the Safavid dynasty a certain 'baroque' element emerged in the complex built by Shah Sultan Husain (1706) and comprising a 200 m. long bazaar, a madrasah with its mosque, and a large caravanserai. The architecture of palaces and pavilions evinces a decorative grace that blossoms amid gardens, pools and fountains. Isfahan, an oasis in the middle of high, arid plateaus, is a city of greenery with its broad squares (the Maidan-i-Shah measures 500 m. by 150 m.), magnificent prospects (the Chahar Bagh is 1.6 km. long), and bridges (the Bridge of the 33 Arches is 300 m. in length).

1 Voûtement de l'iwân ouest de la Mosquée du Vendredi à Ispahan, datant de la période seldjoukide (XIIᵉ siècle).
2 La grande coupole surmontant le sanctuaire de la Mosquée du Shah, à Ispahan, construite par Shah Abbas de 1612 à 1630.
3 Les cellules des maîtres et étudiants à la madrasa de Shah Sultan Husain, à Ispahan, datant de 1706.
4 Iwân d'entrée du sanctuaire de la madrasa de Shah Sultan Husain.

1 Isfahan, Freitagsmoschee, Gewölbe des westlichen Iwan (Seldschukenzeit, 12. Jh.)
2 Isfahan, Große kaiserliche Moschee, Kuppel über dem Betsaal (1612 bis 1630 unter Schah Abbas dem Großen erbaut)
3 Isfahan, Medrese des Schahs Sultan Husein, Zellen der Lehrer und Schüler (1706)
4 Isfahan, Medrese des Schahs Sultan Husein, der zum Betsaal führende Iwan

1 Vaulting of the west *iwan* of the Friday mosque, Isfahan, dating from the Seljuk period (twelfth century).
2 The dome above the sanctuary of the Great mosque of the Shah, Isfahan, built 1612–30 by Shah Abbas the Great.
3 Masters' and students' cells in the Madrasah of Shah Sultan Husain, Isfahan, built in 1706.
4 Entrance *iwan* of the sanctuary of the Madrash of Shah Sultan Husain.

1

2

3

4

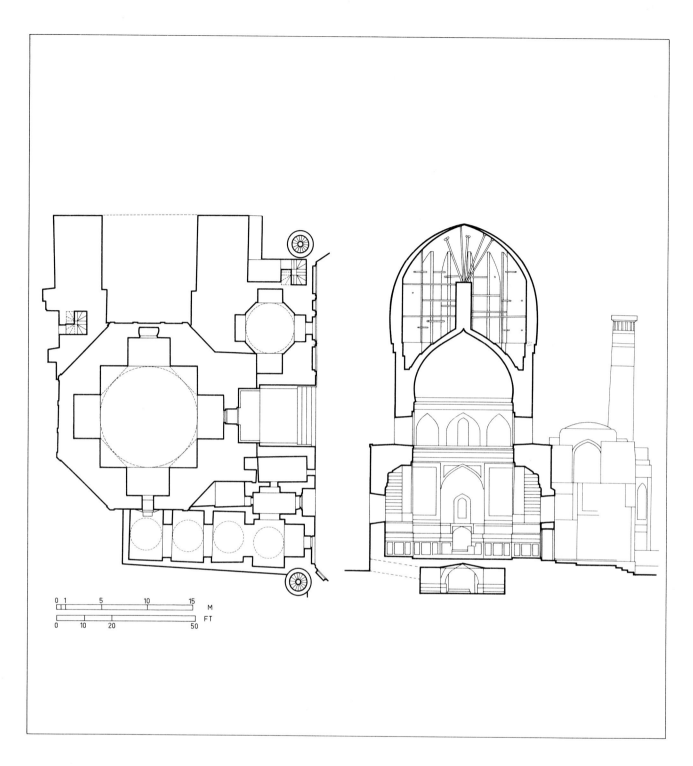

					M
0 1	5	10		15	FT
0	10	20		50	

Mausolée de Gur-é Mir, à Samarcande (U.R.S.S.), tombeau de Tamerlan (Timur Lenk), édifié vers 1405. Plan et coupe longitudinale 1:400. Monument funéraire de plan carré, avec crypte et coupole à double coque. Le dôme extérieur, en bulbe outrepassé, est maintenu par des étançons de bois. Un espace très important et aveugle subsiste entre les deux coupoles. Le haut tambour est percé de quatre baies.

Samarkand (UdSSR), Gur-i-Mir-Mausoleum, Grab Tamerlans, um 1405. Der Innenraum ist quadratisch, von einer zweischaligen Kuppel überwölbt; die Anlage hat eine Krypta. Zwischen der zwiebelförmigen äußeren, mit hölzernen Rippen konstruierten Kuppel und der inneren, kielbogenförmig geschwungenen liegt ein beachtlicher ungenutzter Raum. Der hohe Tambour hat vier Fenster. Grundriß und Längsschnitt 1:400.

Gur-e Amir mausoleum, Samarkand (USSR), tomb of Tamerlane (Timur Lenk), built 1405. Plan and longitudinal section 1:400. Square in plan, the tomb has a crypt and a double-shelled dome. The outer shell with its bulb-shaped section is supported by timber props. Between it and the inner dome is a very large blind space. The tall drum is pierced by four windows.

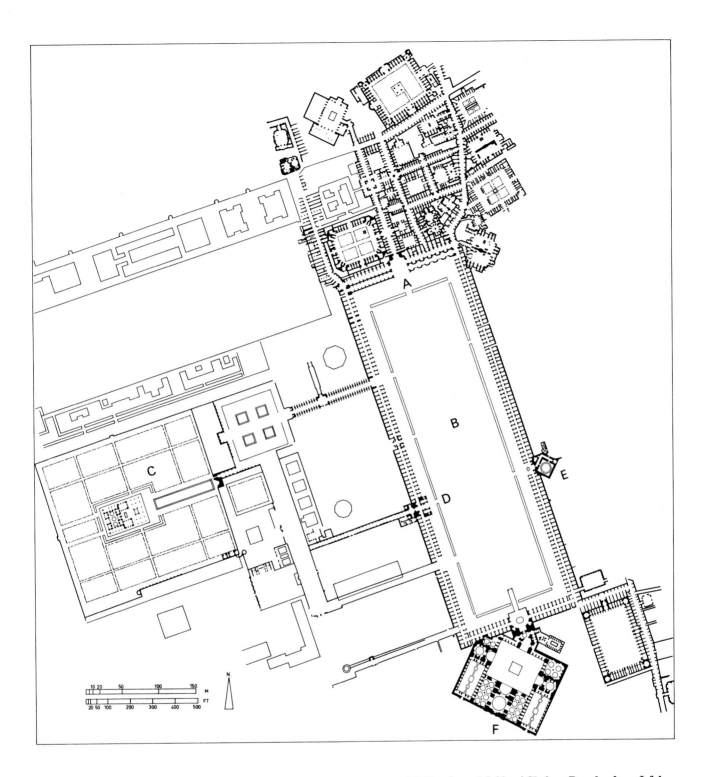

Place Royale ou Meidan-é Shah, à Ispahan (Iran), créée par Shah Abbas-le-Grand de 1597 à 1611. Plan d'ensemble 1:5000. A) Porte du Grand Bazar ou Khaisariyé, B) Meidan-é Shah, mesurant 500 × 150 m et bordé de boutiques, C) Palais aux Quarante Colonnes ou Tchéhel Sotoun, D) Palais d'Ali Kapou, E) Mosquée de Sheikh Lotfallah, F) Grande Mosquée du Shah.

Isfahan (Iran), Königsplatz (Maidan-i-Schah), 1597–1611 von Schah Abbas dem Großen angelegt. Grundriß 1:5000: A) Torbau des Großen Basars (Khaisariye), B) Maidan-i-Schah, 500 × 150 m, von Läden gesäumt, C) Thronhalle der vierzig Säulen (Tschihil Sutun), D) Ali-Kapu-Palast, E) Lutfullah-Moschee, F) Große kaiserliche Moschee.

Maidan-i Shah or Royal palace, Isfahan (Iran), built 1597–1611 by Shah Abbas the Great. Overall plan 1:5000. A) gate of the Qaysariyeh or Great Bazaar, B) Maidan-i Shah, measuring 500 m. by 150 m. and edged with booths, C) Chehel Sotun or Palace of the 40 Columns, D) Ali Qapu palace, E) Sheikh Lutfullah mosque, F) Great mosque of the Shah.

357

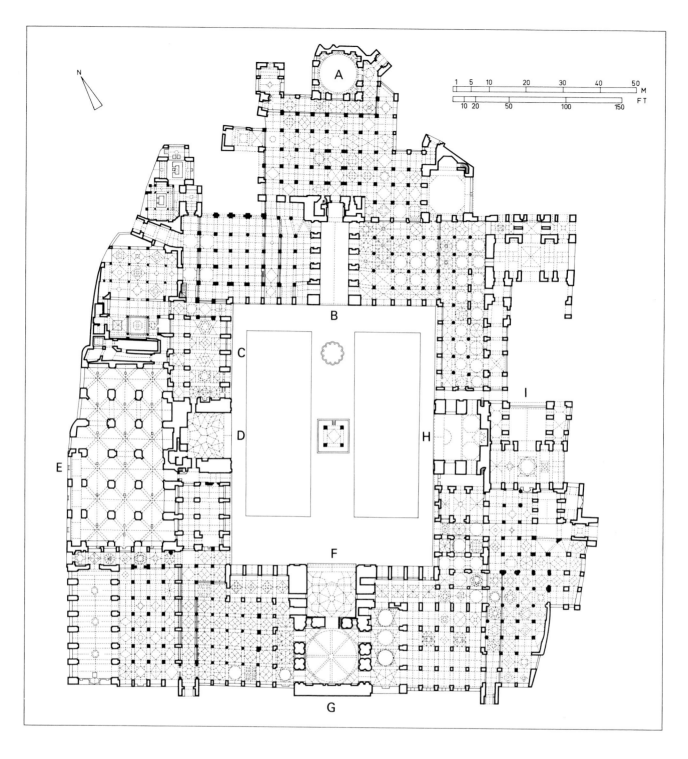

Mosquée du Vendredi, à Ispahan (Iran), dont la construction se poursuit de 1073 à 1800 environ. Plan 1:1000. A) Salle à coupole nord, datant de 1088, B) Iwân nord, après 1121, C) Salle du mihrab d'Uldjaïtu, vers 1315, D) Iwân ouest, du XIIᵉ s., E) Salle d'Hiver, de 1447, F) Iwân sud, du XIIᵉ s., G) Salle à coupole de Nizam al-Mulk de 1073, H) Iwân oriental, I) Madrasa édifiée en 1366.

Isfahan (Iran), Freitagsmoschee, 1073 bis um 1800. Grundriß 1:1000: A) nördlicher Kuppelsaal (1088), B) nördlicher Iwan (nach 1121), C) Saal des Mihrab des Sultans Uldschaitu (um 1315), D) westlicher Iwan (12.Jh.), E) Wintersaal (1447), F) südlicher Iwan (12.Jh.), G) Kuppelsaal des Sultans Nizam al-Mulk (1073), H) östlicher Iwan, I) Medrese (1366).

Friday mosque, Isfahan (Iran), begun 1073 and completed around 1800. Plan 1:1000. A) north domed hall (1088), B) north iwan (after 1121), C) hall of the mihrab of Uljaitu (c.1315), D) west iwan (twelfth century), E) Winter hall (1447), F) south iwan (twelfth century), G) domed hall of Nizam al-Mulk (1073), H) east iwan, I) madrasah or Koran school (1366).

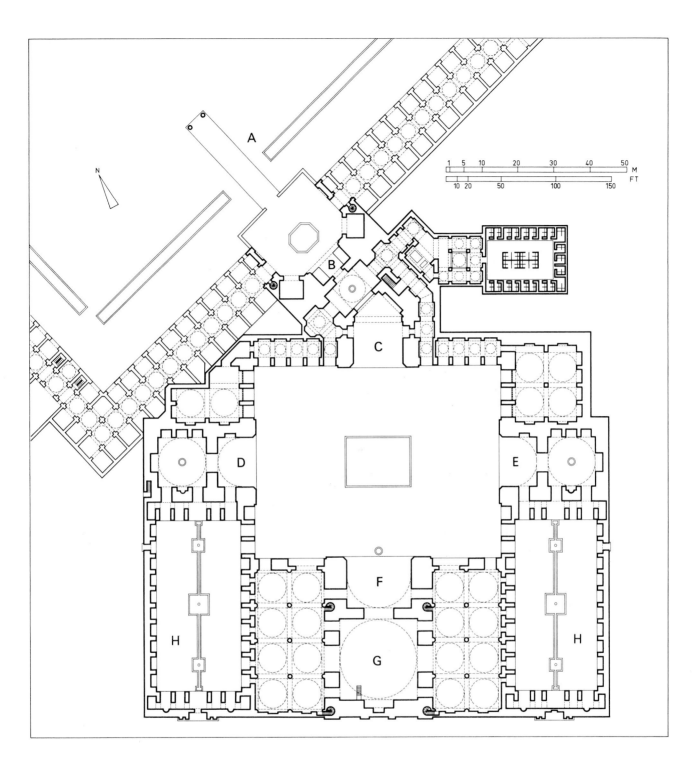

Grande Mosquée du Shah, à Ispahan (Iran), construite par Shah Abbas-le-Grand de 1612 à 1630. Plan 1:1000. Pour les besoins de l'orientation rituelle du mihrab, la mosquée forme un angle de 45° avec le Meidan-é Shah (A) sur lequel donne le portail d'entrée (B). C) Iwân nord, D) Iwân ouest, E) Iwân est, F) Iwân principal, G) Sanctuaire à coupole, H) Madrasas latérales.

Isfahan (Iran), Große kaiserliche Moschee, 1612–1630 von Schah Abbas dem Großen erbaut. Die Achsabweichung um 45° zum Königsplatz ist durch die Qibla bedingt. Grundriß 1:1000: A) Königsportal, B) Eingangsportal, C) nördlicher Iwan, D) westlicher Iwan, E) östlicher Iwan, F) Hauptiwan, G) Kuppelsaal, H) flankierende Medresen.

Great mosque of the Shah, Isfahan (Iran), built 1612–30 by Shah Abbas the Great. Plan 1:1000. Because of the necessity for the *mihrab* to point east the mosque forms an angle of 45° with the Maidan-i Shah (A), on to which the entrance portal (B) gives. C) north iwan, D) west iwan, E) east iwan, F) main iwan, G) domed sanctuary, H) lateral madrasahs.

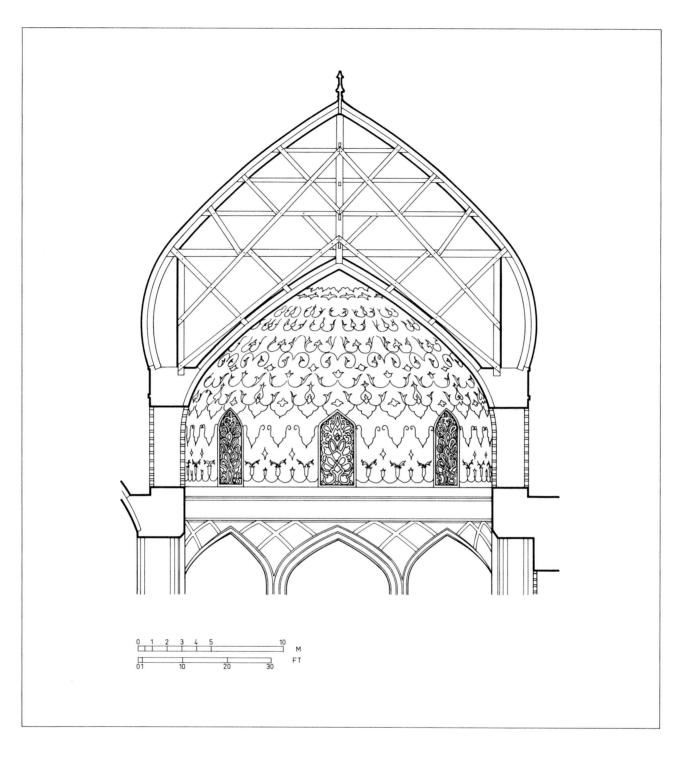

| 0 | 1 | 2 | 3 | 4 | 5 | | 10 | M |

| 01 | | 10 | | 20 | | 30 | FT |

Mosquée du Shah, à Ispahan (Iran). Coupe de la grande coupole montrant le système de construction à double coque 1:250. La coque interne, qui couvre la salle de prière, est séparée par une dizaine de mètres de la coupole outrepassée en bulbe qui forme le dôme externe. Ce dernier est maintenu par un jeu d'étançons de bois dans l'espace aveugle. Construction en brique revêtue de faïence.

Isfahan, Große kaiserliche Moschee. Zwischen der den Betsaal überwölbenden inneren Kuppelschale und der zwiebelförmigen, von hölzernen Rippen getragenen Außenkuppel liegt ein Abstand von etwa 10 m. Der Ziegelbau ist mit Fayencen verkleidet. Schnitt durch die zweischalige Hauptkuppel mit Darstellung des Konstruktionssystems 1:250.

Great mosque of the Shah. Section of the great dome showing the double-shelled construction 1:250. The inner shell covering the prayer-hall is separated from the bulbous outer dome by some ten metres. The outer shell is supported by a system of wooden props inside the blind space. Built of brick, the dome is faced with ceramic tiles.

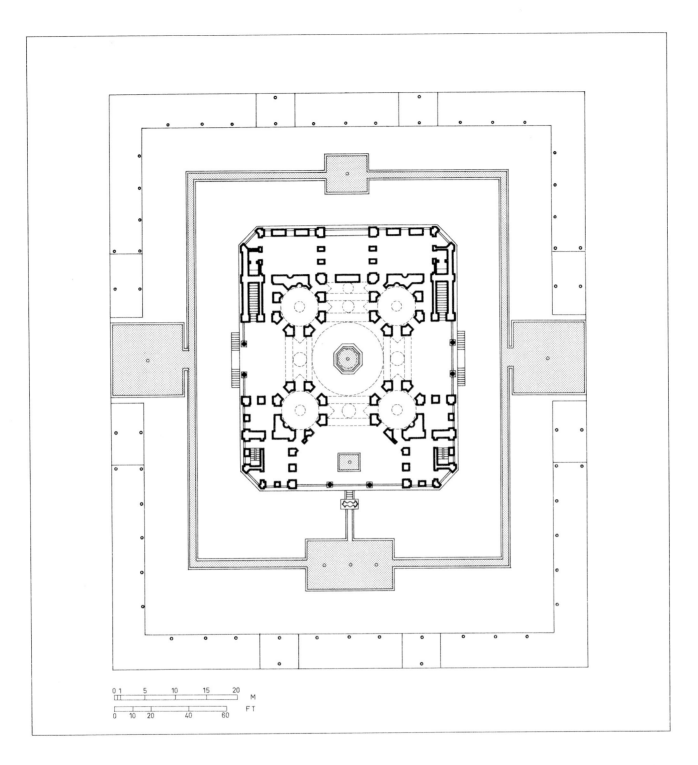

| 0 1 | 5 | 10 | 15 | 20 | M |
| 0 | 10 | 20 | 40 | 60 | F T |

Pavillon de Hecht Behecht (Les Huit Paradis), à Ispahan (Iran), édifié vers 1670. Plan 1:600. Edifice léger, sis au milieu d'un parc et formé de quatre iwâns entourant une pièce ouverte ou jaillit une fontaine. A l'étage, les appartements d'agrément. Tout un système hydraulique alimente les bassins entourant le pavillon.

Isfahan (Iran), Pavillon Hescht Behischt (Acht Paradiese), um 1670. Der inmitten eines Parks gelegene, luftige Bau besteht aus vier Iwanen um einen offenen Raum mit Springbrunnen; im Obergeschoß Räume für die Gartenfeste. Ein kunstvolles Wasserversorgungssystem speist die Bassins rund um den Pavillon. Grundriß 1:600.

Pavilion of Hecht Behecht (The Eight Paradises), Isfahan (Iran), built c. 1670. Plan 1:600. Situated in the middle of a park, this airy building consists of four *iwans* surrounding an open room in which a fountain gushes. The upper storey contains the pleasure apartments. The pools around the pavilion are fed by a special hydraulic system.

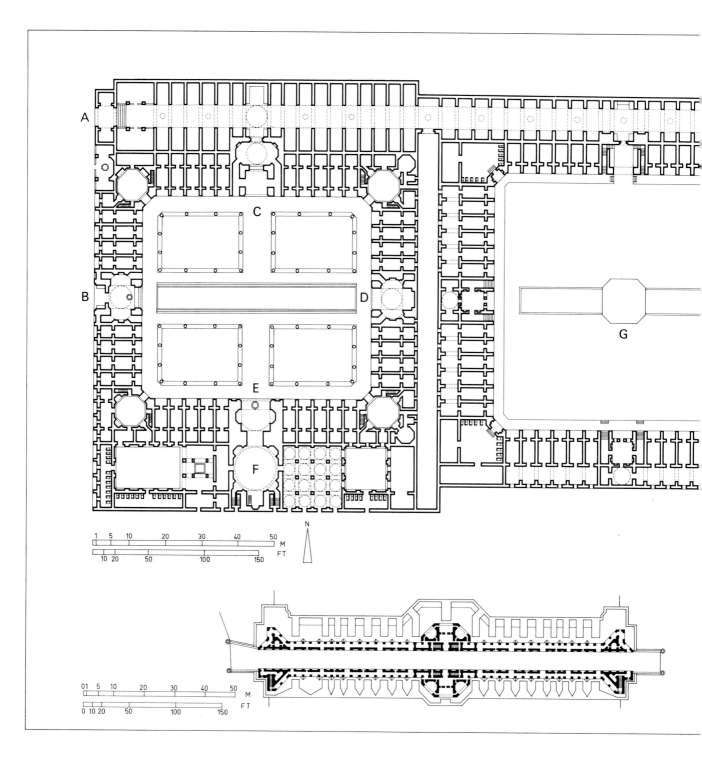

Madrasa de Shah Sultan Husain, ou de la Mère du Shah, à Ispahan (Iran), édifiée de 1706 à 1714. Plan 1:1000. A) Entrée du Bazar, B) Entrée de la Madrasa sur le Tchahar Bagh, C) Iwân nord, communiquant avec le Bazar, D) Iwân est, E) Iwân sud conduisant à la salle de prière, F) Sanctuaire de la mosquée, G) Grand Caravansérail, H) Cour des écuries. A droite: coupe du vestibule d'entrée: 1:150.

Oben: **Isfahan (Iran), Medrese des Schahs Sultan Husein oder der Schah-Mutter,** 1706–1714. Grundriß 1:1000: A) Eingang zum Basar, B) Eingang zur Medrese über den Tschahar Bagh, C) nördlicher Iwan mit Verbindung zum Basar, D) östlicher Iwan, E) südlicher Iwan, Zugang zum Betsaal, F) Sanktuarium der Moschee, G) Große Karawanserei, H) Hof mit Stallungen; Nebenseite: Schnitt durch die Eingangshalle 1:150.

Madrasah of Shah Sultan Husain or of the Shah's Mother, Isfahan (Iran), built 1706–14. Plan 1:1000. A) bazaar entrance, B) entrance to the madrasah on the Chahar Bagh, C) north iwan, communicating with the bazaar, D) east iwan, E) south iwan, leading into the prayer-hall, F) sanctuary of the mosque, G) Great caravanserai, H) stable yard. Right, section of the entrance vestibule 1:150.

362

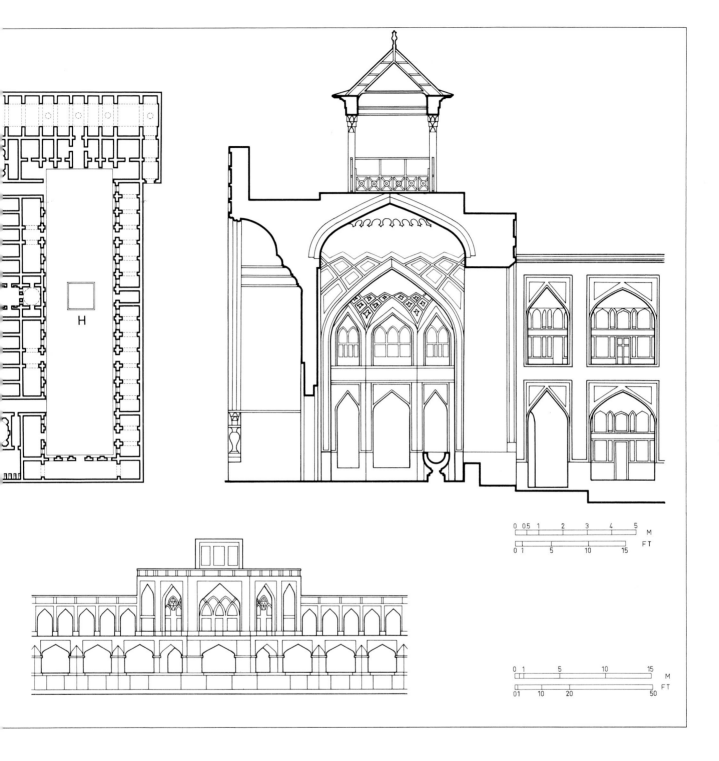

En bas: **Pont-barrage de Khadjou, sur le Zayandeh Roud, à Ispahan** (Iran), construit par Shah Abbas II vers 1650. Plan avec coupe du niveau supérieur 1:1200. A droite, élévation de la partie centrale du pont de Khadjou 1:400. Cette réalisation comporte des vannes pour contrôler le débit de la rivière et irriguer la ville.

Unten: **Isfahan, Brücke Pul-i-Khwaju über den Zayandeh Rud,** um 1650. Von Schah Abbas II. als Stauwehr zur Kontrolle der Wasserführung und zur Wasserversorgung der Stadt angelegt. Aufriß des Mittelteils der Khwaju-Brücke 1:400; Nebenseite: Grundriß des unteren und des oberen Geschosses 1:1200.

Below, **Khaju bridge on the Zayandeh Rud, Isfahan** (Iran), built c.1650 by Shah Abbas II. Plan with section of the upper level 1:1200. Right, elevation of the central part 1:400. The bridge includes sluice gates to control the flow of the river and irrigate the city.

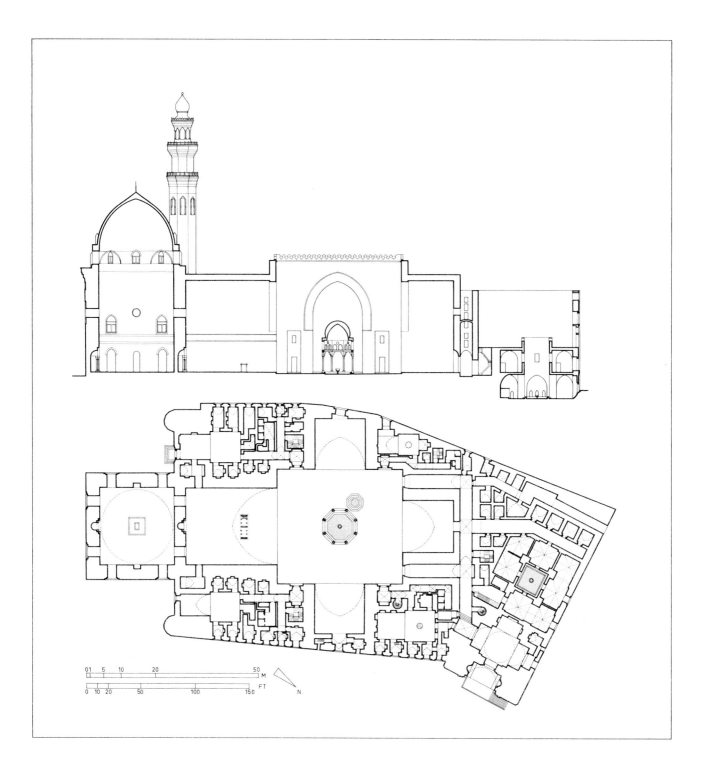

**Mosquée-madrasa de Sultan Hassan, Le
Caire** (Egypte), édifiée de 1356 à 1361
par les Mamelouks turcomans. Coupe
longitudinale et plan 1:1000. Par le recours aux quatre iwâns, cet édifice
s'inspire directement de l'architecture
persane. Mais l'usage de la pierre de
taille, en lieu et place de la brique, lui
confère son caractère propre. Les iwâns
sont voûtés en carènes.

Kairo, Grabmedrese des Sultans Hasan,
1356–1361 von turkmenischen Mame-
luken erbaut. Mit seinen vier Iwanen
folgt der Bau dem persischen Medresen-
schema, ist jedoch nicht aus Ziegeln,
sondern aus Steinquadern erbaut. Die
Iwane tragen Kielbogengewölbe. Längsschnitt und Grundriß 1:1000.

**Madrasah mosque of Sultan Hassan,
Cairo** (Egypt), built 1356–61 by the
Turcoman Mamelukes. Longitudinal
section and plan 1:1000. In using four
iwans this building draws directly on
Persian architecture. It is distinctive,
however, in using freestone instead of
brick. The *iwans* are keel-vaulted.

Turquie seldjoukide et ottomane

Türkei

Seljuk and Ottoman Turkey

Lorsque les Turcs islamisés – peuple des steppes de l'Asie centrale – battent les Byzantins à la bataille de Mantzikert (1071), l'Anatolie s'ouvre à eux. Ils créent le sultanat de Roum (Roumi = Romains), établissent leur capitale d'abord à Nicée, puis à Konya (1134). De leurs origines nomades, ils n'ont guère de tradition architecturale, si ce n'est les influences subies lors de leur passage en Perse. D'emblée ils adoptent les techniques et les formes propres à leurs prédécesseurs tant Arméniens que Syriens du Nord. Le matériau est la pierre de taille traitée selon une rigoureuse stéréotomie; le langage est d'arcs en tiers-point et de voûtes en carènes.

Les mosquées et madrasas (collèges coraniques), les turbés (tombeaux) et surtout les grands caravansérails qu'ils érigent sur les routes du pays – avec leurs voûtes en berceau brisé, contrebutées par des bas-côtés perpendiculaires, témoignent d'une grande qualité plastique que rehausse un original décor géométrique.

Lorsque Osman fonde la dynastie des Ottomans, qui prennent tout d'abord Brousse pour capitale (1326) avant de s'emparer de Constantinople (1453), l'influence architecturale des Byzantins, de leurs espaces centrés et de leurs coupoles à pendentifs, s'accentue. La vénérable église de Sainte-Sophie va exercer une véritable fascination, surtout sur le génial architecte Sinan. Avec la Suleymaniyé édifiée pour Soliman le Magnifique (1550), il relève le défi: sur le même plan, il donne son interprétation, toute de clarté et de stricte délimitation des formes, par opposition aux espaces qui glissent les uns dans les autres dans son modèle byzantin. Il en résulte une œuvre d'un esprit totalement différent.

Nachdem die islamisierten Türken, ein zentralasiatisches Steppenvolk, in der Schlacht von Mantzikert (1071) die Byzantiner besiegt hatten, stand ihnen Anatolien offen. Sie errichteten das Rum-Sultanat, zunächst mit der Hauptstadt Nicäa, dann – ab 1134 – Konya. Als Nomaden besaßen sie kaum architektonische Tradition, abgesehen von einigen Einflüssen, die sie auf ihrem Weg durch Persien aufgenommen hatten. Sie verwendeten darum Techniken und Formen ihrer Vorgänger, der Armenier und Nordsyrer. Als Material dienten exakt zugehauene Steinquadern; Spitzbogen und Kielbogengewölbe sind die beherrschenden Formen.

Die Moscheen und Medresen, die Türben (Grabbauten) und vor allem die großen Karawansereien an den Straßen, deren Kielbogengewölben rechtwinklige Seitenräume als Widerlager dienen, sind von großer plastischer Kraft, die durch den ihnen eigentümlichen geometrischen Dekor noch gesteigert wird.

Nach der Gründung des Osmanischen Reiches mit der Hauptstadt Bursa (1326) durch Osman, besonders aber nach der Eroberung Konstantinopels (1453) nahm der Einfluß der byzantinischen Architektur mit ihren Zentralbauten und Pendentifkuppeln zu. Von der Hagia Sophia ging eine besondere Wirkung aus, vor allem auf Sinan, den genialen Baumeister, der 1550 bei der für Suleyman den Prächtigen erbauten Suleymaniye wohl denselben Grundriß benutzte, doch seine eigene Interpretation gab: An die Stelle der verschliffenen Räume des byzantinischen Vorbildes setzte er klare, streng begrenzte Formen. So entstand ein Bau von völlig anderem Geist.

Über der bedeutenden Rolle der

When the Moslemised Turks—a people from the steppes of Central Asia—defeated the Byzantines at the battle of Manzikert (1071), Anatolia lay open to them. They created the Sultanate of Rum and set up their capital first at Nicaea and then at Konya (1134). Being of nomad origin, they brought very little architectural tradition with them, with the possible exception of what they had absorbed on their way through Persia. They immediately adopted the techniques and forms of their Armenian and north Syrian predecessors. Their material was freestone used with strict precision, their language one of pointed equilateral arches and keel vaults.

Their mosques and madrasahs, their *türbes* or tomb-towers, and above all the great caravanserais that they built along the country's main roads—with their broken barrel vaults buttressed with aisles at right angles—possess excellent plastic qualities set off by original geometrical decoration.

When Osman I founded the Ottoman dynasty, which took Bursa as its capital (1326) before seizing Constantinople in 1453, the architectural influence of the Byzantines (centralised spaces and domes on pendentives) became more marked. The venerable church of Hagia Sophia exercised what amounted to a fascination, particularly over the brilliant architect Sinan. The great mosque he built for Suleiman the Magnificent in 1550 took up the challenge: using the same plan, he produced a version that was all clarity and strict delineation of form, as opposed to the interflowing spaces of his Byzantine model. The result is a work with a totally different feel to it.

Si l'importance de la mosquée est considérable dans ces réalisations, on se gardera d'omettre toute la kulillié qui l'entoure: hôpital, asile psychiatrique, école coranique, bibliothèque, bains, cuisines, etc.

La recherche de Sinan va culminer dans la Sélimiyé d'Edirné (1569), où il réalise un espace octogonal, centré, quasiment sans contre-butement, que domine une coupole de plus de 40 m de diamètre. Mais sur cette époque s'exerce aussi le rayonnement de la Renaissance italienne: tant la modénature et le décor que les solutions technologiques en porteront témoignage; ce courant ira s'accentuant jusqu'à l'éclosion, au XVIIIe siècle, d'un style baroque turc qui ne manque ni de charme ni de grandeur.

Moschee in der islamischen Architektur dürfen die umgebenden, zur Külliye gehörenden Bauten nicht vergessen werden: Krankenhaus, Irrenhaus, Koranschule, Bibliothek, Bäder, Küchen usw.

Sinans Meisterwerk ist die Selimiye in Edirne (1569), ein oktogonaler Bau, von einer mehr als 40 m überspannenden Kuppel überragt und mit kaum sichtbaren Widerlagern. In dieser Zeit sind in der Formensprache, dem Bauschmuck und den technischen Lösungen Einflüsse der italienischen Renaissance festzustellen; diese Strömung erreicht im 18. Jahrhundert mit einem türkischen Barock voller Anmut und Größe ihren Höhepunkt.

Although the mosque had an important place in all this architectural activity, we must not forget all the buildings that surrounded it: hospital, mental hospital, Koran school, library, baths, kitchens, and so on.

Sinan's masterpiece was the Selimiye Mosque at Edirne (1569), an octagonal, centralised structure virtually without buttressing and crowned by a dome more than 40 m. in diameter. But this period was also subject to Italian Renaissance influence, as can be seen both in outlines and decoration, and in terms of technological achievements. This influence continued to grow until in the eighteenth century there blossomed a kind of Turkish Baroque that combines charm with grandeur.

1 Détail du décor ornant le portail d'entrée du caravansérail de Sultan Han près de Kayseri (Anatolie), datant de 1250 env.
2 La salle d'hiver et son système de voûtement au caravansérail de Sultan Han, près de Kayseri.
3 La coupole de la mosquée de Sokoullou-Mehmet Pacha, à Istanbul, édifiée par Sinan en 1571, sur un tracé hexagonal.

1 Sultanhani bei Kayseri, Detail des Dekors am Haupteingang der Karawanserei (um 1250)
2 Sultanhani bei Kayseri, das Gewölbesystem des Wintersaals
3 Istanbul, Sokullu-Moschee, die Kuppel des von Sinan auf sechsseitigem Grundriß errichteten Baus (1571)

1 Detail of the decoration on the gateway of the Caravanserai of Sultan Han, near Kayseri (Anatolia), built c. 1250.
2 The Winter Hall of the Caravanserai of Sultan Han, showing the vaulting system.
3 The dome of Sokullu Mehmed Pasha mosque, Istanbul, built by Sinan on a hexagonal plan in 1571.

1

2

3

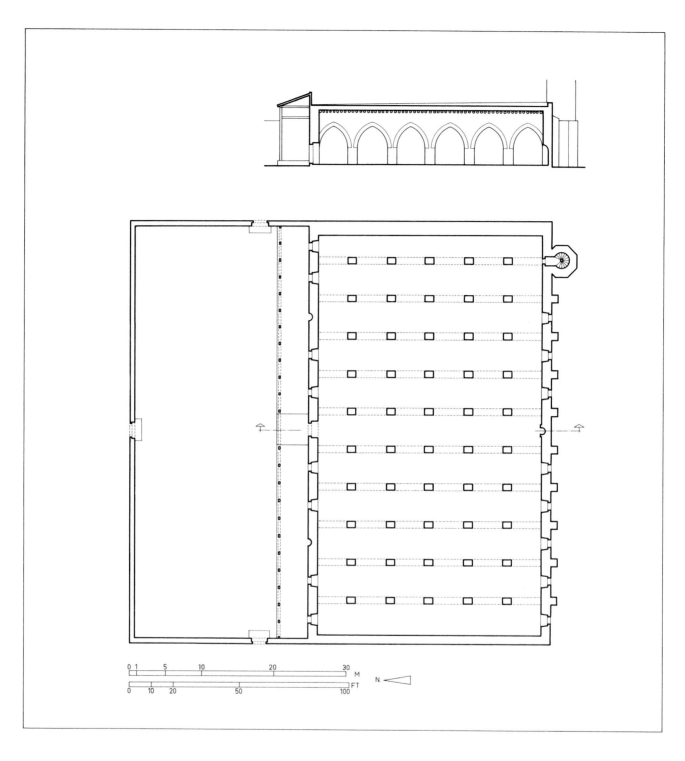

Grande Mosquée, ou Ulu Djami, à Sivas (Anatolie), datant du XIᵉ s. Coupe longitudinale et plan 1:500. Salle hypostyle seldjoukide à couverture en solivage supportée par des travées d'arcades en tiers-point. Au sud-est, un minaret à base octogonale. C'est l'une des premières mosquées turques d'Anatolie.

Sivas (Anatolien), Große Moschee (Ulu Cami), 11.Jh. Seldschukische Säulenhalle mit Balkendecke über Spitzbogenjochen; im Südosten ein oktogonales Minarett. Eine der ältesten türkischen Moscheen in Anatolien. Längsschnitt und Grundriß 1:500.

Ulu Cami, or Great mosque, Sivas (Anatolia), eleventh century. Longitudinal section and plan 1:500. A Seljuk hypostyle hall with a beam roof supported by rows of pointed arches. To the south-east a minaret rises on an octagonal base. This is one of the earliest Turkish mosques in Anatolia.

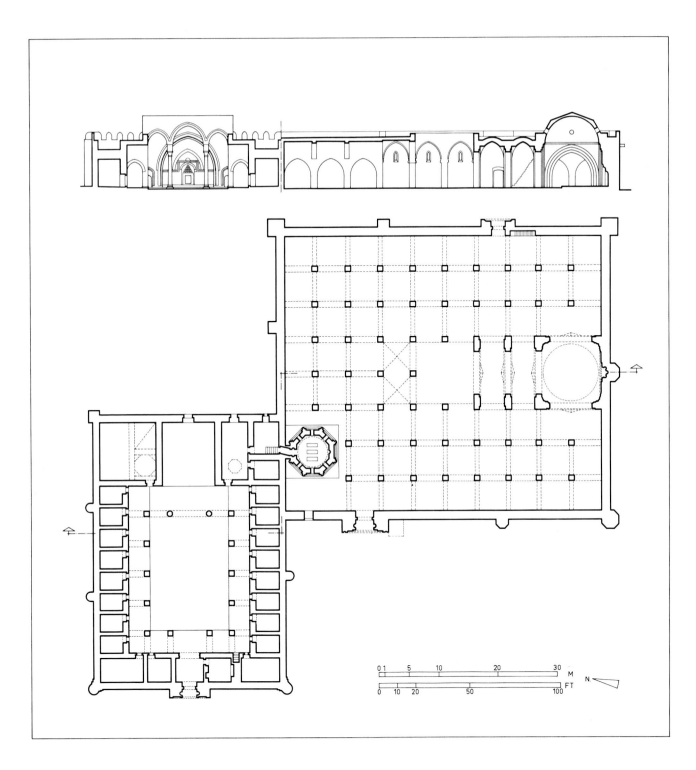

Complexe de Huand Hatun, à Kayseri (Anatolie), la mosquée (à droite) a été édifiée en 1237, la madrasa (à gauche) est postérieure et le tombeau ou turbé, à l'articulation, a été construit en dernier, vers le milieu du XIVᵉ s. Coupe longitudinale et plan 1:600. Mosquée à hypostyle voûtée en berceaux. Madrasa à cour entourée d'arcades.

Kayseri (Anatolien), Huand Hatun, die Moschee (rechts) wurde 1237 erbaut, die Medrese (links) später, zuletzt das Grabmal (Türbe) um Mitte des 14. Jh. Der Säulensaal der Moschee ist tonnengewölbt; Arkaden säumen den Hof der Medrese. Längsschnitt und Grundriß 1:600.

Huand Hatun complex, Kayseri (Anatolia); the mosque (right) was built in 1237, the *madrasah* (left) is later, and the articulated türbe or tomb was the last built, around the mid-fourteenth century. Longitudinal section and plan 1:600. The mosque is a hypostyle with tunnel vaults: the *madrasah* has a courtyard surrounded with arcades.

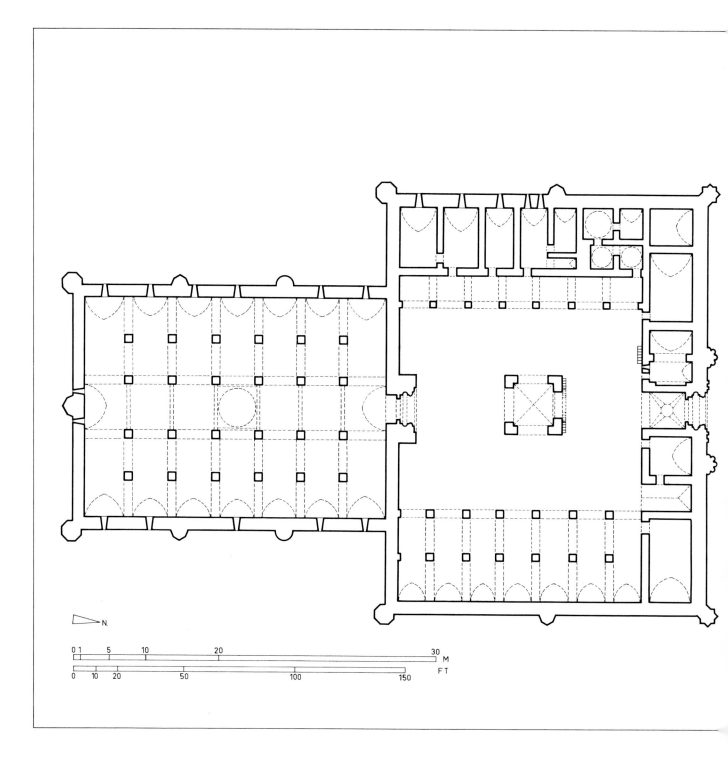

N.

0 1   5   10   20   30
                                                       M
                                                       F T
0 10 20   50   100   150

Caravansérail Sultan Han, près de Kayseri (Anatolie), construit vers 1250.
Plan 1:500. La période seldjoukide est
marquée par l'édification, tous les 30 à
40 km, sur les routes anatoliennes, de
ces relais fortifiés. On distingue, à
gauche, la salle d'hiver à cinq nefs et, à
droite, la cour bordée d'arcades, avec
en son centre, un petit oratoire surélevé
sur quatre arcs.

Karawanserei Sultanhani bei Kayseri,
um 1250. Zur Zeit der Seldschuken
wurden an den anatolischen Straßen
solche befestigten Stützpunkte in 30 bis
40 km Abstand angelegt. Links der
fünfschiffige Wintersaal, rechts der
Arkadenhof, in dessen Zentrum, über
vier Bögen, ein kleines Oratorium.
Grundriß 1:500.

Caravanserai of Sultan Han, near Kayseri (Anatolia), built c.1250. Plan 1:500.
The erection of these fortified stages at
intervals of 30 or 40 km. along the roads
of Anatolia was a feature of the Seljuk
period. Note on the left the five-aisled
Winter hall and, on the right, the arcaded courtyard, in the middle of which
is a small oratory resting on four arches.

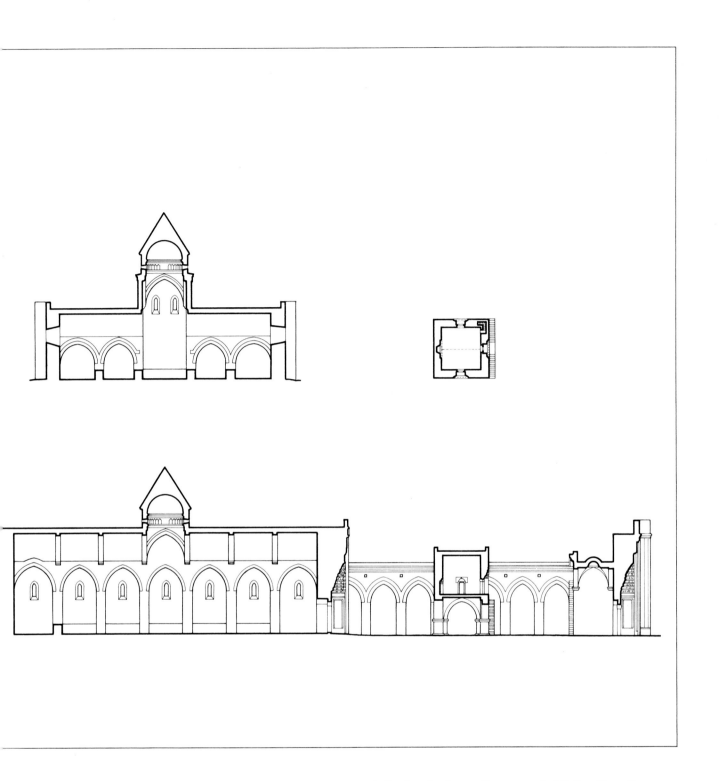

Sultan Han, près de Kayseri. Coupe transversale de la salle d'hiver, plan de l'étage de l'oratoire, et coupe longitudinale 1:500. Par son recours généralisé à l'arc en tiers-point, sa haute nef flanquée d'un double bas-côté de part et d'autre, cette architecture s'apparente à certaines églises arméniennes. L'ornementation très riche du portail et de la salle d'hiver use des stalactites.

Sultanhani bei Kayseri. In der durchgehenden Verwendung des Spitzbogens wie auch in der fünfschiffigen Anlage mit hohem Mittelschiff und beidseits zwei niederen Seitenschiffen ähnelt dieser Bautyp manchen armenischen Kirchen. Das Portal und die Winterhalle sind reich mit Stalaktitendekor geschmückt. Querschnitt und Längsschnitt des Wintersaals, Grundriß vom Obergeschoß des Oratoriums 1:500.

Caravanserai of Sultan Han. Cross section of the Winter hall, plan of the upper storey of the oratory, and longitudinal section 1:500. With its general use of the pointed equilateral arch and its tall nave flanked by pairs of side aisles, this architecture is close to that of certain Armenian churches. The rich decoration of the portal and the Winter hall uses stalactite work.

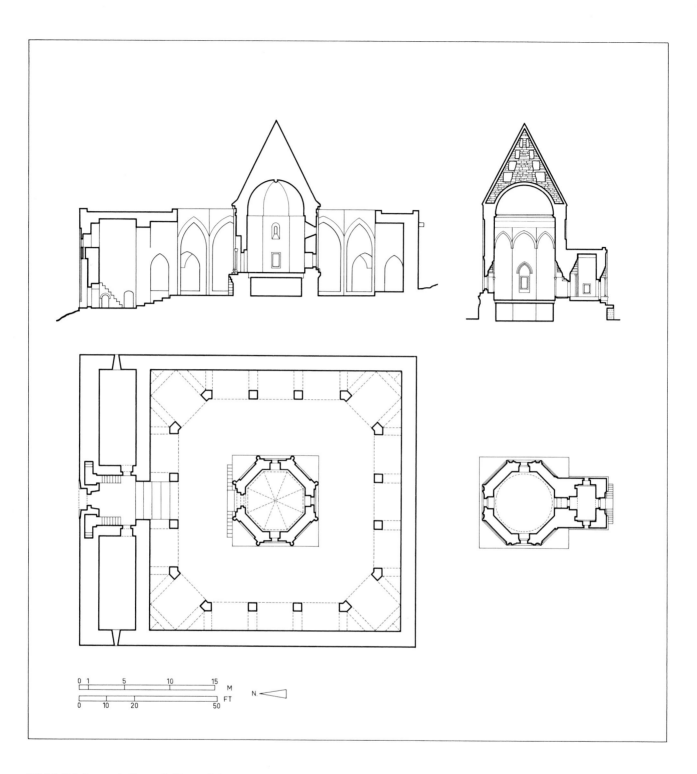

Köshk Madrasa, à Kayseri (Anatolie), construite en 1339. Coupe longitudinale et plan 1:400. Dans un tracé très austère et rigoureux, les arcades entourant une cour carrée présentent aux angles une élégante solution formant un octogone autour du tombeau ou turbé, lui-même octogonal, à chambre voûtée. A droite, **Turbé d'Ali Djafer, à Kayseri,** datant du milieu du XIVe s., et doté d'un vestibule. Coupe longitudinale et plan 1:400.

Links: **Kayseri, Köschk-Medrese, 1339.** Die strengen schmucklosen Arkaden des quadratischen Hofes sind in den Ecken schräg geführt, so daß sie die oktogonale Türbe in Form eines Achtecks umschließen. Der Innenraum der Türbe ist gewölbt. Längsschnitt und Grundriß 1:400. Rechts: **Kayseri, Ali-Djafar-Türbe,** Mitte 14.Jh. Mit Vorraum. Längsschnitt und Grundriß 1:400.

Köshk madrasah, Kayseri (Anatolia), built 1339. Longitudinal section and plan 1:400. In a strict and highly austere design, arcades surround a square courtyard, the corners of which are elegantly modified to form an octagon framing the octagonal vaulted *türbe* or tomb. Right, **Türbe of Ali Jafer, Kayseri,** a tomb with vestibule dating from the mid-fourteenth century. Longitudinal section and plan 1:400.

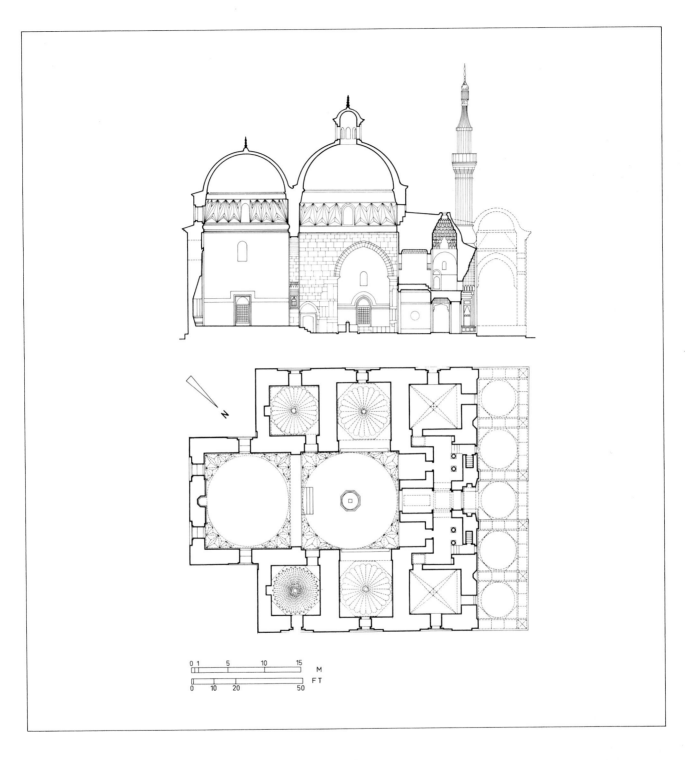

Yéchil-Cami, ou Mosquée Verte de Brousse (Turquie), construite pour Mehmet Ier entre 1413 et 1421. Coupe longitudinale et plan 1:500. Œuvre du gouverneur de Brousse Hadchi-Ivaz Pacha, cette mosquée ottomane présente à l'étage une loge pour le sultan. Grande variété de coupoles, dont la principale est surmontée d'une lanterne. L'intérieur des tambours est décoré de motifs à plissés faisant la liaison avec la coupole.

Bursa, Yeschil-Cami (Grüne Moschee), 1413–1421 für Mehmet I. erbaut. Die Moschee wurde von dem Gouverneur von Bursa, Hadschi-Ivaz-Pascha, errichtet. Im Obergeschoß befindet sich eine Loge für den Sultan. Die Kuppeln sind verschieden ausgebildet, die Hauptkuppel mit Laterne. Der Übergang vom Quadrat zum Rund geschieht durch einen Faltentambour. Längsschnitt und Grundriß 1:500.

Yeshil Cami or Green mosque, Bursa (Turkey), built for Mehmet I between 1413 and 1421. Longitudinal section and plan 1:500. The work of the governor of Bursa, Hadshi-Ivaz Pasha, this Ottoman mosque has a box for the Sultan on the upper storey. It also has a great variety of domes, of which the main one is surmounted by a lantern. The drum interiors are decorated with pleated motifs linking them with their domes.

373

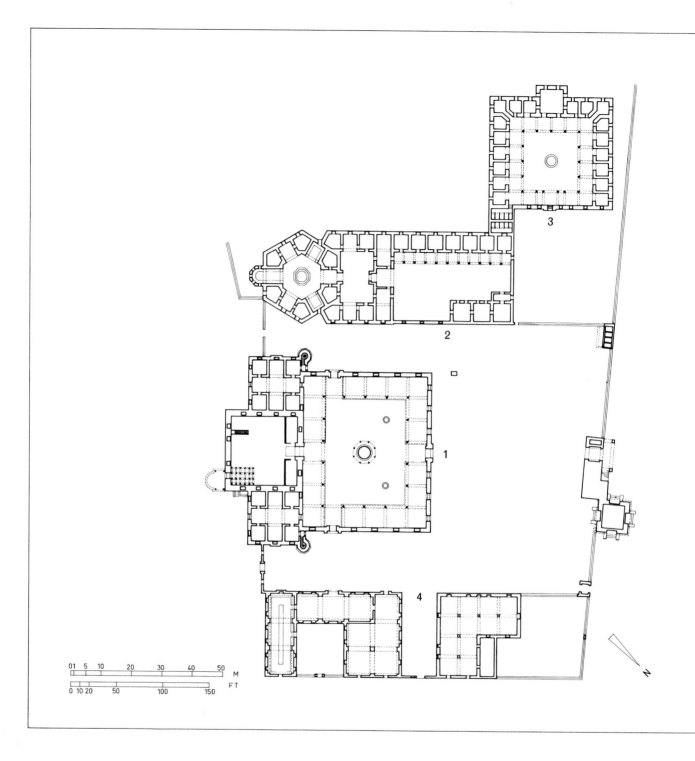

01 5 10   20   30   40   50   M

0 10 20   50   100   150   F T

Kulillié (ensemble comprenant la mosquée et des édifices d'utilité publique) **de Bayazid II à Edirné** (Turquie), construite par Bayazid II entre 1484 et 1488. Plan d'ensemble 1:1200. 1) Mosquée, 2) Hôpital et asile d'aliénés, 3) Ecole de médecine, 4) Cuisines, boulangerie et locaux d'exploitation. L'organisation d'un complexe ottoman relève d'un urbanisme à la fois libre et ordonné.

Edirne, Bayazit-Külliye, 1484–1488 von Bayazit II. angelegt. Der osmanische Städtebau zeichnet sich durch freie und doch geordnete Anlagen aus. Lageplan 1:1200: 1) Moschee, 2) Hospital und Irrenhaus, 3) Medizinschule, 4) Küchen, Bäckereien und Wirtschaftsräume.

Kulilliye of Bayezid II, Edirne (Turkey), a complex comprising a mosque and various public utility buildings, erected 1484–8 by Sultan Bayezid II. Overall plan 1:1200. 1) mosque, 2) hospital and lunatic asylum, 3) medical school, 4) kitchens, bakery, and farm buildings. The layout of an Ottoman complex combined freedom and discipline.

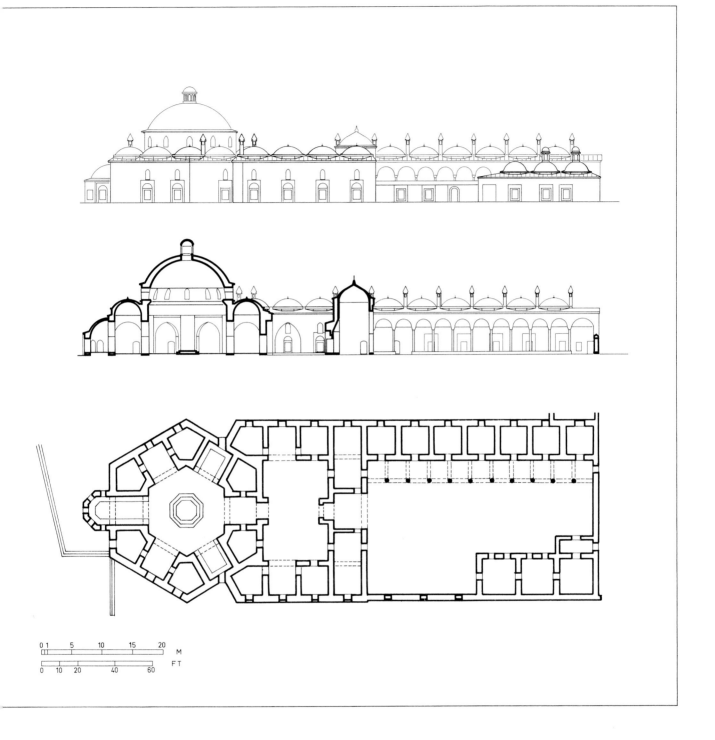

0 1   5   10   15   20   M
0 10 20   40   60 FT

Bâtiments du complexe médical appartenent à la **kulillié de Bayazid II, à Edirné.** Elévation latérale, coupe longitudinale et plan 1:600. On notera le système de couverture individuelle des chambres par des coupoles surbaissées et la solution hexagonale de la salle commune de l'infirmerie.

Edirne, Külliye Bayazits II., Medizinschule. Jeder Raum ist mit einer eigenen Flachkuppel überwölbt, der Gemeinschaftssaal des Krankenhauses ist sechseckig. Aufriß einer Seite, Längsschnitt und Grundriß 1:600.

Kulilliye of Bayezid II: buildings of the medical complex. Side elevation, longitudinal section, and plan 1:600. Note the system of roofing each room separately with a shallow dome and the hexagonal structure of the infirmary common room.

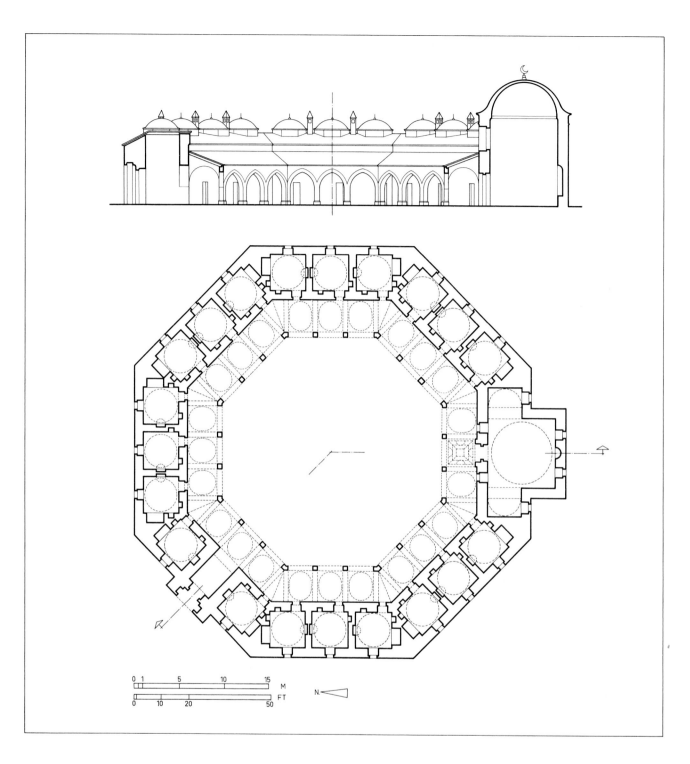

0 1   5   10   15   M
0   10   20   50   FT

N

Kapi Aghasi Madrasa, à Amasya (Anatolie), construite en 1488, sous le règne de Bayazid II. Coupe à travers l'entrée et le sanctuaire et plan 1:400. Cette madrasa, conçue sur un plan octogonal, constitue une originalité. Ce type de plan, originaire de Perse, était généralement appliqué à des caravansérails. On trouve les cellules des étudiants autour d'une cour à portiques.

Amasya (Anatolien), Kapi-Aghasi-Medrese, 1488 unter Bayazit II. erbaut. Die oktogonale Anlage der Medrese ist ungewöhnlich; die Grundrißform stammt aus Persien und wurde im allgemeinen für Karawansereien verwendet. Um den Säulenhof sind die Zellen der Schüler angeordnet. Schnitt durch Eingangs- und Haupthalle und Grundriß 1:400.

Kapi Aghasi madrasah, Amasya (Anatolia), built 1488 in the reign of Bayezid II. Cross section of the entrance and sanctuary, and plan 1:400. This *madrasah* is original in being designed on an octagonal plan, the idea of which came from Persia and was usually applied to caravanserais. The students' cells are arranged round a porticoed courtyard.

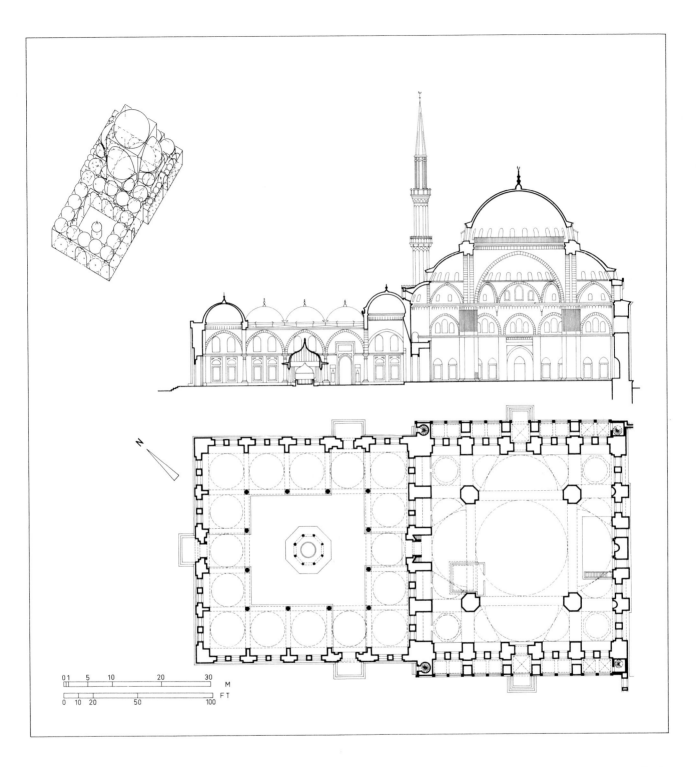

0 1 5 10   20   30   M

0 10 20   50   100   F T

Mosquée de Schézadé, ou Mosquée des Princes, à Istanbul (Turquie), construite par l'architecte Sinan entre 1544 et 1548 pour commémorer le décès prématuré des deux fils de Soliman Ier. Isométrie 1:3000, coupe longitudinale et plan 1:750. C'est le premier plan de mosquée qui s'inspire directement de Sainte-Sophie. Mais il recourt à quatre demi-coupoles contre-butant le dôme central, comme à Sultan Ahmet (1609).

Istanbul, Schehzade-Moschee, 1544 bis 1548 von dem Architekten Sinan zum Gedächtnis der beiden früh verstorbenen Söhne Suleymans I. erbaut. Die erste unmittelbar an der Hagia Sophia orientierte Moschee; hier dienen jedoch vier Halbkuppeln als Widerlager für die Mittelkuppel wie später bei der Sultan-Ahmet-Moschee (1609). Isometrie 1:3000; Längsschnitt und Grundriß 1:750.

Shezade mosque or Mosque of the Princes, Istanbul (Turkey), built 1544–8 by the architect Sinan to commemorate the premature death of the two sons of Suleiman I. Isometric projection 1:3000; longitudinal section and plan 1:750. This was the first mosque plan inspired directly by Hagia Sophia, except that it uses four half-domes to buttress the central dome (as at the mosque of Sultan Ahmed, 1609).

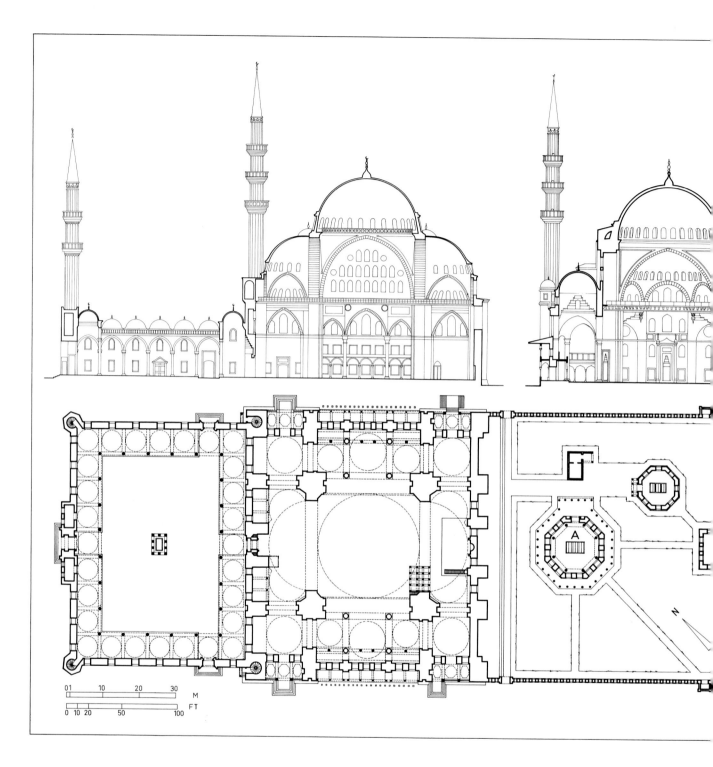

01   10   20   30
                      M
                     FT
0 10 20   50   100

Mosquée de Soliman, ou Suleymaniyé, à Istanbul, édifiée par l'architecte Sinan entre 1551 et 1557. Coupe longitudinale, coupe transversale et plan 1:1000. C'est là que Sinan donne la démonstration de la métamorphose qu'il fait subir au plan de Sainte-Sophie, dont il s'inspire: coupole contre-butée par deux demi-coupoles et deux murs-tympans. On trouve en A) le turbé ou tombeau de Soliman.

Istanbul, Suleymaniye-Moschee, 1551 bis 1557 von Sinan erbaut. Sinan ging hier zwar auch von der Hagia Sophia aus, wandelte das System jedoch ab. Der Hauptkuppel dienen zwei Halbkuppeln als Widerlager, an beiden Seiten befinden sich Schildmauern. Längsschnitt, Querschnitt und Grundriß 1:1000: A) Türbe Suleymans I.

Suleimaniye or Suleiman mosque, Istanbul, built 1551–7 by the architect Sinan. Longitudinal section, cross section, and plan 1:1000. Here Sinan demonstrated his transformation of the Hagia Sophia plan from which he had drawn his inspiration: his dome is buttressed by two half-domes and two tympanum walls. A) Suleiman's tomb.

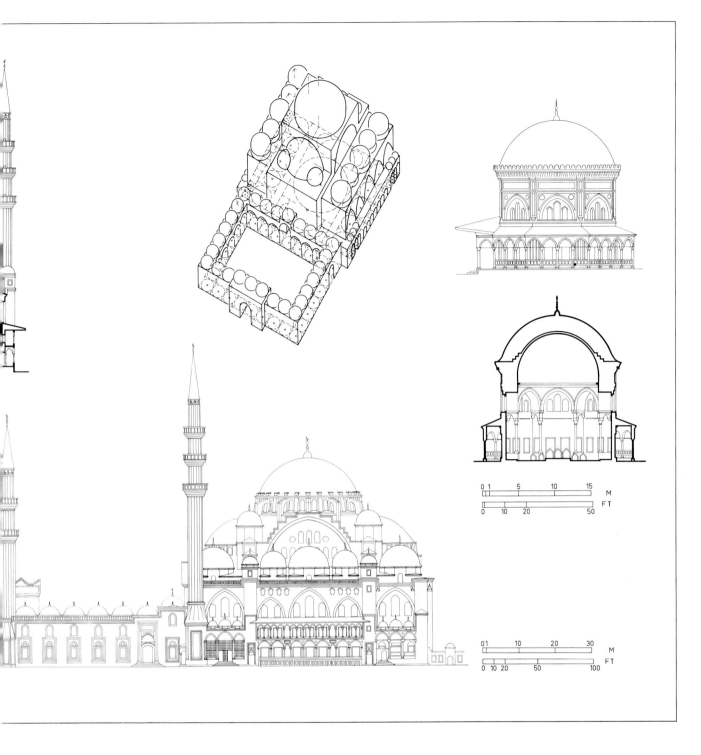

Mosquée de Soliman. Isométrie 1:2000, façade latérale 1:1000. A droite, détail du **Turbé de Soliman.** Elévation et coupe 1:500. La solution des quatre minarets disposés aux angles de la cour à arcades (inspirée de l'atrium) qu'imagine Sinan crée un contre-point entre un volume plein du côté de la mosquée et un espace «négatif» sur la cour.

Links: **Suleymaniye.** Durch Sinans Lösung der vier Minarette an den Ecken des von der Form des Atriums beeinflußten Hofes ergibt sich in der Seitenansicht eine kontrapunktische Wirkung aus dem Gegensatz der Masse der Moschee und der Negativform des Hofes. Isometrie 1:2000; Aufriß einer Seite 1:1000. Rechts: **Türbe Suleymans.** Aufriß und Schnitt 1:500.

Suleiman mosque, Istanbul. Isometric projection 1:2000; lateral façade 1:1000. Right, detail of **Suleiman's tomb.** Elevation and section 1:500. Sinan's solution of putting four minarets at the corners of his arcaded courtyard (inspired by the atrium) sets up a counterpoint between a solid volume on the mosque side and a 'negative' space on the courtyard side.

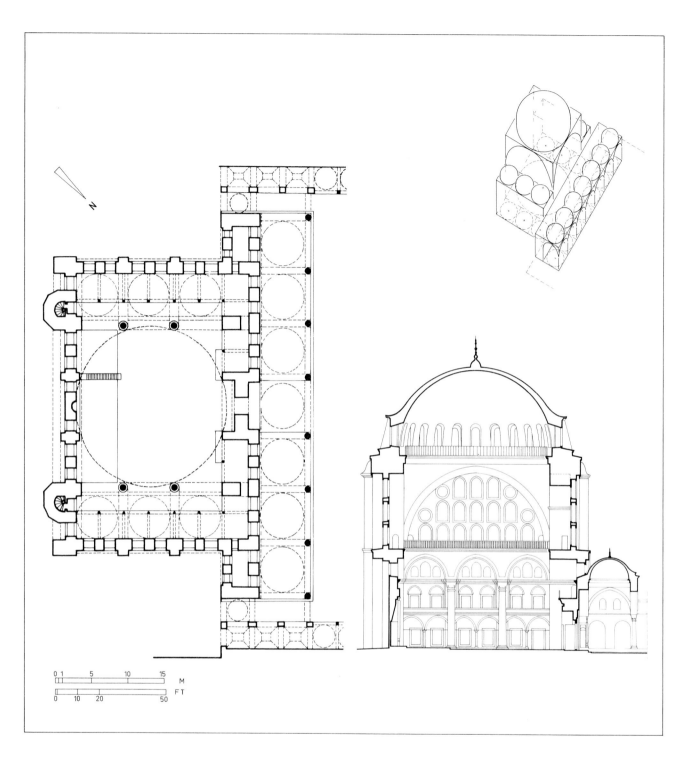

Mosquée de Mihrimah, à Istanbul, construite par Sinan dès 1555 (certains au-
teurs mentionnent 1540). Plan et coupe
longitudinale 1:500, isométrie 1:1500.
Ici l'architecte réussit à ne faire reposer
la coupole que sur les murs extérieurs
de l'édifice, sans recourir à aucun
contre-butement. Il crée ainsi un espace
homogène que ne prolongent latérale-
ment que les galeries des bas-côtés.

Istanbul, Mihrima-Moschee, ab 1555
(oder 1540) von Sinan erbaut. Die Kuppel liegt ohne Halbkuppel-Widerlager
auf den Außenmauern des Baus. So entstand ein einheitlicher Raum, der nur
seitlich durch die Galerien der Seitenschiffe verlängert wird. Grundriß und
Längsschnitt 1:500; Isometrie 1:1500.

Mihrimah mosque, Istanbul, begun by
Sinan in 1555 (some authorities say
1540). Plan and longitudinal section
1:500; isometric projection 1:1500.
Here the architect succeeded in supporting his dome on the outer walls alone
without recourse to buttressing, so
creating a homogeneous interior only
extended sideways by the side-aisle
galleries.

380

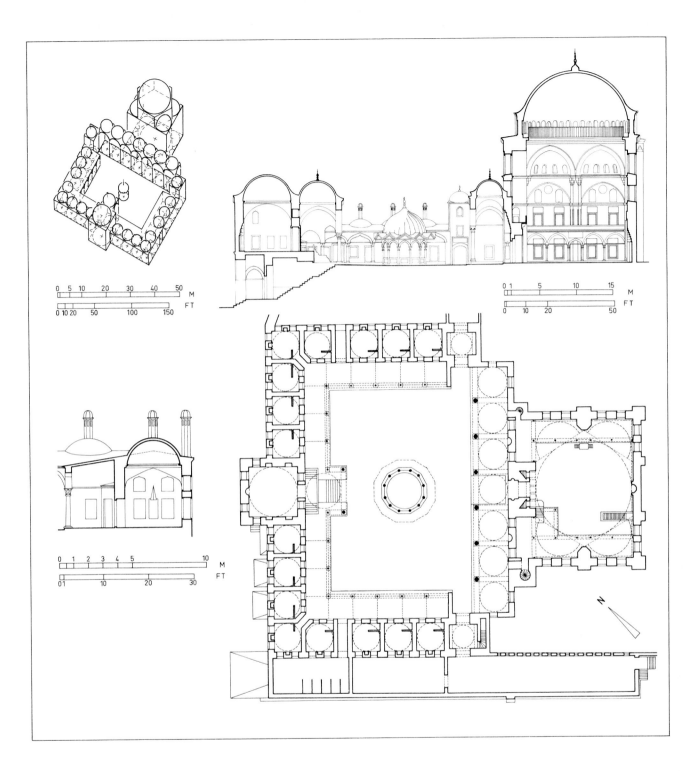

Mosquée de Sokoullou-Mehmet Pacha, à Istanbul, construite par Sinan en 1571. Isométrie 1:1500, détail de la madrasa entourant la cour 1:250, coupe longitudinale et plan 1:500. Sinan recourt ici à un plan hexagonal de la salle de prière s'appuyant de chaque côté sur un puissant pilier. Il obtient comme à Mihrimah un espace en largeur, mais encore plus homogène.

Istanbul, Sokullu-Moschee, 1571 von Sinan erbaut. Sinan wählte für den Betsaal einen sechseckigen Grundriß mit einem mächtigen Pfeiler an jeder Seite. Dadurch ergab sich wie in der Mihrima-Moschee ein breitgelagerter, hier aber noch geschlossener Raum. Isometrie 1:1500; Detail der den Hof umgebenden Medrese 1:250; Längsschnitt und Grundriß 1:500.

Sokollu Mehmed Pasha mosque, Istanbul, built by Sinan in 1571. Isometric projection 1:1500; detail of the *madrasah* surrounding the courtyard 1:250; longitudinal section and plan 1:500. Here Sinan adopted a hexagonal plan for the prayer-hall, using a powerful pier on each side. This gave a broad interior, as in the Mihrimah mosque, but here it is even more homogeneous.

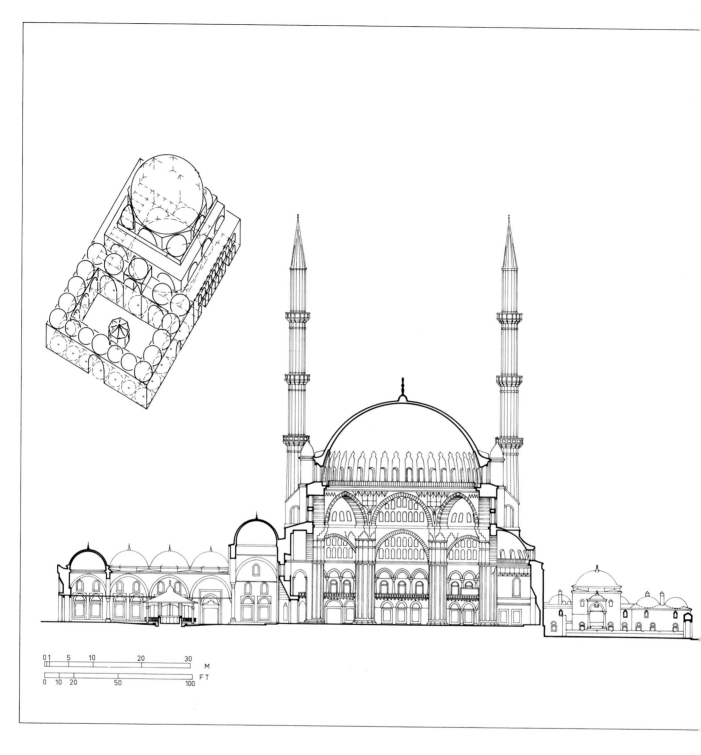

0 1	5	10		20		30

M

F T

0	10	20		50		100

Mosquée de Sélim, ou Sélimiyé, à Edirné, édifiée par Sinan entre 1569 et 1575. Isométrie 1:2000 et coupe longitudinale 1:750. Cet édifice marque l'aboutissement des recherches de Sinan vers un espace de plus en plus homogène: coupole unique reposant sur un octogone. 43 m de diamètre interne, dont le contrebutement n'est guère apparent à l'extérieur.

Edirne, Selimiye-Moschee, 1569–1575 von Sinan erbaut. Mit diesem Bau erreichte Sinan die angestrebte Geschlossenheit in größter Vollendung. Das Oktogon ist mit einer einzigen, 43 m überspannenden Kuppel überwölbt; das Widerlagersystem ist von außen kaum zu erkennen. Isometrie 1:2000; Längsschnitt 1:750.

Selimiye or Selim mosque, Edirne, built by Sinan between 1569 and 1575. Isometric projection 1:2000; longitudinal section 1:750. This building marks the culmination of Sinan's search for a more and more homogeneous interior. A single dome is supported on an octagon; it is 43 m. in diameter, and its buttressing is barely visible on the outside of the building.

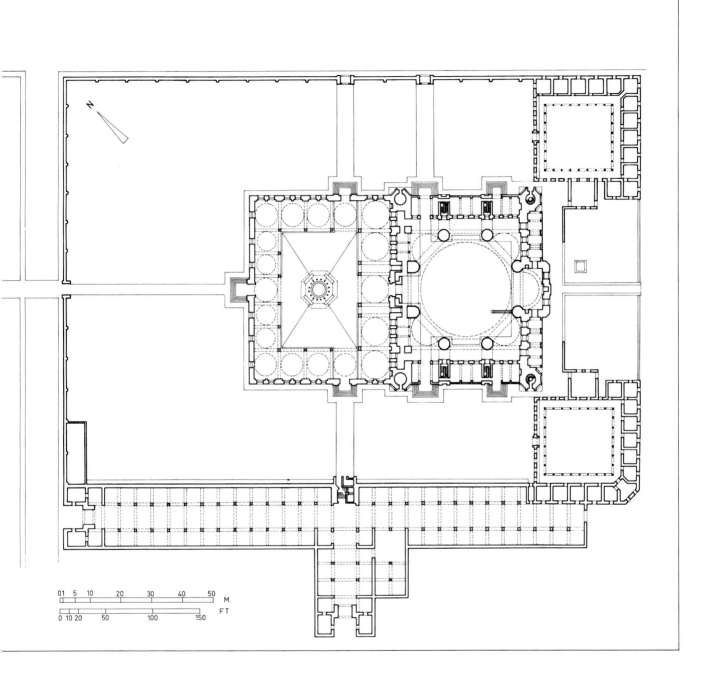

01 5 10   20   30   40   50   M

0 10 20   50   100   150   FT

Kulillié et Mosquée de Sélim, à Edirné. Plan 1:1200. Ici, les quatre minarets contribuent à la stabilité de l'ensemble. Les espaces «secondaires» tels que l'«abside» du mihrab et les quatre petites demi-coupoles d'angles se fondent dans le grand espace central. Le bazar de 225 m de long qui borde l'ensemble au sud-ouest est une adjonction de Mourad III (1575–1595).

Edirne, Külliye und Selimiye-Moschee. Die vier Minarette tragen zur Stabilität des Bauwerks bei. «Nebenräume» wie der Mihrab und die vier kleinen Halbkuppeln in den Ecken verschmelzen mit dem Hauptraum. Der 225 m lange Basar an der Südwestseite wurde von Murad III. (1575–1595) gestiftet. Grundriß 1:1200.

Kulilliye and Selim mosque, Edirne. Plan 1:1200. The four minarets contribute to the stability of the whole composition. The 'secondary' spaces such as the 'apse' of the *mihrab* and the four little half-domes in the corners originate in the great central space. The 225 m. long bazaar bordering the complex to the south-west was added by Murad III (1575–95).

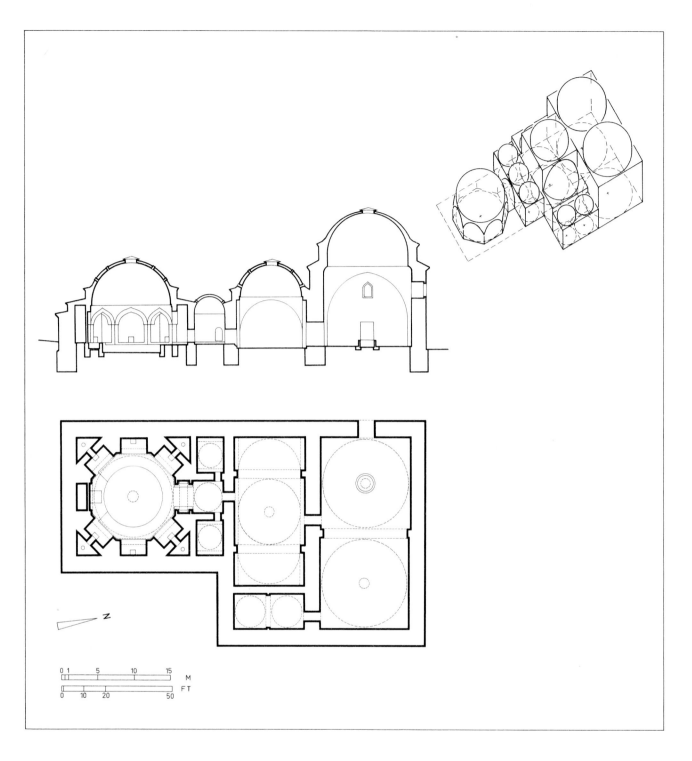

Hamam de Yeni-Kaplidcha, à Brousse, construit en 1560. Coupe longitudinale et plan 1:500, isométrie 1:1000. Cet établissement de bains se caractérise par le plan complexe de son étuve voûtée (à gauche). Les coupoles des salles réservées au bain sont pourvues d'oculi d'éclairage.

Bursa, Yeni-Kaplidscha-Hamam, 1560. Das gewölbte Schwitzbad dieser Badeanlage hat einen kompliziert gegliederten Innenraum (links). Die Kuppeln der Baderäume sind im Scheitel mit einer Lichtöffnung versehen. Längsschnitt und Grundriß 1:500; Isometrie 1:1000.

Yeni-Kaplicha hamam, Bursa, built 1560. Longitudinal section and plan 1:500; isometric projection 1:1000. A notable feature of this bathing establishment is the intricate plan of its vaulted sweating-room (left). The domes of the bath halls have oculi to admit light.

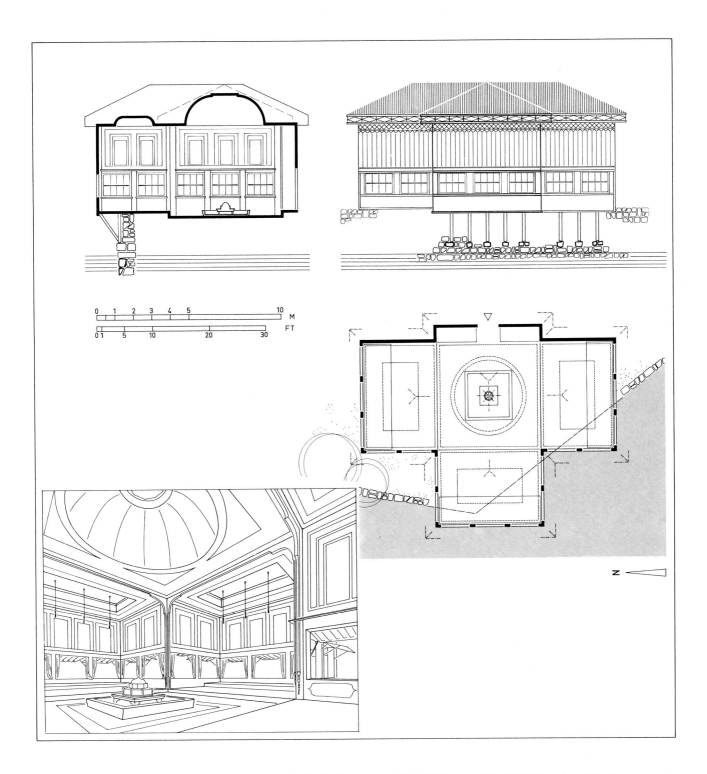

Köprülü-Yalisi, à Anadolu-Hisar, sur le Bosphore, datant de la fin du XVIIᵉ s. Coupe transversale, façade sur le Bosphore et plan 1:200, perspective de la salle de réception. Les yalis sont des résidences d'été propres à Istanbul, situées au bord de l'eau. La salle carrée comporte trois avant-corps identiques surplombant partiellement l'eau.

Anadoluhisari (Bosporus), Köprülü-Yalisi, Ende 17. Jh. Die Yali sind am Meer gelegene Sommerresidenzen der Bewohner von Istanbul. An den quadratischen Hauptraum schließen auf drei Seiten untereinander gleiche Vorbauten an, die zum Teil über dem Wasser liegen. Querschnitt, Fassade zum Bosporus, Grundriß des Empfangsraums 1:200; perspektivische Ansicht des Empfangsraums.

Köprülü-Yalisi, Anadolu-Hisar (on the Bosphorus), late seventeenth century. Cross section, Bosphorus front, and plan 1:200; bottom left, perspective of the reception room. The *yali* was a seaside summer residence peculiar to Istanbul. The square hall has three identical projecting portions over the water.

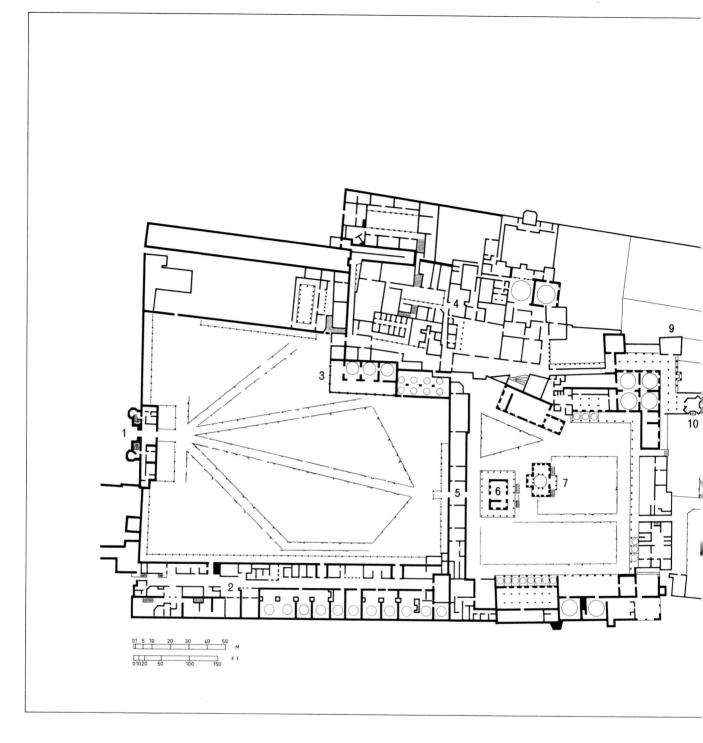

Sérail de Top-Kapi à Istanbul. Commencé vers 1475, ce quartier des palais ne cessa de grandir jusqu'au XVIIᵉ s. Plan d'ensemble 1:2000. 1) Première porte, 2) Cuisines, 3) Salle du Conseil, 4) Aile du Harem, 5) Deuxième porte, 6) Salle d'audience, 7) Bibliothèque, 8) à 10) Kiosques d'agrément, 11) Salle de Bagdad. Le site se trouve à l'extrême pointe entre la Corne d'Or et la mer de Marmara.

Istanbul, Top-Kapi-Sarayi, um 1475 begonnen, bis ins 17.Jh. erweitert. Das Palastviertel liegt auf der Sarayi-Spitze zwischen Goldenem Horn und Marmarameer. Grundriß 1:2000: 1) erstes Tor, 2) Küchen, 3) Ratsaal, 4) Harem, 5) zweites Tor, 6) Audienzsaal, 7) Bibliothek, 8) bis 10) Pavillons, 11) Bagdad-Saal.

Top-Kapi seraglio, Istanbul, palace quarter begun c.1475 and repeatedly enlarged until the seventeenth century. Overall plan 1:2000. 1) first gate, 2) kitchens, 3) council hall, 4) harem wing, 5) second gate, 6) audience room, 7) library, 8–10) pleasure pavilions, 11) Baghdad room. The seraglio is built on the tip of the peninsula between the Golden Horn and the Sea of Marmara.

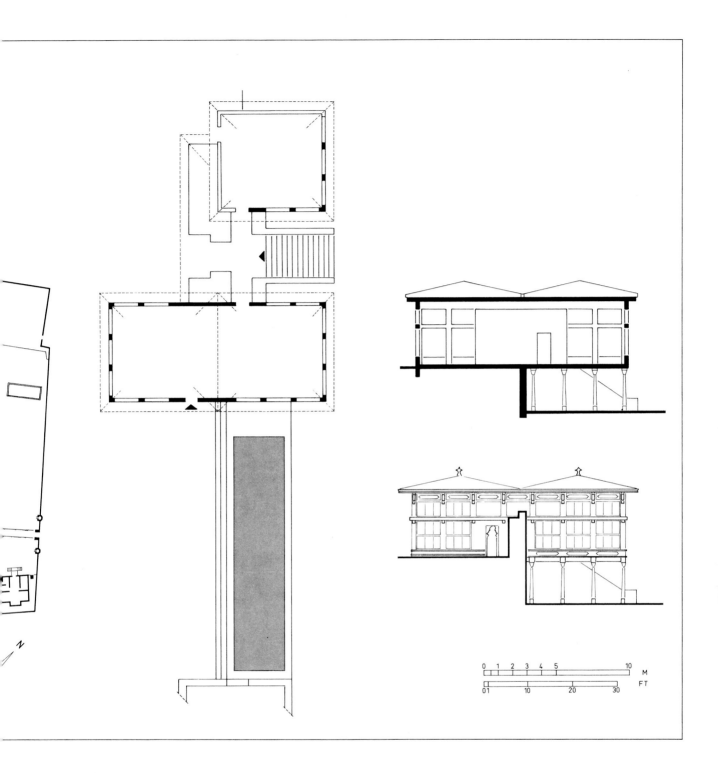

Kara-Mustafa-köchkü, dans les jardins du sérail de Top Kapi (voir N° 8 du plan d'ensemble). Plan, coupe transversale et élévation 1:250. Belvédère classique, avec ses fenêtres qui descendent jusqu'au sol et ses parois presque entièrement en verre. C'est l'un des exemples typiques des kiosques du XVIIIᵉ siècle.

Istanbul, Kara-Mustafa-Köschkü im Garten des Top-Kapi-Sarayi (Lageplan: 8). Der Pavillon ist mit den bis zum Boden reichenden Fenstern und nahezu völlig verglasten Fenstern ein klassisches Belvedere, ein typisches Beispiel für die Lusthäuschen des 18. Jh. Grundriß, Querschnitt und Aufriß 1:250.

Kara-Mustafa-köshkü, in the gardens of the Top-Kapi seraglio (8 on the overall plan). Cross section and elevation 1:250. A typical example of the eighteenth-century Turkish summer pavilion with windows down to the floor and walls almost entirely of glass.

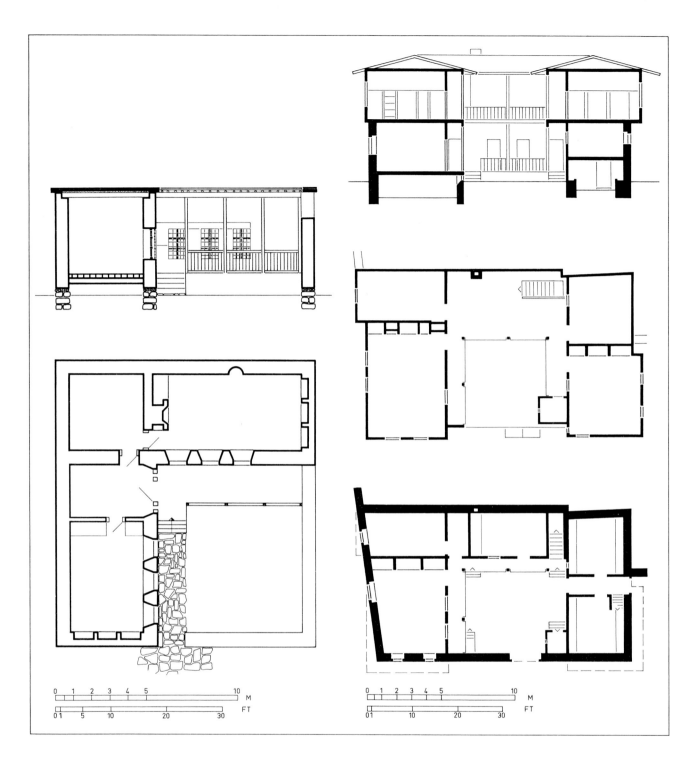

| 0 | 1 | 2 | 3 | 4 | 5 | | | | | | 10 | | M |
| 0 1 | | 5 | | 10 | | | 20 | | | | 30 | | FT |

| 0 | 1 | 2 | 3 | 4 | 5 | | | | | | 10 | | M |
| 0 1 | | 5 | | 10 | | | 20 | | | | 30 | | FT |

Maison d'habitation à Konya (Anatolie). Coupe transversale et plan 1:200. Ces maisons des Hauts Plateaux ne s'ouvrent que sur le petit jardin intérieur. Elles sont construites en brique crue. La couverture de rondins est revêtue de terre, comme isolant thermique.
Maison à Ankara. Coupe longitudinale, plan de l'étage et plan du rez-de-chaussée 1:250. Organisation autour d'une cour.

Links: **Konya (Anatolien), Wohnhaus.** Bei den aus ungebrannten Ziegeln gebauten Häusern der anatolischen Hochebene öffnen sich alle Räume nur auf den kleinen Innengarten. Das Knüppelholzdach ist zur besseren Isolierung mit Lehm bestrichen. Querschnitt, Grundriß 1:200. Rechts: **Ankara, Wohnhaus.** Die Räume sind um einen Hof angeordnet. Längsschnitt, Grundrisse des Ober- und des Erdgeschosses 1:250.

Dwelling-house, Konya (Anatolia). Cross section and plan 1:200. These High Plateau houses only opened inwards, on to a small garden. They were built of unfired brick; the log roof was covered with earth for insulation purposes. **Dwelling-house, Ankara.** Longitudinal section, plan of the upper storey, and ground-floor plan 1:250. The house is laid out round a courtyard.

Inde islamique

Islamisches Indien

Moslem India

Si l'invasion islamique en Inde débute avec la dynastie turque des Ghaznévides, au Xe siècle, il ne s'agit d'abord que de raids. Le premier sultan d'Inde est un ancien esclave, Qoutoub-ed-din Aibek, qui établit sa capitale à Delhi en 1206. Il y construit une grande mosquée, pour laquelle il se sert de matériaux de remploi, prélevés sur les temples hindouistes et jaïns qu'ont détruits les musulmans. Cette mosquée nommée Qouat-el Islam possède le plus haut minaret (Qoutoub Minar) jamais édifié en Inde (73 m).

Les musulmans, d'origine turque ou persane, vont progressivement importer la culture issue du monde iranien, sans assimiler vraiment les modes d'expression locaux. Ils créeront une architecture qui, sur la base des formes et décors hérités de Boukhara, Ispahan, Hérat ou Ghazna, va donner naissance à un style propre. C'est dans le sultanat de Gulbarga (Inde centrale) que naît un art original au XIVe siècle. La Djami-Masdjid ou Mosquée du Vendredi de Gulbarga (1367) apporte une formule quasiment standardisée, fondée sur l'arc brisé, la voûte en carène et la coupole.

Aux XVe et XVIe siècles, la dynastie des Lodi, à Delhi, laisse une série de remarquables tombeaux, dont va dériver la lignée des admirables constructions funéraires qui éclôt avec l'époque moghole (1526–1858). Cette période, marquée par la domination des Mongols en Inde, débute avec un grand conquérant, Baber ou Babur, auquel succède Humayun, qui crée à Delhi l'un des plus beaux mausolées moghols (1565). Désormais, des forteresses, comme à Delhi ou Agra, enserrent dans leurs puissantes murailles des palais de marbre blanc ou de grès rouge aux déli-

Die islamische Invasion in Indien begann im 10. Jahrhundert unter der Ghaznaviden-Dynastie, allerdings handelte es sich zunächst nur um vereinzelte Überfälle. Der erste indische Sultan, Kutub-ud-din-Aibak, der 1206 Delhi zu seiner Hauptstadt machte, war ein ehemaliger Sklave. Aus dem Material der von den Muselmanen zerstörten hinduistischen und jainistischen Tempel erbaute er in Delhi die Moschee Quwwat-ul-Islam (Kutub-Moschee) mit dem höchsten Minarett (Kutub Minar, 73 m), das je auf indischem Boden errichtet wurde.

Die Muselmanen türkischen oder persischen Ursprungs führten nach und nach die Kultur der persischen Welt ein, ohne sie jedoch mit den lokalen Ausdrucksmöglichkeiten zu verbinden. Ihre Architektur beruhte zwar auf dem von Buchara, Isfahan, Herat oder Ghazna übernommenen Formenschatz und Dekor, entwickelte sich aber zu einem eigenen Stil. Eine eigenständige Kunst bildete sich im 14. Jahrhundert im Sultanat Gulbarga (Zentralindien) aus. Die Jami-Masjid (Freitagsmoschee) in Gulbarga (1367) ist nach einer typisierten Formel aus Spitzbögen, Kielbogengewölben und Kuppeln konstruiert.

Die im 15. und 16. Jahrhundert in Delhi residierenden Lodi-Sultane haben bemerkenswerte Grabbauten geschaffen, die ersten einer Reihe, die in den Grabmonumenten der Mogul-Zeit (1526 bis 1858) gipfelt. Die Epoche der Mogul-Herrscher in Indien begann mit dem großen Eroberer Babur, dessen Nachfolger Humayun in Delhi eines der schönsten Mogul-Mausoleen errichten ließ (1565). Von dieser Zeit an umschlossen Festungen mit mächtigen Mauern wie Delhi und Agra Paläste aus weißem Marmor oder rotem Sandstein mit

The Moslem invasion of India began with the Turkish Ghaznavid dynasty in the tenth century, although at first it was only in the form of raids. The first Sultan of India was a former slave, Qutb ud-Din Aybak, who set up his capital at Delhi in 1206. There he built a great mosque, Quwat-el Islam, re-using materials from the Hindu and Jain temples destroyed by the Moslems. This mosque has the highest minaret (Qutb Minar, 73 m.) ever built in India.

The Moslems, who were of Turkish or Persian origin, progressively introduced the civilisation of the Iranian world without really assimilating local modes of expression. Their architecture, based on the formal and decorative legacy of Bukhara, Isfahan, Herat and Ghazna, eventually achieved a style of its own. An original art can be said to have emerged in the fourteenth century in the Sultanate of Gulbarga (central India). The Jami-Masjid or Friday Mosque at Gulbarga (1367) uses an almost standardised formula based on broken arch, keel vault and dome.

In the fifteenth and sixteenth centuries the Lodi dynasty of Delhi built a series of remarkable tombs, the first in a line of splendid funerary monuments that was to reach its culmination in the Mogul period (1526–1858). This period of Mongol dominion in India began with a great conqueror, Babur, whose successor Humayun erected at Delhi one of the finest Mogul mausoleums (1565). From then on cities such as Delhi and Agra became fortresses, enclosing within powerful walls delicately arcaded palaces of white marble or red sandstone, and mosques with elegantly festooned arches (the Pearl Mosque at Agra). Sumptuous tombs (the Itimad-ud

cates arcades, des mosquée aux élégants arcs festonnés (Mosquée de la Perle, à Agra). Des tombeaux fastueux (Itimour-ed Daula et Tadj Mahall, à Agra au XVIIᵉ s.), et de merveilleux observatoires astronomiques vont joncher les cités islamiques de l'Inde.

Il faut faire une place à part aux créations d'un empereur exceptionnel: Akbar, le «Grand Moghol» (1556 à 1605), fondateur d'une religion syncrétique et d'une capitale étonnante: Fathepour Sikri. Cette ville située non loin d'Agra, avec ses palais, sa salle du trône, sa mosquée, ses maisons nobles, entièrement construits en grès rouge, témoigne d'une trop rare synthèse avec les techniques de construction indiennes. Mais cette tentative n'aura pas de postérité.

feinen Arkaden, Moscheen mit elegant geschweiften Bogen (Perlenmoschee in Agra), prächtige Grabmäler (Itimud-uddaula und Taj Mahal in Agra, 17. Jahrhundert); in allen islamischen Städten Indiens entstanden herrliche Sternwarten.

Ein besonderer Platz gebührt den Schöpfungen eines ungewöhnlichen Herrschers, Akbars, des «Großmoguls» (1556–1605). Er begründete nicht nur eine synkretistische Religion, sondern schuf auch eine erstaunliche Hauptstadt, Fatehpur Sikri. Mit ihren ausschließlich aus rotem Sandstein erbauten Palästen, dem Thronsaal, der Moschee, den Adelshäusern ist diese unweit von Agra gelegene Stadt das Beispiel einer – leider nur allzu seltenen – geglückten Synthese islamischer und indischer Konstruktionstechniken, die allerdings ohne Nachfolge blieb.

Daula and the Taj Mahal, Agra, seventeenth century) and magnificent astronomical observatories were strewn throughout the cities of Moslem India.

Of particular note are the creations of one outstanding emperor, Akbar, the 'Great Mogul' (1556–1605), founder of a syncretic religion and of a dazzling capital—Fatehpur Sikri. Situated not far from Agra, this city of palaces with its throne room, mosque, and noble houses built entirely of red sandstone bears witness to an all too rare synthesis with indigenous construction techniques: unfortunately the experiment was never repeated.

1 Vue axiale du Tadj Mahall, mausolée de Moumtaz Mahall, à Agra, construit de 1632 à 1654 par le Grand Moghol Chah Jahan.
2 Le centre de la ville de Fathepour Sikri, capitale qu'Akbar fit construire de 1569 à 1574. Au fond, le Diwan-i Khas ou salle des audiences privées.
3 Mausolée d'Itimour-ed-Daula, à Agra, construit à la demande de Nour Mahall pour son père en 1628.

1 Agra, axiale Ansicht des Taj Mahal, Grabmal des Mumtaz Mahal (unter dem Großmogul Shah Jahan erbaut, 1632–1654)
2 Fatehpur Sikri, das Zentrum der von Akbar errichteten Hauptstadt (1569 bis 1574); im Hintergrund der private Audienzsaal
3 Agra, Grabmal des Itimud-ud-daula, das von Nur Mahal für ihren Vater erbaut wurde (1628)

1 Axial view of the Taj Mahal, Agra, the mausoleum of Mumtaz Mahal built by the Great Mogul Shah Jahan in 1632–54.
2 Centre of Fatehpur Sikri, the capital that Akbar had built between 1569 and 1574. In the background is the Diwan-i Khas or private audience room.
3 Mausoleum of Itimad-ud Daula, Agra, built by order of Nur Mahal for her father in 1628.

1

2

3

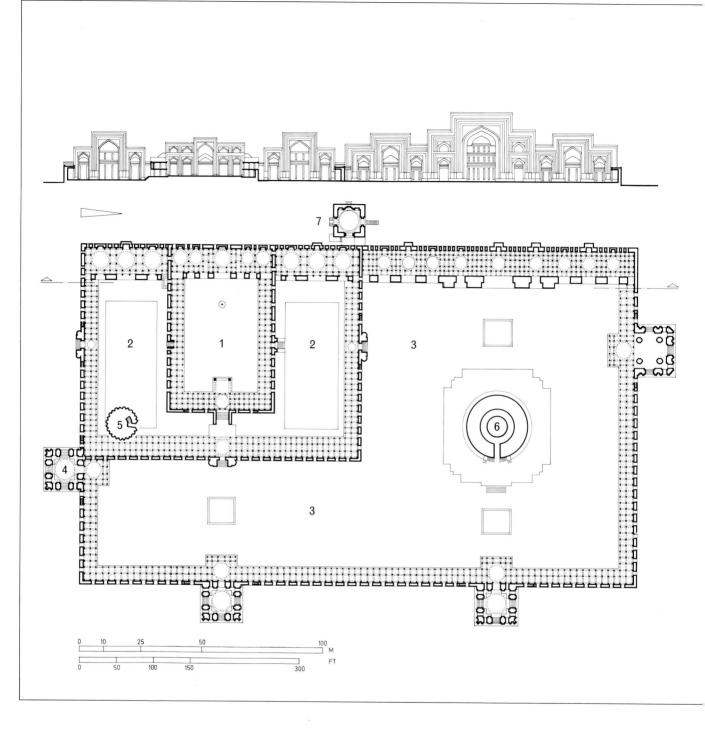

Mosquée Qouat-el Islam, ou Mosquée de Qoutoub, dans le Vieux-Delhi, dont la construction débute en 1200 et se poursuit jusqu'en 1315. Coupe et plan 1:1500. 1) Mosquée originelle, symétrique (1200), 2) Premier agrandissement (1210–1229), 3) Deuxième agrandissement (1295–1315), 4) Porte Alai Derwaze (1305), 5) Qoutoub Minar (1200), 6) Minaret inachevé, 7) Tombeau d'Iltoutmich (1236).

Alt-Delhi, Moschee Quwwat-ul-Islam (Kutub-Moschee), 1200–1315. Schnitt und Grundriß 1:1500: 1) ursprüngliche, symmetrische Moschee (1200), 2) erste Erweiterung (1210–1229), 3) zweite Erweiterung (1295–1315), 4) Alai Derwaze (1305), 5) Kutub Minar (1200), 6) unvollendetes Minarett, 7) Grab des Iltutmish (1236).

Quwat-el Islam or Qutb mosque, Old Delhi, built 1200–1315. Section and plan 1:1500. 1) the original, symmetrical mosque (1200), 2) first extension (1210–29), 3) second extension (1295 to 1315), 4) Alai Darwazah (gate; 1305), 5) Qutb Minar (1200), 6) unfinished minaret, 7) tomb of Iltutmish (1236).

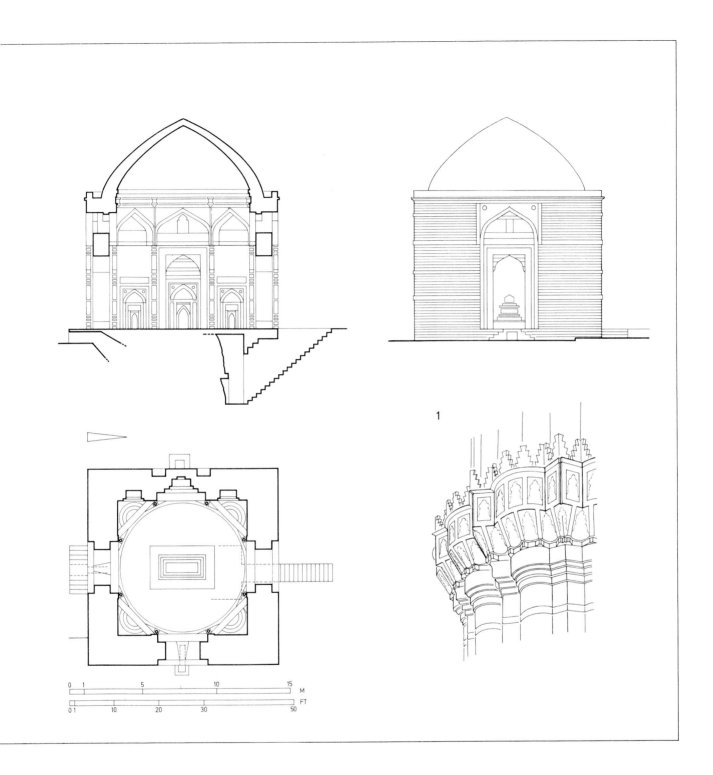

Tombeau du sultan Iltoutmich, construit en 1236. Coupe, élévation et plan 1:250. Edifice de plan carré, dont la coupole repose sur quatre trompes, issu de l'influence persane, mais réalisé par des artisans hindous. En 1), détail des stalactites supportant les balcons du Qoutoub Minar, minaret haut de 72,5 m pour une base de 15 m de diamètre.

Grabmal des Sultans Iltutmish, 1236. Der von einer Trompenkuppel überwölbte Bau mit quadratischem Grundriß ist persisch beeinflußt, aber von hinduistischen Handwerkern ausgeführt. Schnitt, Aufriß und Grundriß 1:250. 1) Detail der die Balkone des Kutub Minar stützenden Stalaktiten. Dieses Minarett hat an der Basis einen Durchmesser von 15 m und ist 72,5 m hoch.

Qutb mosque: tomb of Sultan Iltutmish, built 1236. Section, elevation, and plan 1:250. Built on a square plan with its dome resting on four squinches, the tomb was Persian-influenced but executed by Indian craftsmen. 1) detail of the stalactite work supporting the balconies of Qutb Minar, a minaret that rises 72.5 m. high on a 15 m. diameter base.

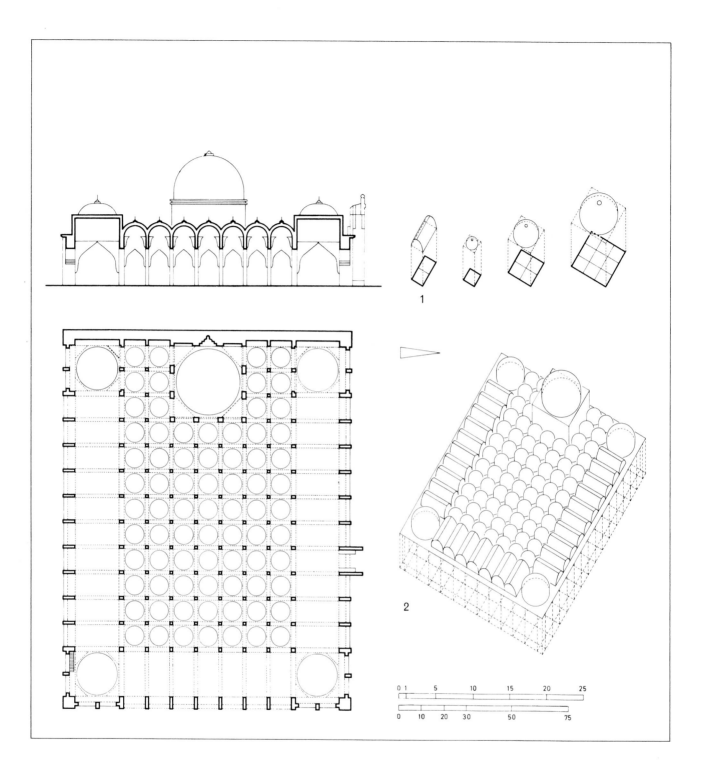

Djami-Masdjid, ou Mosquée du Vendredi, à Gulbarga (Inde méridionale), construite en 1367. Coupe et plan 1:500, 1) Eléments de construction, 2) Axonométrie du système. Edifice bâti exclusivement à l'aide d'arcs et de coupoles, selon un système modulaire unique en Inde. Salle de prière en éléments unitaires, voûtes de la galerie à deux unités, coupoles d'angles à quatre unités, sanctuaire à neuf unités.

Gulbarga (Südindien), Jami-Masjid (Freitagsmoschee), 1367. Der Bau wurde ausschließlich mit Hilfe von Bögen und Kuppeln konstruiert; sein Modulsystem ist in Indien einzigartig. Der Betsaal ist aus einzelnen Grundeinheiten zusammengesetzt, für die Galeriegewölbe wurden zwei Einheiten, für die Eckkuppeln vier und für das Sanktuarium neun verwendet. Schnitt und Grundriß 1:500; 1) Konstruktionselemente, 2) Axonometrie.

Jami-Masjid or Friday mosque, Gulbarga (south India), built 1367. Section and plan 1:500. 1) structural elements, 2) axonometric projection of the system. The building was erected exclusively with the aid of arches and domes following a modular system unique in India. The prayer-hall uses unitary elements, the gallery vaults two units, the corner domes four units and the shrine nine units.

Djami-Masdjid, ou Mosquée du Vendredi, à Champanir (Inde moyenne, côte ouest), construite en 1485. Plan schématique 1:800 et axonométrie ouverte. Fondée sur un principe d'alternance de petites et grandes coupoles, supportées par des piliers de type hindou, cette mosquée comporte, pour les travées centrales, un exhaussement de deux niveaux.

Champanir (zentralindische Westküste), Jami-Masjid (Freitagsmoschee), 1485. Die Moschee zeigt einen Wechsel von großen und kleinen Kuppeln über Säulen vom Hindu-Typ. Das Mittelschiff ist um zwei Geschosse überhöht. Grundrißschema 1:800 und axonometrischer Schnitt.

Jami-Masjid or Friday mosque, Shampanir (west coast of central India), built 1485. Diagrammatic plan 1:800 and open axonometric projection. This mosque uses the principle of alternate small and large domes supported by Indian-style pillars. The middle bays are two levels higher.

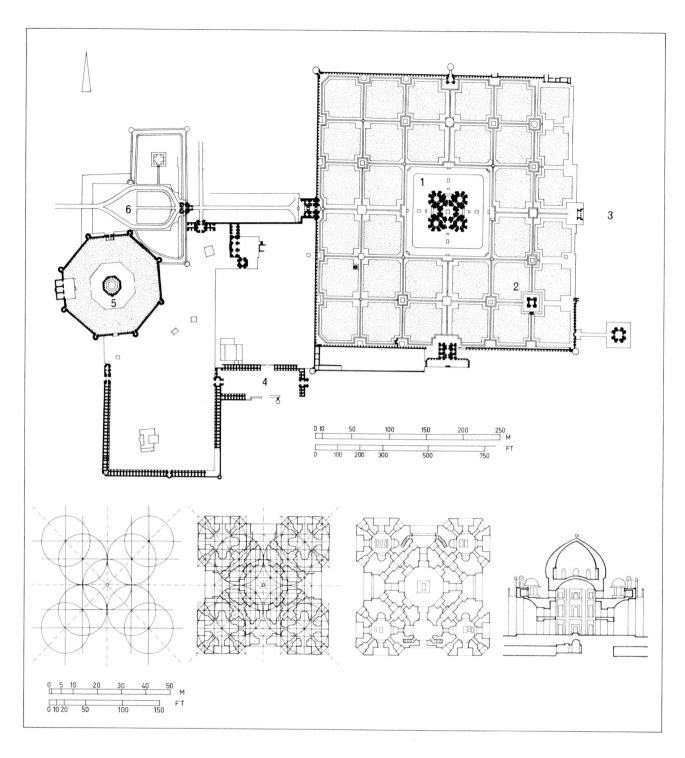

Mausolée d'Humayun, à Delhi, construit en 1565 par l'architecte Mirak Mirza Ghiyas. Plan général 1:5000, analyse géométrique, plan et coupe 1:1500. 1) Mausolée d'Humayun, 2) Tombe du barbier, 3) Rivière Jumna, 4) Sérail arabe, 5) Tombeau d'Isa Khan, 6) Rampe d'accès. Œuvre d'un architecte persan qui travailla pour Haji Begum, veuve du souverain moghol, ce mausolée annonce le Tadj Mahall.

Delhi, Grabmal des Humayun, 1565, Architekt Mirak Mirza Ghiyas. Der persische Architekt arbeitete im Auftrag von Haji Begum, der Witwe des Mogulherrschers. Das Mausoleum weist bereits auf das Taj Mahal voraus. Grundriß 1:5000: 1) Grabmal des Humayun, 2) Grab des Barbiers, 3) Fluß (Jumna), 4) arabisches Serail, 5) Grabmal des Isa Khan, 6) Auffahrt; geometrische Analyse mit Grundriß und Schnitt 1:1500.

Mausoleum of Humayun, Delhi, built by the architect Mirak Mirza Ghiyas in 1565. Overall plan 1:5000; geometrical analysis, plan, and section 1:1500. 1) mausoleum of Humayun, 2) barber's tomb, 3) river Jumna, 4) Arab seraglio, 5) tomb of Isa Khan, 6) access ramp. Built by a Persian architect working for Haji Begum, widow of the Mogul ruler, this mausoleum foreshadows the Taj Mahal.

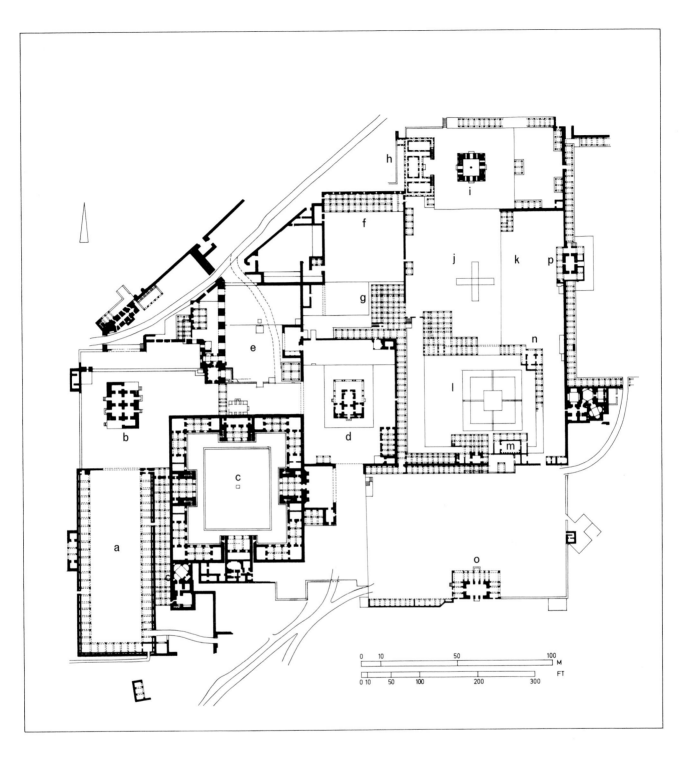

Ville de Fathepour Sikri, résidence du Grand Moghol Akbar, construite de 1569 à 1574. Plan du quartier palatin 1:2000. a) Ecuries, b) Maison du rajah Birbal, c) Palais de Jodh Bai, d) Maison de Miriam, e) Jardin de Miriam, f) Hôpital, g) Panch Mahall, h) Salle de travail d'Akbar, i) Salle des audiences privées, j) Cour, k) Jardin, l) Salle de séjour d'Akbar, m) Chambre à coucher d'Akbar, n) Harem, o) Administration, p) Cour des audiences publiques.

Fatehpur Sikri, die Residenz des Großmoguls Akbar, 1569–1574. Plan des Palastbezirks 1:2000: a) Stallungen, b) Haus des Raja Birbal, c) Palast der Kaiserin Jodh Bai, d) Miriams Haus, e) Miriams Garten, f) Hospital, g) Panch Mahal, h) Arbeitsraum des Kaisers, i) Saal für Privataudienzen, j) Hof, k) Garten, l) Wohnraum Akbars, m) Schlafgemach Akbars, n) Harem, o) Verwaltung, p) Hof für öffentliche Audienzen.

City of Fatehpur Sikri (Uttar Pradesh), residence of the Great Mogul Akbar, built 1569–74. Plan of the palace quarter 1:2000. a) stables, b) Rajah Birbal's house, c) palace of Jodh Bai, d) Miriam's house, e) Miriam's garden, f) hospital, g) Panch Mahal, h) Akbar's study, i) private audience room, j) courtyard, k) garden, l) Akbar's drawing-room, m) Akbar's bedroom, n) harem, o) offices, p) courtyard for public audiences.

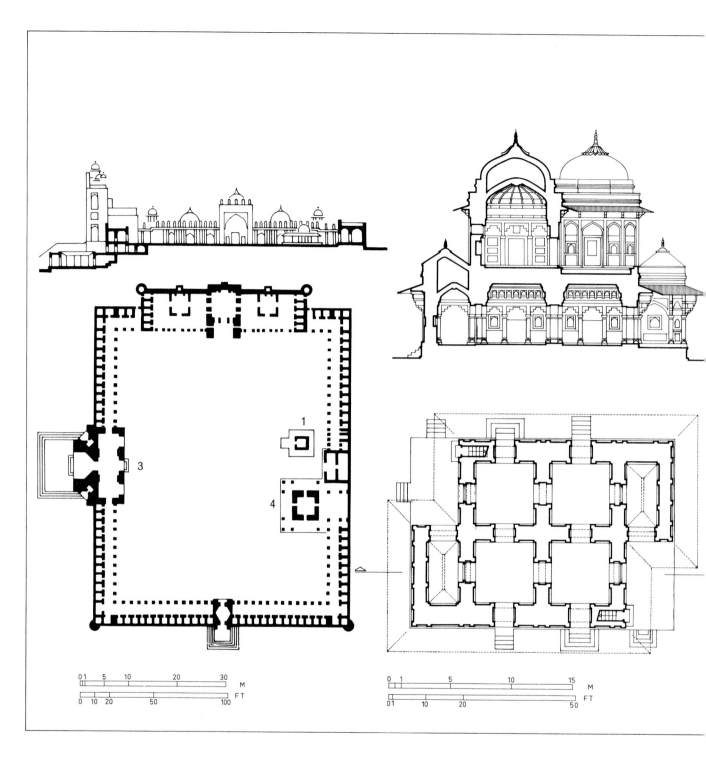

Djami-Masdjid de Fathepour Sikri, construite en 1571. Coupe longitudinale et plan 1:750. État après les adjonctions du temps d'Akbar. 1) Tombeau de Sélim Chisti, 2) Porte royale, 3) Arc triomphal, 4) Tombeau d'Islam Khan. Mosquée à cour entourée de portiques. A droite, **Maison du rajah Birbal, à Fathepour Sikri,** construite en 1569. Coupe et plan du rez-de-chaussée 1:300.

Links: **Fatehpur Sikri, Jami-Masjid,** 1571. Moschee mit Säulenhof; Zustand nach den Erweiterungsbauten unter Akbar. Längsschnitt und Grundriß 1:750: 1) Grabmal des Salem Chishti, 2) Königstor, 3) Triumphtor, 4) Grabmal des Islam Khan. Rechts: **Fatehpur Sikri, Haus des Raja Birbal,** 1569. Schnitt, Grundriß des Erdgeschosses 1:300.

Jami-Masjid, Fatehpur Sikri, built 1571. Longitudinal section and plan (as it was after Akbar's additions) 1:750. 1) tomb of Selim Chishti, 2) royal gate, 3) triumphal arch, 4) tomb of Islam Khan. The mosque has a porticoed courtyard. Right, **Rajah Birbal's house, Fatehpur Sikri,** built 1569. Section and plan of the ground floor 1:300.

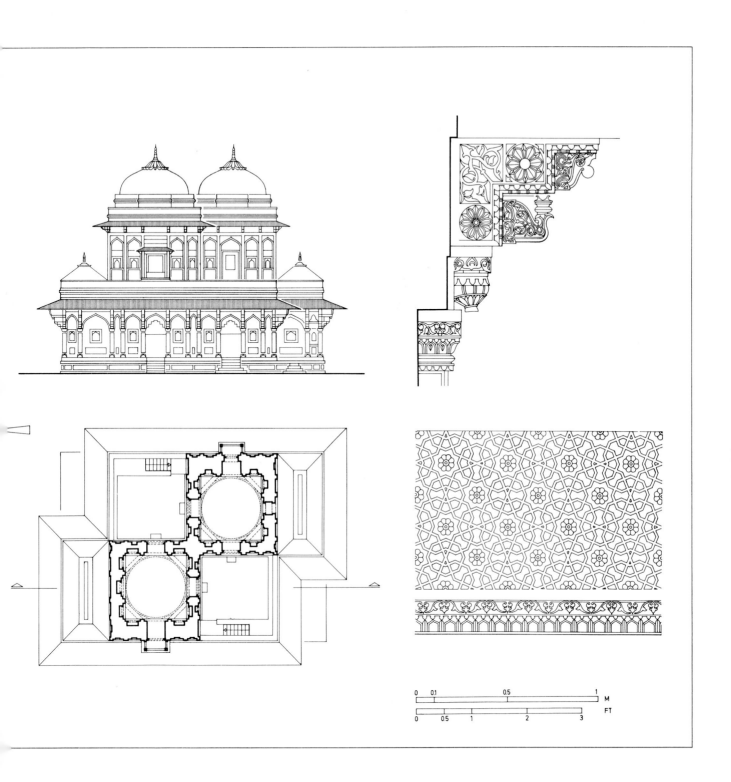

| 0 | 0.1 | | 0.5 | | 1 | M |
| 0 | 0.5 | 1 | | 2 | 3 | FT |

Maison du rajah Birbal. Elévation et plan de l'étage 1:300. Détail d'une console et structure géométrique sculptée dans le grès rouge 1:20. Le caractère de Fathepour Sikri est de mêler les arcs et coupoles islamiques aux consoles et architraves d'origine hindoue. Ce trait découle de la philosophie religieuse dont Akbar se voulait le prophète.

Fatehpur Sikri, Haus des Raja Birbal. In Fatehpur Sikri sind islamische Bögen und Kuppeln zusammen mit hinduistischen Konsolen und Architraven verwendet. Diese Eigenheit ist eine Folge der Religionsphilosophie, als deren Prophet sich Akbar sah. Aufriß, Grundriß des Obergeschosses 1:300; Konsole und Detail eines in roten Sandstein gehauenen geometrischen Ornaments 1:20.

Rajah Birbal's house, Fatehpur Sikri. Elevation and plan of upper storey 1:300; detail of a bracket and geometrical structure carved in red sandstone 1:20. Fatehpur Sikri is characterised by a blending of Moslem arches and domes with brackets and architraves of native Indian origin. This was a deliberate expression of the religious philosophy of which Akbar saw himself as the prophet.

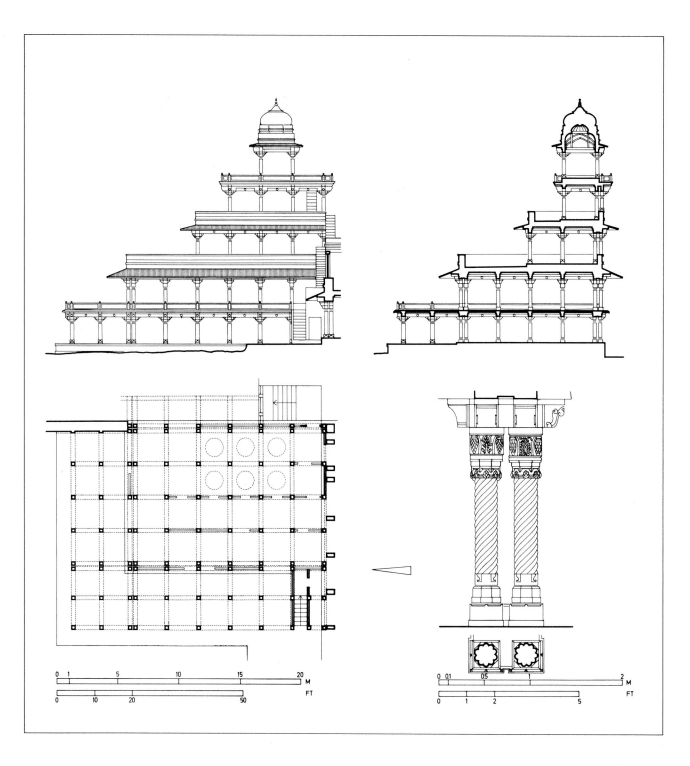

Panch Mahall, à Fathepour Sikri, construit en 1570. Elévation, plan et coupe 1:300, détail de colonnes jumelles 1:40. Cette halle, haute de cinq étages, à structure asymétrique, qui dérive des couvents de bois érigés au temps du bouddhisme hinayana, reste mystérieuse. Sa destination n'est pas clairement déterminée au sein du quartier palatin.

Fatehpur Sikri, Panch Mahal, 1570. Die fünfgeschossige asymmetrische Halle ist von den hölzernen Klosterbauten des Hinayana-Buddhismus abgeleitet. Ihre Bestimmung innerhalb des Palastbezirks ist nicht gesichert. Aufriß, Grundriß und Schnitt 1:300; Doppelsäule 1:40.

Panch Mahal, Fatehpur Sikri, built 1570. Elevation, plan, and section 1:300; detail of the paired columns 1:40. This hall—five storeys high, asymmetrical in structure and inspired by the wooden monasteries of the days of Hinayana Buddhism—remains a mystery; it is not clear what it was for, nor why it was situated at the heart of the palace quarter.

400

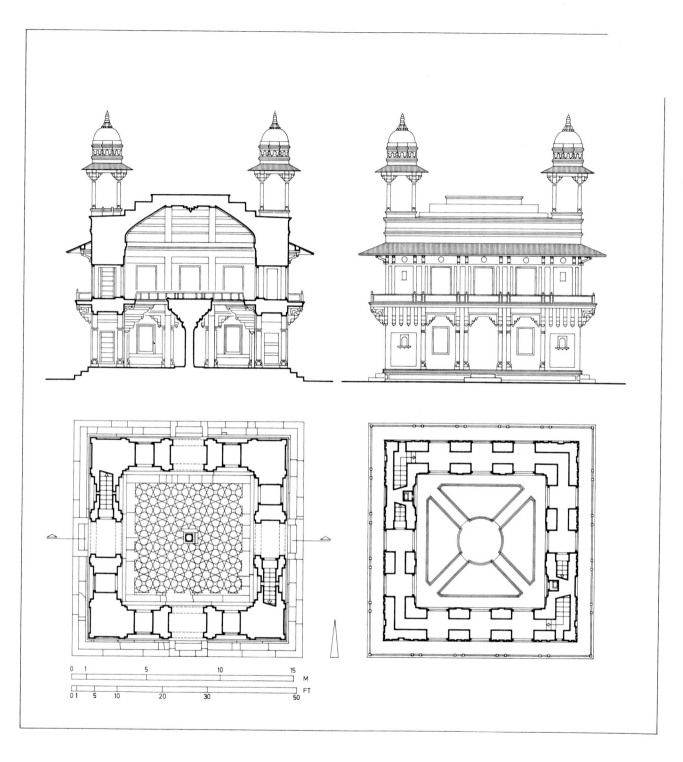

0	1		5		10		15	
								M

| 0 1 | 5 | 10 | 20 | 30 | | 50 | FT |

Diwan-i-Khas, ou salle des audiences privées de l'empereur Akbar, à Fathepour Sikri, construit en 1570. Coupe et plan du rez-de-chaussée, élévation et plan de l'étage 1:250. Sur la sorte de «champignon» érigé au centre de la salle carrée, et auquel conduisent des passerelles en diagonales, Akbar siégeait sur son trône. La coupole qui devait couronner l'édifice n'a pas été réalisée.

Fatehpur Sikri, Diwan-i-Khas (Halle für Privataudienzen) des Großmoguls Akbar, 1570. Auf einer pilzförmigen Stütze in der Mitte des quadratischen Saals befand sich der Thron Akbars, zu dem diagonal Stege führten. Die ursprünglich geplante Kuppel wurde nicht ausgeführt, Schnitt, Grundriß des Erdgeschosses, Aufriß, Grundriß des Obergeschosses 1:250.

Diwan-i Khas, private audience room of Emperor Akbar, Fatehpur Sikri, built 1570. Section and plan of the ground floor, elevation and plan of upper storey 1:250. Akbar's throne was set on a sort of 'mushroom' arrangement in the centre of the square room, approached by diagonal walkways. The dome with which the building was to be crowned was never built.

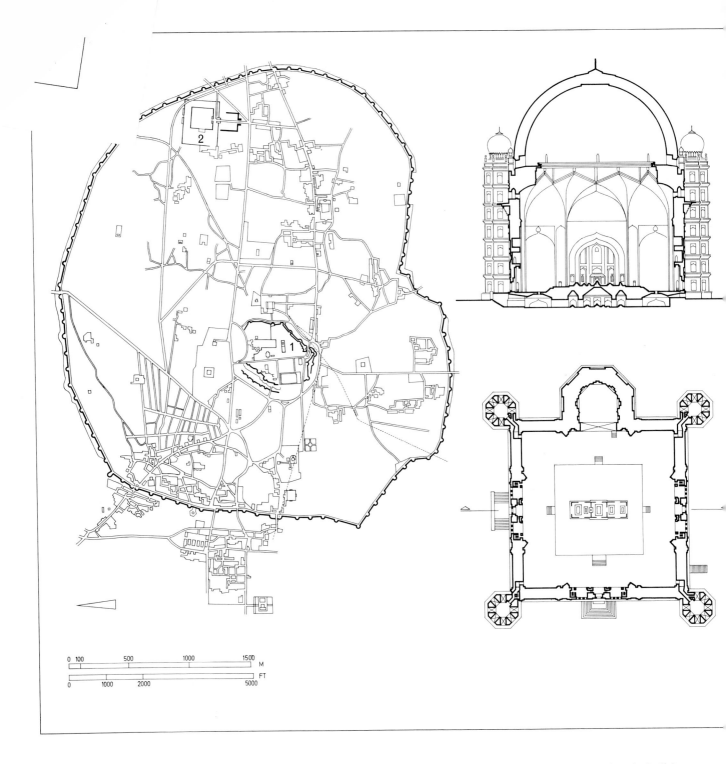

Ville de Bijapour (Inde méridionale), cité ceinte de murailles. Plan 1:30000. 1) Citadelle, 2) Gol Gumbaz. A droite, **Gol Gumbaz, mausolée du sultan Muhammad Adil Chah,** construit de 1626 à 1656. Coupe et plan 1:1000. Le Gol Gumbaz est une construction énorme, dont la coupole avoisine les dimensions de celle du Panthéon à Rome, et s'élève sur une structure carrée sans contre-butement.

Links: **Bijapur (Südindien),** durch Mauern befestigte Stadt. Stadtplan 1:30000: 1) Zitadelle, 2) Gol Gumbaz. Rechts: **Gol Gumbaz,** Grabmal des Sultans Mohammed Adil Shah, 1626–1656. Die Kuppel des gewaltigen Baus nähert sich in ihren Dimensionen denen des Pantheons; sie erhebt sich ohne Widerlagersystem über dem quadratischen Unterbau. Schnitt und Grundriß 1:1000.

Walled City of Bijapur (south India). Plan 1:30,000. 1) citadel, 2) Gol Gumbaz. Right, **Gol Gumbaz, mausoleum of Sultan Muhammad Adil Shah, Bijapur,** built 1626–56. Section and plan 1:1000. This enormous building has a dome almost as big as that of the Pantheon, Rome, supported on a square structure without buttressing.

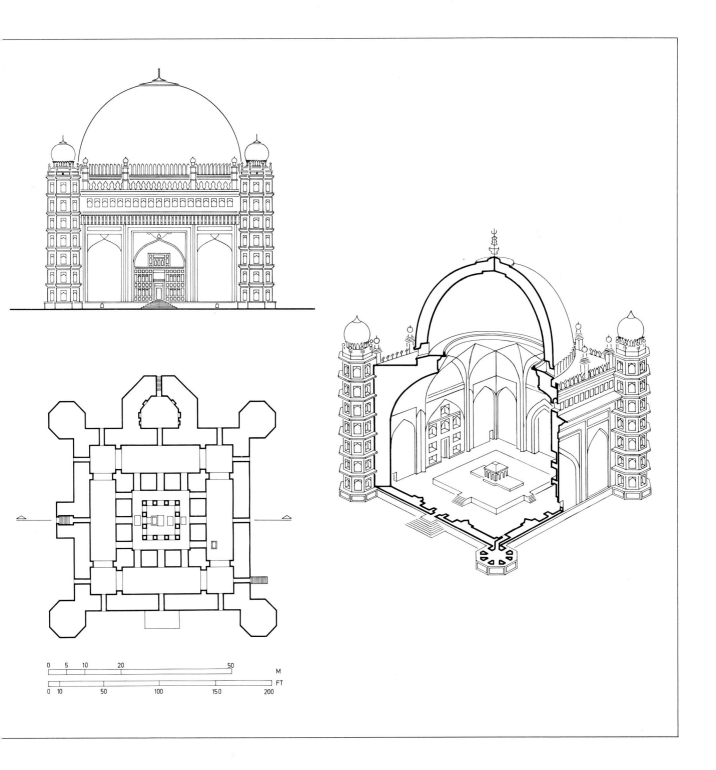

| 0 | 5 | 10 | 20 | | 50 | | M |
| 0 | 10 | | 50 | 100 | 150 | 200 | FT |

Gol Gumbaz. Elévation de la façade d'entrée, plan du sous-sol 1:1000, et axonométrie. Les tours d'angles octogonales donnent sa cohésion à l'édifice, dont le système de liaison entre le plan carré et la base circulaire de la coupole est réalisé par l'intermédiaire de nervures entrecroisées (deux carrés décalés à 45°). En sous-sol, la crypte funéraire.

Gol Gumbaz. Die oktogonalen Ecktürme verleihen dem Bau Geschlossenheit. Der Übergang vom quadratischen Unterbau zum Rund des Kuppelauflagers wird durch gekreuzte Rippen (zwei um 45° verschobene Quadrate) erreicht. Aufriß der Eingangsseite, Grundriß des Untergeschosses 1:1000; Axonometrie.

Gol Gumbaz, Bijapur. Elevation of the entrance façade, plan of the basement 1:1000, and axonometric projection. The octagonal angle towers give the building cohesion. The link between the square plan and the circular base of the dome is achieved by means of intersecting ribs (two squares, one at 45° to the other). The basement contains the burial crypt.

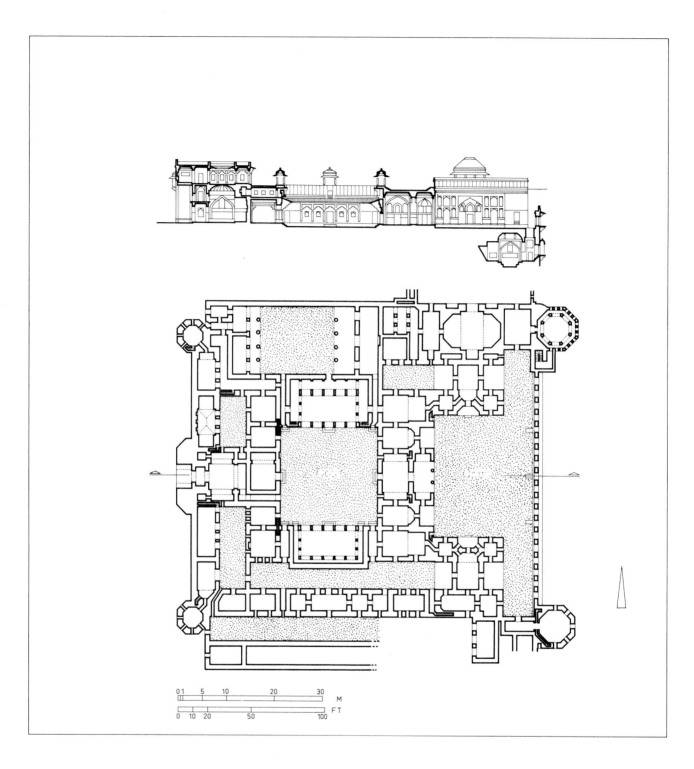

0 1 5 10   20   30
                          M
0 10 20   50   100
                          FT

Jahangiri Mahall, dans le Fort Rouge d'Agra, construit par Akbar en 1570. Coupe et plan 1:750. Portant le nom du fils d'Akbar, ce palais, par son style, rappelle la maison du rajah Birbal à Fathepour Sikri. Les pièces s'ordonnent autour des cours et non selon un plan libre comme à Fathepour Sikri. La terrasse à l'est donne sur la rive de la Jumna.

Agra, Jahangiri Mahal in der Roten Feste, 1570 unter Akbar erbaut. Der nach Akbars Sohn benannte Palast ist stilistisch dem Haus des Raja Birbal in Fatehpur Sikri ähnlich, die Räume sind aber nicht wie dort frei, sondern um Höfe angeordnet. Die Ostterrasse geht auf den Jumna. Schnitt und Grundriß 1:750.

Jahangiri Mahal, in the Red Fort, Agra, built by Akbar in 1570. Section and plan 1:750. This palace, named after Akbar's son, bears a stylistic resemblance to Rajah Birbal's house at Fatehpur Sikri. The rooms are laid out round courtyards and not on a free plan, as at Fatehpur Sikri. The east terrace opens on to the bank of the Jumna.

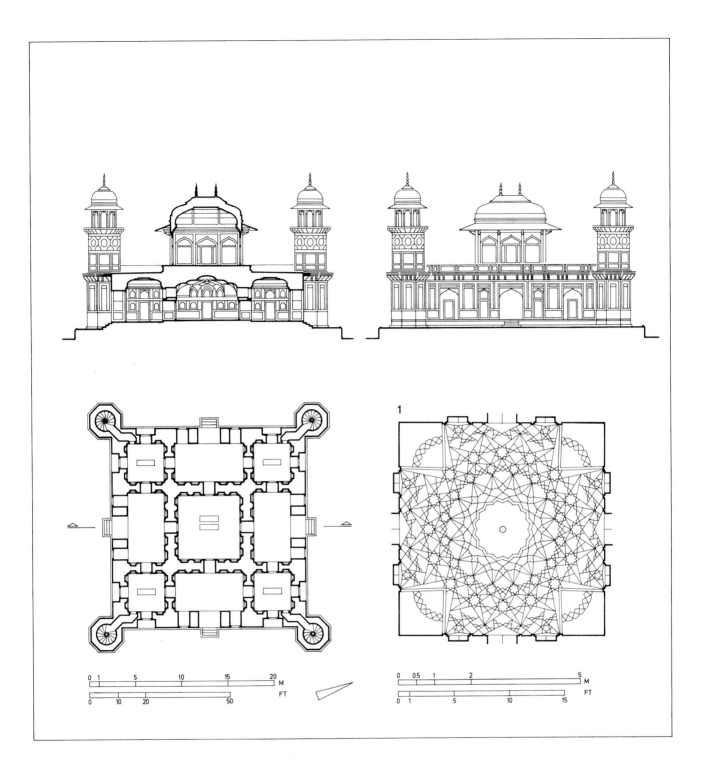

Mausolée d'Itimour-ed-Daula, à Agra, construit en 1628. Coupe, plan et élévation 1:400; en 1, le plafond de la salle funéraire 1:100. Consacré par Nour Mahall à son père Itimour-ed-Daula, trésorier et grand vizir de l'empereur, ce mausolée se dresse dans un jardin carré au bord de la Jumna. Le plan dérive d'une demeure d'habitation de l'époque, avec sa chambre haute à claires-voies.

Agra, Grabmal des Itimud-ud-daula, 1628. Das von Nur Mahal für ihren Vater Itimud-ud-daula erbaute Grabmal liegt in einem quadratischen Garten am östlichen Ufer des Jumna. Der Bau mit Dachpavillon und vergitterten Bogenöffnungen ist vom zeitgenössischen Wohnbau abgeleitet. Schnitt, Grundriß und Aufriß 1:400; 1) Decke der Grabkammer 1:100.

Mausoleum of Itimad-ud Daula, Agra, built 1628. Section, plan, and elevation 1:400. 1) ceiling of the burial chamber 1:100. The mausoleum was dedicated by Nur Mahal to her father Itimad-ud Daula, the emperor's treasurer and grand vizier. It stands in a square garden on the bank of the Jumna. The plan is derived from the contemporary dwelling-house with its high ceiling and openwork windows.

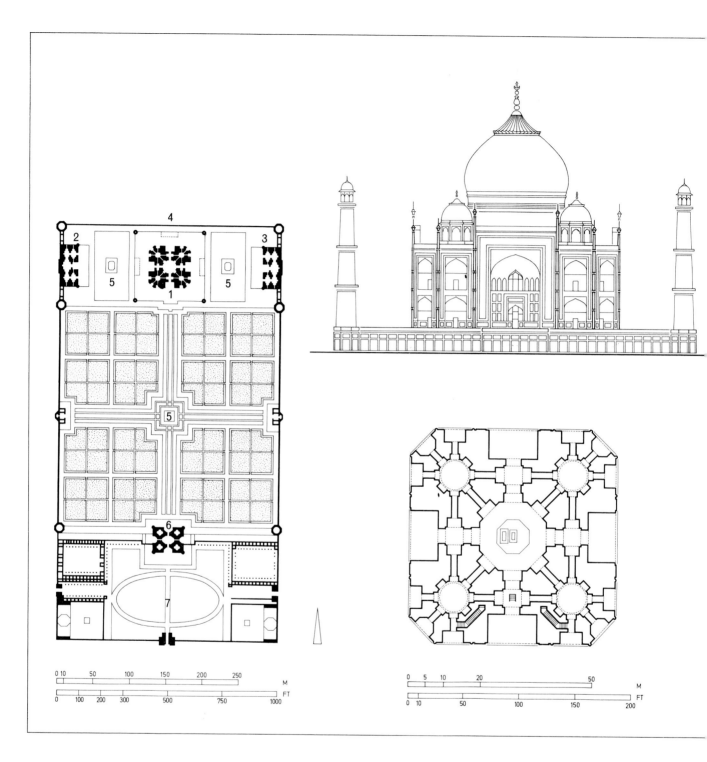

Tadj Mahall, mausolée de Moumtaz Mahall, à Agra, construit de 1632 à 1654, par le Grand Moghol Chah Jahan. Situation 1:5000. 1) Tombeau, 2) Mosquée funéraire, 3) Maison des hôtes, 4) Rivière Jumna, 5) Bassin, 6) Porte monumentale d'entrée, 7) Cour d'entrée. Elévation et plan du rez-de-chaussée du mausolée 1:1000. Edifice à plan centré, entouré de quatre minarets hauts de 45 m.

Agra, Taj Mahal, das Grabmal des Mumtaz Mahal, 1632–1654 durch den Großmogul Shah Jahan errichtet. Dem Grabbau (1), einem Zentralbau, sind vier Minaretts beigegeben. Lageplan 1:5000: 1) Grabbau, 2) Grabmoschee, 3) Gästehaus, 4) Fluß (Jumna), 5) Wasserbecken, 6) monumentaler Torbau, 7) Vorhof; Aufriß und Erdgeschoßgrundriß des Grabbaus 1:1000.

Taj Mahal, the mausoleum of Mumtaz Mahal, Agra, built 1632-54 by the Great Mogul Shah Jahan. Site plan 1:5000. 1) tomb, 2) funerary mosque, 3) guest house, 4) river Jumna, 5) pool, 6) monumental entrance gate, 7) entrance courtyard. Elevation and plan of the ground floor of the mausoleum 1:1000. The centrally-planned building is surrounded by four minarets 45 m. in height.

Tadj Mahall. Coupe et plan des couvertures 1:1000. Au-dessus de la crypte, une salle voûtée que surmonte un énorme espace aveugle situé sous le bulbe monumental du dôme supérieur. A droite, **Monument funéraire de Khan Khanan, à Delhi,** construit vers 1630. Elévation et plan 1:1000. L'architecte du Tadj Mahall s'est inspiré des façades de cet édifice légèrement antérieur.

Links: **Taj Mahal, Grabbau.** Über der Krypta ist ein gewölbter Saal, darüber eine monumentale Zwiebelkuppel mit einem riesigen Blindraum. Schnitt, Grundriß des Dachgeschosses 1:1000. Rechts: **Delhi, Grabmal des Khan Khanan,** um 1630. Der Architekt des Taj Mahal nahm Anregungen von der Fassade dieses etwas älteren Grabbaus auf. Aufriß und Grundriß 1:1000.

Taj Mahal. Section and plan of the roof 1:1000. Above the crypt is a vaulted hall and above that an enormous blind space beneath the monumental bulb of the outer dome. Right, **Funerary monument of Khan Khanan, Delhi,** built c.1630. Elevation and plan 1:1000. The architect of the Taj Mahal drew his inspiration from the façades of this slightly earlier building.

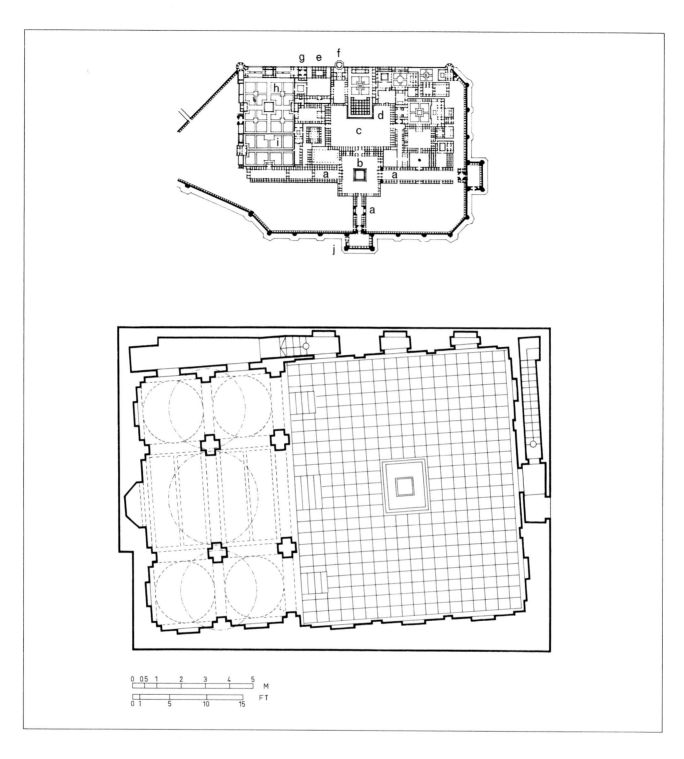

0 05 1   2   3   4   5   M

0 1   5   10   15   FT

Fort Rouge, construit à Delhi, pour Chah Jahan, en 1638. 1:10000. a) Bazar, b) Pavillon de musique, c) Cour des audiences publiques, d) Salle des audiences publiques, e) Salle des audiences privées, f) Pavillon sur la Jumna, g) Maison de bain, h) et i) Jardins, j) Entrée. En bas, **Oratoire privé de l'empereur, dit Mosquée de la Perle, au Fort Rouge de Delhi,** construit par Aurangzeb. Plan 1:150.

Oben: **Delhi, die Rote Feste,** 1638 für Shah Jahan erbaut. Plan 1:10000: a) Basar, b) Musikpavillon, c) Hof für öffentliche Audienzen, d) Halle für öffentliche Audienzen, e) Halle für Privataudienzen, f) Pavillon über dem Jumna, g) Badehaus, h) und i) Gärten, j) Eingang. Unten: **Oratorium des Kaisers (Perlenmoschee)** in der Roten Feste von Delhi, von Aurangzeb erbaut. Grundriß 1:150.

Red Fort, Delhi, built for Shah Jahan in 1638. Plan 1:10,000. a) bazaar, b) music pavilion, c) courtyard for public audiences, d) public audience room, e) private audience room, f) pavilion overlooking the Jumna, g) bath-house, h) and i) gardens, j) entrance. Below, the **Pearl mosque, Red Fort, Delhi,** the emperor's private oratory built by Aurangzeb. Plan 1:150.

Mexique ancien   Altes Mexiko   Ancient Mexico

Les civilisations précolombiennes du Mexique, malgré leurs diversités, s'élaborent sur un fonds culturel commun, dont l'homogénéité repose tant sur une parenté des systèmes religieux que sur un avancement technologique de caractère néolithique, avec apparition tardive de la métallurgie réservée essentiellement au culte et à la parure. Mais c'est l'architecture qui constitue l'élément unitaire essentiel. Partout, le lieu de culte est une pyramide. Partout, on pratique un «sport sacré», le jeu de pelote, dont les aires sont aménagées. Partout, la caste au pouvoir édifie des palais. A l'exception des Mayas (traités à part), toutes ces cultures ignorent la voûte.

Les origines de l'architecture apparaissent dès l'époque olmèque de La Venta (800 av. J.-C.) dans les régions basses du golfe, avec des monuments de terre battue. L'apogée classique éclate en revanche sur les hauts plateaux, à Teotihuacan (450 avant à 450 après J.-C.). Immenses perspectives rectilignes constituées de plates-formes et de gradins, bordées de pyramides aux faces habillées de blocs sommairement appareillés et revêtues d'une couche de stuc peint (la Pyramide du Soleil mesure 225 × 222 m et 63 m de haut, totalisant 2,5 millions de tonnes de matériaux!), palais à patios bordés de piliers sculptés et ornés de fresques jalonnent un urbanisme à croissance organique sur trame orthogonale.

Dans le Mexique moyen, la cité sacrée des Zapotèques à Monte Alban reprend à peu près les mêmes formules, avec des pyramides moins colossales, surmontées de sanctuaires en dur. Envolées de gradins et d'escaliers, esplanades, appareil parfois cyclopéen caractérisent cet art austère et puissant.

Die präkolumbischen Kulturen Mexikos entwickelten sich bei aller Verschiedenheit auf einer gemeinsamen kulturellen Basis, die sich einmal aus der Verwandtschaft der religiösen Systeme ergab, dann durch eine «neolithische» Stufe der Technik und die sehr späte Einführung der Metallbearbeitung, die ausschließlich auf Zwecke des Kults und der Schmuckherstellung beschränkt blieb. Das wesentliche einigende Element ist jedoch die Architektur. In allen präkolumbischen Kulturen hatte die Kultstätte die Form einer Pyramide; alle spielten ein «heiliges Spiel» – Pelote –, für das besondere Spielplätze angelegt wurden; überall ließ die Herrscherschicht Paläste bauen. Mit Ausnahme der Maya kannte keine der präkolumbischen Kulturen Wölbungsformen.

Die Anfänge der Architektur gehen auf die Olmeken-Zeit, auf La Venta (800 v. Chr.) zurück, auf Lehmbauten im Tiefland am Golf von Mexiko. Die klassische Blüte entfaltete sich jedoch auf der Hocheben in Teotihuacán (450 v. Chr. bis 450 n. Chr.). Gewaltige, gradlinig fluchtende Plattformen und Terrassen sind von Pyramiden mit Verkleidungen aus Steinblöcken mit bemaltem Stuck gesäumt (die Sonnenpyramide ist 63 m hoch über einer Grundfläche von 225 × 222 m; das Material, aus dem sie errichtet wurde, wiegt insgesamt 2,5 Millionen Tonnen) und von Palästen, deren Innenhöfe mit skulptierten und freskierten Säulen umgeben sind – organisch gewachsene Städte auf der Basis eines rechtwinkligen Systems.

Monte Albán, die heilige Stadt der Zapoteken, wurde nach nahezu gleichen Prinzipien angelegt, allerdings mit kleineren, von steinernen Tempeln be-

For all their diversity, the pre-Columbian civilisations of Mexico had a common cultural basis, rendered homogeneous by religious affinities on the one hand and by a 'neolithic' technology on the other, with metallurgy appearing very late and being reserved exclusively for ritual and ornamental purposes. But it was architecture that constituted the essential unifying element. For all the pre-Columbian civilisations, the place of worship was the pyramid; all of them played the 'sacred game' of pelota, which needed special courts; and in every case the ruling caste built palaces. With the exception of the Mayas, whom we shall be dealing with separately, none of these civilisations knew the vault.

The origins of Mexican architecture go back to the Olmec period of La Venta (800 B.C.) and the monuments of beaten earth erected in the low-lying Gulf regions. Its classical apogee, however, was reached in the high plateaux—at Teotihuacan, built between 450 B.C. and A.D. 450. Vast rectilinear perspectives made up of platforms and tiers are bordered by pyramids faced with roughly jointed blocks of stone and finished with a painted plaster rendering (the Pyramid of the Sun measures 225 m. by 222 m., is 63 m. high, and uses 2.5 million tons of material). Palaces with patios bordered with sculptured pillars and decorated with frescoes punctuate a town plan based on organic growth along a grid.

The sacred city of the Zapotecs at Monte Alban in central Mexico largely echoes the same formulae, with less colossal pyramids surmounted by stone sanctuaries. Flights of tiers, staircases, esplanades and, occasionally, cyclo-

Vers 800 de notre ère, des vagues d'invasions venues du nord ruinent ces cultures que remplaceront celles des Toltèques, des Mixtèques et des Totonaques. Le gigantisme des origines y fait place à une architecture plus élaborée, à des espaces internes plus importants (salles hypostyles à patio de Tula), à un décor subtil et géométrique (palais de Mitla), à des colonnades élégantes (Tajin).

Au XIIe siècle, nouvelle invasion barbare et régression qui va permettre aux Aztèques de s'imposer dans tout le Mexique au XVe siècle et de créer de vastes complexes cultuels avec pyramides, ainsi que de gigantesques palais où la salle de réception, aux dires des conquistadores, pouvait contenir 3000 personnes. Cet essor s'écroule lors du sac de Tenochtitlan par Cortès en 1525.

krönten Pyramiden. Terrassen, Treppenfluchten, Esplanaden und ein manchmal fast zyklopisches Mauerwerk sind für diese strenge, machtvolle Architektur charakteristisch.

Einfälle aus dem Norden zerstörten diese Kulturen, an deren Stelle diejenigen der Tolteken, Mixteken und Totonaken traten. Die gigantischen Bauten der Frühzeit wurden durch architektonisch ausgefeiltere mit größeren Innenräumen (Säulensäle mit Innenhof in Tula), subtilem geometrischem Dekor (Palast von Mitla) und eleganten Kolonnaden (Tajín) abgelöst.

Im 12. Jahrhundert kam es zu einer erneuten Barbareninvasion und zu einem Zerfall, der es den Azteken ermöglichte, im 15. Jahrhundert ihre Herrschaft über ganz Mexiko auszudehnen. Sie errichteten große Kultstätten mit Pyramiden, aber auch gewaltige Paläste, deren Audienzsäle nach Aussage der Konquistadoren 3000 Personen faßten. Mit der Einnahme von Tenochtitlán durch Cortéz im Jahre 1525 brach auch diese Kultur zusammen.

pean masonry characterise its austere and powerful architecture.

Waves of invasions from the north around A.D. 800 destroyed these civilisations, succeeded by those of the Toltecs, Mixtecs and Totonacs. Gigantic size gave way to a more elaborate type of architecture with more spacious interiors (the patioed hypostyle halls of Tula), delicate, geometrical decoration (the Palace at Mitla), and elegant colonnades (Tajin).

The twelfth century saw a further wave of barbarian invasion come and go, as a result of which the Aztecs were able to dominate the whole of Mexico by the fifteenth century, creating vast ritual complexes with pyramids as well as enormous palaces with reception rooms that, according to the Conquistadores, were capable of accommodating 3000 people. This final fling ended with the sack of Tenochtitlan by Cortés in 1525.

1 Le palais de Quetzalpapalotl, à Teotihuacan, datant de 250 apr. J.-C. Un patio entouré de galeries et de chambres.
2 Une pyramide zapotèque de l'esplanade sacrée à Monte Alban, édifiée vers le milieu du Ier millénaire de notre ère.
3 Le Palais des Colonnes à Mitla, œuvre mixtèque des XIe et XIIe siècles, avec ses frises en mosaïque géométrique.
4 La pyramide aztèque de Santa Cecilia, avec son temple haut (XVe siècle).

1 Teotihuacán, Palast des Quetzalpapalotl, ein von Galerien und Räumen umgebener Patio (250 n. Chr.)
2 Monte Albán, eine zapotekische Pyramide auf der Terrasse der heiligen Bergstadt (Mitte 1. Jahrtausend)
3 Mitla, mixtekischer Säulenpalast mit geometrischen Tuffsteinfriesen (11./12. Jh.)
4 Santa Cecilia, aztekische Pyramide mit bekrönendem Tempel (15. Jh.)

1 Palace of Quetzalpapalotl, Teotihuacan, A.D. 250. A patio surrounded by galleries and chambers.
2 Zapotec pyramid on the sacred esplanade, Monte Alban, built around the middle of the first millennium A.D.
3 Palace of the Columns, Mitla, an eleventh- and twelfth-century Mixtec building with geometrical friezes.
4 The Aztec pyramid of S. Cecilia with its raised temple (fifteenth century).

1

2

3

4

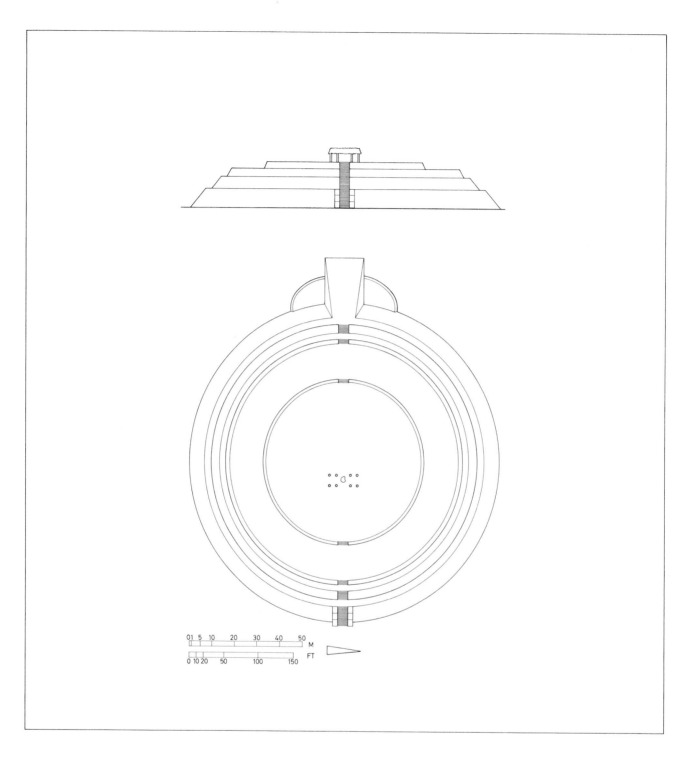

| 0 1 5 10 | 20 | 30 | 40 | 50 |
| | | | | M |

FT

| 0 10 20 | 50 | 100 | 150 |

Pyramide circulaire de Cuicuilco, sur les Hauts Plateaux, près de Mexico, datant du Ve s. avant notre ère. Elévation et plan 1:1500. Cette pyramide archaïque de 135 m de diamètre fut édifiée en deux temps, les deux degrés supérieurs remontant au IVe siècle avant notre ère. Un sanctuaire en bois et chaume la couronnait. Elle fut recouverte par l'éruption de lave du volcan Xitlé.

Cuicuilco (bei Mexico City, Meseta Central), 5.Jh.v.Chr. Die Pyramide hat an der Basis einen Durchmesser von 135 m. Sie wurde in zwei Etappen errichtet: Die beiden oberen Stufen stammen erst aus dem 4.Jh.v.Chr. Auf der Plattform befand sich ein Heiligtum aus Holz und Flechtwerk. Die Pyramide wurde bei einem Ausbruch des Vulkans Xitle verschüttet. Aufriß und Grundriß 1:1500.

Circular pyramid, Cuicuilco (near Mexico City), fifth century B.C. Elevation and plan 1:1500. The pyramid measures 135 m. in diameter and was built in two stages, the two top steps having been added in the fourth century B.C. It was originally crowned by a wood-and-thatch shrine. An eruption of the volcano Xitle buried it in lava.

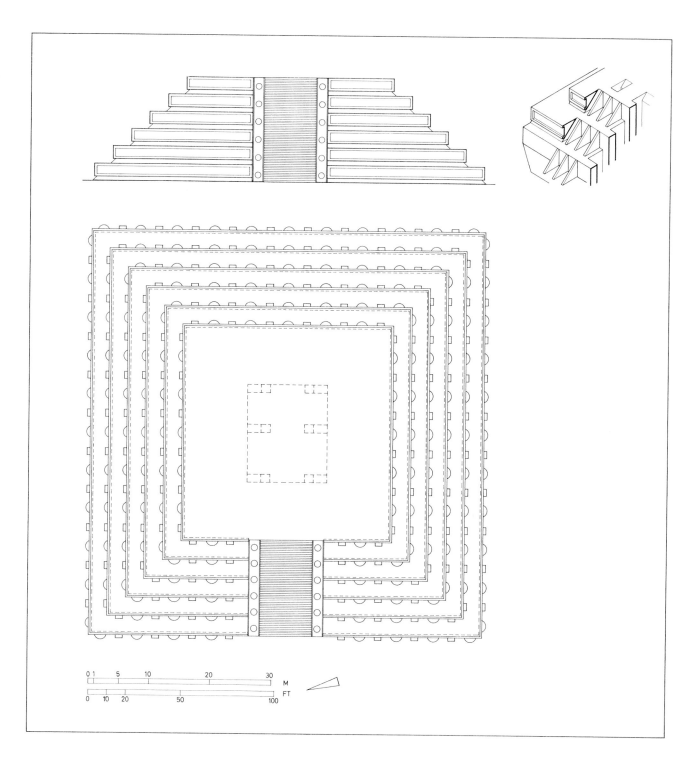

0 1	5	10	20	30 M
0	10 20	50		100 FT

Pyramide du Temple de Quetzalcoatl, à Teotihuacan, sur les Hauts Plateaux, au nord de Mexico, datant de 50 à 100 apr. J.-C. Elévation et plan 1:600 et détail de construction. Les échiffres et les panneaux en gradins sont ornés de gueules du Serpent à Plume et de masques du dieu Tlaloc, symbole de la pluie. Au sommet, un sanctuaire en matériaux périssables a disparu.

Teotihuacán (nördlich Mexico City, Meseta Central), Quetzalcoatl-Pyramide, 50–100 n.Chr. Treppenrampen und Tafelfüllungen der Stufen sind mit dem Kopf der Gefiederten Schlange und der Maske des Regengottes Tlaloc geschmückt. Der Tempel auf der Pyramide war aus vergänglichem Material und ist nicht erhalten. Aufriß und Grundriß 1:600; Konstruktionsdetail.

Pyramid of the temple of Quetzalcoatl, Teotihuacan (near Mexico City), A.D. 50–100. Elevation and plan 1:600; detail of the construction. The string walls and tiered panels are decorated with Plumed Serpent heads and masks of the god Tlaloc, symbol of rain. The shrine on top was built of perishable materials and has not survived.

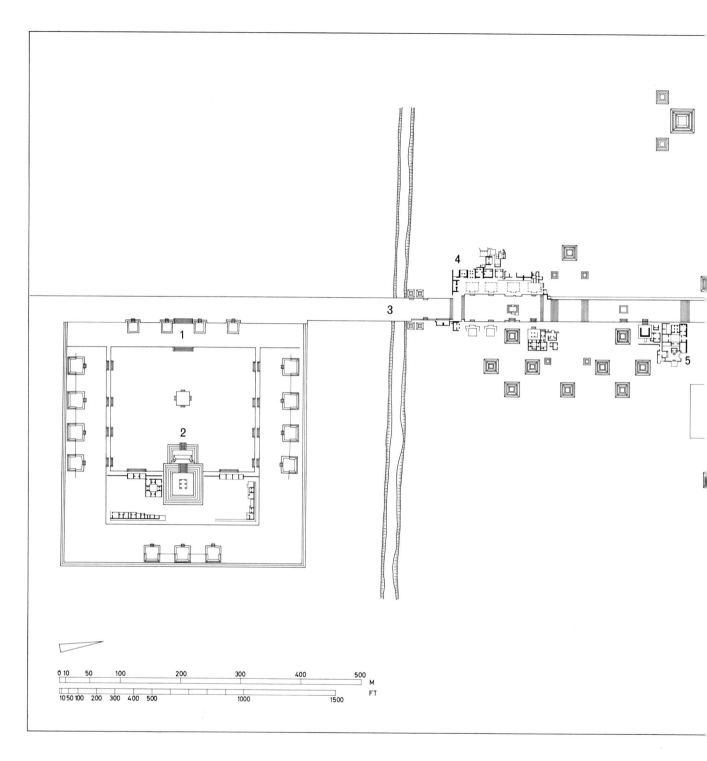

Ensemble cultuel de Teotihuacan, près de Mexico, état au IIIe ou IVe s. de notre ère. Plan général 1:6000. 1) Enceinte de la Citadelle, 2) Temple de Quetzalcoatl, 3) Allée des Morts, 4) Ensemble dit du Souterrain, 5) Groupe Viking, 6) Complexe de la Pyramide du Soleil, 7) Place des Colonnes, 8) Palais de Quetzalpapalotl, 9) Place de la Lune, 10) Pyramide de la Lune. Urbanisme organique et orthogonal.

Teotihuacán, Kultzentrum («Stadt der Götter»), Zustand im 3./4.Jh.n.Chr. Eine organische Anlage im rechtwinkligen System. Lageplan 1:6000: 1) Umfassung der Zitadelle, 2) Quetzalcoatl-Pyramide, 3) Totenstraße, 4) «Subterraneo»-Gruppe, 5) «Viking»-Gruppe, 6) Sonnenpyramide, 7) Säulenplatz, 8) Palast des Quetzalpapalotl, 9) Mondplatz, 10) Mondpyramide.

Teotihuacan: the sacred complex as it was in the third or fourth centuries A.D. Overall plan 1:6000. 1) La Ciudadela, 2) temple of Quetzalcoatl, 3) avenue of the Dead, 4) the 'underground' complex, 5) the Viking group, 6) Sun pyramid complex, 7) plaza of the Columns, 8) palace of Quetzalpapalotl, 9) plaza of the Moon, 10) pyramid of the Moon. An organic, rectangular piece of town-planning.

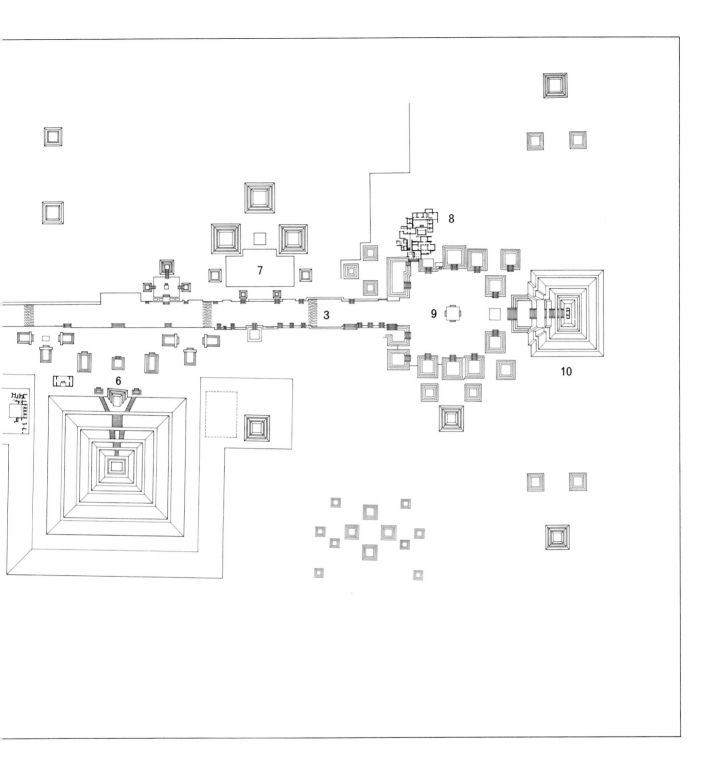

Le principe original qui régit la croissance de cet **Ensemble cultuel de Teotihuacan** se fonde sur des éléments symé-
triques agencés dans une asymétrie générale. Cette formule autorise un agrandissement urbain constant par des adjonctions qui se greffent sur l'Allée des
Morts comme sur un tronc principal.

Die Anlage des **Kultbezirks von Teotihuacán** beruht auf der Vereinigung von
symmetrischen Elementen zu einem
asymmetrischen Ganzen. Dieses System
ermöglichte eine stetige Erweiterung
durch Quartiere, die der Totenstraße
wie einer durchgehenden Hauptader zu-
geordnet sind.

The growth of the **sacred complex in
Teotihuacan** was originally due to symmetrical elements being fitted together
asymmetrically. By adding elements that
are grafted on the avenue of the Dead,
thus resembling a tree-trunk, this principle makes for constant urban growth.

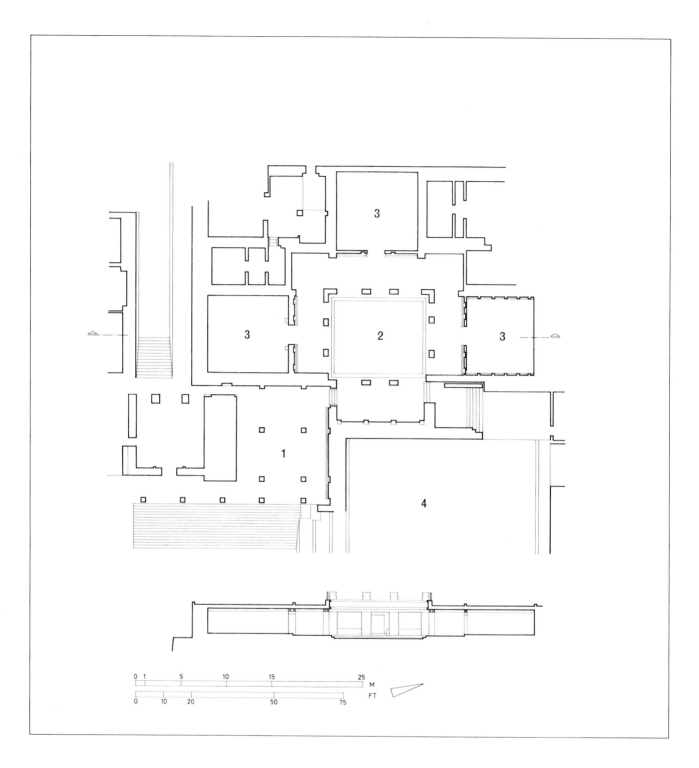

Palais de Quetzalpapalotl, à Teotihuacan, datant de 250 apr. J.-C. Plan et coupe 1:400. 1) Vestibule hypostyle, 2) Patio, 3) Chambres d'habitation, 4) Plateforme de la Place de la Lune. Cette habitation typique à patio, qui a fait l'objet d'une anastylose exemplaire, doit remonter à la période d'apogée de Teotihuacan.

Teotihuacán, Palast des Quetzalpapalotl, 250 n.Chr. Der charakteristische Wohnpalast mit Patio entstand vermutlich zur Blütezeit von Teotihuacán. Er wurde vorbildlich rekonstruiert. Grundriß 1:400: 1) Pfeilervorhalle, 2) Patio, 3) Wohnräume, 4) Plattform am Mondplatz; Schnitt 1:400.

Palace of Quetzalpapalotl, Teotihuacan, A.D. 250. Plan and section 1:400. 1) hypostyle vestibule, 2) patio, 3) living quarters, 4) platform of the plaza of the Moon. This typical patioed dwelling, on which an exemplary theoretical reconstruction has been done, must date from the heyday of Teotihuacan.

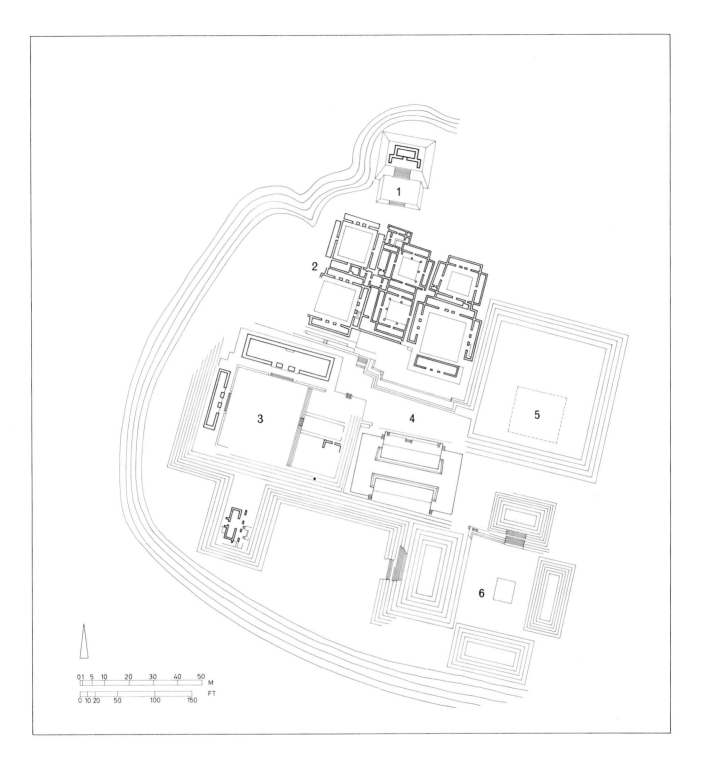

Cité de Yagul, dans le Mexique Moyen, près d'Oaxaca, état au IXᵉ–Xᵉ s. de notre ère. Plan 1:1500. 1) Pyramide nord, 2) Quartier des palais, 3) Grand patio occidental, 4) Jeu de pelote, 5) Soubassement du patio oriental, 6) Patio méridional. Outre un jeu de pelote très bien conservé, Yagul présente une organisation des palais en quadrilatères qui annonce celle de Mitla.

Yagul (bei Oaxaca, Mittelmexiko), Zustand im 9./10. Jh. n. Chr. In Yagul hat man außer einem sehr gut erhaltenen Ballspielplatz auch Paläste gefunden, deren vierseitige Anordnung bereits die Palastform von Mitla ankündigt. Stadtplan 1:1500: 1) Nordpyramide, 2) Palastbezirk, 3) Großer Westhof, 4) Ballspielplatz, 5) Unterbau des Ostplatzes, 6) Südplatz.

City of Yagul (near Oaxaca, central Mexico), as it was in the ninth and tenth centuries A.D. Plan 1:1500. 1) north pyramid, 2) palace quarter, 3) great west patio, 4) tlachtli or ball court, 5) base of the east patio, 6) south patio. In addition to a very well-preserved ball-court, Yagul is distinguished by a quadrilateral palace layout that anticipates that of Mitla.

Ensemble cultuel de Monte Alban, près d'Oaxaca, dans le Mexique Moyen, vers le milieu du Iᵉʳ millénaire de notre ère. Plan général de l'esplanade 1:1750. 1) Plate-forme sud, 2) Temple dit «Système M», 3) Palais des «Danzantes», 4) Temple dit «Système IV», 5) Observatoire, 6) Complexe central, 7) Edifice «S», 8) Jeu de pelote, 9) Grand escalier de la plate-forme nord, 10) Quadrilatère nord, 11) Pyramide «A», 12) Complexe nord de quatre pyramides.

Monte Albán (bei Oaxaca, Mittelmexiko), Kultzentrum, um Mitte des 1. Jahrtausends n. Chr. Um die Bauten der zapotekischen Bergstadt Monte Albán errichten zu können, mußte man die Kuppe des drei Täler beherrschenden Berges abtragen. Auf allen Pyramiden standen steinerne Tempel, deren Holzdecken nicht erhalten sind. Die unterirdischen Grabkammern sind mit steinernen Platten gedeckt.

Sacred complex of Monte Alban (near Oaxaca, central Mexico), built around the middle of the first millennium A.D. Overall plan of the esplanade 1:1750. 1) south platform, 2) 'System M' temple, 3) palace of the 'Danzantes', 4) 'System IV' temple, 5) observatory, 6) central complex, 7) 'S' building, 8) ball-court, 9) great stairway of the north platform, 10) north quadrangle, 11) 'A' pyramid, 12) northern complex of four pyramids.

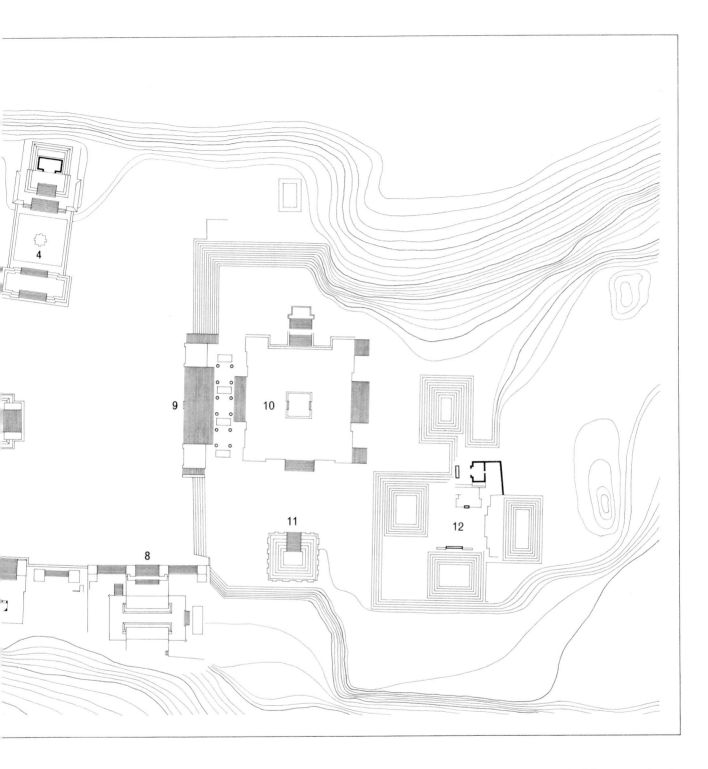

Pour bâtir les édifices couronnant **l'acropole zapotèque de Monte Alban,** il a fallu araser la colline qui domine la jonction de trois vallées. Toutes les pyramides étaient surmontées de sanctuaires construits en dur, dont la couverture a disparu. Elle était réalisée en rondins. En sous-sol, une série de sépultures à couverture de dalles.

Monte Albán, Kultzentrum. Lageplan 1:1750: 1) südliche Plattform, 2) Heiligtum, System «M», 3) Palast der «Danzantes», 4) Heiligtum, System «IV», 5) Observatorium, 6) Mittelbau, 7) Gebäude «S», 8) Ballspielplatz, 9) große Treppe zur nördlichen Plattform, 10) Nordplatz, 11) Pyramide «A», 12) Nordkomplex mit vier Pyramiden.

To construct the buildings crowning the **Zapotec 'acropolis' of Monte Alban** it was necessary to flatten off the top of the hill, which dominates the junction of three valleys. All the pyramids were topped with stone shrines, the log roofs of which have disappeared. Below ground was a series of slab-roofed tombs.

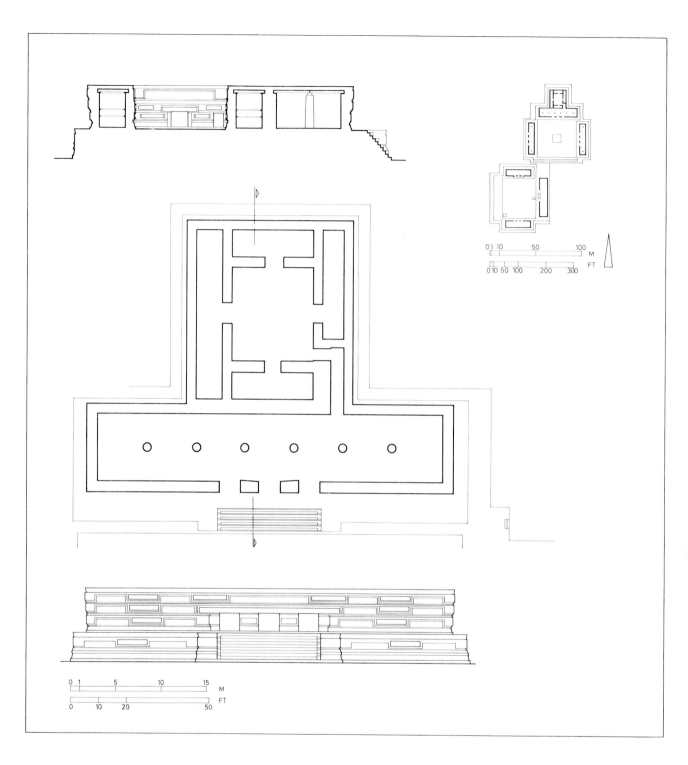

Palais de Colonnes à Mitla, dans le Mexique Moyen. Coupe transversale, plan et élévation de la façade 1:400, situation 1:4000. Par ses frises à motifs géométriques, réalisées en mosaïque de tuf, par l'apparition de colonnes monolithiques dans la grande salle et par son patio, ce palais mixtèque, datant des XIe et XIIe s., marque l'éclosion d'un style original.

Mitla (Mittelmexiko), Säulenpalast, 11. u. 12. Jh. Dieser Mixtekenpalast bezeichnet mit seinen geometrischen, mosaikartig gefügten Tuffsteinfriesen, mit den Monolith-Säulen im großen Saal und dem Patio das Erblühen eines Stils von großer Eigenart. Querschnitt, Grundriß, Aufriß der Fassade 1:400; Lageplan 1:4000.

Palace of the Columns, Mitla (near Oaxaca, central Mexico), a Mixtec palace built in the eleventh and twelfth centuries. Cross section, plan, and front elevation 1:400; site plan 1:4000. The friezes with their geometrical motifs done in tuff mosaic, the patio and the use of monolithic columns in the great hall all mark the emergence of an original Mixtec style.

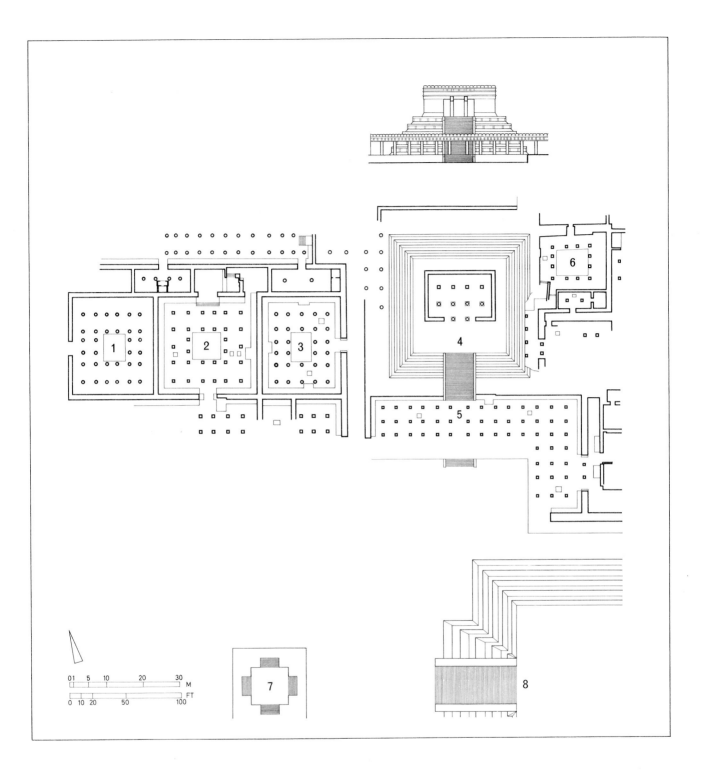

Complexe central de Tula, capitale des Toltèques des Hauts Plateaux, aux IXᵉ et Xᵉ s. Elévation restituée de la pyramide «B» ou Temple de Tlahuizcalpantecuhtli et plan des édifices fouillés 1:1000. 1) à 3) Salles hypostyles à patio, 4) Pyramide «B», 5) Vestibule hypostyle à patio, 6) Petite salle hypostyle à patio, 7) Adoratoire central, 8) Pyramide principale «C». Apparition des hypostyles à vastes espaces internes.

Tula, zentrale Gebäudegruppe. Tula war im 9. und 10. Jh. Hauptstadt der Tolteken. Erstes Auftreten von Hypostylen mit großem innerem Freiraum. Rekonstruierter Aufriß der Pyramide «B» (Tempel des Tlahuizcalpantecuhtli), Grundriß der ausgegrabenen Bauten 1:1000: 1) bis 3) Säulensäle mit Patio, 4) Pyramide «B», 5) Säulenvorhalle, 6) kleiner Säulensaal mit Patio, 7) zentrale Kultplattform, 8) Hauptpyramide «C».

Central complex of Tula, the capital of the High Mesa Toltecs in the ninth and tenth centuries. Reconstructed elevation of 'B' pyramid or temple of Tlahuizcalpantecuhtli and plan of the excavated buildings 1:1000. 1–3) patioed hypostyle halls, 4) 'B' pyramid, 5) hypostyle vestibule, 6) small hypostyle hall with patio, 7) central place of worship, 8) main or 'C' pyramid. These were the first hypostyles creating vast interiors.

421

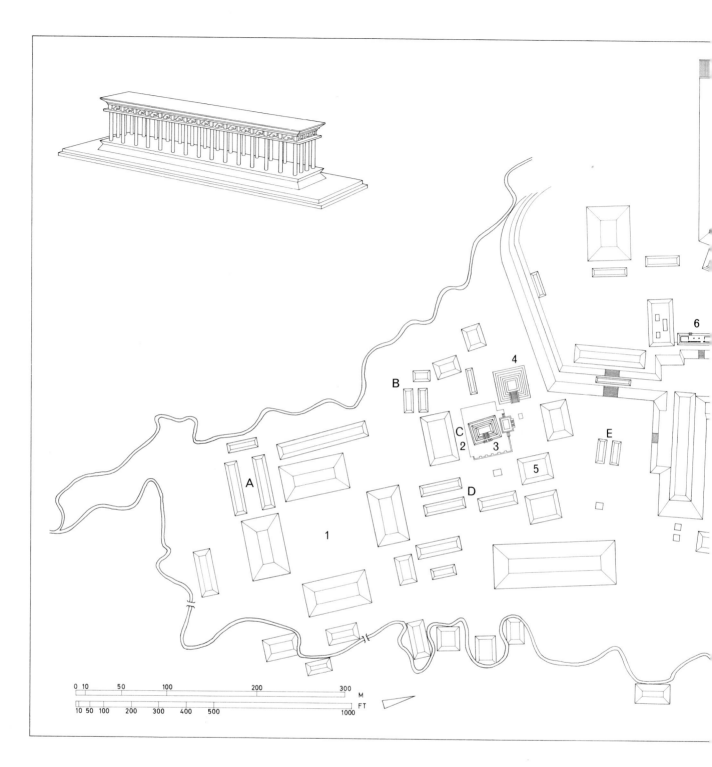

Ensemble cultuel du Tajin, dans le Golfe, capitale des Totonaques entre le IIe et le VIIe s. de notre ère. Plan général 1:4000; en vignette à gauche, restitution de l'**Edifice «Q» à colonnettes.** 1) Place du Ruisseau, 2) Jeu de pelote aux bas-reliefs, 3) Pyramides N° 5 et N° 2, 4) Pyramide des Niches, 5) Edifice N° 3, 6) Place du Tajin Chico, 7) Edifice «C», 8) Edifice «B», 9) Edifice «A», 10) Edifice «Q», 11) Pyramide de l'acropole, A)–H): huit jeux de pelote.

El Tajín, Kultbezirk. El Tajín war vom 2. bis 7. Jh. Hauptstadt der Totonaken. Lageplan 1:4000: 1) Bachplatz, 2) Ballspielplatz mit Flachreliefs, 3) Pyramiden «5» und «2», 4) Nischenpyramide, 5) Gebäude «3», 6) Platz des Tajín Chico, 7) Gebäude «C», 8) Gebäude «B», 9) Gebäude «A», 10) Gebäude «Q», 11) Pyramide auf der Akropolis, A) bis H) Ballspielplätze. Oben links: **Säulenbau «Q»,** Rekonstruktion.

Sacred complex, Tajin (near the Gulf coast), the Totonac capital between the second and seventh centuries A.D. Overall plan 1:4000. Inset left, reconstruction of **'Q' building with its small columns.** 1) plaza of the Stream, 2) ball court with bas-reliefs, 3) no. 5 and no. 2 pyramids, 4) pyramid of the Niches, 5) no. 3 building, 6) Tajin Chico plaza, 7) 'C' building, 8) 'B' building, 9) 'A' building, 10) 'Q' building, 11) acropolis pyramid, A to H) eight ball-courts.

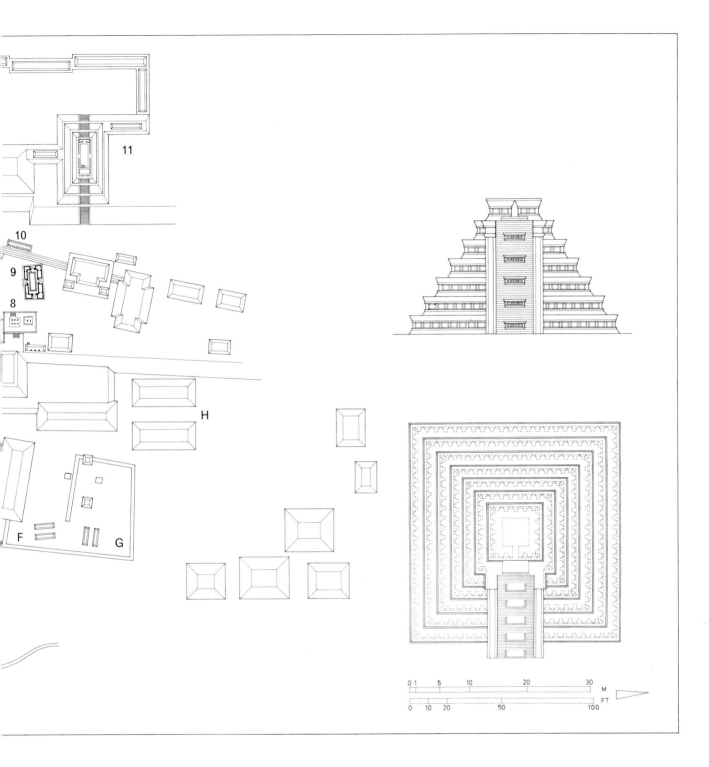

0 1	5	10		20		30	
---	---	---	---	---	---	---	M
0	10	20		50		100	FT

L'ensemble du Tajin, non loin du golfe du Mexique, est encore incomplètement fouillé et recèle des dizaines de pyramides ensevelies. A droite, grande **Pyramide des Niches.** Elévation et plan 1:600. L'édifice comporte au total 365 niches, symboles des jours de l'année solaire. Au sommet, une chambre devait exister, réalisée en dur, et mesurant environ 5×5 m.

El Tajín, Kultzentrum. Der Kultbezirk ist erst zum Teil ausgegraben, es sind noch zahlreiche Pyramiden freizulegen. Rechts: **Nischenpyramide.** Die 365 Nischen der großen Pyramide symbolisieren die Tage des Sonnenjahres. Auf der oberen Plattform muß sich ein steinerner Tempel von 5 × 5 m befunden haben. Aufriß und Grundriß 1:600.

The **Tajin complex,** which has not yet been excavated completely, includes dozens of buried pyramids. Right, the huge **Pyramid of the Niches.** Elevation and plan 1:600. The building has a total of 365 niches, symbolising the days of the solar year. At the top there must have been a stone chamber measuring about 5 m².

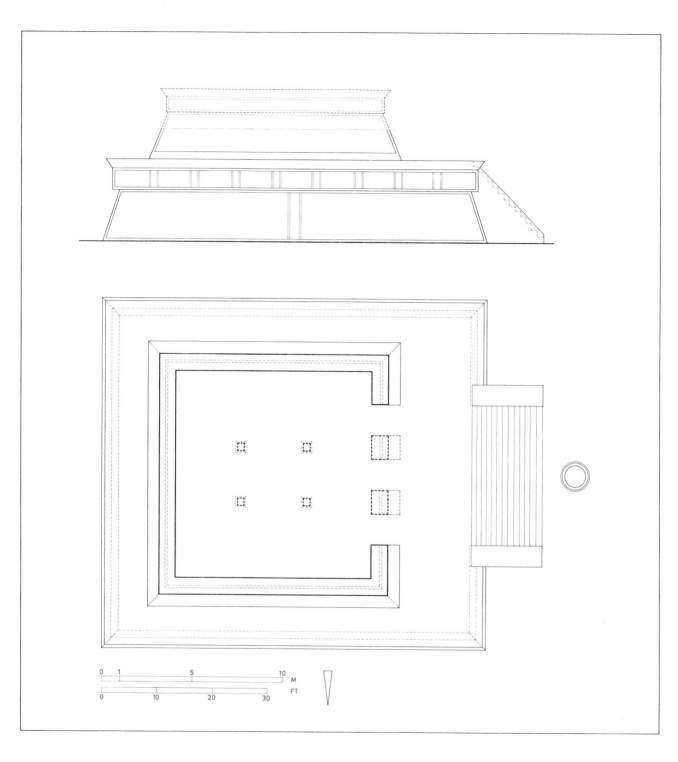

Pyramide du Serpent à Plumes, à Xochi-calco (Hauts Plateaux), datant des VIIIᵉ–IXᵉ s. Elévation latérale et plan 1:200. Ainsi nommée en raison des bas-reliefs qui font le tour du degré in-férieur, cette pyramide devait présenter un sanctuaire en dur, couvert de ma-driers, qui est reconstitué ici en éléva-tion. Cette culture assure le relais entre les civilisations classiques et le monde chichimèque et aztèque.

Xochicalco, Pyramide der Gefiederten Schlange (Quetzalcoatl-Pyramide), 8. bis 9. Jh. Die Pyramide trägt ihren Na-men nach den Schlangenkopf-Reliefs der unteren Stufe. Auf ihrer Plattform stand ein steinerner Tempel mit Bohlendecke (im Aufriß rekonstruiert). Diese Kultur verbindet die alten Kulturen mit denen der Chichimeken und Azteken. Aufriß einer Seite, Grundriß 1:200.

Plumed Serpent pyramid, Xochicalco (south of Mexico City), eighth to ninth century. Side elevation and plan 1:200. The pyramid received its name from the bas-reliefs running round the lower step. It must have had a stone shrine roofed with planks (reconstructed in the ele-vation). This civilisation provided the link between the ancient civilisations and the Chichimec and Aztec worlds.

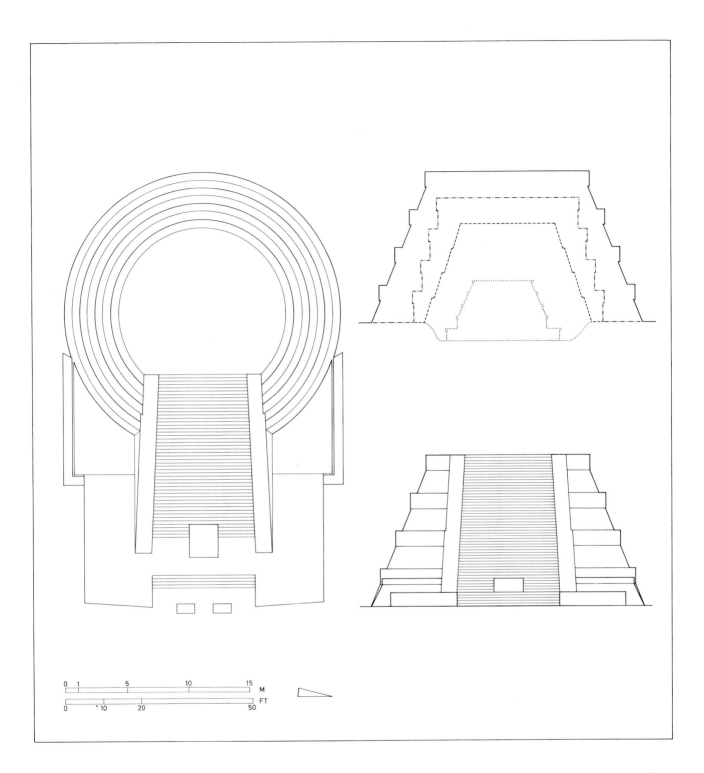

Pyramide circulaire de Calixtlahuaca, datant de l'époque aztèque (XIVe et XVe s.). Plan du dernier état, coupe montrant les superpositions successives et élévation du dernier état 1:300. A la fin du monde précolombien, on retrouve la forme circulaire qui existait à l'aube de la civilisation, à Cuicuilco, deux millénaires plus tôt. Cette pyramide est dédiée au dieu du Vent.

Calixtlahuaca, Rundpyramide, aztekische Zeit (14. u. 15. Jh.). Am Ende der präkolumbianischen Epoche taucht die Rundpyramide wieder auf, die es bereits 2000 Jahre früher in Cuicuilco gegeben hatte. Die Pyramide ist dem Windgott geweiht. Grundriß (letzter Zustand), Schnitt mit den verschiedenen Bauschichten, Aufriß (letzter Zustand) 1:300.

Circular pyramid, Calixtlahuaca, Aztec period (fourteenth and fifteenth centuries). Plan of the final state, section showing the successive superpositions, and elevation of the final state 1:300. At the end of the pre-Columbian period men rediscovered the circular form that had been used at Cuicuilco two millennia before. This pyramid is dedicated to the wind god.

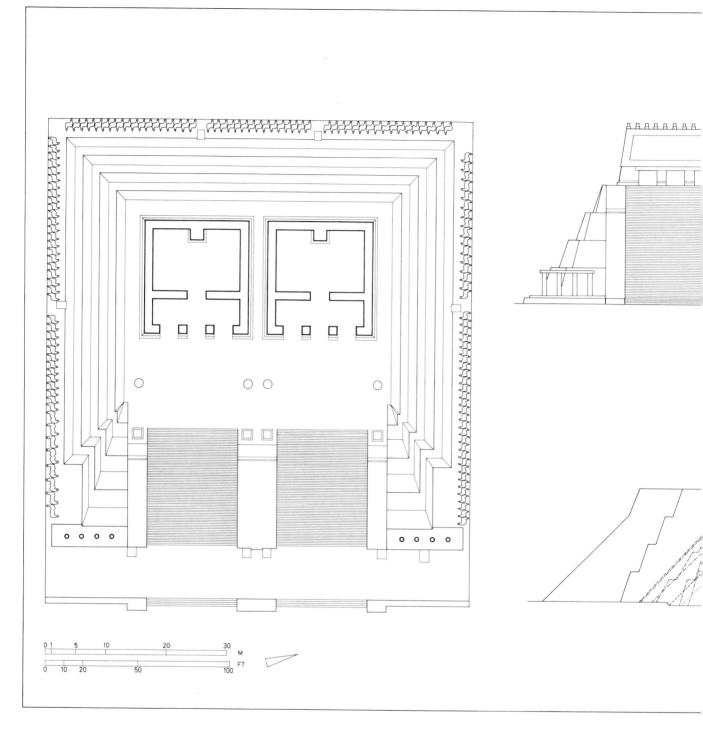

Pyramide double de Tenayuca, près de Mexico, sur les Hauts Plateaux, cité qui fut d'abord la capitale des Chichimèques, puis passa aux mains des Aztèques. Etats successifs entre le XIIIe et le XVIe s., plan des sanctuaires jumeaux, élévation avec sanctuaires restitués et coupe montrant les six superpositions 1:600. Autour de la pyramide court un cordon de serpents en hautrelief.

Tenayuca (Meseta Central), Doppeltempel-Pyramide, 13. u. 16. Jh. (mehrere Bauphasen). Tenayuca war zunächst Hauptstadt der Chichimeken und fiel dann an die Azteken. Um die Pyramide läuft eine Einfassung aus steinernen Schlangen. Grundriß mit Doppeltempel, Aufriß mit Rekonstruktion der Tempel, Schnitt mit Angabe der sechs übereinanderliegenden Schichten 1:600.

Double pyramid, Tenayuca (near Mexico City). Originally the Chichimec capital, Tenayuca later passed into the hands of the Aztecs. It was built in stages between the thirteenth and sixteenth centuries. Plan of the twin shrines; elevation with the shrines reconstructed; and section showing the six superpositions 1:600. A band of serpents carved in high relief runs round the pyramid.

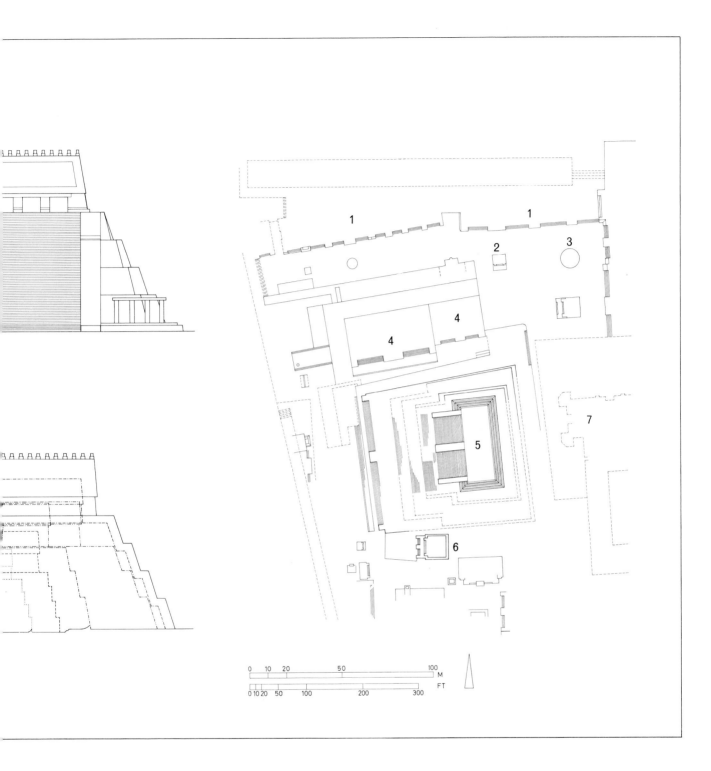

Ensemble cultuel aztèque de Tlatelolco, à Mexico, datant des XVe et XVIe s. Plan général 1:2000. 1) Plates-formes bordées d'escaliers, 2) Petites pyramides annexes, 3) Plate-forme gladiatoire, 4) Pyramides secondaires à double escalier, 5) Pyramide principale avec superpositions multiples, 6) Pyramide du Calendrier, 7) Emplacement de l'église de Santiago Tlatelolco.

Tlatelolco, Aztekisches Kultzentrum, 15. u. 16. Jh. Lageplan 1:2000: 1) Plattformen mit Treppen, 2) kleine Nebenpyramiden, 3) Plattform für Gladiatorenkämpfe, 4) Nebenpyramiden mit Doppeltreppen, 5) Hauptpyramide (mehrere übereinandergesetzte Bauschichten), 6) Kalenderpyramide, 7) Kirche Santiago Tlatelolco.

Aztec sacred complex, Tlatelolco (Mexico City), fifteenth and sixteenth centuries. Overall plan 1:2000. 1) platforms edged with stairways, 2) small outlying pyramids, 3) gladiators' platform, 4) secondary pyramids with double stairways, 5) main pyramid with multiple superpositions, 6) Calendar pyramid, 7) Site of the church of Santiago Tlatelolco.

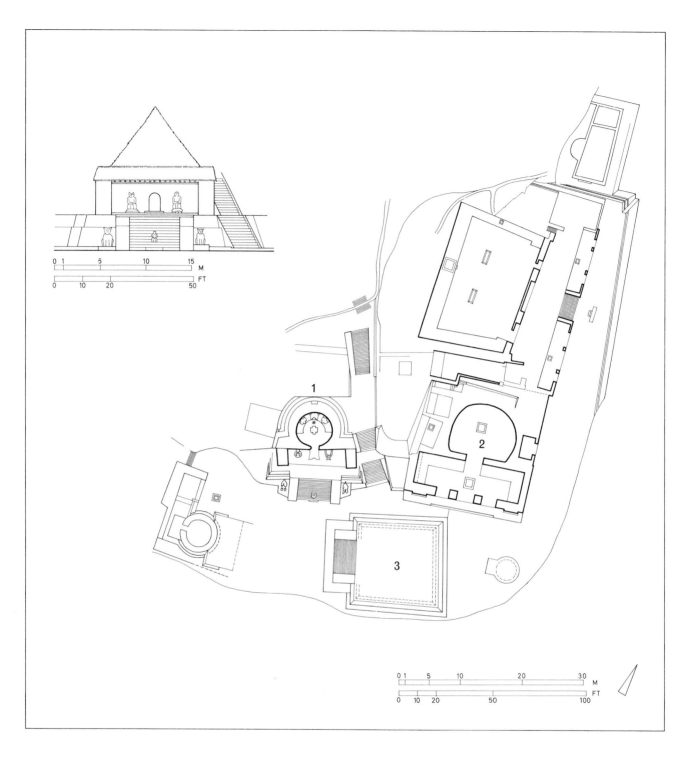

Centre cultuel de Malinalco, près de Toluca (Hauts Plateaux), ensemble aztèque en grande partie rupestre, datant de la fin du XVe s. Elévation du temple circulaire des Aigles et des Jaguars 1:400, disposition des principaux édifices 1:600. 1) Temple rupestre des Aigles et des Jaguars, 2) Second sanctuaire circulaire, 3) Pyramide de plan carré, édifiée en deux degrés.

Malinalco (bei Toluca, Meseta Central), Kultzentrum, Ende 15.Jh. Große Teile der aztekischen Anlage wurden aus dem Fels gehauen. Aufriß des Rundtempels der Adler und Jaguare 1:400; Lageplan der wichtigsten Bauwerke 1:600: 1) Felsentempel der Adler und Jaguare, 2) zweiter Rundtempel, 3) zweistufige quadratische Pyramide.

Sacred complex, Malinalco (near Toluca), an Aztec complex dating from the late fifteenth century, much of it carved out of the rock. Elevation of the circular temple of the Eagles and Jaguars 1:400; layout of the principal buildings 1:600. 1) rock temple of the Eagles and Jaguars, 2) second circular shrine, 3) two-stepped pyramid on a square plan.

Monde maya

Maya

The Mayas

Parmi les civilisations mésoaméricaines dont les vestiges précolombiens nous sont parvenus, celle des Mayas est la plus avancée du point de vue architectural. Dans la zone méridionale du Mexique (Yucatan et Peten), au Guatémala et dans le nord du Honduras, des cités se sont développées par centaines dans la forêt vierge ou la brousse tropicale.

Les principaux édifices mayas sont les pyramides et les palais; mais on se gardera d'oublier les jeux de pelote, les bains, les observatoires astronomiques et même les fortifications tardives. Le trait spécifique de l'architecture maya réside dans l'utilisation d'une fausse voûte en encorbellement qui reproduit, à l'intérieur des édifices, l'espace des huttes de chaume et de torchis dans lesquelles vivent encore les populations indiennes. Grâce à l'utilisation d'un mortier de chaux, pour lier un blocage analogue à un béton rudimentaire, ces couvertures voûtées, qui présentent des faces orthogonales à l'extérieur, constituent de véritables toitures monolithiques dont la masse énorme surplombe les salles. Ces dernières sont de proportions modestes, eu égard à l'immensité de certains palais qui dépassent 90 m de façade (Palais du Gouverneur à Uxmal). Une vaste frise à décor géométrique court autour des édifices.

Les pyramides, qui peuvent atteindre 45 m de haut, présentent des escaliers très abrupts permettant d'accéder à un temple haut. Contrairement aux pyramides égyptiennes, la pyramide maya – comme celles du Mexique en général – supporte un sanctuaire. La découverte en 1952 par Alberto Ruz d'une crypte funéraire dans la Pyramide des Inscriptions de Palenque a permis de constater

Unter allen präkolumbischen mittelamerikanischen Kulturen, von denen uns Spuren erhalten sind, ist in architektonischer Hinsicht die Maya-Kultur am weitesten entwickelt. Im Süden Mexikos (Yucatán, Petén), in Guatemala und Nordhonduras entstanden Hunderte von Städten im Urwald oder im tropischen Busch.

Pyramiden und Paläste sind die wichtigsten Maya-Bauten, doch dürfen darüber die Ballspielplätze, Bäder, Observatorien und auch die Festungen der Spätzeit nicht vergessen werden. Die besondere Eigenart der Maya-Architektur liegt in der Verwendung eines Kraggewölbes, durch das im Innern der Steinbauten Räume von gleichem Charakter entstanden wie in den Steinhütten und Adobebauten, in denen die Indio-Bevölkerung heute noch lebt. Dank der Verwendung von Kalkmörtel zum Binden der Bruchsteine (ähnlich einem rudimentären Beton) bilden diese Gewölbe, die nach außen rechtwinklig erscheinen, monolithische Überdachungen, die schwer auf den Innenräumen lasten. Im Verhältnis zu den Ausmaßen mancher Paläste mit Fassaden von mehr als 90 m (Gouverneurspalast in Uxmal) sind die Innenräume recht klein. Ein breiter Fries mit geometrischem Dekor läuft um den Bau.

Bei den bis zu 45 m hohen Pyramiden führen steile Treppen zu einem bekrönenden Tempel. Im Unterschied zu ägyptischen Pyramiden tragen die der Maya – und alle übrigen mexikanischen – einen solchen Tempel. Die Entdeckung einer Grabkammer in der Inschriftenpyramide von Palenque 1952 durch Alberto Ruz zeigt, daß manche Pyramiden der Maya Grabbauten sind.

Of all the pre-Columbian civilisations of Central America of which traces have come down to us, the most advanced in terms of architecture was that of the Mayas. In the southern part of Mexico (Yucatan and Peten), in Guatemala, and in northern Honduras, hundreds of cities have been uncovered in the primeval forest and the tropical bush.

The Mayas mainly built pyramids and palaces, but their pelota courts, baths, astronomical observatories, and even their belated fortifications are not to be ignored. The distinctive feature of Mayan architecture was a false, corbelled vault that gave their interiors the same shape as the straw and adobe huts the Indians still live in today. Thanks to their use of lime mortar (not unlike a rudimentary form of concrete) to bind rubble-work, these vaulted roofs, which from outside are all rectangular faces, present a truly monolithic appearance as they rise massively above the halls of palaces and other buildings. The halls themselves are of modest dimensions when one thinks of the size of certain palaces, with façades more than 90 m. in length (the Governor's Palace at Uxmal). Vast friezes of geometrical decoration run round these buildings.

The pyramids, some of which are as high as 45 m., have very steep staircases leading up to a raised temple. Unlike their Egyptian counterparts, Mayan pyramids—indeed, Mexican pyramids in general—support a shrine. The discovery by Alberto Ruz of a burial crypt in the Pyramid of Inscriptions at Palenque in 1952 was evidence that certain Mayan pyramids served as tombs.

Major Mayan cities dating from the so-called Old Empire (second century

que certaines pyramides mayas servaient parfois de tombeaux.

Parmi les grandes cités mayas, il faut mentionner, pour la période dite de l'Ancien Empire (IIe s. av. J.-C. au VIIe s. apr. J.-C.), Uaxactun, Tikal, Copan et Palenque, ainsi que, pour la période dite du Nouvel Empire (VIe au Xe siècle), Uxmal, Kabah, Sayil et la partie ancienne de Chichen Itza. Cette dernière ville deviendra le centre d'une remarquable renaissance après l'invasion toltèque de 987. Jusqu'en 1185 de notre ère, elle donnera le jour à une architecture de vastes salles hypostyles (Mille Colonnes du Temple des Guerriers).

Unter den großen Maya-Städten des sogenannten Alten Reiches (2. vorchristliches bis 7. nachchristliches Jahrhundert) sind Uaxactun, Tikal, Copan und Palenque zu nennen, unter denen des Neuen Reiches (6. bis 10. Jahrhundert) Uxmal, Kabah, Sayil und der alte Teil von Chichén Itzá. Diese Stadt wurde nach dem Tolteken-Einfall 987 zum Zentrum einer bemerkenswerten Renaissance; bis 1185 baute man dort gewaltige Säulensäle (Tausend Säulen des Kriegertempels).

B.C. to seventh century A.D.) include Uaxactun, Tikal, Copan, and Palenque; the New Empire (sixth to tenth century) produced, among others, Uxmal, Kabah, Sayil, and the old part of Chichen Itza. The last-named city was to become the centre of a remarkable renaissance following the Toltec invasion of 987. Between then and 1185 it produced an architecture of vast hypostyle halls (the Thousand Columns of the Temple of the Warriors).

1 Façade latérale de la Maison des Tortues, à Uxmal, œuvre caractéristique du style «puuc» du Yucatan (IXe siècle).
2 La Pyramide des Inscriptions à Palenque, dans le Chiapas, dans laquelle fut découverte une crypte funéraire. L'édifice date de 692.
3 L'entrée du Temple des Guerriers, à Chichen Itza, avec les deux serpents à l'effigie du dieu Kukulkan, œuvre de la civilisation maya-toltèque, au XIe siècle.

1 Uxmal, Seitenansicht des Schildkrötenhauses; ein charakteristisches Beispiel des Puuc-Stils in Yucatán (9. Jh.)
2 Palenque, Inschriftenpyramide; Archäologen entdeckten darin eine Grabkammer (692)
3 Chichén Itzá, Eingang des Kriegertempels, zu beiden Seiten die Gefiederte Schlange, Bild des Gottes Kukulkan (Maya-Tolteken-Bau, 11. Jh.)

1 Lateral façade of the House of the Turtles, Uxmal, a typical example of the 'puuc' style of Yucatan (ninth century).
2 Pyramid of Inscriptions, Palenque (Chiapas), in which archaeologists discovered a burial crypt. The building dates from A.D. 692.
3 Entrance to the Temple of Warriors, Chichen Itza, with its twin serpents in the image of the god Kukulcan, built by the Maya-Toltec civilisation in the eleventh century.

1

2

3

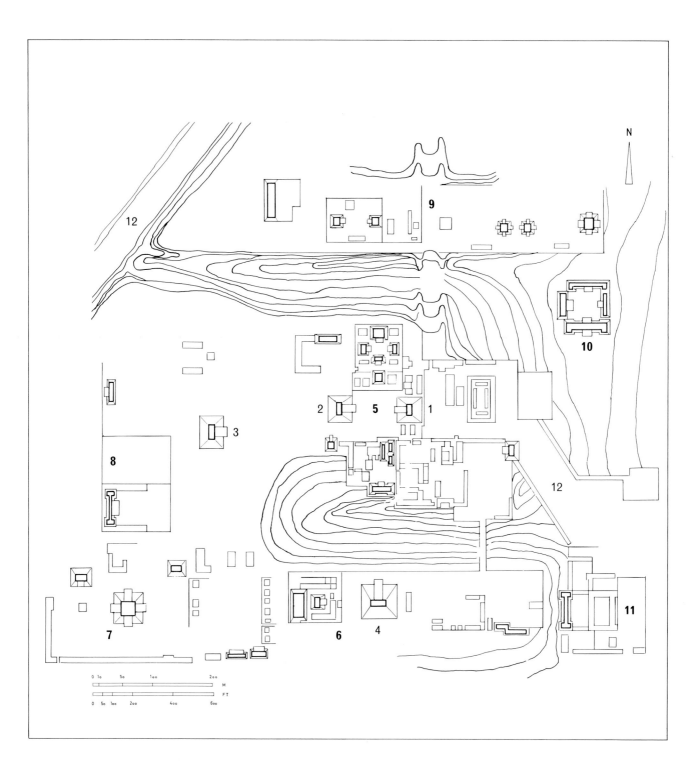

Cité de Tikal, dans le Peten (Guatémala), état vers le VIIᵉ s., avant la décadence maya. Plan général 1:6000. 1) Temple I, 2) Temple II, 3) Temple III, 4) Temple V, 5) Groupe A, 6) Groupe B, 7) Groupe C, 8) Groupe D, 9) Groupe E, 10) Groupe F, 11) Groupe G, 12) Grandes routes. C'est le centre cérémoniel, mesurant environ 1 km², que présente ce plan. Une organisation orthogonale.

Tikal (Petén, Guatemala), Zustand im 7. Jh. vor dem Niedergang der Maya. Das in rechtwinkligem System angelegte Kultzentrum der Stadt bedeckt etwa 1 km². Lageplan 1:6000: 1) Tempel I, 2) Tempel II, 3) Tempel III, 4) Tempel V, 5) Gruppe A, 6) Gruppe B, 7) Gruppe C, 8) Gruppe D, 9) Gruppe E, 10) Gruppe F, 11) Gruppe G, 12) Hauptstraßen.

Tikal (Peten, Guatemala), as it was in the seventh century before the decline of Mayan civilisation. Overall plan 1:6000. 1) temple I, 2) temple II, 3) temple III, 4) temple V, 5) group A, 6) group B, 7) group C, 8) group D, 9) group E, 10) group F, 11) group G, 12) main roads. The plan shows the ceremonial centre of the city, which was rectangular in layout and covered about 1 km².

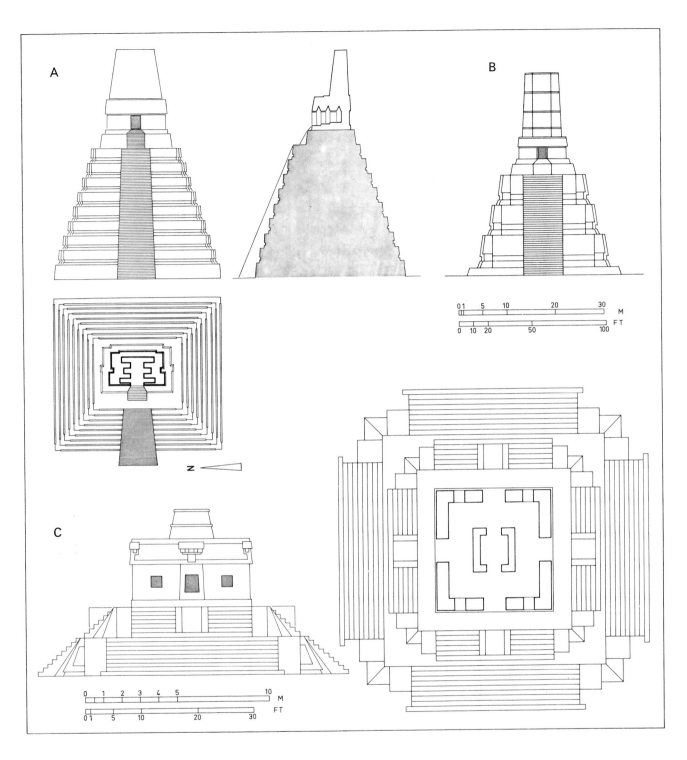

A) **Temple I de Tikal,** pyramide à degrés surmontée d'un sanctuaire à cresteria, haute de 47 m et datant du Vᵉ s. de notre ère. Elévation, coupe et plan 1:750. **B) Temple II de Tikal.** Elévation 1:750. La pente des pyramides mayas est très raide, le sanctuaire supérieur exigu. C) **Temple I de Dzibilchaltun,** au Yucatan (Mexique), vers 485 apr. J.-C., structure à plan centré. Elévation et plan 1:200.

A) **Tikal, Tempel I,** 5. Jh. n. Chr. Stufenpyramide, auf der Plattform Tempel mit Cresteria. Aufriß, Schnitt und Grundriß 1:750. B) **Tikal, Tempel II.** Die Maya-Pyramiden sind steil, der krönende Tempel ist eng. C) **Dzibilchaltun (Yucatán, Mexiko), Tempel I,** um 485 n. Chr. Der Bau ist zentriert, die vier Seiten gleichen sich. Aufriß und Grundriß 1:200.

A) **Temple I, Tikal,** fifth century A.D., a 47 m. high stepped pyramid topped by a roof-combed shrine. Elevation, section and plan 1:750. **B) Temple II, Tikal.** Elevation 1:750. C) **Temple I of Dzibilchaltun** (Yucatan, Mexico), a centrally planned structure dating from A.D. c.485. Elevation and plan 1:200.

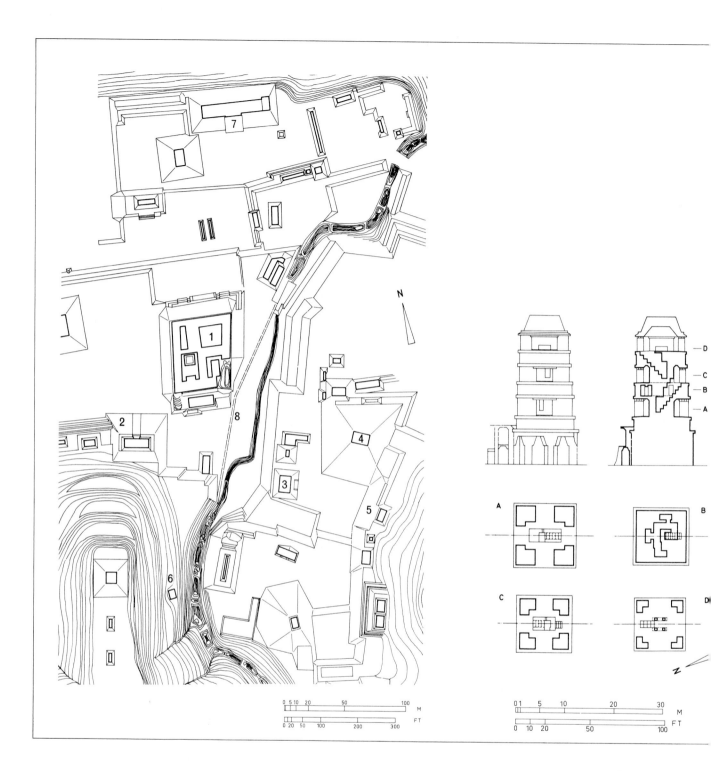

Cité de Palenque, dans le Chiapas (Mexique). Plan général 1:3000. L'essor de cette ville se situe aux VIIᵉ et VIIIᵉ s. 1) Grand Palais, 2) Pyramide des Inscriptions, 3) Temple du Soleil, 4) Temple de la Croix, 5) Temple de la Croix Feuillue, 6) Temple du Beau Relief, 7) Temples nord, 8) Aqueduc. A droite, **Tour du Grand Palais**. Elévation, coupe et plans des étages 1:750.

Links: **Palenque** (Chiapas, Mexiko), Blütezeit der Stadt im 7. und 8.Jh. Lageplan 1:3000: 1) Großer Palast, 2) Inschriftenpyramide, 3) Sonnentempel, 4) Kreuztempel, 5) Tempel des Brabanter Kreuzes (Blattkreuzes), 6) Tempel des Schönen Reliefs, 7) Nordtempel, 8) Äquadukt. Rechts: **Palenque, Turm des Großen Palastes**. Aufriß, Schnitt und Grundrisse 1:750.

Palenque (Chiapas, Mexico), a city that had its heyday in the seventh and eighth centuries. Overall plan 1:3000. 1) Great palace, 2) pyramid of Inscriptions, 3) temple of the Sun, 4) temple of the Cross, 5) temple of the Leafy Cross, 6) temple of the Beautiful Relief, 7) north temples, 8) aqueduct. Right, **Tower of the Great palace**. Elevation, section, and plans of the storeys 1:750.

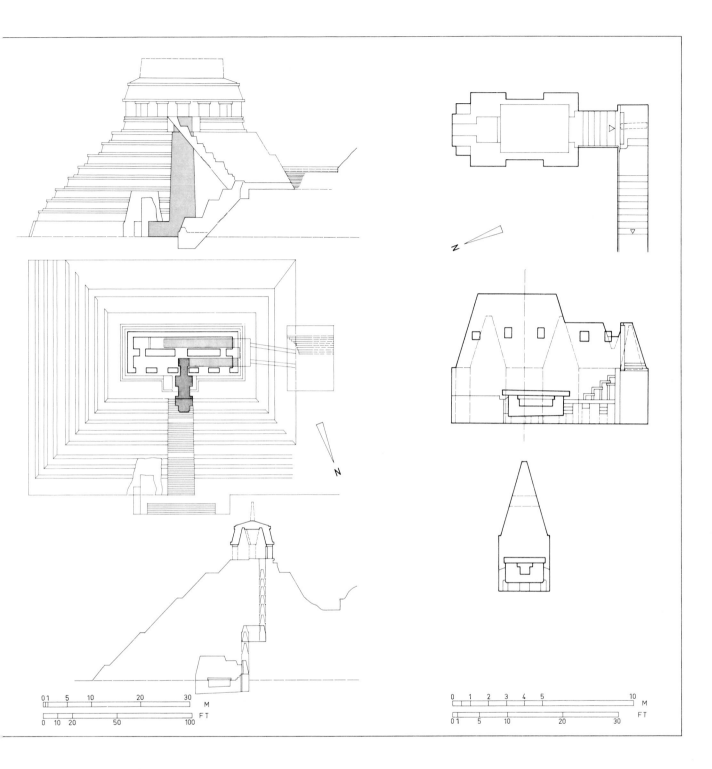

Pyramide des Inscriptions, à Palenque, datant de 692 apr. J.-C. Elévation ouverte, plan et coupe montrant la situation de la crypte funéraire voûtée en encorbellement et des escaliers d'accès 1:750. A droite, **Détail de la Crypte** de la Pyramide des Inscriptions. Plan, coupe longitudinale et coupe transversale 1:200. La découverte de cette crypte en 1952 a révolutionné l'archéologie maya.

Links: **Palenque, Inschriftenpyramide,** 692. Die Entdeckung der Grabkammer dieser Pyramide im Jahr 1952 hat die Maya-Forschung revolutioniert. Aufriß mit Teilschnitt, Grundriß, Schnitt mit gewölbter Krypta und Treppen 1:750. Rechts: **Grabkammer der Inschriftenpyramide.** Grundriß, Längsschnitt und Querschnitt 1:200.

Pyramid of Inscriptions, Palenque, A.D. 692. Open elevation, plan and section (1:750) showing the positions of the corbel-vaulted burial crypt and the stairways. Right, **Detail of the crypt** of the pyramid of Inscriptions. Plan, longitudinal section, and cross section 1:200. The discovery of this crypt in 1952 revolutionised Mayan archeology.

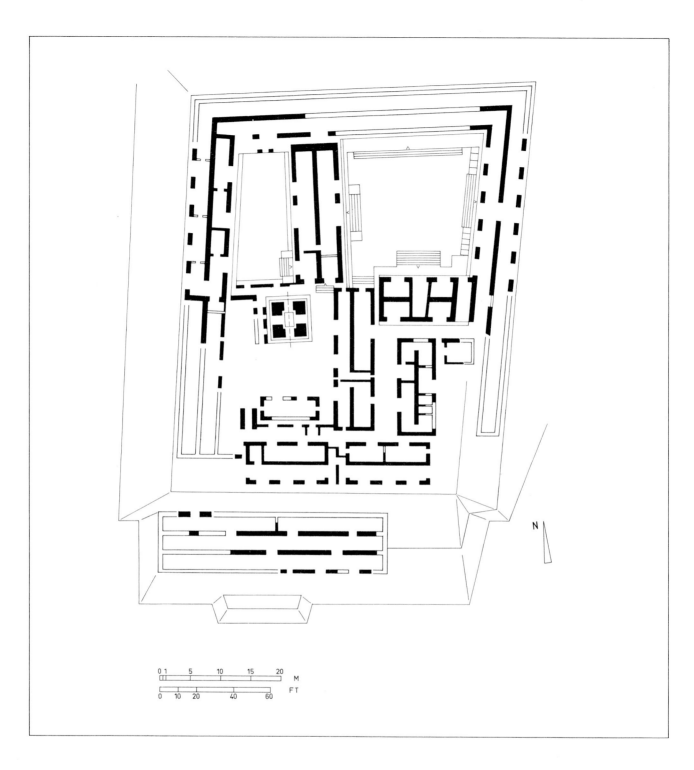

Grand Palais de Palenque, datant de 672 apr. J.-C. Plan 1:600. Cet édifice, bâti sur une esplanade artificielle dans laquelle s'enfoncent des galeries souterraines, est composé de trois patios entourés de couloirs et de portiques. Au centre, la position de la Tour qui avait peut-être une fonction astronomique. Certaines parties du palais devaient être habitées.

Palenque, Großer Palast, 672. Der auf einer künstlichen Terrasse mit unterirdischen Gängen errichtete Bau umfaßt drei Innenhöfe, um die Gänge und Portiken führen. Im Zentrum der Turm, der vielleicht astronomischen Zwecken diente. Teile des Palastes waren sicher bewohnt. Grundriß 1:600.

Great palace, Palenque, c. A.D. 672. Plan 1:600. The palace stands on an artificial esplanade containing underground galleries. It consists of three patios surrounded by corridors and porticoes. Centre, site of the tower, which may have served as an astronomical observatory. Certain parts of the palace must have been inhabited.

Cité d'Uxmal, au Yucatan (Mexique), dont l'apogée se situe du VIIIᵉ au Xᵉ s. Plan d'ensemble 1:6000. Contrairement au Peten et au Chiapas où le déclin débute au VIIIᵉ s., le Yucatan voit éclore une architecture monumentale jusqu'au Xᵉ s. 1) Palais du Gouverneur, 2) Maison des Tortues, 3) Pyramide du Devin, 4) Quadrilatère des Nonnes, 5) Quadrilatère des Colombes, 6) Grande Pyramide, 7) Temple sud-ouest, 8) Pyramide de la Vieille.

Uxmal (Yucatán, Mexiko). Blütezeit der Stadt vom 8. bis 10. Jh. Während in Petén und Chiapas der Niedergang bereits im 8. Jh. einsetzte, schufen die Maya in Yucatán noch bis ins 10. Jh. herrliche Bauten. Lageplan 1:6000: 1) Gouverneurspalast, 2) Schildkrötenhaus, 3) Pyramide des Zauberers, 4) «Nonnenkloster», 5) «Taubenbau», 6) Große Pyramide, 7) Südwesttempel, 8) Pyramide der Alten Frau.

Uxmal (Yucatan, Mexico), which had its heyday in the eighth to tenth century. Overall plan 1:6000. Unlike Peten and Chiapas, which began to decline in the eighth century, Yucatan enjoyed a florescence of monumental architecture until the tenth century. 1) Governor's palace, 2) house of the Turtles, 3) pyramid of the Magician, 4) Nunnery quadrangle, 5) quadrangle of the Pigeons, 6) Great pyramid, 7) south-west temple, 8) pyramid of the Old Woman.

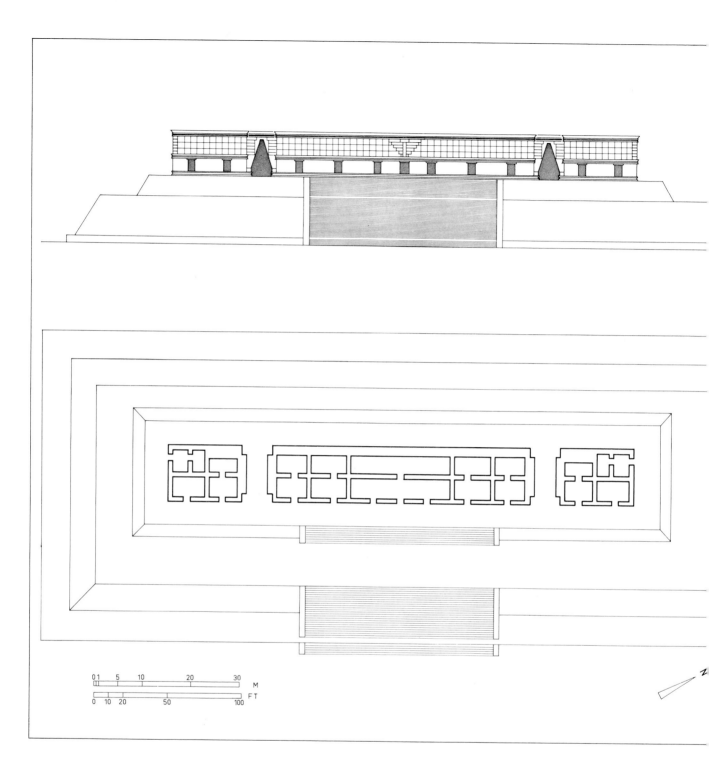

Palais du Gouverneur, à Uxmal, datant des VIIIe–IXe s. Elévation et plan 1: 750. Construit sur deux énormes soubassements artificiels que gravit une volée d'escaliers monumentaux, l'édifice long de 100 m présente un corps central flanqué de deux ailes reliées par des arcs mayas typiques. Les chambres sont voûtées en encorbellement. L'appareil sert de coffrage à un béton rudimentaire.

Uxmal, Gouverneurspalast, 8.–9. Jh. Das 100 m lange Gebäude steht auf einem mächtigen zweistufigen Unterbau. Eine breite Treppe führt zum Mitteltrakt, der durch typische Maya-Bögen mit den Flügelbauten verbunden ist. Kraggewölbe überspannen die Räume. Das Mauerwerk dient als Schalung für eine Art primitiven Beton. Aufriß und Grundriß 1:750.

Governor's palace, Uxmal, eighth to ninth century. Elevation and plan 1:750. Built on two enormous artificial platforms climbed by a flight of monumental stairways, this 100 m. long palace comprises a central corps with two wings, linked by typically Mayan arches. The interiors are corbel-vaulted. The stonework provided shuttering for a rudimentary form of concrete.

438

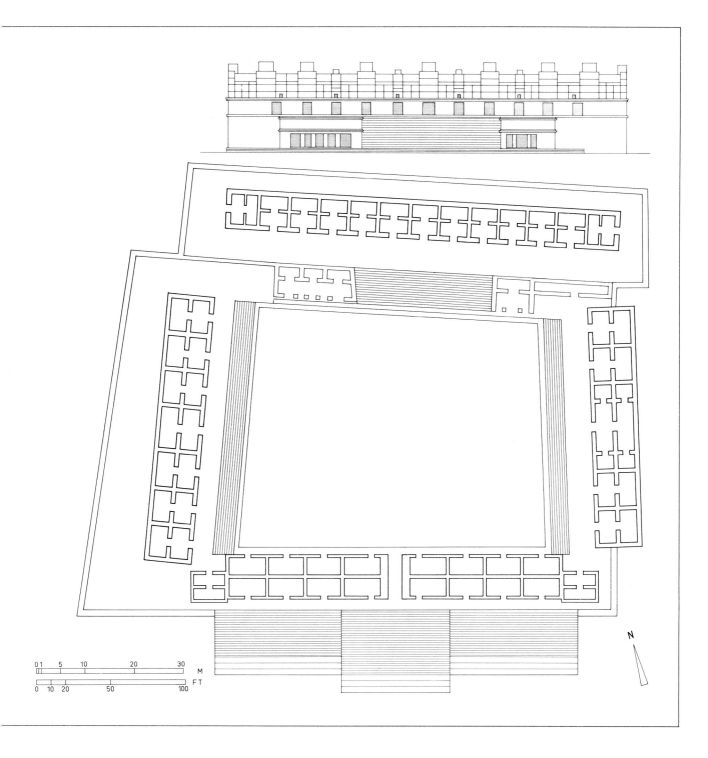

Quadrilatère des Nonnes, à Uxmal, datant de 909. Elévation du palais septentrional et plan d'ensemble 1:750. Composition monumentale à angles ouverts, fondée sur des édifices longs auxquels conduisent de larges escaliers monumentaux, le Quadrilatère des Nonnes doit son nom aux premiers explorateurs. Comme le Palais de Gouverneur, les édifices présentent de grandes frises à décor géométrique.

Uxmal, «Nonnenkloster», 909. Die mächtige, an den Ecken offene Anlage ist aus langgestreckten Bauten gebildet, zu denen breite Treppen führen. Sie verdankt ihren Namen den ersten Forschern, die die Stadt untersuchten. Wie der Gouverneurspalast sind auch diese Bauten mit breiten geometrischen Friesen geschmückt. Aufriß des Nordtrakts, Grundriß der Gesamtanlage 1:750.

Nunnery quadrangle, Uxmal, built 909. Elevation of the north palace and overall plan 1:750. This vast composition with open corners is based on long buildings approached by monumental stairways. It was named by the first explorers. Like the Governor's palace, it is decorated with large geometrical friezes.

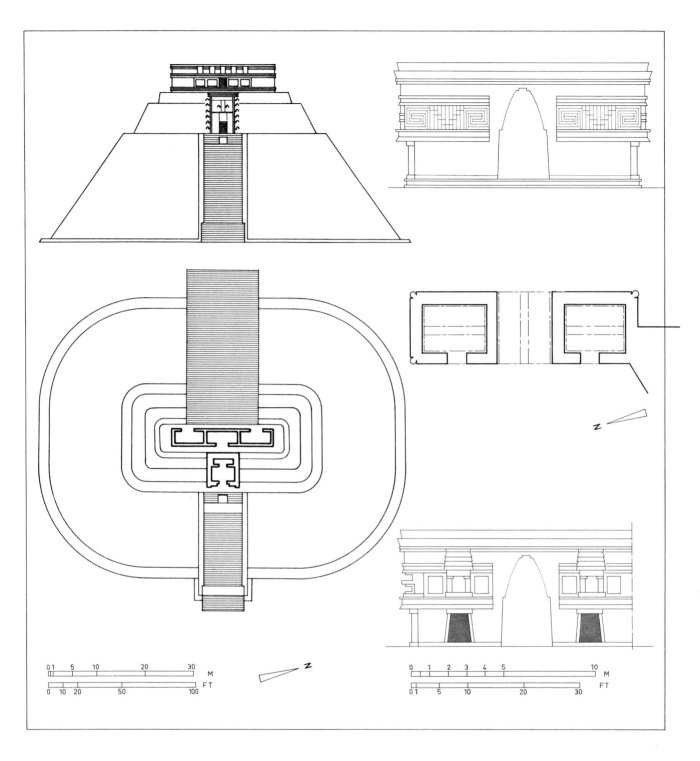

Pyramide du Devin, à Uxmal, dont le premier état remonte au début du VIIIᵉ s. Elévation de la face occidentale et plan 1:750. Deux escaliers permettent d'accéder aux sanctuaires hauts situés à des niveaux différents. A droite, **Arc de Labna** (Yucatan). Elévations occidentale et orientale, et plan 1:200. L'arc triomphal est une création des Mayas du Yucatan.

Links: **Uxmal, Pyramide des Zauberers,** ältester Teil 8.Jh. Zwei Treppen führen zu den verschieden hoch gelegenen Tempeln. Aufriß der Westseite, Grundriß 1:750. Rechts: **Labna (Yucatán, Mexiko), Triumphbogen.** Der Triumphbogen ist eine Schöpfung der in Yucatán lebenden Maya. Aufriß der West- und der Ostseite, Grundriß 1:200.

Pyramid of the Magician, Uxmal, begun in the early eighth century. West elevation and plan 1:750. Two stairways lead to the raised shrines situated at different levels. Right, **Arch of Labna** (Yucatan, Mexico). West and east elevations and plan 1:200. The triumphal arch was an invention of the Mayas of Yucatan.

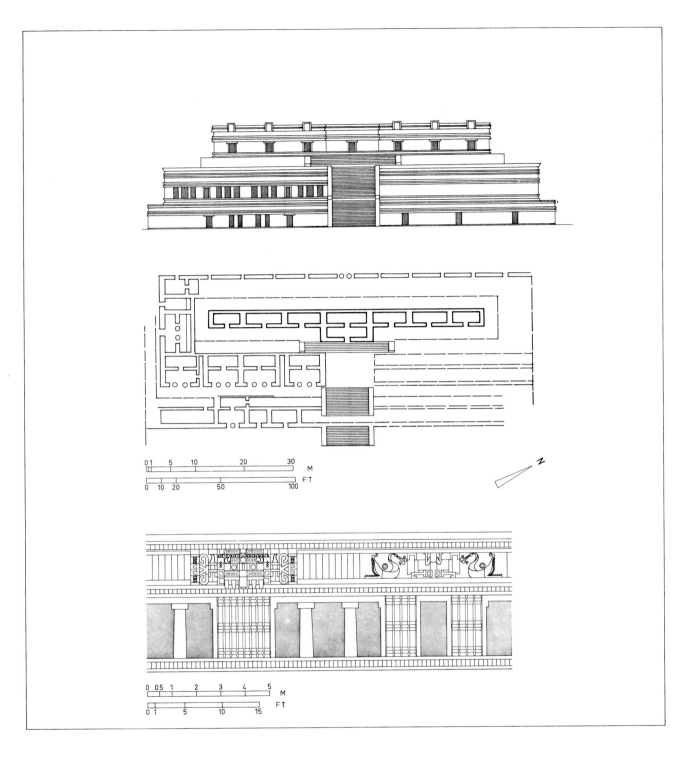

0 1 5 10 20 30 M
0 10 20 50 100 F T

0 05 1 2 3 4 5 M
0 1 5 10 15 F T

Grand Palais de Sayil, au Yucatan (Mexique), datant des VIIIe–IXe s. Elévation et plan 1:750 et détail de la façade du 1er étage 1:150. Chaque étage est constitué par un terre-plein présentant des salles en façade. La superposition des salles n'est pas réalisable en raison de la pesanteur du mode de construction maya, avec ses voûtements massifs.

Sayil (Yucatán, Mexiko), Großer Palast, 8.–9. Jh. Jedes der zurückgestuften Stockwerke besteht aus einem Erdkern, dem die Räume fassadenartig vorgeblendet sind. Das Gewicht der Wölbungen ließe ein Aufeinandersetzen der Stockwerke nicht zu. Aufriß und Grundriß 1:750; Detail der Obergeschoßfassade 1:150.

Great palace, Sayil (Yucatan, Mexico), eighth to ninth century. Elevation and plan 1:750; detail of the first-storey façade 1:150. Each storey consists of a terrace with rooms facing on to it. The rooms could not be placed one above the other because of the heavy construction and massive vaults used by the Mayas.

441

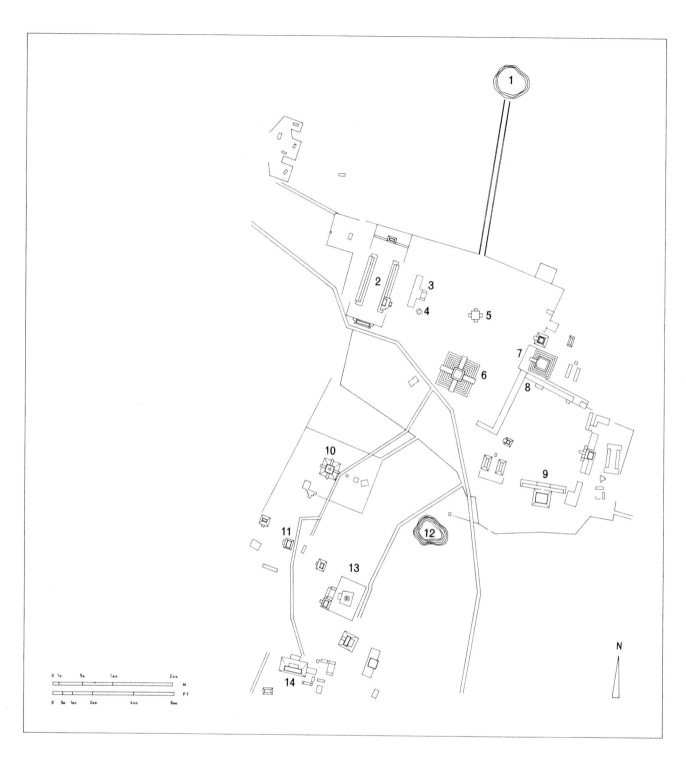

Cité maya-toltèque de Chichen Itza, au Yucatan (Mexique). Plan général 1: 6000. Ville maya aux VIIIᵉ et IXᵉ s., elle est envahie en 987 par les Toltèques. 1) Cenote des sacrifices, 2) Jeu de Pelote, 3) Tzompantli, 4) Plate-forme des Aigles, 5) Temple de «Vénus», 6) Castillo, 7) Temple des Guerriers, 8) Mille Colonnes, 9) Marché, 10) Tombe du Grand Prêtre, 11) Maison Rouge, 12) Cenote, 13) Caracol, 14) Nonnes.

Chichén Itzá (Yucatán, Mexiko). Im 8. und 9. Jh. von den Maya bewohnt, 987 von den Tolteken erobert. Lageplan 1:6000: 1) Opferbrunnen, 2) Ballspielplatz, 3) Tzompantli, 4) Plattform der Adler, 5) «Venustempel», 6) Castillo, 7) Kriegertempel, 8) Tausend Säulen, 9) Markt, 10) Grab des großen Priesters, 11) Rotes Haus, 12) Cenote de Xtoloc, 13) Caracol, 14) Nonnen.

Chichen Itza (Yucatan, Mexico), Mayan city of the eighth and ninth centuries, overrun by the Toltecs in 987. Overall plan 1:6000. 1) sacrificial cenote, 2) ball-court, 3) Tzompantli, 4) platform of the Eagles, 5) temple of 'Venus', 6) El Castillo, 7) temple of Warriors, 8) group of the Thousand Columns, 9) market, 10) tomb of the High Priest, 11) Red House, 12) cenote, 13) caracol, 14) Nunnery.

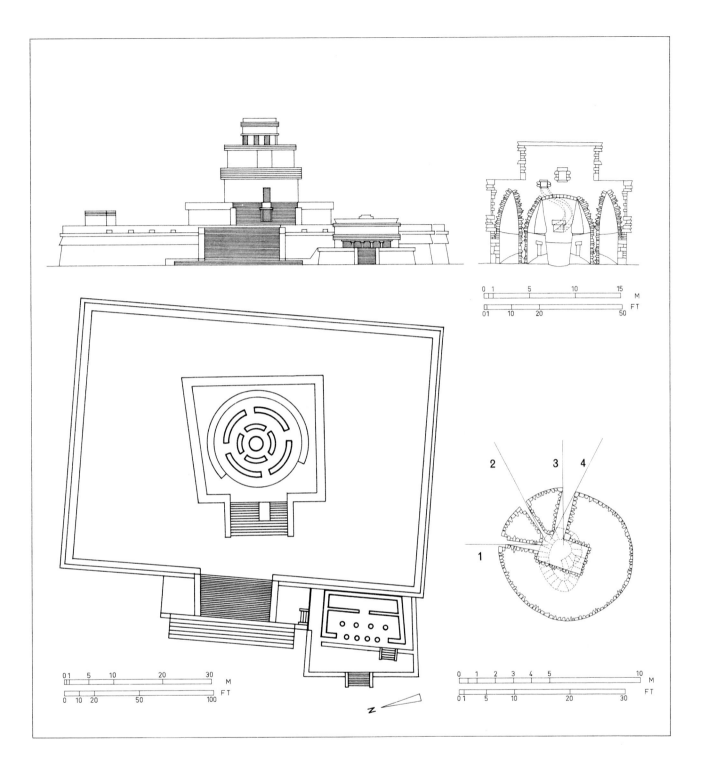

Caracol ou Observatoire de Chichen Itza, construction antérieure à l'invasion toltèque. Elévation et plan 1:750. A droite, coupe de la **Tour du Caracol**, avec escalier hélicoïdal 1:400, et plan de la chambre haute 1:200, avec lignes de visées: 1) Sud, 2) Coucher de Lune le 21 III, 3) Ouest et coucher de Soleil aux 21 III et 21 IX, 4) Coucher de Soleil au 22 VI, solstice d'été.

Links: **Chichén Itzá, Caracol (Observatorium)**, vor dem Tolteken-Einfall erbaut. Aufriß und Grundriß 1:750. Rechts: **Turm des Caracol.** Schnitt mit Wendeltreppe 1:400; Grundriß der oberen Kammer 1:200 mit Visierlinien: 1) Süden, 2) Monduntergang am 21. März, 3) Westen, Sonnenuntergang am 21. März und 21. September, 4) Sonnenuntergang zur Sonnenwende 22. Juni.

Caracol or observatory, Chichen Itza, built prior to the Toltec invasion. Elevation and plan 1:750. Right, section of **Caracol tower** with its spiral stairway 1:400, and plan of the upper room 1:200 with its pointing lines: 1) south, 2) moonset on 21 III, 3) west and sunset on 21 III and 21 IX, 4) sunset on 22 VI, the summer solstice.

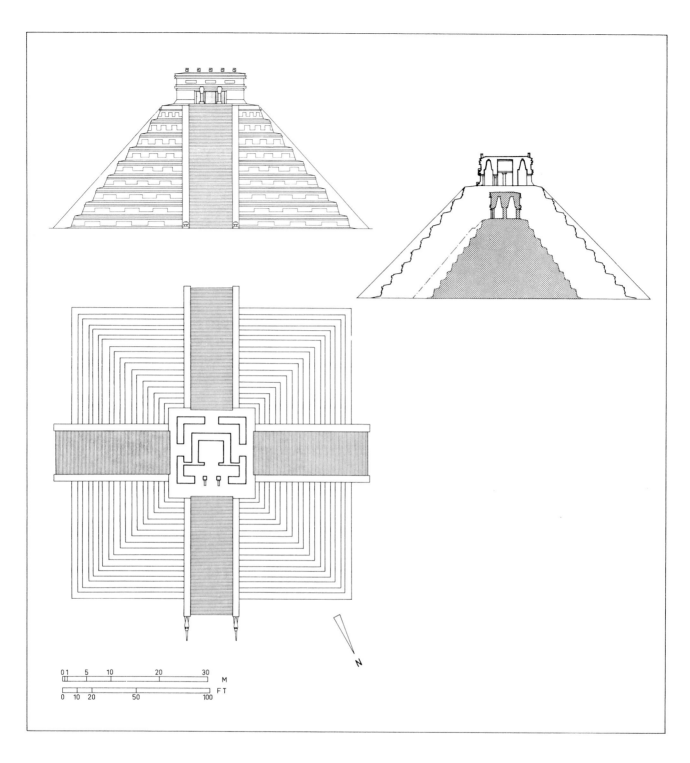

0 1   5   10   20   30   M
0   10 20   50   100   F T

N

Pyramide ou Castillo de Chichen Itza, création maya-toltèque du XIᵉ s. Elévation et plan 1:750, avec à droite, le schéma en coupe des superpositions (en grisé, le 1ᵉʳ Castillo). Pyramide à degrés surmontée d'un sanctuaire bien conservé. Quatre escaliers axiaux comptant 91 marches chacun, soit 364 marches, plus une à l'entrée du temple haut, soit 365. Dédié au dieu Kukulkan, Serpent à Plumes.

Chichén Itzá, Castillo (Pyramide), 11. Jh., Maya-Tolteken-Bau. Stufenpyramide, auf der Plattform ein gut erhaltener Tempel; vier axiale Treppen mit je 91, zusammen also 364 Stufen, dazu am Tempeleingang eine weitere Stufe, also insgesamt 365. Dem Gott Kukulkan, der Gefiederten Schlange, geweiht. Aufriß und Grundriß 1:750; rechts Schnittschema mit Bauschichten (grau: 1. Bau).

El Castillo pyramid, Chichen Itza, a Mayan-Toltec structure dating from the eleventh century. Elevation and plan 1:750 with, on the right, a diagrammatic section of the superpositions (shaded, the first castillo). The stepped pyramid is surmounted by a well-preserved shrine. The four axial stairways have 91 steps each, totalling 364, and the one at the entrance of the raised temple makes 365. The temple is dedicated to the god Kukulcan, the Plumed Serpent.

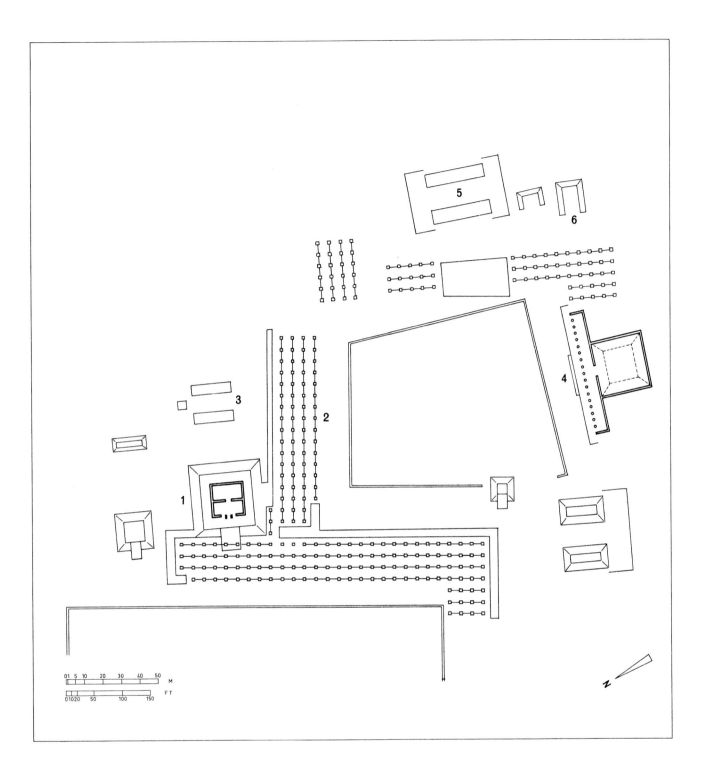

Ensemble des Mille Colonnes de Chichen Itza, d'époque toltèque (XIe s.). Plan général 1 : 2000. 1) Temple des Guerriers (on notera la grande analogie avec le temple principal de Tula) précédé de la salle hypostyle voûtée des Mille Colonnes, 2) Colonnade nord-est, 3) Jeu de Pelote, 4) Marché couvert, 5) Jeu de Pelote, 6) Bain de vapeur.

Chichén Itzá, Komplex mit den Tausend Säulen, Toltekenzeit, 11.Jh. Lageplan 1 : 2000 : 1) Kriegertempel (viele Entsprechungen zum Haupttempel von Tula), davor der überwölbte Saal der Tausend Säulen, 2) Nordost-Kolonnade, 3) Ballspielplatz, 4) überdachter Markt, 5) Ballspielplatz, 6) Dampfbad.

Group of the Thousand Columns, Chichen Itza, dating from the Toltec period (eleventh century). Overall plan 1 : 2000. 1) temple of Warriors (note the great similarity with the principal temple at Tula), with in front the vaulted hypostyle hall of the Thousand Columns, 2) north-east colonnade, 3) ball-court, 4) covered market, 5) ball-court, 6) steam bath.

445

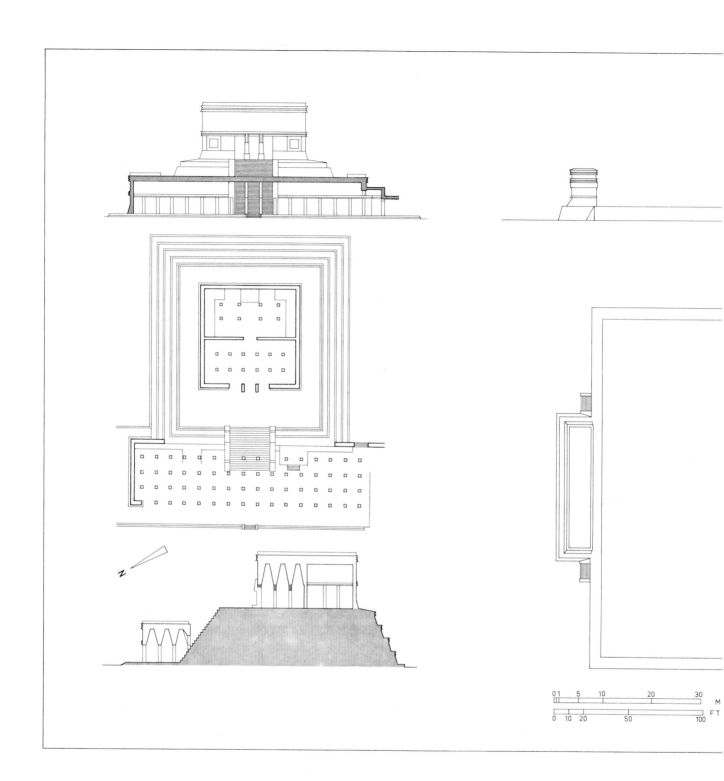

Temple des Guerriers de Chichen Itza, datant du XIᵉ s. Elévation, plan et coupe longitudinale 1:750. L'arrivée des Toltèques au Yucatan crée des espaces nouveaux, issus de la combinaison des salles hypostyles de Tula et des voûtes bétonnées mayas. Ainsi le sanctuaire de ce temple est-il très vaste en regard de ceux de Tikal ou Palenque. Mais c'est la grande hypostyle précédant la pyramide qui marque le renouveau capital.

Chichén Itzá, Kriegertempel, 11.Jh. Die Tolteken schufen in Yucatán einen neuen Raumtypus aus der Verbindung der Säulensäle von Tula mit den betonierten Gewölben der Maya. Verglichen mit Tikal oder Palenque ist der Innenraum des Tempels hier groß. Die bedeutendste Neuerung ist jedoch der große Säulensaal vor der Pyramide. Aufriß, Grundriß und Längsschnitt 1:750.

Temple of Warriors, Chichen Itza, eleventh century. Elevation, plan and longitudinal section 1:750. The arrival of the Toltecs in Yucatan gave rise to quite new interiors resulting from a combination of the hypostyle halls of Tula with the Mayas' concrete vaults. The shrine of this temple, for example, is enormous in comparison with those of Tikal or Palenque; but it is the vast hypostyle in front of the temple that marks the real renewal.

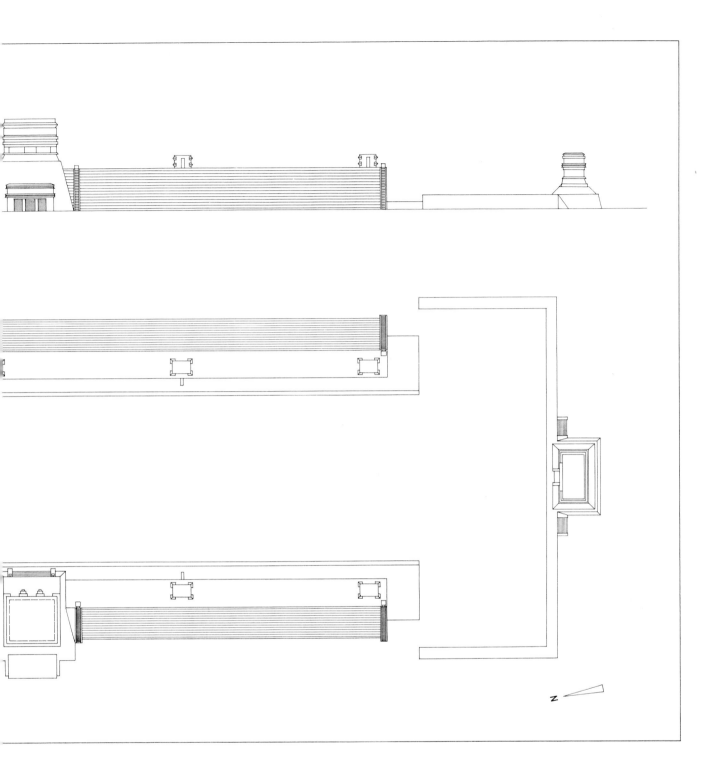

Grand Jeu de Pelote de Chichen Itza flanqué du **Temple des Tigres**, création maya-toltèque (XIe s.). Elévation et plan 1:750. L'espace de jeu qui forme un plan en H allongé est bordé, dans la partie médiane, de hauts murs soutenus par des talus. Au centre, des anneaux de pierre que devait traverser la balle de caoutchouc massif, à laquelle les joueurs ne devaient toucher ni avec les mains ni avec les pieds.

Chichén Itzá, großer Ballspielplatz, daneben Tigertempel, Maya-Tolteken-Anlage, 11.Jh. Der Platz in Form eines breitgestreckten H ist im mittleren Teil von hohen nach außen abgeböschten Mauern begrenzt. In deren Mitte ist innen der Steinring angebracht, durch den der massive Latexball geworfen werden mußte, ohne ihn mit Händen oder Füßen zu berühren. Aufriß und Grundriß 1:750.

Great ball-court, Chichen Itza, flanked by the temple of the Tigers, Mayan-Toltec (eleventh century). Elevation and plan 1:750. The playing space, an elongated H in plan, is bounded in the middle by high walls supported by banks of earth. Centre, the stone rings through which the solid rubber ball had to pass without the players touching it with either hands or feet.

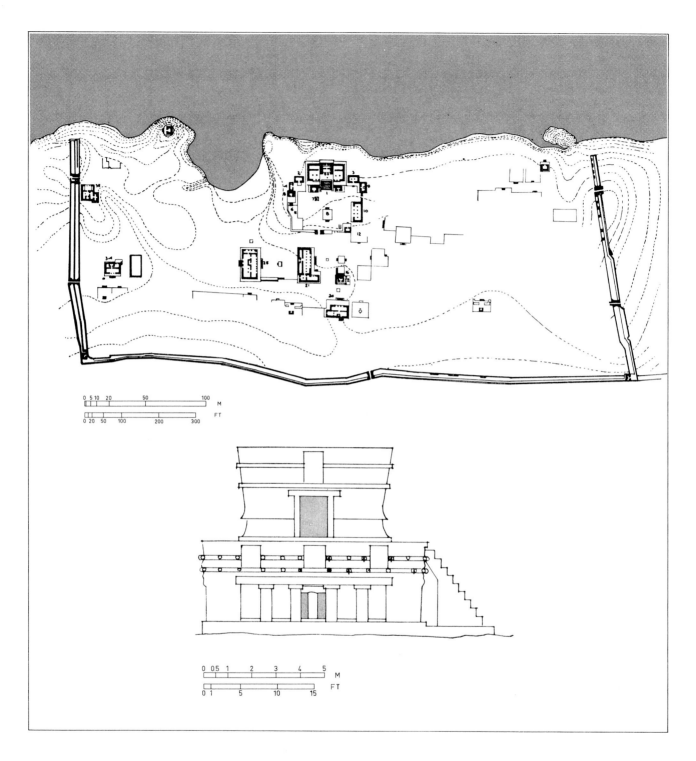

		M
0 5 10 20	50	100
0 20 50 100	200	300	FT

		M
0 05 1	2 3 4 5	
0 1	5 10 15	FT

Cité de Tulum, Quintana Roo (Mexique), construite en bordure de la mer des Caraïbes et fortifiée au XIIᵉ ou XIIIᵉ s. Plan 1:3000. A la fin de la civilisation maya, l'insécurité nécessite de fortifier les villes. En bas, **Temple des Fresques, à Tulum.** Elévation 1:150. Œuvre tardive caractérisée par l'évasement des murs vers le haut. Le bel appareil des parements mayas s'est abâtardi.

Oben: **Tulúm** (Quintana Roo; an der Karibischen See), im 12. oder 13. Jh. befestigt. Die unsicheren Verhältnisse am Ende der Maya-Zeit zwangen zur Befestigung der Städte. Stadtplan 1:3000. Unten: **Tulúm, Tempel der Fresken.** Bau der Spätzeit mit den charakteristischen, nach außen geneigten Mauern im oberen Teil. Die Wandverkleidung hat nicht mehr die schöne Qualität früherer Mayabauten. Aufriß 1:150.

Tulum (Quintana Roo, Mexico), a city on the shore of the Caribbean, fortified in the twelfth or thirteenth century. Plan 1:3000. Insecurity at the end of the Maya period made it necessary to fortify cities. Below, **Temple of Frescoes, Tulum.** Elevation 1:150. A late work characterised by the splaying of the walls towards the top. The beautiful precision of Mayan stonework is already a thing of the past.

Pérou   Peru   Peru

L'aire andine que couvrent le Pérou et la Bolivie a donné naissance à une série de civilisations, dont les réalisations architecturales s'étendent sur plus de 2000 ans, jusqu'à la conquête espagnole. Malheureusement, les documents sérieux, relatifs aux principaux monuments de ces cultures précolombiennes, sont encore trop rares pour qu'il soit possible d'envisager une publication globale des plans de l'architecture ancienne du Pérou. Force nous est donc de nous en tenir à des notions très sommaires.

On distingue essentiellement entre les cultures occupant les côtes du Pacifique et celles qui se développent sur les hauts plateaux et dans les vallées montagneuses des Cordillères. Les premières, qui pratiquent une irrigation très évoluée, érigent des cités construites en adobes, ou brique crue. Elles bâtissent des pyramides qui offrent parfois des similitudes avec certaines créations archaïques du Mexique, comme à Mojeque, dans la vallée de Casma, ou d'énormes montagnes artificielles, comme à Moche (Pyramides de la Lune et du Soleil). Pacatnamu, Cajamarquilla, Tambo Colorado sont des agglomérations clairement planifiées. Mais c'est la cité chimu de Chanchán (vers 1100 de notre ère) qui constitue la plus vaste capitale de l'Amérique australe, avec ses quelque 20 km² et sa dizaine de quartiers quadrangulaires, enfermés dans des murs d'enceinte et dotés de réserves d'eau, de palais et de sanctuaires.

L'époque incaïque (XVᵉ siècle), sur les hauts plateaux, succède aux réalisations de Chavin (IIᵉ s. av. J.-C.) et de Tiahuanaco (500 à 1000 apr. J.-C.) qui avaient élaboré le vocabulaire architec-

Im mittleren Andengebiet (Peru und Bolivien) entstand eine Reihe von Kulturen, deren Bauschöpfungen während zweitausend Jahren, in der Zeit bis zur Eroberung dieses Gebietes durch die Spanier, entstanden. Die präkolumbischen Bauten dieser Kulturen sind allerdings noch zu wenig erforscht, als daß es möglich wäre, hier in umfassender Weise Grundrisse und Pläne altperuanischer Bauten vorzulegen. Wir müssen uns auf eine summarische Darstellung beschränken.

Man unterscheidet grundsätzlich zwischen den Kulturen des Küstenlandes und denen der Hochebenen und Kordillerentäler. Die Küstenkulturen entwickelten komplizierte Bewässerungssysteme; sie errichteten ihre Städte in Adobe-Bauweise, das heißt aus ungebrannten Ziegeln. Ihre Pyramiden – etwa Mojeque im Casma-Tal – haben eine gewisse Ähnlichkeit mit manchen altmexikanischen, andere sind gewaltige künstliche Hügel, so in Moche (Mond- und Sonnenpyramide). Pacatnamu, Cajamarquilla und Tambo Colorado sind eindeutig geplante Siedlungen. Die größte Hauptstadt Südamerikas war jedoch die Chimú-Stadt Chan-Chan (um 1100) mit einer Fläche von etwa 20 km², unterteilt in rechteckige, mauerumschlossene Quartiere mit Wasserreservoiren, Palästen und Tempeln.

Auf die Kulturen von Chavín (2. Jahrhundert v. Chr.) und Tiahuanaco (500 bis 1000 n. Chr.), die mit ihren oft megalithischen Bauten ein Vokabular der Steinarchitektur ausgebildet hatten, folgte auf den Hochebenen die Inka-Periode (15. Jahrhundert). Befestigte Städte wie Machu Picchu und Pisac, Festungen wie Sacsayhuaman und Städte wie Cuzco und Viracochapampa

The Andean region of what are now Peru and Bolivia cradled a series of civilisations whose architectural output extended over more than two thousand years, right down to the Spanish conquest. Unfortunately not enough serious work has yet been done on the principal monuments of these pre-Columbian civilisations for it to be possible to envisage comprehensive publication of the plans of ancient Peruvian architecture. We can give no more than a very brief outline.

One essential distinction is between the civilisations that occupied the Pacific coastal regions and those that developed on the high plateaux and in the mountain valleys of the Cordilleras. The former, who practised a highly sophisticated form of irrigation, built cities of adobe or unfired brick. They constructed pyramids that occasionally resembled certain early Mexican works, such as that at Moxeke in the Casma valley, or enormous artificial mountains, as at Moche (the Moon and Sun Pyramids). Pacatnamu, Cajamarquilla and Tambo Colorado are clearly-planned agglomerations. But it is the Chimu city of Chan Chan, built around A.D. 1100, that constitutes the largest capital in South America with its 20 km² and ten walled quadrangular quarters complete with reservoirs, palaces and shrines.

The Inca period (fifteenth century) on the high plateaux was heir to the achievements of Chavin (second century B.C.) and Tiahuanaco (A.D. 500–1000), cities that had extended the architectural vocabulary of stone with monuments that were often of megalithic construction. The fortified Inca cities of Machu Picchu and Pisac, bastions such as Sacsahuaman, and towns such as

tural de la pierre, avec des monuments souvent construits en éléments mégalithiques. Des cités fortes incaïques comme Machu Picchu et Pisac, des bastions comme Sacsahuaman ou des villes comme Cuzco et Viracochapampa témoignent des progrès considérables qui marquent l'avènement de la dernière grande civilisation antérieure à la conquête.

La technique d'appareillage des blocs, les moyens nécessaires à leur transport, les formules de taille et d'ajustement d'éléments polygonaux sont encore insuffisamment étudiés pour faire l'objet d'un exposé. Mais la fabuleuse cité de Machu Picchu, découverte en 1911 seulement, prouve qu'une architecture de pierre très élaborée a vu le jour sur le continent sud-américain.

zeugen von den beträchtlichen Fortschritten der letzten großen Kultur vor der Eroberung durch die Spanier.

Die Technik der Steinbearbeitung, die Transportarten, die Formeln, nach denen polygonale Elemente zugehauen und gefügt wurden, sind noch zu wenig erforscht, als daß eine zusammenfassende Darstellung möglich wäre. Doch die ungewöhnliche und erstaunliche, erst 1911 entdeckte Stadt Machu Picchu beweist, daß es in Südamerika eine sehr hoch entwickelte Steinarchitektur gegeben hat.

Cuzco and Viracochapampa indicate the considerable progress made by this last major civilisation before the Conquest.

Their technique of jointing, the way they transported their blocks of stone, and the formulae they used for cutting and fitting polygonal elements have still not been studied sufficiently for it to be possible to give a full account of them. But the fabulous city of Machu Picchu, which was not discovered until 1911, is proof that a highly sophisticated stone architecture evolved on the South American continent.

1 Vestiges de la grande cité de Tiahuanaco, sur les hauts plateaux boliviens. Une architecture de pierre du début du Ier millénaire.
2 La Pyramide de la Lune, à Moche, construite en adobes au Ve s. apr. J.-C.
3 Vue aérienne d'un des quartiers de l'immense capitale côtière des Chimu, à Chanchán (XIIe siècle).
4 Vue d'ensemble de la cité-forteresse inca de Machu Picchu, dans les Andes (XVe–XVIe siècles).

1 Tiahuanaco, die Ruinen der auf dem bolivianischen Hochplateau gelegenen, aus Stein erbauten Stadt (Anfang 1.Jahrtausend)
2 Moche, die Mondpyramide, ein Adobe-Bau (5.Jh.)
3 Chan-Chan, Blick auf ein Quartier der im Küstengebiet gelegenen, riesigen Chimú-Stadt (12.Jh.)
4 Machu Picchu (Anden), Gesamtansicht der befestigten Inka-Stadt (15.Jh.)

1 Remains of the great city of Tiahuanaco on the high plateaux of Bolivia, with stone architecture dating from the beginning of the first millennium.
2 Pyramid of the Moon, Moche, a fifth-century A.D. adobe structure.
3 Aerial view of one of the quarters of the vast Chimu capital on the coast at Chan Chan (twelfth century).
4 General view of the Inca fortified city of Machu Picchu in the Andes (fifteenth–sixteenth century).

1

2

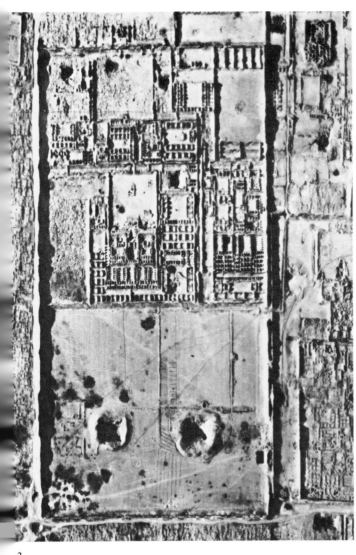

3

4

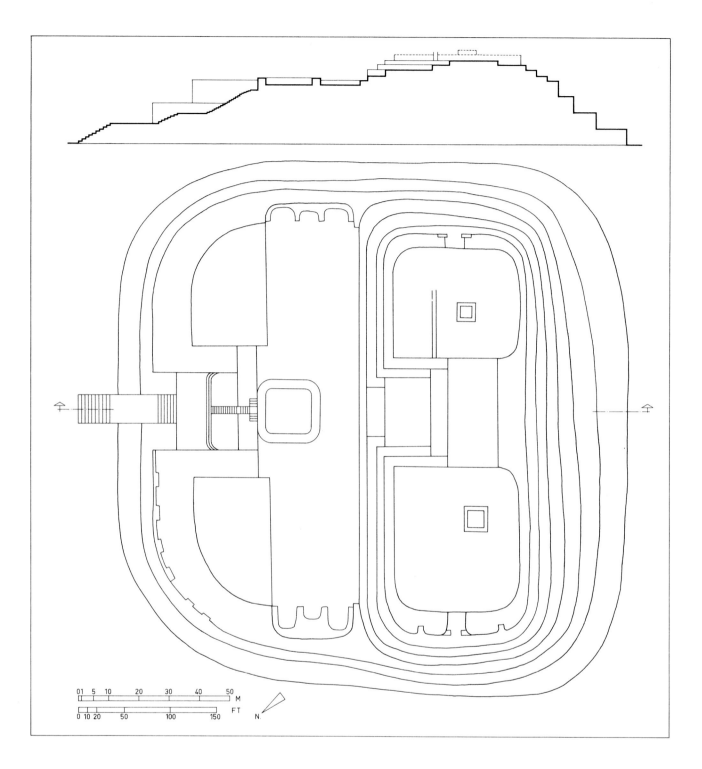

Temple de Mojeque, dans la vallée de Casma (Pérou côtier). Structure remontant au début de notre ère, style Chavin. Coupe et plan 1:1200. Ce grand temple à soubassement pyramidal, de structure complexe, est réalisé en terre battue, avec décor en relief et escalier axial. L'édifice, relativement érodé, devait comporter deux lieux de culte à la manière des temples-jumeaux aztèques du Mexique.

Mojeque (Casma-Tal, Küstengebiet), Tempel, Beginn unserer Zeitrechnung, Chavínstil. Das große Heiligtum auf pyramidenartigem Unterbau hat einen vielteiligen Grundriß mit axialer Treppe. Es ist aus Lehm erbaut und mit Reliefs geschmückt. Wahrscheinlich trug der ziemlich verwitterte Bau zwei Tempel in der Art der aztekischen Zwillingstempel in Mexiko. Schnitt und Grundriß 1:1200.

Temple of Moxeke (in the Casma valley, near the coast), built in the Chavin style around the beginning of our era. Section and plan 1:1200. This large, structurally complex temple on a pyramidal base is built of beaten earth and decorated with reliefs. It has an axial stairway. Fairly heavily eroded now, it must have included two shrines in the manner of the twin temples of the Aztecs.

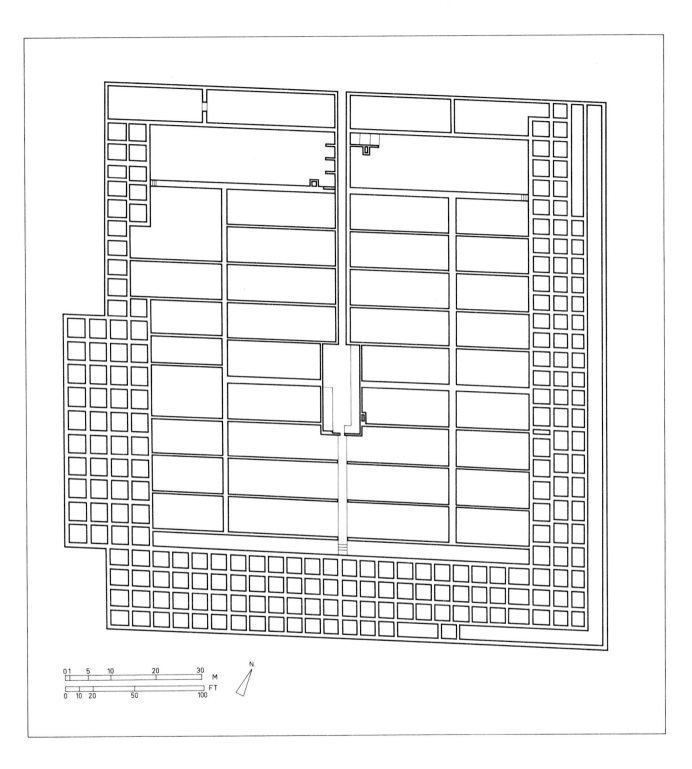

Entrepôts incas de Incahuasi, XVᵉ s.(?). Plan 1:800. Caractéristique de la société de type socialiste instaurée par les Incas au Pérou et de l'organisation économique, avec stockage de denrées dans de grands silos à grain, cette structure régulière reflète la planification centralisée. Chacun des carrés de 4 × 4 m est situé en contrebas des voies d'accès.

Incahuasi, Magazine der Inka, 15. Jh.(?). Die regelmäßige Anlage ist für die Gesellschaftsstruktur und das Wirtschaftssystem der Inka charakteristisch. Die Vorratshaltung in großen Getreidemagazinen spiegelt die zentrale Planung. Jedes Quadrat mißt 4 × 4 m und liegt tiefer als die Zugangswege. Grundriß 1:800.

Inca ware-houses, Incahuasi, possibly fifteenth century. Plan 1:800. A feature of the socialist social and economic organisation established in Peru by the Incas was the stockpiling of food supplies in enormous grain silos. This regular structure is an example of such centralised planning. Each of the 4 m. by 4 m. squares is situated at a lower level than the approach roads.

0 50 100 500 1000 2000 M

100 500 1000 2000 3000 4000 5000 6000 FT

N.

Grande cité de Chanchán, capitale des Chimu, vers l'an 1100, sur la côte nord du Pérou. Plan d'ensemble 1:30000. Cette immense métropole, bâtie en bordure du Pacifique, dans une zone aujourd'hui presque désertique, mais soigneusement irriguée autrefois, est divisée en quartiers murés de 300 à 500 m de long. Des pyramides et des réservoirs artificiels complètent ces vestiges impressionnants.

Chan-Chan (Küstengebiet), um 1100 Hauptstadt der Chimú. Die gewaltige Stadt an der Pazifikküste in einem heute wüstenartigen, einst aber gut bewässerten Gebiet ist in ummauerte, 300 × 500 m messende Quartiere unterteilt. Pyramiden und künstliche Wasserreservoirs ergänzen die eindrucksvolle Anlage. Stadtplan 1:30000.

Chan Chan, the capital set up by the Chimu on the coast of northern Peru around 1100. Overall plan 1:30,000. This vast metropolis, built on the shore of the Pacific in what is now virtually a desert zone but was once carefully irrigated, is divided into walled quarters 300 to 500 m. long. Pyramids and man-made reservoirs complete these imposing remains.

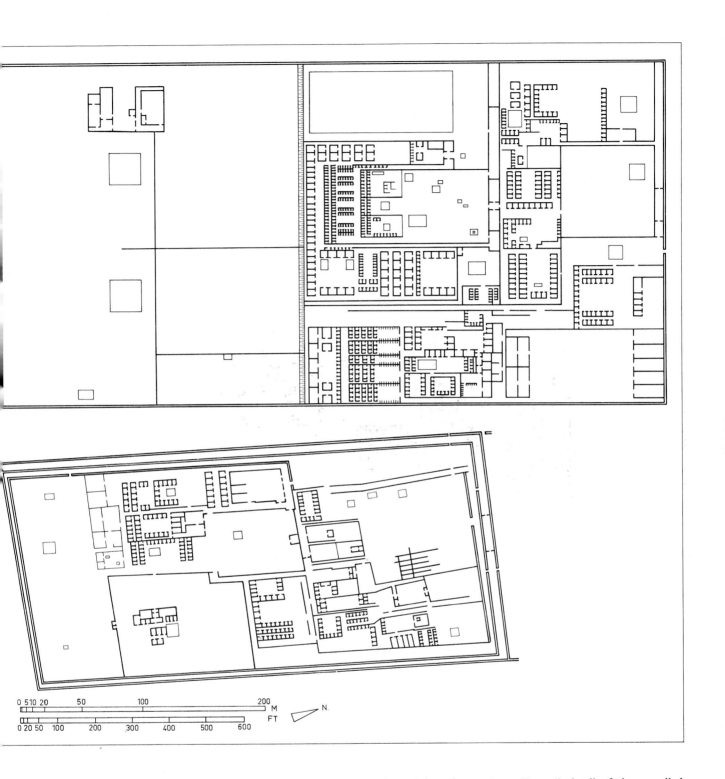

0 5 10 20   50   100   200 M

0 20 50 100   200   300   400   500   600 FT   N.

Chanchán, 1) Détail de **l'un des quartiers murés, dit le «Labyrinthe»,** 1:3000. Habitations et silos de stockage sont disposés selon une stricte organisation orthogonale à l'intérieur de l'enceinte de 530 × 265 m. 2) Détail du **quartier dit «Rivero»,** doté d'une double et triple enceinte, dont les murs en adobes devaient atteindre 8 à 10 m de hauteur.

Chan-Chan, 1) «**Labyrinth**», eines der ummauerten Stadtviertel. Innerhalb der Umfassungsmauer sind auf 530 × 265 m Wohnhäuser und Magazine nach exakt rechtwinkligem Plan angelegt. 2) «**Rivero**»-**Quartier** mit doppeltem und teils dreifachem Mauergürtel; die Adobe-Mauern waren 8–10 m hoch. Quartierpläne 1:3000.

Chan Chan. 1) detail of the so-called **'Maze', one of the walled quarters** 1:3000. Dwelling-houses and storage silos were laid out on a strictly rectangular plan within a 530 m. by 265 m. enclosing wall. 2) detail of the **'Rivero' quarter,** with a double and triple enclosure of adobe walls that must have been between 8 and 10 m. high.

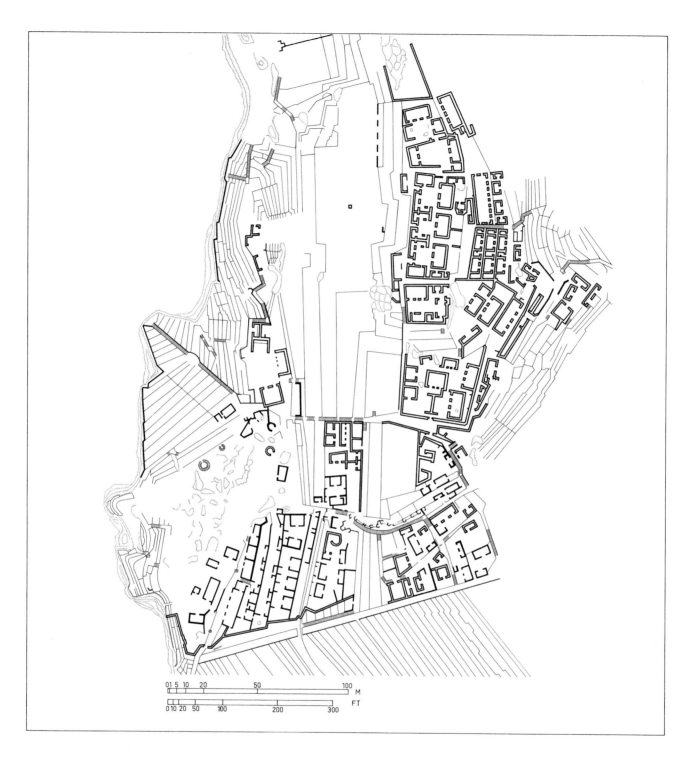

01 5 10 20   50   100
                                    M
                                    FT
0 10 20 50   100   200   300

Cité-forteresse de Machu Picchu, dans les montagnes de la Cordillère, sur le versant amazonien du Pérou, datant de la fin de l'époque inca aux XVᵉ et XVIᵉ s. Plan général 1:2000. Découverte en 1911 seulement, cette place forte en nid d'aigle, sur le cours de l'Urubamba, est entièrement édifiée en pierres de taille, parfois cyclopéennes. Places, lieux de culte, habitations et magasins s'articulent dans un relief tourmenté.

Machu Picchu (Kordilleren), Spätzeit der Inka, 15. und 16. Jh. Die erst 1911 entdeckte, wie ein Adlerhorst hoch über dem Urubamba errichtete Bergfeste ist völlig aus zum Teil riesigen Steinblöcken gebaut. Plätze, Kultstätten, Wohnhäuser und Magazine schmiegen sich dem unregelmäßigen Relief des Berges an. Lageplan 1:2000.

Machu Picchu (on the Amazon slope of the Cordilleras), dating from the late Inca period of the fifteenth and sixteenth centuries. Overall plan 1:2000. This fortified 'eyrie' overlooking the River Urubamba, which was only discovered in 1911, is built entirely in masonry, some of it cyclopean. Plazas, cult sites, dwelling-houses, and storerooms form a tangled plan on several levels.

456

L'architecture internationale

Zeitgenössische Architektur

International architecture

C'est avec les années 20 que débute l'essor de l'architecture de type international qui recouvrira bientôt la plantète entière, se superposant progressivement aux courants nationaux et aux traditions autochtones, comme aux options politiques fondamentales. L'âge de la technologie, amorcé par les créations de fer du XIXᵉ siècle, va trouver sa formulation dans le style fonctionnel, ennemi du rétro et de l'éclectisme. Désormais, la construction se concrétise en béton armé (inventé en 1890), en verre et en métal. Elle s'exprime dans des volumes purs de tout décor, orthogonaux et réduits à des formes géométriques aux sobres articulations, qui récusent souvent la symétrie.

La naissance de cette architecture contemporaine avait été annoncée par les Guimard, Mackintosh, Berlage, Loos, Behrens ou Mendelsohn, qui présagent les divers courants qui s'épanouiront durant le dernier demi-siècle, du fonctionnalisme aux structures organiques et au brutalisme... Mais le style moderne se concrétise avant tout par la création de la Weissenhofsiedlung de Stuttgart et du Bauhaus de Gropius, dans les années 1925-27. Il trouvera son expression théorique avec le Congrès des CIAM en 1928, qui agit comme un phare sur les architectes «modernistes». C'est désormais l'idée de «machine» qui prévaut dans la construction de masse: mur rideau, parallélépipèdes, formes cubistes, s'imposent dans le monde entier au lendemain de la deuxième guerre mondiale. On construit les mêmes édifices à New York, Berlin, Sydney, Tokyo, Mexico, Moscou ou Rio. Car on doit faire face aux reconstructions massives et à la pénétration de l'automobile dans les cités. Cette

In den zwanziger Jahren setzte die Entwicklung einer internationalen Architektur ein, die sich sehr schnell über die ganze Welt verbreitete und das Übergewicht über nationale, traditionelle Strömungen und auch politisch bestimmte Richtungen gewann. Das durch die Eisenkonstruktionen des 19. Jahrhunderts eingeleitete technische Zeitalter fand seinen Ausdruck im Funktionalismus, einer deutlichen Absage an die Vergangenheit und den Eklektizismus. Seither sind Eisenbeton (1890 eingeführt), Glas und Metall die beherrschenden Konstruktionselemente; die Baukörper sind frei von jeglichen dekorativen Zutaten, sie sind rechtwinklig, auf geometrische Formen und einfache Verbindungen reduziert, oft unter Verzicht auf Symmetrie.

Die zeitgenössische Architektur wurde durch Architekten wie Guimard, Mackintosh, Berlage, Loos, Behrens und Mendelsohn vorbereitet, die die verschiedenen Strömungen des letzten halben Jahrhunderts – Funktionalismus, Organisches Bauen, Brutalismus – ankündigten. In der Stuttgarter Weißenhofsiedlung und in Gropius' Bauhaus (1925 bis 1927) fand die moderne Architektur ihre Ausprägung, mit dem CIAM-Kongreß 1928 – einem Signal für alle fortschrittlichen Architekten – ihre theoretische Formulierung. Seitdem beherrschte der Begriff der «Wohnmaschine» die Konstruktionen: Vorhangwände, Parallelipipede, kubistische Formen setzten sich nach dem Zweiten Weltkrieg auf der ganzen Welt durch. In New York, Berlin, Sydney, Tokyo, Mexico City, Moskau und Rio entstanden völlig gleichartige Bauten, denn überall bestand die Notwendigkeit eines Wiederaufbaus in großem Maß-

The nineteen-twenties saw the beginning of a style of architecture that soon spread throughout the world, steadily overlaying and obscuring national currents, indigenous traditions, and even fundamental political differences. The technological age ushered in by the iron architecture of the nineteenth century was to find expression in a functional style that turned its back on the past and on eclecticism. This was an architecture of reinforced concrete (invented in 1890), glass and metal. It used stark, rectangular volumes stripped of all decoration and reduced to geometrical shapes linked together with great sobriety and often with deliberate asymmetry.

The birth of this modern style had been heralded by such architects as Guimard, Mackintosh, Berlage, Loos, Behrens and Mendelsohn, representing the various currents that were to emerge during the last half-century from functionalism through organic structures to brutalism. But it was in the years 1925-7, in the Weissenhofsiedlung in Stuttgart and in Gropius's Bauhaus, that it really crystallised, and its theoretical confirmation came with the 1928 CIAM conference, which became a sort of beacon for all 'modernist' architects. From now on 'machine' was the key word in the language of mass construction: curtain walls, parallelepipeds, and cubist shapes conquered the world in the years following the Second World War. Whether the city was New York, Berlin, Sydney, Tokyo, Mexico City, Moscow or Rio, the buildings that went up were the same. And the world was faced with rebuilding on a massive scale and in particular with the new penetration of the city by the motor car.

dernière pose des problèmes tant aux architectes qu'aux urbanistes, et va commander toute la conception des villes nouvelles – telle Brasilia.

Mais, dès les années 50 aussi, se dessine un mouvement qui va s'opposer au style standardisé et simpliste dont l'essor est porté par le boom économique. Ce modernisme formaliste des émules de Le Corbusier, de Mies ou de Gropius est remis en question par des structures plus souples, qui ne tardent pas à faire «éclater la boîte». C'est la création de la chapelle de Ronchamp, du Guggenheim, des voiles de Candela, du Terminal TWA, à la suite des Aalto, Scharoun et Nervi, qui aboutissent à un renouvellement du langage architectural. De plus, une série de préoccupations sociologiques et de recherches dans le domaine de la sémiologie, de l'environnement et de l'écologie viennent battre en brèche les idées purement technologiques et remettre en question les credo de l'ère fonctionnaliste.

stab. Ebenso drang überall der motorisierte Verkehr in die Städte ein und brachte für Architekten und Städtebauer neue Probleme, die zu einer neuen Stadtkonzeption – wie Brasilia – führen müssen.

In den fünfziger Jahren begann sich eine Gegenbewegung zu dem von der Woge des wirtschaftlichen Aufschwungs getragenen standardisierten und simplifizierten Stil abzuzeichnen. Der formalistische Modernismus der Nachfolger von Le Corbusier, Mies van der Rohe und Gropius wurde durch flexiblere Strukturen abgelöst, die zwar überraschten, sich aber entschieden durchsetzten. Die Kapelle von Ronchamp, das Guggenheim-Museum, Candela, der TWA-Terminal des Kennedy Airport, die Bauten von Aalto, Scharoun und Nervi führen zu einer Erneuerung der architektonischen Ausdrucksmöglichkeiten. Dazu haben soziologische Ideen, Forschungen auf den Gebieten der Semiologie, der Umweltkunde und der Ökologie die beherrschende Stellung der Technologie erschüttert und die Glaubenssätze des Funktionalismus in Frage gestellt.

The latter posed problems for architects and planners alike and was to dictate the entire conception of new cities such as Brasilia.

In the fifties, however, a new movement started to emerge in opposition to the standardised, simplistic style that had flourished with the economic boom. The formalist modernism of the followers of Le Corbusier, Mies van der Rohe and Gropius was challenged by more flexible structures that before long had 'burst the cigar box'. The chapel at Ronchamp, the Guggenheim Museum, Candela's membranes, the TWA Terminal, and the work of Aalto, Scharoun and Nervi led to a renewal of the language of architecture. A variety of sociological preoccupations as well as research in the fields of semiology and ecology then further discredited the purely technological approach to architecture, questioning all the credos of the functionalist period.

1 Façade de la Villa Savoye, à Poissy, par Le Corbusier, 1929–1931.
2 La «Villa sur la Cascade», ou Falling Water, à Bear Run, Pennsylvanie, par Frank Lloyd Wright, 1936 à 1937.
3 Terminal TWA, à Kennedy International Airport, New York, par Eero Saarinen, 1956–1961.
4 Le bassin olympique construit par Kenzō Tange à Tokyo entre 1960 et 1964.
5 La Philharmonie de Berlin, édifiée par Hans Scharoun de 1960 à 1963.

1 Poissy, Villa Savoye, Fassade (Le Corbusier, 1929–1931)
2 Bear Run (Pennsylvanien), Falling Water (Frank Lloyd Wright, 1936 bis 1937)
3 New York, Kennedy Airport, TWA-Terminal (Eero Saarinen, 1956–1961)
4 Tokyo, olympisches Schwimmbad (Kenzo Tange, 1960–1964)
5 Berlin, Philharmonie (Hans Scharoun, 1960–1963)

1 Façade of the Villa Savoye, Poissy, by Le Corbusier (1929–31).
2 'Falling Water', Bear Run, Pennsylvania, by Frank Lloyd Wright (1936 to 1937).
3 TWA Terminal, Kennedy International Airport, New York, by Eero Saarinen (1956–61).
4 Olympic swimming-pool, Tokyo, by Kenzo Tange (1960–4).
5 Philharmonie, Berlin, by Hans Scharoun (1960–3).

1

2

3

4

5

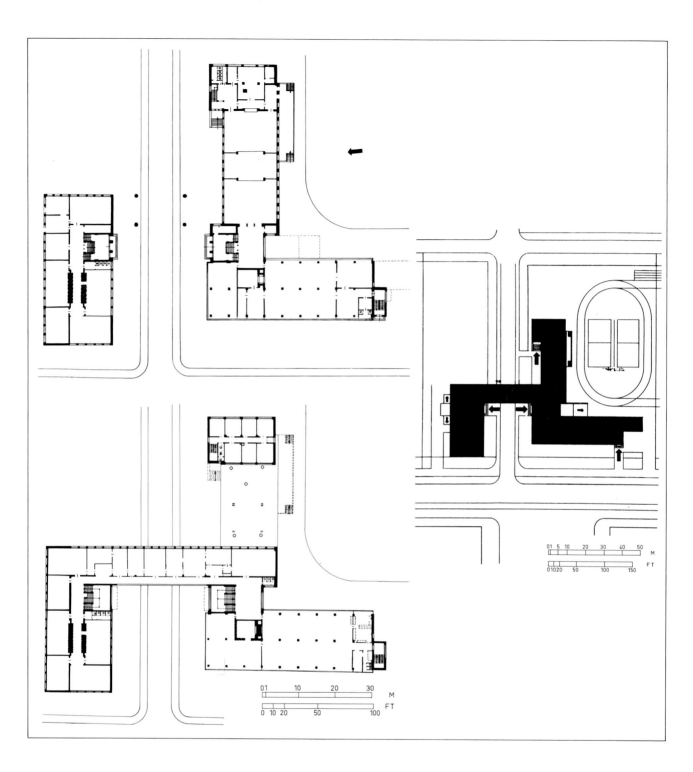

Le Bauhaus, à Dessau, construit en 1924 par Walter Gropius. Plan du rez-de-chaussée et plan de l'étage 1:1000, situation 1:2000. Ce complexe est caractéristique des tendances nouvelles et de la liberté du plan, dans un schéma orthogonal, qui sera celui de l'architecture fonctionnelle du XXᵉ s. Les éléments édifiés sur des piliers porteurs, laissant le sol libre, se retrouveront chez Le Corbusier.

Dessau, Bauhaus, 1924, Walter Gropius. Der Bau ist für die neuen Tendenzen und die freie Grundrißgestaltung, wie sie die funktionelle Architektur des 20. Jh. vertritt, charakteristisch. Die auf Stützpfeiler gesetzten Baukörper, die den Boden freilassen, treten bei Le Corbusier wieder auf. Grundriß des Erd- und des Obergeschosses 1:1000; Lageplan 1:2000.

Bauhaus, Dessau, built by Walter Gropius in 1924. Plans of the ground and first floors 1:1000; site plan 1:2000. The complex is typical of the trend towards freedom of plan within a rectangular system that was to characterise the functional architecture of the twentieth century. This device of supporting the building on pillars and leaving the ground plan open was also used by Le Corbusier.

460

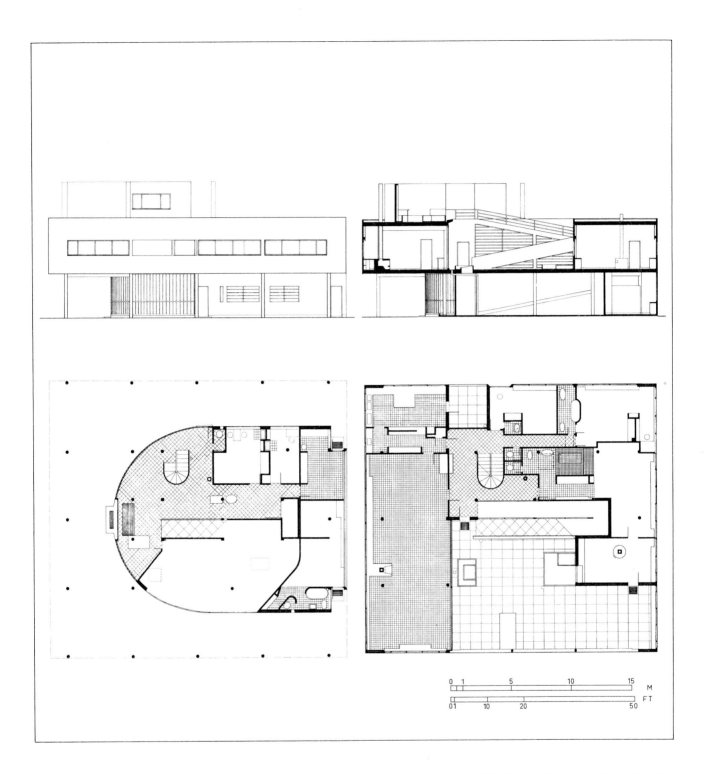

0 1   5   10   15
▭▭▭▭▭▭▭▭▭▭▭▭▭▭▭▭▭▭▭▭▭▭   M
01   10   20   50   FT

La Villa Savoye, à Poissy, construite en 1929 par Le Corbusier. Elévation ouest et coupe nord-sud, plan du rez-de-chaussée et de l'étage 1:300. Cette maison individuelle, avec son plan rigoureux s'inscrivant dans un rectangle, son patio supérieur, ses rampes d'accès et une grande partie du sol restant libre sous les poteaux porteurs, influencera toute une génération d'architectes.

Poissy, Villa Savoye, 1929, Le Corbusier. Dieses Wohnhaus beeinflußte eine ganze Architektengeneration: Der Grundriß ist völlig einem Rechteck einbeschrieben, der Patio nach oben verlegt, Rampen führen ins oberste Geschoß, ein großer Teil des Bodens bleibt frei. Aufriß der Westseite, Schnitt Nord–Süd, Grundriß des Ober- und des Hauptgeschosses 1:300.

Villa Savoye, Poissy, built by Le Corbusier between 1929 and 1931. West elevation and north-south section, plans of the ground and first floors 1:300. This highly individual house with its strict plan contained within a rectangle, its upstairs patio, its access ramps and its supporting posts, leaving much of the ground floor free, was to influence a whole generation of architects.

461

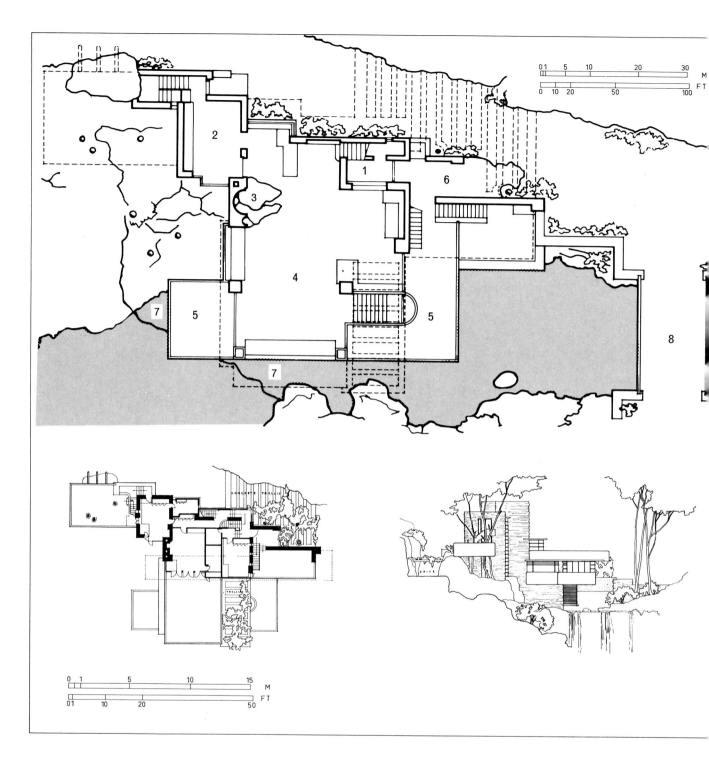

La Villa sur la Cascade, ou Falling Water, à Bear Run, Pennsylvanie, construite en 1936 par Frank Lloyd Wright. Plan de l'étage principal 1:150, plan de l'étage supérieur et élévation de la façade ouest 1:300. A l'opposé de la Villa Savoye, strictement délimitée, la Villa sur la Cascade fait éclater les limites, se modèle dans l'espace. 1) Entrée, 2) Cuisine, 3) Cheminée, 4) Séjour, 5) Terrasse, 6) Loggia, 7) Chute d'eau, 8) Pont.

Bear Run (Pennsylvanien), Falling Water, 1936, Frank Lloyd Wright. Im Gegensatz zur Villa Savoye, die sich streng an gesetzte Grenzen hält, sprengt dieses Haus solche Grenzen und ist seiner Lage entsprechend frei gestaltet. Grundriß des Hauptgeschosses 1:150: 1) Eingang, 2) Küche, 3) Kamin, 4) Wohnraum, 5) Terrasse, 6) Loggia, 7) Wasserfall, 8) Brücke; Grundriß des Obergeschosses, Aufriß der Westfassade 1:300.

'Falling Water', Bear Run, Pennsylvania, built by Frank Lloyd Wright between 1936 and 1937. Plan of the main floor 1:150; plan of the upper floor and elevation of the west front 1:300. In contrast to the severely self-contained Villa Savoye, Wright's house almost explodes into the space around it. 1) entrance, 2) kitchen, 3) fireplace, 4) living-room, 5) terrace, 6) loggia, 7) waterfall, 8) bridge.

462

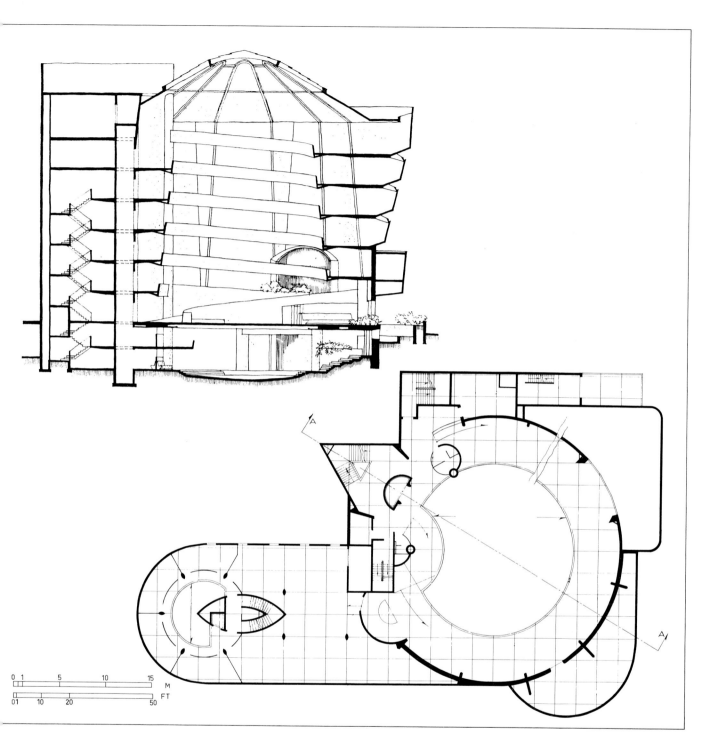

Le Musée Guggenheim, à New York, conçu dès 1943 par Frank Lloyd Wright. Coupe transversale et plan du premier étage 1:400. La solution du musée à rampe hélicoïdale formant un espace continu pour le visiteur a constitué l'une des réalisations les plus audacieuses de la première moitié du XXᵉ s. Le musée fut ouvert en 1959, après de longues recherches nécessitées par le caractère novateur de l'œuvre.

New York, Guggenheim-Museum, ab 1943 von Frank Lloyd Wright geplant. Die Lösung eines Museums mit gewendelter Rampe, die für den Besucher einen sich dauernd fortsetzenden Raum bildet, ist einer der kühnsten architektonischen Gedanken des 20. Jh. Die neue Bauidee erforderte eine lange Entwicklungszeit, das Museum wurde 1959 eröffnet. Querschnitt, Grundriß des ersten Geschosses 1:400.

Guggenheim Museum, New York, designed by Frank Lloyd Wright from 1943 onward. Cross section and plan of the first floor 1:400. Designing a museum as a spiral ramp, thus offering the visitor a single interior, was one of the boldest conceits of the first half of the twentieth century. The museum was not opened until 1959, its innovatory character having necessitated extensive research.

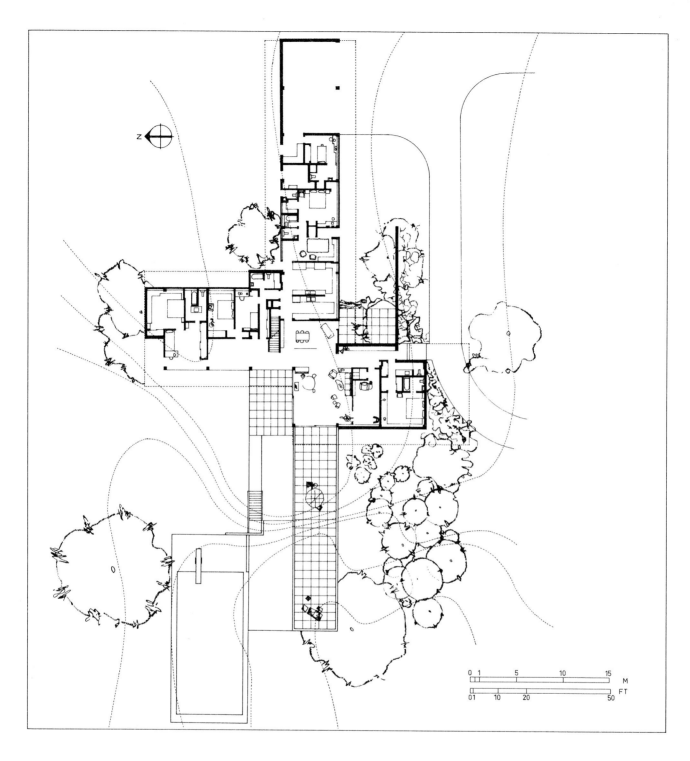

	0	1		5		10		15	
									M
	01		10		20			50	FT

Maison Tremaine, à Mantecito, Santa Barbara (Californie), construite en 1948 par Richard Neutra. Plan 1:400. Villa typique de l'après-guerre, noyée dans la végétation et fondée sur un plan très libre à plusieurs niveaux constamment en contact avec la nature, par de vastes baies et de légères structures d'acier couvertes de béton armé. Des galeries et vérandas créent des zones intermédiaires intérieur/extérieur.

Mantecito, Santa Barbara (Kalifornien), Tremaine House, 1948, Richard Neutra. Typische Nachkriegsvilla, eingebettet in die Vegetation. Sehr freizügige Organisation auf mehreren Ebenen, durch weite Öffnungen und leichte, mit armiertem Beton gedeckte Stahlstrukturen in engem Kontakt mit der Natur. Galerien und Veranden bilden Zwischenzonen in der Aufteilung des Innen und Außen. Grundriß 1:400.

Tremaine House, Mantecito, Santa Barbara, California, built by Richard Neutra in 1948. Plan 1:400. This is a typical post-war villa, surrounded by vegetation and based on a very free ground plan on several levels in constant contact with nature through vast windows and light steel structures roofed with reinforced concrete. Galleries and verandas create intermediate zones between interior and exterior.

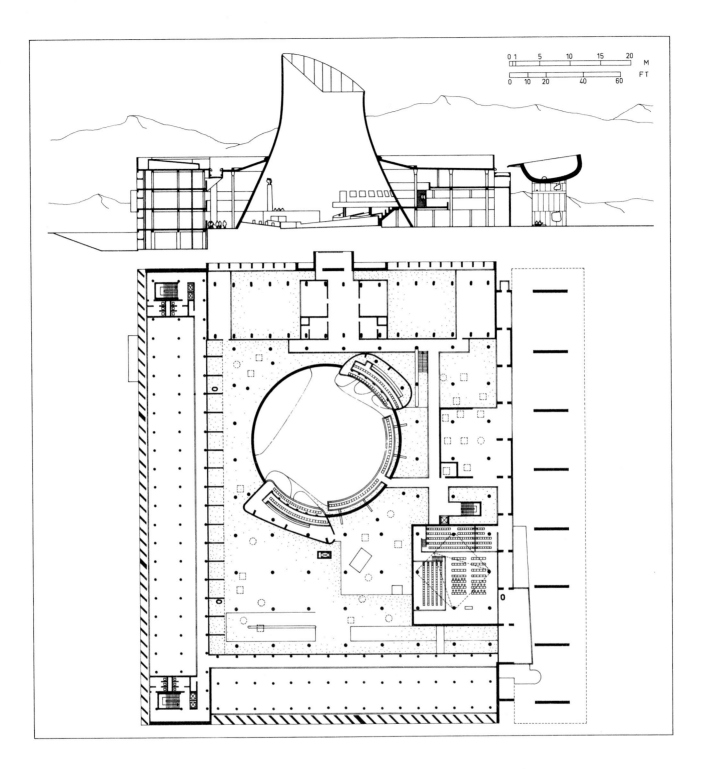

Le Palais de l'Assemblée, à Chandigarh (Inde), construit de 1951 à 1956 par Le Corbusier. Coupe transversale et plan 1:600. Chargé de concevoir la capitale du Penjab, Le Corbusier réalise une série d'ouvrages monumentaux à structure claire et aux lignes audacieuses, dotées de brise-soleil gigantesques. On y retrouve le plan clairement délimité de la Villa Savoye et le béton brut de décoffrage.

Chandigarh (Indien), Parlament, 1951 bis 1956, Le Corbusier. Für die Hauptstadt des Bandschab schuf Le Corbusier eine ganze Reihe von monumentalen Werken mit klaren Strukturen und kühner Linienführung, ausgestattet mit gigantischen Sonnenblenden. Der Plan entspricht in seiner strengen Begrenzung der Villa Savoye; auch der Sichtbeton findet sich wieder. Querschnitt und Grundriß 1:600.

Assembly Building, Chandigarh (India), built 1951–6 by Le Corbusier. Cross section and plan 1:600. Commissioned to design the new capital of the Punjab, Le Corbusier produced a series of monumental works of great structural clarity and boldness of line, fitted with gigantic *brise-soleil*. Here again we find the clearly outlined plan of the Villa Savoye as well as the use of unrendered shuttered concrete.

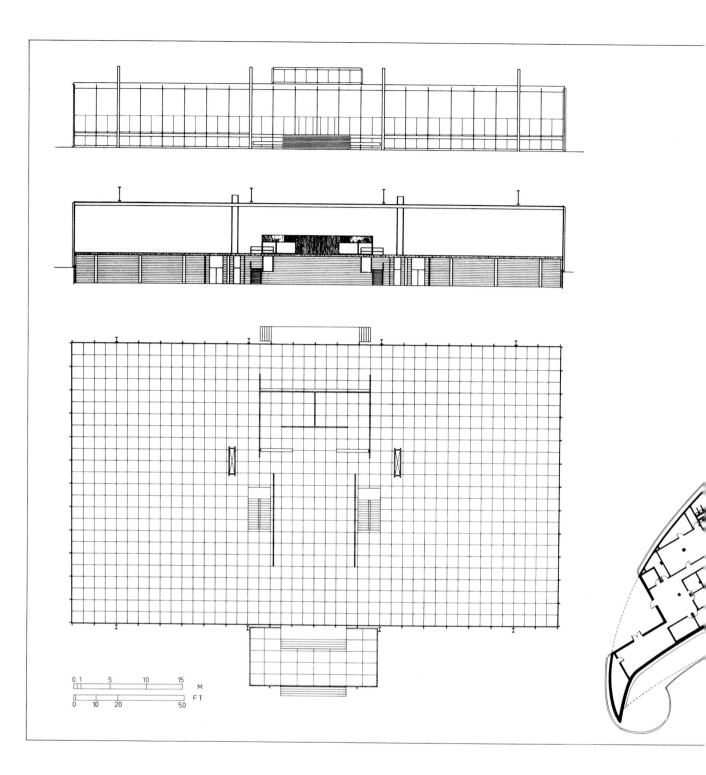

La Crown Hall de l'Illinois Institute of Technology, à Chicago, construite en 1952 par Mies van der Rohe. Elévation de la façade, coupe longitudinale et plan 1:500. C'est l'une des grandes réalisations de cet architecte. Il y développe la formule de l'espace libre, sans piliers internes, où les supports sont des poutrelles d'acier. Aucune structure porteuse aux angles et façade rideau.

Chicago, Illinois Institute of Technology, Crown Hall, 1952, Mies van der Rohe. Eines der großen Bauwerke dieses Architekten, der hier die Formel des freien Raumes entwickelt, ohne Innenstützen, mit Stahlbalken als Trägern. In den Ecken keine tragenden Strukturen, vorgeblendete Fassaden. Längsschnitt und Grundriß 1:500.

Crown Hall, Illinois Institute of Technology, Chicago, built by Mies van der Rohe in 1952. Front elevation, longitudinal section and plan 1:500. This was one of the architect's major works. In it he developed the formula of free space without internal pillars; the supports are steel girders; there are no supporting structures at the corners; and the façade is a 'curtain'.

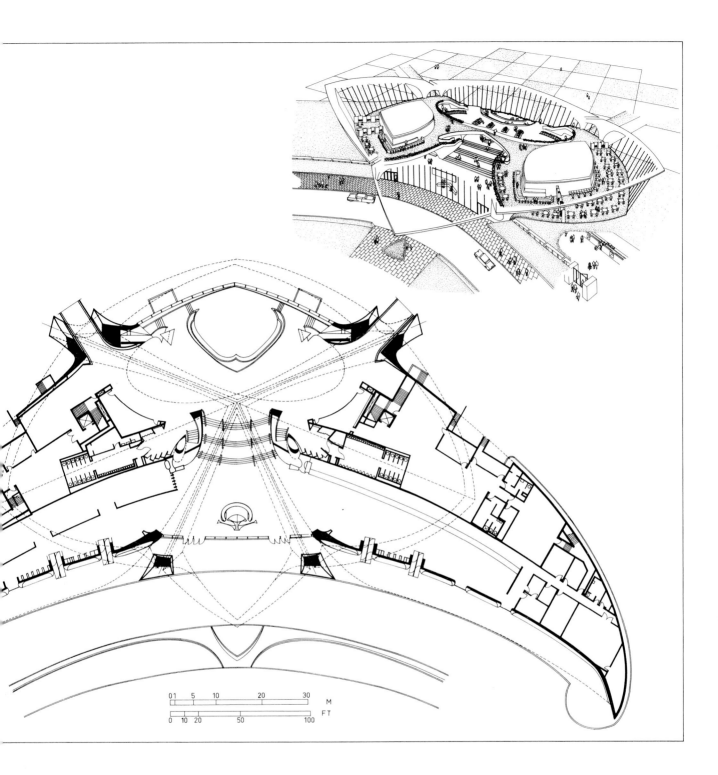

Bâtiment du Terminal de la TWA à l'aéroport Kennedy, New York, construit en 1956 par Eero Saarinen. Plan général 1:800 et axonométrie ouverte. Création d'un espace dynamique grâce à des voiles de béton armé qui allient l'architectonique et le génie civil, cette œuvre du grand bâtisseur finlandais est une véritable sculpture dans l'espace avec ses formes qui récusent entièrement le système orthogonal des fonctionnalistes.

New York, Kennedy Airport, TWA-Terminal, 1956, Eero Saarinen. Durch die segelartig gespannten Dächer aus armiertem Beton entsteht ein dynamischer Raum, in dem sich Architektur und Ingenieurkunst verbinden. Dieser Bau des finnischen Architekten bildet eine eigentliche Skulptur im Raum, deren Formen das orthogonale System der Funktionalisten völlig negieren. Übersichtsplan 1:800 und Axonometrie.

TWA Terminal, Kennedy International Airport, New York, built by Eero Saarinen between 1956 and 1961. Overall plan 1:800 and open axonometric projection. The great Finnish architect here used reinforced-concrete membranes to create a dynamic interior that is a combination of architectonics and brilliant civil engineering. His building is a veritable sculpture in space, using shapes that wholly reject the rectangular system of the functionalists.

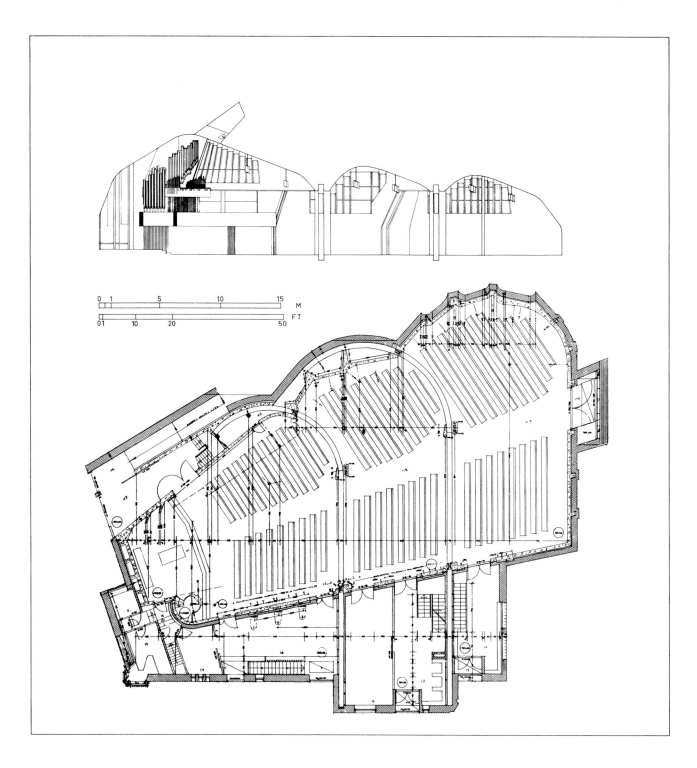

Eglise de Vuoksenniska, dans la commune d'Imatra (Finlande), conçue en 1956 par Alvar Aalto. Coupe des espaces internes et plan 1:300. Réalisation entièrement asymétrique qui recourt, tant en plan qu'en élévation, à une organisation très libre, cette église peut se subdiviser en trois salles indépendantes. Les plafonds incurvés répondent à des critères acoustiques.

Vuoksenniska, Imatra (Finnland), Kirche, 1956, Alvar Aalto. Völlig asymmetrischer Bau mit sehr freizügigem Grund- und Aufriß. Die Kirche kann in drei unabhängige Säle unterteilt werden. Die einwärts gekrümmte Decke sorgt für eine bessere Akustik. Schnitt durch die Innenräume und Grundriß 1:300.

Church at Vuoksenniska, Imatra district (Finland), designed in 1956 by Alvar Aalto. Section of the interior areas and plan 1:300. A totally asymmetrical building organised very freely in both plan and elevation, this church can be subdivided into three independent halls. The curved ceilings were dictated by acoustic requirements.

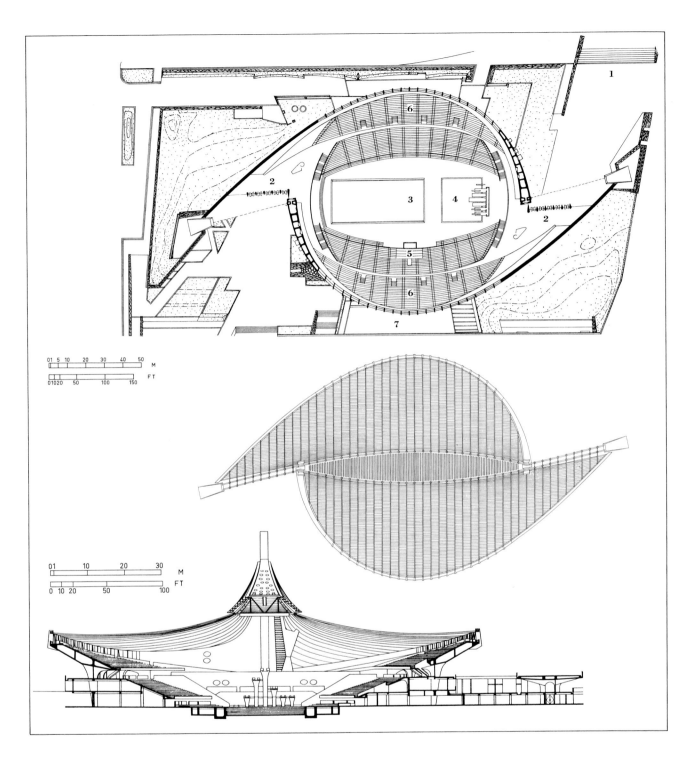

Grande Halle olympique de Tokyo, par Kenzo Tange, construite dès 1959 pour les Jeux Olympiques de 1964. Plan et structure de la toiture suspendue 1: 2000, coupe transversale 1:1000. 1) Entrée, 2) Accès au grand stade, 3) Piscine, 4) Plongeoirs, 5) Loge, 6) Gradins, 7) Jardin intérieur. L'immense voile de la toiture est supporté par deux énormes piliers en béton armé et par des cables noyés dans des ancrages au sol.

Tokyo, Große olympische Halle, 1959 begonnen (für Olympische Spiele 1964), Kenzo Tange. Die riesige Segelstruktur des Daches wird von zwei Pfeilern aus armiertem Beton und im Boden verankerten Kabeln getragen. Grundriß mit Struktur des Hängedaches 1:2000; 1) Zugang, 2) Eingang ins große Stadion, 3) Schwimmbad, 4) Becken für Turmspringen, 5) Loge, 6) stufenweise erhöhte Bänke, 7) Innengarten; Querschnitt 1:1000.

Great Olympic Hall, Tokyo, built by Kenzo Tange (beginning in 1959) for the 1964 Olympic Games. Plan and structure of the suspended roof 1:2000; cross section 1:1000. 1) entrance, 2) access to main stadium, 3) pool, 4) diving boards, 5) box, 6) stands, 7) indoor garden. The enormous sweep of the roof is supported by two vast reinforced-concrete pillars and by cables sunk in anchorages on the ground.

469

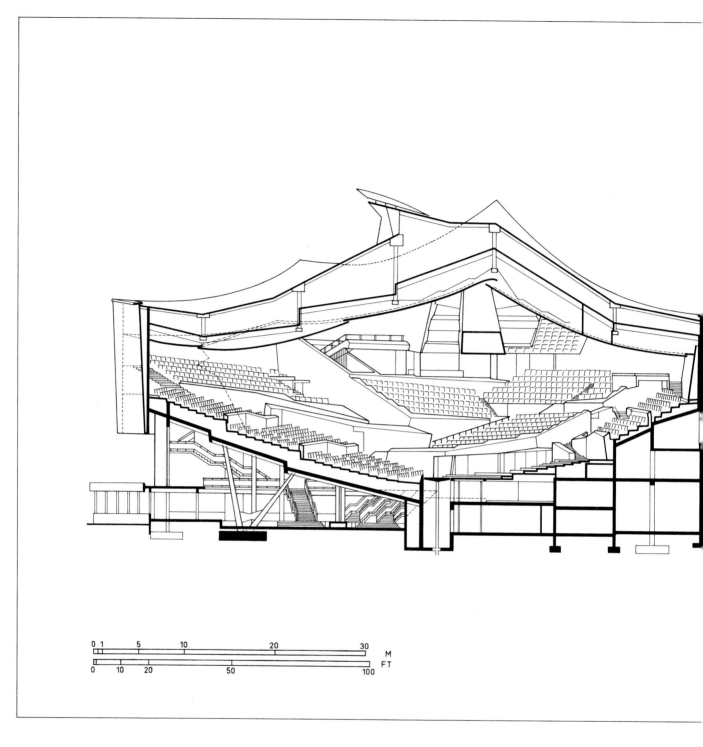

0 1   5   10   20   30   M
0   10 20   50   100   FT

La Philharmonie de Berlin, construite en 1963 par Hans Scharoun. Coupe longitudinale 1:400 et plan 1:800. Œuvre type du mouvement expressionniste et de l'architecture organique, cette salle de concert qui permet de distribuer le public autour de l'orchestre, est calculée en fonction des lois acoustiques.

Berlin, Philharmonie, 1963, Hans Scharoun. Typischer Bau des Expressionismus und der «organischen» Architektur. In diesem Konzertsaal sind die Sitze den akustischen Gesetzen entsprechend um das Orchester herum angeordnet. Längsschnitt 1:400.

Philharmonie, Berlin, built by Hans Scharoun between 1960 and 1963. Longitudinal section 1:400; plan 1:800. A typical product of the Expressionist movement and of organic architecture, this concert hall in which the audience is seated around the orchestra was worked out in accordance with the laws of acoustics.

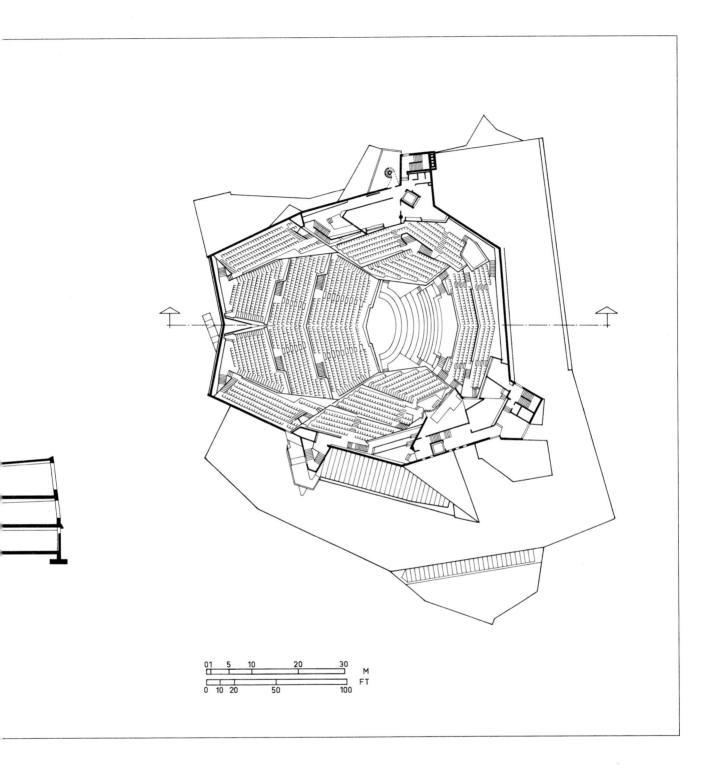

01 5 10 20 30 M
FT
0 10 20 50 100

Avec la **Philharmonie de Berlin,** Hans Scharoun a réalisé sa création la plus achevée. Il y refuse autant l'organisation orthogonale que la symétrie. Toitures et plafonds à lignes courbes s'apparentent aux formes d'une vaste tente de nomades. L'aspect extérieur est sacrifié aux nécessités de l'espace interne.

Berlin, Philharmonie. Der Bau ist das vollendetste Werk von Hans Scharoun. Rechtwinklige Organisation und Symmetrie sind vermieden. Die gekurvten Dächer und Raumdecken gleichen den Formen eines großen Nomadenzeltes. Die Außenarchitektur folgt zwangsläufig der Innenarchitektur. Grundriß 1:800.

Philharmonie, Berlin, Hans Scharoun's most finished work, rejects both rectangular organisation and symmetry. Its curved roofs and ceilings are reminiscent of some vast nomad tent. External appearance has here been subordinated to the requirements of the interior.

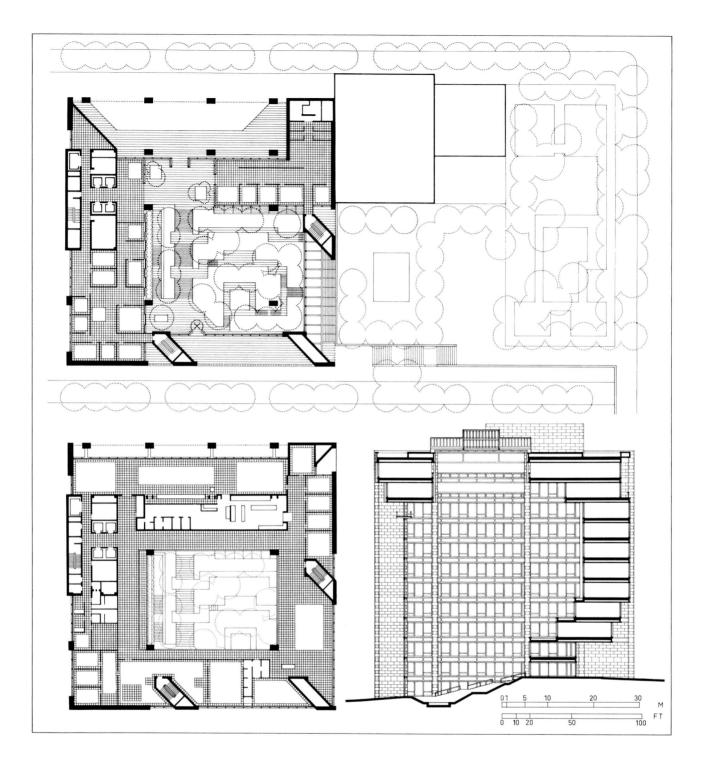

La Fondation Ford, à New York, édifiée en 1963 par Kevin Roche, John Dinkeloo and Associates. Plan du rez-de-chaussée, plan d'un étage type et coupe transversale 1:800. Cet édifice, dont les deux ailes bordant le plan carré enferment un jardin intérieur vitré, est un immeuble de bureaux non commercial. C'est l'introduction des préoccupations écologiques dans l'architecture de la seconde moitié du XXᵉ s.

New York, Ford Foundation, 1963, Kevin Roche, John Dinkeloo and Associates. Die beiden Flügel dieser quadratischen Anlage bilden den Rahmen für einen verglasten Innengarten. Mit diesem Bau finden die oekologischen Gesichtspunkte der zweiten Hälfte des 20. Jh. Eingang in die Architektur. Grundriß des Erdgeschosses, Plansystem eines Obergeschosses, Längsschnitt 1:800.

Ford Foundation, New York, built by Kevin Roche, John Dinkeloo and Associates in 1963. Ground floor plan, plan of a typical upper floor and cross section 1:800. The two wings of this non-commercial office block border a square plan and enclose a glazed indoor garden. The building marks the advent of ecological considerations in the architecture of the second half of the twentieth century.

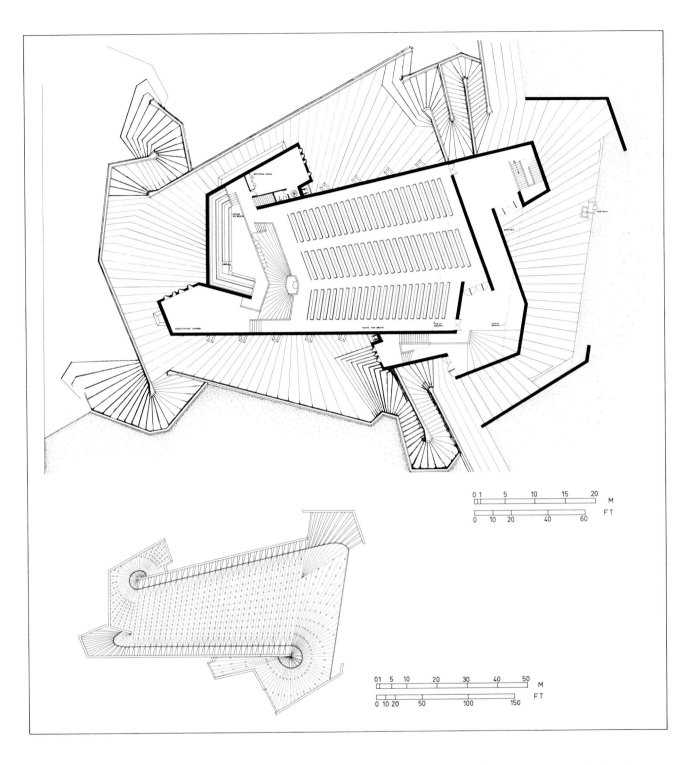

La Chapelle de Tuskegee, ou Interdeno-minational Chapel du Tuskegee Institute (Alabama), construite en 1960–69 par Paul Rudolph. Plan 1:600 et structure des toitures 1:1200. De structure libre et de conception expressionniste, cette chapelle au plan tourmenté élabore un espace puissamment articulé entre des murs de brique. Les lames de la toiture jouent avec des transparences qui créent un éclairage très élaboré.

Tuskegee Institute (Alabama), Inter-denominational Chapel, 1960–1969, Paul Rudolph. Die Kapelle ist frei von archi-tektonischen Systemen und expressio-nistisch konzipiert. Der verzogene Grundriß läßt innerhalb der Ziegel-mauern einen stark gegliederten Innen-raum entstehen. Grundriß 1:600; Dach-struktur 1:1200.

Interdenominational chapel, Tuskegee Institute, Alabama, built 1960-9 by Paul Rudolph. Plan 1:600; roof structure 1:1200. This building is Expressionist in concept and free in terms of struc-tural design. With its contorted plan it creates an interior that is powerfully ar-ticulated between brick walls. The leaves of the roof play with transparencies to set up highly elaborate lighting effects.

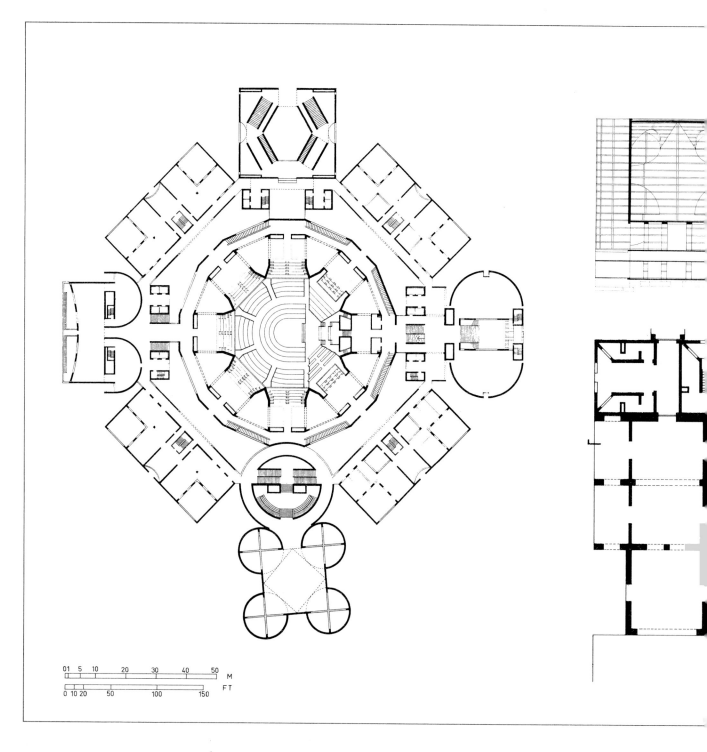

01 5 10   20   30   40   50   M

0 10 20 50   100   150   FT

Le Centre gouvernemental de Dacca, ou «Banglanagar» (Bengladesh), Palais de l'Assemblée, construit dès 1962 par Luis I. Kahn, plan 1:1200, coupe longitudinale 1:800, et **Hôtellerie des secrétaires,** plan et coupe 1:400. Le sens de la monumentalité et des réalisations colossales dont témoigne Luis I. Kahn a pu s'exprimer pleinement dans cette immense réalisation qu'est la création d'une capitale moderne.

Dacca, auch **Banglanagar (Bangladesch), Government Centre, Parlamentssaal,** Baubeginn 1962, Luis I. Kahn. Kahns Sinn für Monumentalität und kolossale Projekte findet in dieser riesigen Anlage, dem Werk einer modernen Großstadt, seinen Ausdruck. Grundriß 1: 1200, Längsschnitt 1:800. **Hotel der Sekretäre.** Grundriß und Schnitt 1:400.

Government Centre, Dacca or Banglanagar (Bangla Desh): Assembly Building by Luis I. Khan, begun 1962, plan 1:1200, longitudinal section 1:800; **Residence of the Secretaries,** plan and section 1:400. Kahn's feeling for the monumental found full expression in this colossal project, namely the creation of a modern capital.

474

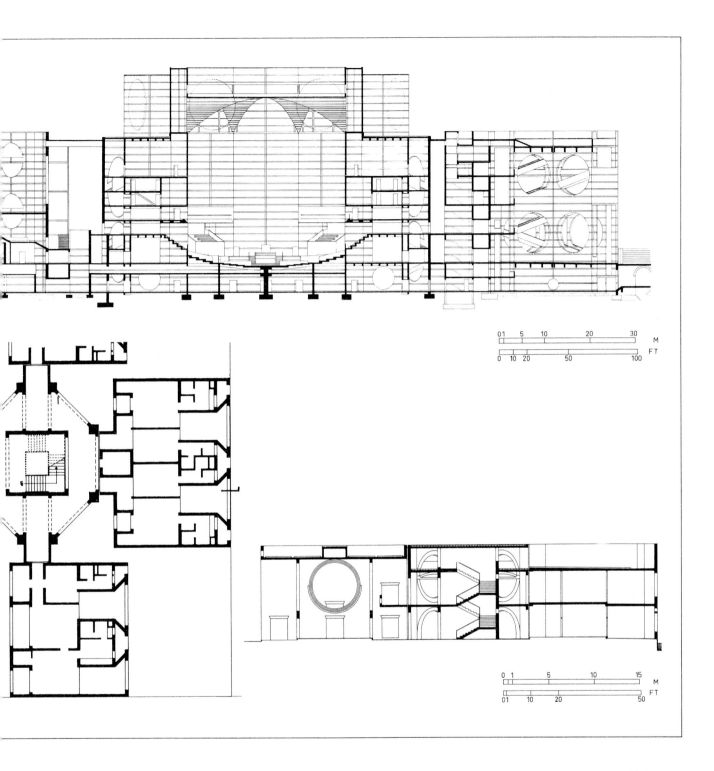

Le Palais de l'Assemblée de Dacca, avec son plan centré qui évoque des réminiscences de la Rome antique et ses ouvertures circulaires qui trouent les parois monolithiques de béton que soulignent des joints de marbre blanc, est l'une des créations les plus spectaculaires du style kahnien. Pour les habitations des secrétaires et des ministres, l'architecte recourt aux structures de brique, mariées au béton.

Dacca, Government Centre, Parlamentssaal. Der zentralisierte Grundriß, der an das antike Rom erinnert, und die kreisrunden Öffnungen in den monolithischen Betonmauern, die durch ein weißes Marmorgefüge hervorgehoben sind, machen dieses Gebäude zu einem der spektakulärsten Werke Kahns. Für die Wohnbauten der Sekretäre und Minister benutzte er Ziegel und Beton.

Assembly Building, Dacca, with its centralised plan evoking ancient Rome and its circular openings in monolithic concrete walls accented with white marble joints, one of Kahn's most spectacular works. For the secretaries' and ministers' residences the architect turned to brick used in conjunction with concrete.

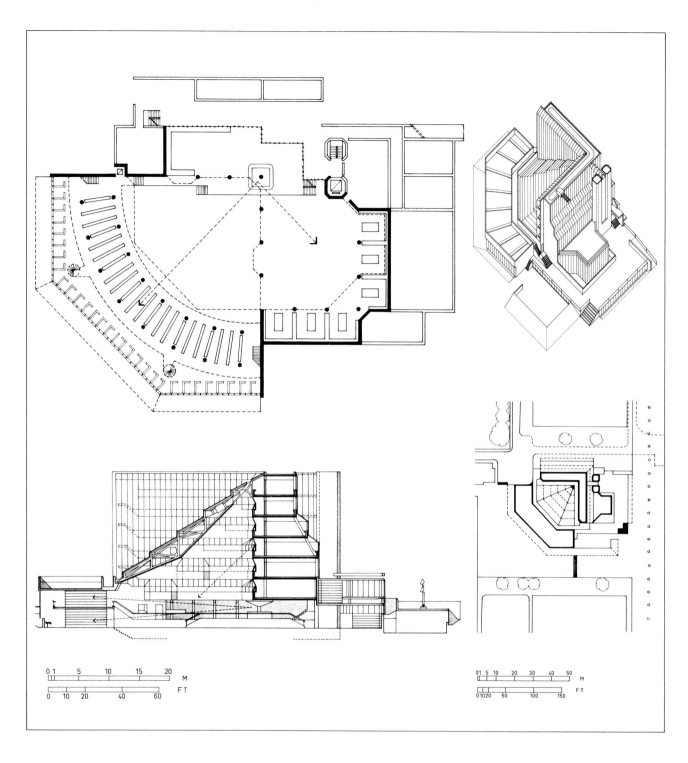

La Bibliothèque de la Faculté d'Histoire, à l'Université de Cambridge (Grande-Bretagne), construite de 1964 à 1968 par James Stirling. Plan du rez-de-chaussée et coupe 1:600, axonométrie et plan de situation 1:2000. A l'intérieur des deux ailes à angle droit se déploie la verrière inclinée qui abrite la salle de lecture. L'emploi généralisé des surfaces de verre en plans inclinés a exercé une influence considérable sur l'architecture de la dernière décennie.

Cambridge (England), Universität, Bibliothek der Geschichtswissenschaft, 1964–1968, James Stirling. Zwischen den beiden, rechtwinklig zueinander stehenden Flügeln ist das geneigte Glasdach des Lesesaals ausgespannt. Der weitverbreitete Gebrauch geneigter Glasflächen hat erheblichen Einfluß auf die Architektur der letzten Jahrzehnte gehabt. Grundriß des Erdgeschosses, Schnitt 1:600; Axonometrie, Lageplan 1:2000.

History Faculty Library, Cambridge University, built 1964–8 by James Stirling. Ground floor plan and section 1:600; axonometric projection and site plan 1:2000. Inside the two right-angled wings is the sloping glass roof of the reading room. This widespread use of glass surfaces and inclined planes has been an influential factor in the architecture of the last decade.

Auteurs des plans

Tous les plans de ces deux volumes ont été dessinés expressément par José Conesa, architecte, Genève, à l'exception des documents suivants:

pp. 21–33, 76–96, 204–216, 432–448: Georges Berthoud, architecte EPF-Z, SIA, Genève;

pp. 264–280, 392–408: Andreas Volwahsen et Gerd Mader, architectes, Munich;

pp. 324–340: en collaboration avec l'atelier Masuda, Tokyo.

Enfin, pour ce qui est des plans d'architectes contemporains, et afin de respecter le style graphique de ces derniers, on a recouru aux publications de leurs œuvres. Les plans du dernier chapitre sont extraits des ouvrages suivants:

p. 466: Carter, Peter, *Mies van der Rohe at Work*, Phaidon, Londres 1974;

p. 468: Fleig, Karl, *Alvar Aalto*, 2e éd., vol. I, Artemis, Zurich 1974;

pp. 461, 463, 464, 465, 467, 473, 476: Futagawa, Yukio, *Global Architecture*, A.D.A. Edita, Tokyo;

p. 472: Futagawa, Yukio, et autres, *Kevin Roche, John Dinkeloo and Associates, 1962–1975*, A.D.A. Edita, Tokyo 1975;

pp. 474–475: Giurgola, Romaldo et Mehta, Jaimini, *Louis I. Kahn*, Artemis, Zurich 1975;

p. 469: Kultermann, Udo, *Kenzo Tange, Architecture and Urban Design 1946 to 1969*, trad. Henry A. Frey, Artemis, Zurich 1970;

p. 460: Wingler, Hans M., *Das Bauhaus: 1919–1933*, 2e éd., Rasch und Du Mont Schauberg, Cologne 1968.

Planverfasser

Die Pläne für diese beiden Bände wurden mit Ausnahme der unten aufgeführten von José Conesa, Architekt, Genf, eigens für dieses Werk gezeichnet. Es stammen von:

Georges Berthoud, Architekt EPF-Z, SIA, Genf: S. 21–33; 76–96; 204–216; 432–448;

Andreas Volwahsen und Gerd Mader, Architekten, München: S. 264–280; 392–408;

Atelier Masuda, Tokyo: S. 324–340.

Um den persönlichen graphischen Stil der zeitgenössischen Architekten zu wahren, wurden die Pläne ihrer Bauten aus Werk-Veröffentlichungen entnommen. Die Pläne des letzten Kapitels stammen aus den folgenden Publikationen:

S. 461, 463, 464, 465, 467, 473, 476: Futagawa, Yukio, Global Architecture, A.D.A. Edita, Tokyo;

S. 468: Fleig, Karl, Alvar Aalto, 2. Aufl., Bd. 1, Verlag für Architektur/Artemis, Zürich 1974;

S. 469: Kultermann, Udo (Hrsg.), Kenzo Tange. Architecture and Urban Design 1946–1969, Verlag für Architektur/Artemis, Zürich 1970;

S. 474–475: Giurgola, Romaldo und Jaimini Mehta, Louis I. Kahn, Verlag für Architektur/Artemis, Zürich 1975;

S. 460: Wingler, Hans M. (Hrsg.), Das Bauhaus: 1919–1933, Rasch und Co. und DuMont Schauberg, Köln, 2. Aufl., Köln 1968;

S. 466: Carter, Peter, Mies van der Rohe at Work, Phaidon, London 1974;

S. 472: Futagawa, Yukio (Hrsg.) und andere, Kevin Roche, John Dinkeloo and Associates, A.D.A. Edita, Tokyo 1975.

Acknowledgements

All the plans in volumes 1 and 2 are by José Conesa, architect, Geneva, with the exception of those reproduced on the following pages:

pp. 21–33, 76–96, 204–16, 432–48, by Georges Berthoud, architect, EPF-Z, SIA, Geneva;

pp. 264–80, 392–408, by Andreas Volwahsen and Gerd Mader, architects, Munich;

pp. 324–40, collaboration with the Masuda atelier, Tokyo.

For the plans by modern architects we were able to use publications relating to their achievements. The plans in the last chapter are taken from the following works:

Futagawa, Yukio, *Global Architecture*, A.D.A. Edita, Tokyo, for pp. 461, 463, 464, 465, 467, 473, 476.

Fleig, Karl, *Alvar Aalto*, 2nd ed., vol. I, Artemis, Zurich 1974, for p. 468.

Kultermann, Udo (ed.), *Kenzo Tange. Architecture and Urban Design 1946 to 1969*, trsl. Henry A. Frey, Artemis, Zurich 1970, for p. 469.

Giurgola, Romaldo and Mehta, Jaimini, *Louis I. Kahn*, Artemis, Zurich 1975, for pp. 474–5.

Wingler, Hans M. (ed.), *Das Bauhaus: 1919–1933*, 2nd ed., Rasch and Du Mont Schauberg, Cologne, 1968, for p. 460.

Carter, Peter, *Mies van der Rohe at Work*, Phaidon, London 1974, for p. 466.

Futagawa, Yukio (ed.) and others, *Kevin Roche, John Dinkeloo and Associates, 1962–1975*, A.D.A. Edita, Tokyo 1975, for p. 472.

Photos

Babey-Ziolo: 203 (3)
Bersier, René: 167 (2)
Butler, Yvan: 75 (3)
Corboz, André: 203 (2), 223 (1), 243 (1)
Etienne, Gilbert: 307 (3)
Futagawa: 243 (3), 459 (1–5)

Gigon, Fernand: 307 (2)
Hinous-Ziolo: 223 (3)
Kersting-Ziolo: 39 (1), 187 (3)
Kumasegawa-Ziolo: 307 (1)
Nimatallah-Ziolo: 187 (1–2, 4)
Oronoz-Ziolo: 223 (2)
Percheron-Ziolo: 99 (2)
Rouiller, Jacques: 147 (2)

Schneider-Ziolo: 75 (2), 123 (4), 203 (1)
Stierlin, Henri: 19 (1–4), 39 (3), 55 (1–4), 75 (1), 99 (1, 3), 123 (1–3), 147 (1, 3), 167 (1, 3), 203 (4), 223 (4), 263 (1–3), 283 (1–3), 323 (1–3), 343 (1–3), 355 (1–4), 367 (1–3), 391 (1–3), 411 (1–4), 431 (1–3), 451 (1–4)
Takase-Ziolo: 39 (2), 243 (2)

Index

Index

Index

Table des Matières   Inhaltsverzeichnis   Table of Contents

Printed in Switzerland